Gender, Law and Justice in a Global Market

Theories of gender justice in the twenty-first century must engage with global economic and social processes. Using concepts from economic analysis associated with global commodity chains and feminist ethics of care, Ann Stewart considers the way in which 'gender contracts' relating to work and care contribute to gender inequalities worldwide. She explores how economies in the Global North stimulate desires and create deficits in care and belonging, which are met through transnational movements, and traces the way in which transnational economic processes and discourses of rights and care create relationships between Global South and North. She focuses on African women who produce fruit and flowers for European consumption; body workers who migrate to meet deficits in 'affect' through provision of care and sex; and British-Asian families who seek belonging through transnational marriages.

Ann Stewart is a reader in Law and Associate Professor in the School of Law, at the University of Warwick, where she specialises in the area of gender and the law, particularly in the context of international development.

The Law in Context Series

Editors: William Twining (University College London)
Christopher McCrudden (Lincoln College, Oxford)
Bronwen Morgan (University of Bristol)

Since 1970 the Law in Context series has been in the forefront of the movement to broaden the study of law. It has been a vehicle for the publication of innovative scholarly books that treat law and legal phenomena critically in their social, political and economic contexts from a variety of perspectives. The series particularly aims to publish scholarly legal writing that brings fresh perspectives to bear on new and existing areas of law taught in universities. A contextual approach involves treating legal subjects broadly, using materials from other social sciences, and from any other discipline that helps to explain the operation in practice of the subject under discussion. It is hoped that this orientation is at once more stimulating and more realistic than the bare exposition of legal rules. The series includes original books that have a different emphasis from traditional legal textbooks, while maintaining the same high standards of scholarship. They are written primarily for undergraduate and graduate students of law and of other disciplines, but most also appeal to a wider readership. In the past, most books in the series have focused on English law, but recent publications include books on European law, globalisation, transnational legal processes, and comparative law.

Books in the series
Anderson, Schum & Twining: *Analysis of Evidence*
Ashworth: *Sentencing and Criminal Justice*
Barton & Douglas: *Law and Parenthood*
Beecher-Monas: *Evaluating Scientific Evidence: An Interdisciplinary Framework for Intellectual Due Process*
Bell: *French Legal Cultures*
Bercusson: *European Labour Law*
Birkinshaw: *European Public Law*
Birkinshaw: *Freedom of Information: The Law, the Practice and the Ideal*
Cane: *Atiyah's Accidents, Compensation and the Law*
Clarke & Kohler: *Property Law: Commentary and Materials*
Collins: *The Law of Contract*
Cranston: *Legal Foundations of the Welfare State*
Dauvergne: *Making People Illegal: What Globalisation Means for Immigration and Law*
Davies: *Perspectives on Labour Law*
Dembour: *Who Believes in Human Rights?: The European Convention in Question*
de Sousa Santos: *Toward a New Legal Common Sense*
Diduck: *Law's Families*
Fortin: *Children's Rights and the Developing Law*
Glover-Thomas: *Reconstructing Mental Health Law and Policy*

Goldman: *Globalisation and the Western Legal Tradition: Recurring Patterns of Law and Authority*

Gobert & Punch: *Rethinking Corporate Crime*

Harlow & Rawlings: *Law and Administration*

Harris: *An Introduction to Law*

Harris, Campbell & Halson: *Remedies in Contract and Tort*

Harvey: *Seeking Asylum in the UK: Problems and Prospects*

Hervey & McHale: *Health Law and the European Union*

Holder and Lee: *Environmental Protection, Law and Policy*

Kostakopoulou: *The Future Governance of Citizenship*

Lewis: *Choice and the Legal Order: Rising above Politics*

Likosky: *Transnational Legal Processes*

Likosky: *Law, Infrastructure and Human Rights*

Maughan & Webb: *Lawyering Skills and the Legal Process*

McGlynn: *Families and the European Union: Law, Politics and Pluralism*

Moffat: *Trusts Law: Text and Materials*

Monti: *EC Competition Law*

Morgan & Yeung: *An Introduction to Law and Regulation: Text and Materials*

Norrie: *Crime, Reason and History*

O'Dair: *Legal Ethics*

Oliver: *Common Values and the Public–Private Divide*

Oliver & Drewry: *The Law and Parliament*

Picciotto: *International Business Taxation*

Reed: *Internet Law: Text and Materials*

Richardson: *Law, Process and Custody*

Roberts & Palmer: *Dispute Processes: ADR and the Primary Forms of Decision-Making*

Rowbottom: *Democracy Distorted: Wealth, Influence and Democratic Politics*

Scott & Black: *Cranston's Consumers and the Law*

Seneviratne: *Ombudsmen: Public Services and Administrative Justice*

Stapleton: *Product Liability*

Stewart: *Gender, Law and Justice in a Global Market*

Tamanaha: *Law as a Means to an End: Threat to the Rule of Law*

Turpin and Tomkins: *British Government and the Constitution: Text and Materials*

Twining: *Globalisation and Legal Theory*

Twining: *Rethinking Evidence*

Twining: *General Jurisprudence: Understanding Law from a Global Perspective*

Twining: *Human Rights, Southern Voices: Francis Deng, Abdullahi An-Na'im, Yash Ghai and Upendra Baxi*

Twining & Miers: *How to Do Things with Rules*

Ward: *A Critical Introduction to European Law*

Ward: *Law, Text, Terror*

Ward: *Shakespeare and Legal Imagination*

Wells and Quick: *Lacey, Wells and Quick: Reconstructing Criminal Law*

Zander: *Cases and Materials on the English Legal System*

Zander: *The Law-Making Process*

Gender, Law and Justice in a Global Market

ANN STEWART

CAMBRIDGE
UNIVERSITY PRESS

CAMBRIDGE UNIVERSITY PRESS
Cambridge, New York, Melbourne, Madrid, Cape Town,
Singapore, São Paulo, Delhi, Tokyo, Mexico City

Cambridge University Press
The Edinburgh Building, Cambridge CB2 8RU, UK

Published in the United States of America by Cambridge University Press,
New York

www.cambridge.org
Information on this title: www.cambridge.org/9780521763110

First published 2011

Printed in the United Kingdom at the University Press, Cambridge

A catalogue record for this publication is available from the British Library

ISBN 978-0-521-76311-0 Hardback
ISBN 978-0-521-74653-3 Paperback

This book is dedicated to the memory of Sybil and Norman
Stewart and to the future of Arthur, Sidney and Sofia.

Contents

Figures

Acknowledgements

Caring in all its forms engulfed the time and energy necessary to write this book. At the same time its gestation has involved huge amounts of caring by many people in many locations stretching from Sheffield to Delhi and places in between. I hope everyone knows how enriched I feel by their care. However I would like to thank in particular William Twining for his support and willingness to stick with this project; Geeta Oberoi for her determination and research assistance; George and William Stewart for being there; and Geoffrey Green for never giving up on me.

Abbreviations

ABA	American Bar Association
ACP	African, Caribbean and Pacific countries
ADB	Asian Development Bank
AIDS	acquired immunodeficiency syndrome
AOA	Agreement on Agriculture
APWLD	Asia Pacific Forum on Women, Law and Development
ASBO	Anti-social behaviour order
ASEAN	Association of Southeast Asian Nations
BIS	Department for Business, Innovation and Skills
BMA	Bilateral migration agreement
BrAsian	British Asian
CAP	European Common Agricultural Policy
CEDAW	Convention on Elimination of All Forms of Discrimination Against Women
CIPD	Chartered Institute of Personnel and Development
CIS	Commonwealth of Independent States
CRE	Commission for Racial Equality
CrPC	Criminal Procedure Code
DFID	Department of International Development
DTI	Department of Trade and Industry
DH	Department of Health
DIR	Domestic Incident Report
ECHR	European Convention on Human Rights
ECJ	European Court of Justice
EEA	European Economic Area
EIC	East India Company
EOC	Equal Opportunities Commission
EPA	Economic Partnership Agreement
ETI	Ethical Trading Initiative
ETLR	Evolutionary theory of land rights
EU	European Union
FAO	Food and Agriculture Organization
FCO	Foreign and Commonwealth Office

FDI	foreign direct investment
FFV	fresh fruits and vegetables
FMU	Forced Marriage Unit
FSC	Federal Shariat Court
GATS	General Agreement on Trade in Services
GATT	General Agreement on Tariffs and Trade
GCC	Global commodity chain
GDP	Gross domestic product
GHS	Ghana Health Service
GVC	Global value chain
HIV	human immunodeficiency virus
ICCPR	International Convention on Civil and Political Rights
ICESCR	International Covenant on Economic, Social and Cultural Rights
IFIs	International Financial Institutions
ILO	International Labour Organization
IMF	International Monetary Fund
IOM	International Organization for Migration
IPC	Indian Penal Code
LDCs	Least Developed Countries
MDGs	Millennium Development Goals
MFLO	Muslim Family Law Ordinance
MFN	Most Favoured Nation
MNC	Multinational Corporation
MPL	Muslim Personal Law
NCW	National Commission for Women
NGO	Non-governmental organisation
NHS	National Health Service
NRI	Non-resident Indian
NTAE	non-traditional agricultural exports
OECD	Organisation for Economic Co-operation and Development
OFW	Overseas Foreign Workers
OSCE	Organization for Security and Co-operation in Europe
OWWA	Overseas Workers Welfare Association
PPC	Pakistan Penal Code
POEA	Philippines Overseas Employment Administration
PO	Protection Officer
PSI	private standards initiative
SAP	Structural Adjustment Programmes
TNC	Transnational corporation
TNF	Transnational family
TNM	Transnational marriage
UDHR	Universal Declaration of Human Rights
UN	United Nations

UNCTAD	United Nations Conference on Trade and Development
UNICEF	United Nations Children's Fund
UNIFEM	United Nations Development Fund for Women
UNRISD	United Nations Research Institute for Social Development
VAW	Violence against women
WHO	World Health Organization
WILDAF	Women in Law and Development in Africa
WLSA	Women and Law in Southern Africa
WTO	World Trade Organization

Introduction

Living in a Global North consumer society: a contextual vignette

I live in an inner city neighbourhood in the United Kingdom (UK). When I visit the well women's clinic, at a surgery where all the doctors are practising Christians, I sit next to a middle-aged Somalian Muslim woman. We live on the same street, share a lawn mower, and struggle to grow plants under large trees. I know that she will probably be circumcised because I am familiar with the statistics – a 95 per cent prevalence rate for women in Somalia (UNICEF 2004). She laughs, and expresses incomprehension, when, as a middle-aged woman, I run along the street, sweating profusely and clad in very little.

Behind my house, a group of boys aged between seven and fifteen regularly play football. They argue vociferously about the rules in fluent 'street' English. Many are Somalis by origin although there are white and African Caribbean boys as well. Their sisters emerge to congregate around the public bench to chat and occasionally to play ball games but always on the margins of the 'pitch'. On Saturday mornings I see the boys returning from their classes in the Koran while one white young man delivers newspapers to my door. His father used to clean our windows until he had a bad accident. He now works for a landscape garden firm but the work is precarious and does not provide an adequate income, so his wife has started to work part time as a social carer for a local disabled adult. His daughter and her female partner look through household items in my cellar which used to belong to my parents to see whether anything would be useful for their flat because they are setting up home together.

Behind me lives an African Caribbean woman with young twin boys. For many years she worked at the end of our street, selling sex, but is now involved with a voluntary organisation which offers support to street sex workers. She chats regularly to her friend and neighbour, another African Caribbean woman, who has recently retired as a probation officer and knows a number of the local young men well. At the end of my street there are two residential care homes for the vulnerable elderly. Black women care workers, who look after the white residents, walk past to catch buses at the start or finish of their shifts. The Malawian woman who cared for my parents in our house until they died recently tells me that a number are, like herself, recent migrants from southern Africa. Around the corner is the local shop and post office run by a couple originally from the Punjab in India. The woman, who is the holder of the post office licence, and I discuss the weather in North India, because we are both going there soon, she for the first time in fifteen years, me for the third time in a year. She tells me about the difficulties she is facing in obtaining an entry visa for her husband's brother who wishes to attend a family wedding.

From my house I walk for 500 metres, past newly erected, luxury flats, to my local supermarket, Waitrose, which used to be Safeway. The local property paper tells me its presence will increase the price of my house because the change in ownership is an indication that there are significant numbers of affluent consumers within the vicinity. When I shop there, I see an overwhelmingly working-age, white clientele (including friends and acquaintances but never neighbours), choosing between a huge range of imported food products, which are presented and packaged in ways designed for the convenience of 'money rich/time poor' consumers.

This vignette of life and work raises a number of issues, which will be explored in this book. The first of these relates to the plurality and diversity of a multicultural consumer society that is located in the Global North. While there are many ways of telling a story of urban life at the beginning of the twenty-first century, this narrative is told primarily through particular identities, which are ascribed to individuals. This discourse of difference and individuality tends to be dominant within feminist narratives. It describes a white middle-aged professional woman; a Somalian refugee woman; a black African care worker; a Punjabi small businesswoman; an African Caribbean sex worker; a young working-class lesbian and so on. Some of the women are also mothers and citizens; all are family members and consumers. These identities are rooted in communities some of which seem more 'solid' than others. The Somali, Punjabi and African Caribbean communities, albeit in different ways, are identified according to group membership while Waitrose customers are identified via patterns of consumption and lifestyle and lesbian women via their sexuality. The only thing that women seem to share collectively, and not through their status as women, is a neighbourhood. Even then, their use and perceptions of this space, including how safe it is, probably differs substantially (Massey 1994).

It is unlikely that there is much consensus among the local residents on values, for instance in relation to the expression of individual sexual identities. One can presume that the dominant view of the practising Muslim and Christian communities would be that sexual intercourse should be contained within heterosexual marriages and that public expressions of diverse sexual identities are to be actively discouraged. Views on the extent to which women's sexuality is a matter for regulation by family members or through state institutions, or available in the market place for purchase, would vary considerably. Many residents do not like the public transactions relating to the purchase of sex that take place nearby, although there are regular supplies of (male) customers. Yet a wide range of sexual identities and family forms are in evidence in the neighbourhood. The tensions within particular ascribed communities, when values are not shared between individual members, or between communities and state institutions, when these values differ, are not immediately obvious or seemingly of concern to close neighbours if they are not members of the constituent community. Physical proximity does not produce connectedness.

A second, alternative way of seeing this neighbourhood is through the wider economic and social processes that have contributed to its creation and which continue to shape social and economic relations (Massey 1994: chapters 6 and 7). This narrative would chart the contribution of imperialism and colonialism to the development of the steel industry and the economic prosperity built upon this legacy. It would see the effects on local wages and social relations of the defeat of the once-dominant white male industrial working class, which had secured relatively high 'family wages' through unionisation. It would focus on the shift in mass production to developing countries in the restructuring of the steel industries, which led to a huge loss of male jobs and their replacement by more precarious and poorly paid service jobs and the commensurate increase in women's paid employment. The African Caribbean and South Asian communities would be explained as a product of labour market policies, based on former colonial relationships, which initially brought workers to Britain to work in specific manufacturing and service sectors.

The neighbourhood is also shaped by present forms of globalisation which have contributed to the development of the UK as a consumer-based market economy. The huge range of food products available in Waitrose and other supermarkets is the result of these global processes. Those who grow and process these products are largely invisible to consumers, who do not come into contact with farm workers, many of whom are now seasonal workers from the newer member states of the European Union (EU), in the UK, let alone those working on farms or plantations in Chile, Kenya or the Windward Islands.

The battle for a favourable position within the global market place leads to domestic UK economic and social policies which encourage women to enter and remain within the labour market but also seek to limit the social welfare responsibilities of the state. The care workers who look after the young or the elderly in the local private homes or public institutions are part of the wider service economy, taking over or supplementing activities which until relatively recently have been seen as the unpaid responsibility of female family members. Migrant women, along with local working-class women and some men, are filling the 'care gap'. These care service workers earn very little and do not shop at Waitrose.

Immigration policies based on the colonial legacy have enabled women migrant workers to fill these gaps in health and care services. Now immigration policy does not grant access based on membership of the Commonwealth and relies on the regional labour market of the EU to meet unskilled labour requirements. Because they work with the bodies of their clients or service users and therefore share a proximity, such workers, including migrants, may be thought to be less invisible than those who produce our food and other consumer goods. However the workers' insecure status as non-citizens or as undocumented migrants, working often in informal employment contexts, ensures a precarious and socially invisible existence. The African care workers will soon not be seen in the neighbourhood either because they have been replaced by EU citizens or because they have been absorbed into less public spaces due to the loss of rights to work legally. The migrant women who work in the most exploited sectors of the commercial sex industry are almost totally invisible.

Introducing the framework

This book introduces a number of specific contexts, albeit not so local as the one described above, which provide similar narratives around constructions of identities and the impact of wider economic and social processes. The villages in the Punjab in India, Mirpur in Pakistan and Sylhet in Bangladesh, border towns in Moldova, the outskirts of Nairobi and farms in Naivasha in Kenya are not chosen at random or as discrete case studies but because they are shaped by, and themselves shape, identities within contemporary Britain. They are all affected by social and economic processes that have created and continue to create inequalities, not only within their neighbourhoods, but also within wider society. These processes, which create relationships of power between people living in the neighbourhoods, also create profound disparities in life chances between citizens of Global North and Global South states. They distribute many of the benefits of globalisation to the Global North.

Figure 1 provides the basic conceptual structure for this book. It seeks to capture the importance of the network of relationships that spans jurisdictions and affects gender relations within jurisdictions. The gender pyramids are adapted from Barrientos et al. (2001) and represent state jurisdictions in the Global North and Global South. Overall, the figure seeks to capture two networks of relationships. The first considers the way in which gender relations within a state are constructed through the institutions of the market, state and family/community (the vertical). The vertical 'up' and 'down' arrows represent the relationships between the three institutions of market, state and community/family, leading to the distribution of activities. Whereas identity was traditionally moulded by relationships in families and communities, it is increasingly conferred by sophisticated and segmented market choices (represented by the 'up' arrows). Consumers now buy an affective service, an interpersonal relationship, which was once associated with caring within families and community. The vertical 'down' arrows represent the expansion of market values into the domain of state and family. The final decades of the twentieth century were characterised by neoliberal policies, which either shrunk the state or introduced market relations into the provision of state services. The extent and impact of these developments varies according to the location of a particular jurisdiction.

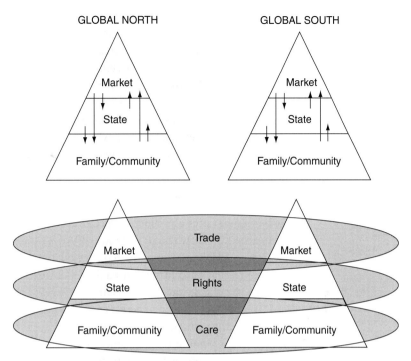

Fresh Fruit & Vegetables ∗ Bodywork ∗ Diasphoric Belonging

Figure 1: The framework.

The second set of relationships under consideration in this book spans jurisdictions. Global supply chains link the jurisdictions through the horizontal sets of interactions and discourses represented in the ellipses which encompass the lower two pyramids (the horizontal). The processes and their governance (through trade, rights and care 'talk') mould gender relations and construct gender identities. Throughout the book the demand end of the particular chain is focused on the UK. Chapters 3 and 9 discuss the way in which the demand is created for a particular resource. Chapter 3 concentrates on the demand for 'exotic' food products and body work services (involving care and sex). Chapter 9 reviews the way in which South Asian families seek to satisfy their sense of belonging in multicultural Britain. Chapters 4 and 5 consider the African context from which the food products are supplied. Chapter 4 provides an introduction to gender issues in sub-Saharan African countries that experienced British colonialism, while Chapter 5 focuses more specifically on the Kenyan context for the fresh fruit and flowers value chain. Chapters 6 and 7 are concerned with the home contexts for the supply of body workers. Chapter 6 discusses gender issues in Moldova, the Philippines, Poland and Ghana as source countries for women migrants. Chapter 7 concentrates on the particular body work chains involving nurses, care and domestic workers and sex workers from these countries. The next two chapters are concerned with the family chain involving South

Asian transnational families. Chapter 8 introduces the reader to gender relations in South Asia, while the specific issues relating to the family chains that link Pakistan, Bangladesh, India and the UK are addressed in Chapter 9.

Two conceptual 'tools' are used to explain these networks: one drawn from political economy analysis, the global value chain; and the other from feminism, the relational framework of ethics of care analysis. The reasons why global value chain analysis provides a useful framework in which to discuss social and economic processes and their governance are discussed in Chapter 1, while the contribution of the ethics of care analysis, set within a wider discussion of difference, is assessed in Chapter 2. These two chapters between them provide the framework for the rest of the book.

To refer back to the opening vignette, the economically focused framework of global commodity/value chain addresses the narrative told through the social and economic processes but is not sufficiently aware of the impact of gendered identities on these processes (Yeates 2009). Households are seen in current economic models as consumers of goods and public services rather than as producers of valuable inputs to both public and private sectors of any economy. Feminist analyses (Ferguson and Folbre 1981; Badgett and Folbre 1999; Elson 2000) have distinguished activities associated with production from those associated with what they describe as social reproduction, the biological and social activities necessary to sustain ourselves and essential for any functioning society. Production attracts economic value, and is the basis for national budgets, while social reproduction outside the market does not (Hoskyns and Rai 2007). There is therefore very little debate over the levels of care that are sustainable in economies that reward self-interest far more than the altruistic provision of care for others (Badgett and Folbre 1999). When activities are transferred to the market and become services they attract value but usually they are not seen as particularly valuable. The way that production and social reproduction are organised in any society is of central importance to a gendered understanding. Responsibilities for productive and reproductive work are dis-tributed to men and women differently although the particular ways in which this occurs varies between societies.

A major theme of this book will be to explore the gender consequences of the distribution of activities that are associated with social reproduction between the institutions of the market, state, family and community and the contribution of law to this distribution. Assessing the effects of globalisation from the standpoint of how women's lives are organised in households is central to this process (Harding 2008: 225). I will argue that the lack of recognition of the value of social reproduction within any society contributes to global gender inequalities because it tends to distribute the benefits of globalisation to the Global North at the expense of women and their families and communities in the Global South. I use and adapt the concept of global commodity/value chains to explore this claim.

We will see the way in which fruit and vegetables grown in East Africa are prepared and packaged to add value, then exported to Europe to be sold in supermarkets, creating a commodity/value chain. A care service chain is created when women migrate from Poland or the Philippines, entrusting family care to others, in order to provide care within European economies. The provision of sexual services is now a global industry, entailing both the movement across borders of consumers and service providers but also the creation and circulation of global cultural constructions of sexualities. I use the concept of body work, which avoids a division between sexual and physical nurture, to look at the way in which the social relationships involved in health, care and sex service provision are understood and regulated within global body work chains.

I extend the commodity/value chain concept even further to explore activities associated with transnational families, which involve the movement of individuals but relate also to the movement of norms, particularly those relating to the regulation of women's sexuality. Cultural and ideological identities are constructed within transnational 'imagined communities' (Anderson 1991) which offer citizens of different nation states a sense of belonging to a wider community constructed around shared beliefs (such as the Islamic Umma) or goals (such as the achievement of women's international human rights). Thus the horizontal processes illustrated in Figure 1 affect the way in which men and women work and organise family life within specific (vertical) jurisdictions.

While Chapter 1 critiques analyses rooted in social and economic processes, Chapter 2 addresses the feminist analyses of difference and intersectionality (Grabham et al. 2009). The opening narrative of differing identities presents a challenge for the political solidarity that is essential to support the redistributive strategies which would tackle gender-based inequality (Fraser 1995). Contemporary forms of globalisation affect gender relations in complex ways. It is clearly not the case that all men are winners and that all women are losers. This book is based upon the premise that there is no identifiable universal community of women who experience disadvantage based on their sex alone. However, assumptions about gender roles, and the way in which social reproductive activities, in particular, are organised and valued within any society and then integrated into global market processes, contribute to gender-based injustices, which differentially affect women and men. I contend that care analysis, which assumes that our individual identities are formed through relationships with others, can play a major role in a critique of existing trade and rights discourses and can be used in wider strategies designed to tackle global gender inequalities. The market is absorbing and reconstructing care as affect – something that can be bought and sold as a good or service. The provision of affective services is central to the development of the global economy and forms the core of the UK's consumer society, discussed in Chapter 4. Such consumer markets are developing rapidly across the world and are reconstructing gender identities. Markets offer women and men identities imbued with high degrees of autonomy, which raises challenges for the promulgation of a state-based discourse of women as rights-holding citizens, as a means of expanding 'civil' space for women outside the existing power relationships of the family. The feminist ethic of care provides the basis for a critical assessment of these changes in the relations between market, state and family.

I intend, therefore, to address the challenges relating to feminist legal analysis in the context of globalisation not primarily through a 'rights question' but through a care question although I take due account of the role of rights in women's struggles for greater justice. I ask: who do we care about and how? not, do all women have human rights? Care thinking will feature in three ways. First, the substantive activities variously defined as social reproduction, caring and affective labour (and associated with a labour process) are the subject matter for discussion in particular jurisdictions and in the global chains; secondly, the values associated with care thinking, such as attentiveness and responsibility, will play a major role in the critiques of existing policies and discourses of trade, development and rights; and thirdly, care is used as a method to support the discussion of the global chains. I will argue that a more relational basis to rights and trade discourses will contribute towards tackling global gender inequalities. Thus I aim to combine and apply commodity/value chain analysis and feminist discussions of ethical caring to the specific contexts under discussion.

The processes of globalisation link people together in new ways within and across societies. They create new divisions and differences. These processes affect gender relations and are in part constructed through legal norms. They are built upon often invisible relationships that need to be understood if the injustices contained within them are to be tackled. This process of understanding requires equal attentiveness to the various contexts in which these relationships are constructed. The actors involved in the chains are located within a range of countries with varying socio-economic and political histories and legal contexts, primarily in the Global South but also, in the case of the body work chains, in 'transitional' states. These histories and contexts affect the interactions between the actors and need our attention. It is important to listen to the ways in which the issues that form the subject matters of the chains, whether they be food exports or transnational marriages, are debated not only internationally but also locally within Kenya and Bangladesh as well as within the UK. Listening carefully tends to reconfigure the perception of the issue under consideration: instead of seeing Moldova through the lens of trafficking, trafficking is seen through an understanding of Moldova.

It is a practical impossibility to cover each 'originating' jurisdiction comprehensively but Chapter 4 provides a wider gender perspective on sub-Saharan African jurisdictions, Chapter 6 discusses Moldova in depth and Chapter 8 does the same for South Asia. Poland, Ghana and the Philippines receive less comprehensive, but still relatively detailed, coverage in Chapter 6. The 'chains' are set within particular jurisdictions and associated with specific transnational activities in order to conduct a more detailed contextual legal analysis. I have chosen these examples because they have attracted wider gender analysis and are also subject to various forms of gender-based policy initiatives. They open up the potential for a wider analysis of specific issues within and across jurisdictions, such as how difference is understood and dealt with within law.

I contend that constructions of gender are moulded through the plural governance measures within the chains. They contribute to the distribution of power relations between the social actors in the chains. A gender perspective reveals the ways in which the benefits of globalisation are unequally distributed and assesses the potential to redistribute these benefits. I look at the way in which discourses of trade, rights and care contribute to the existing processes of governance and regulation. I will argue that trade discourse is associated with the market and with an individual consumer identity; that rights are associated with the state and a citizen identity; and that care discourse is presently associated with family and community institutions and constructs a relational carer identity but that it is increasingly incorporated into market-oriented consumer discourse, producing a caring consumer.

1

Constructing relationships in a global economy

Introduction

The last chapter told a story of cultural identities and economic processes. This chapter considers the impact of the global economy on gender relations, in particular its effects on divisions of labour. The chapter is divided into two sections that introduce two conceptual 'tools', which underpin the framework set out in Figure 1 in the Introduction. The first is the gender pyramid, which provides a gender perspective on the ways in which the distribution of productive and socially reproductive labour embodied in 'gender contracts' impacts on women's position within formal labour markets in contemporary processes of globalisation. It considers the effect of regulatory interventions on the construction of the 'worker', which reinforce gender injustices. It therefore addresses issues relating to the vertical relationships between state, market and family within the framework of this book. It assesses the implications of the increasing involvement of women as workers within global production processes that have relocated much mass production to countries in the Global South. The basis for historic gender contracts, in which women took responsibility for maintaining the household while men provided its income, are undermined, while the gender norms upon which these contracts are based are yet to change significantly, producing gender injustice.

The same developments are creating consumer, service-based markets and societies. The chapter moves on to consider the impact of consumerism on the relationship between production and social reproduction and on the construction of gendered identities. Relationships of care once within the unpaid socially reproductive sphere increasingly involve intimate service relationships involving the body of the worker and that of the consumer, which supplement or substitute familial caring relationships. The chapter assesses the gender implications of this move, which can also contribute to the exploitation of women. The final sections in this part of the chapter address the challenges to, and potential for, political action based upon consumer identities to address these injustices and pose an alternative vision, which would wrest the value of social production from the market and place it within the political domain. Feminism needs to reaffirm the importance and value of social reproduction in all societies to reduce gender injustice.

The second part of the chapter focuses on the second conceptual tool, the commodity/value chain framework, which provides the basis for the specific chains discussed in subsequent chapters. It is discussed in relation to a conventional commodity chain involving the importation of food from Kenya and then to body work service migration and finally, stretching the concept, to apply to transnational family formation and norm-creation. This section therefore provides the basis for the horizontal relationships across jurisdictions under discussion in this book. The conclusion draws the threads together and relates them to the challenges they pose to feminist analysis and action to address global injustices.

Feminisation of work and the gender pyramid

Hardt argues that there have been a 'succession of economic paradigms in dominant capitalist countries ... each defined by a privileged sector of the economy' (1999: 89). The first was dominated by agriculture and the extraction of raw materials; the second by industry and the manufacture of durable goods; and a third and current one 'in which providing services and manipulating information are at the heart of economic production' (Hardt 1999: 89). The second of these paradigms was characterised in the Global North by Fordist mass production and 'state organized capitalism' in which welfare states used the economic policies of Keynes to 'soften the boom bust cycles endemic to capitalism' by investing in infrastructure, adopting redistributive taxation, regulating business, providing social welfare and decommodifying public goods (Fraser 2009: 2). In the Global South, newly independent states adopted state-based development policies (although without the resources for more than rudimentary welfare provisions) to try to 'jump-start national economic growth' (Fraser 2009: 2).

Second-wave feminism, born in this era, challenged dominant progressive understandings of social injustice, linked to the public economic sphere, to include injustices, which occurred in the family, in cultural traditions and within civil society, and which involved unequal distribution based on gender, race, sexuality and nationality, as well as class. Feminism uncovered a gender division of labour: production associated with the world of paid work, and the role of men, and social production assumed to be women's role and involving 'biological reproduction; unpaid production in the home (both goods and services); social provisioning (... voluntary work directed at meeting needs in the community); the reproduction of culture and ideology; and the provision of sexual, emotional and affective services (such as are required to maintain family and intimate relationships)' (Hoskyns and Rai 2007: 300).

In the last two decades of the twentieth century, neoliberalism has been defined as 'A theory of political economic practices that proposes that human wellbeing can best be advanced by liberating individual entrepreneurial freedoms and skills within an institutional framework characterized by strong private property rights, free markets, and free trade. The role of the state is to create and preserve an institutional framework appropriate to such practices' (Harvey, 2005: 2). It has swept aside many of the underpinnings of state-based capitalism, although the processes were slower and more uneven in northern states in comparison to the rigours of structural adjustment policies in the Global South, and unleashed the economy from the constraints of the state. In Hardt's third post-Fordist paradigm, new technologies are harnessed to produce goods, and increasingly services, targeted at specific types of consumer. Technological innovation has created 'knowledge' economies which use information and communication processes to drive production and enable elements in the production process to be spatially separated. The post-industrial era involves a move in dominant economies from manual to mental labour to produce 'immaterial' products such as knowledge, ideas and cultures (Radin and Sunder 2005). While mass assembly has moved from northern locations to economies with the capacity to provide this process by using cheaper labour, the 'value added' elements such as product development, design and advertising are largely retained in the North.

These developments are associated with the 'feminisation' of work. First, many more women worldwide are involved in productive work. They form the labour force in many of the mass-production sectors located across the world. Secondly, the combination of neoliberal ideology and post-industrial production has extended commodification to aspects of life that once would have been associated with the 'social' (whether utilities formerly provided through the state or unpaid socially reproductive activities) (Kelsey 2008). It has also brought ways of thinking associated with this social realm into that of paid work. Thus productive work increasingly relies upon the attributes (skills) associated with the feminine and with the values associated with care thinking such as attentiveness to relationships. Some argue that this 'affective' form of labour is 'not only directly productive of capital but at the very pinnacle of the hierarchy of labouring forms' (Hardt 1999: 89). 'Affect' particularly produced through services has more 'living' labour content than that of other commodities. The cost of labour is thus very important for productivity and profit margins (Kelsey 2008: 12), creating huge incentives to restructure northern labour markets in a bid to compete in world markets while capital also searches for cheap sources of suitable labour for mass production or for outsourced affective services within other countries. Because it is far easier to move operations across national borders, global competition renders jobs more flexible and precarious in the Global North and reinforces insecurity and precariousness in the South. 'Flexible' forms of work are now characteristic of labour markets worldwide (Beneria et al. 2000: xii).

Thus while it is important to recognise that access to labour markets provides women with much-needed income and a measure of social and economic independence, it is also necessary to consider whether inclusion as these precarious/flexible workers has produced a net improvement in women's overall well-being or has resulted in a diminution of the well-being of all members of societies. The Fordist 'gender contract' in the Global North was based on a household model of a man working for a 'family wage', which was deemed sufficient to support his family, while his wife provided her unpaid labour in exchange. Public paid work attracted economic value while unpaid familial labour did not. State social welfare policies largely reinforced these divisions of labour and gendered forms of dependency. The content of the gender contract in Global South contexts differed depending on imperial and colonial histories as well as on local social and cultural norms. Productive and reproductive work in non-industrial economies, such as those in sub-Saharan Africa, or agrarian sectors in South Asia, as we shall see, is far more highly integrated (Rai 2002). In the Global South, the majority of women live in households that have been described as 'semi proletarianised' in which workers receive low or unstable recompense for their waged labour (not a collectively bargained-for family or living wage) and so must engage in a range of activities to survive (Wallerstein and Smith 1992).

The northern model of a breadwinning man who collectively bargains for a family income is being replaced by universal adult worker households containing a new type of idealised worker: the 'free unencumbered self fashioning individual' (Fraser 2009: 7). While a few professional women worldwide may fit the 'high end' free floating worker profile, most must seek to gain their freedom from the traditional forms of authority associated with family labour through working for 'minimum' wages, with little job security and for long hours. Feminist aspirations to 'transform the system's deep structures and animating values – in part by decentring wage work and valorizing unwaged activities, especially the socially necessary carework performed by women' (Fraser 2009: 4) seems to have become associated with the promotion of women's total absorption into the waged economy without a reassessment of the value of, and responsibility for, unpaid socially reproductive labour.

Gendered worker subjectivity: constructing the working body

Labour, family and, particularly in northern jurisdictions, social welfare laws within states (which can be both state- and 'non state'-based) contribute to the gendered construction of workers; produce understandings of what constitutes work and how it is valued in a society; and reinforce social norms relating to the responsibilities for social reproduction (Conaghan and Rittich 2005). They construct and reflect specific gender contracts and affect the ways in, and the terms upon, which women access paid work. Each regulatory form brings its own constructions of worker and carer which, in a global market, may have originated in very different contexts to the ones in which they are applied with often unforeseen consequences for gender relations.

The 'gender pyramid' developed by Barrientos and her colleagues (Barrientos, Dolan and Tallontire 2001; 2003), and adapted here in Figure 2, provides a framework through which to explore the way in which specific gender contracts are reflected in production-related regulation.

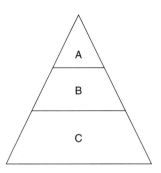

A = Formal Employment Conditions and Entitlements
(e.g. contracts, wages, discrimination)

B = Employment-Related Issues and Entitlements
(e.g. childcare, occupational health, training, housing)

C = Social Issues and Entitlements (e.g. domestic responsibilities,
education, gender relations)

Figure 2: The gender production-focused pyramid. Source: Barrientos et al. (2001: 11)

Segment A represents the regulation and provision of formal employment, which operate within a framework that tends to treat workers as abstract factors of production ('free unencumbered worker'). Labour costs are lowest for employers who restrict their responsibilities to this first level. The second segment (B) represents the regulation and provision of work-related benefits which treat workers as embodied individuals ('*worker*/citizen/carer'). Workers' organisations seek to extend rights to, and employers sometimes voluntarily adopt responsibilities for, the second level. States also provide rights either as a result of welfarism or as a result of international labour or human rights obligations. The third segment (C) represents the wider social entitlements which recognise and support those who work as social reproducers or carers. Within any jurisdiction (or region such as the EU), full-time employees generally enjoy the most rights (A and B) while 'live in' domestic workers and 'home workers' may be entitled to few and sex workers none. Women generally will obtain the same rights as men if they enter labour markets as employees and formally gain entitlements within segments A and B. However as we shall see in subsequent chapters, women face widespread discrimination, including work-based sexual harassment, even as such workers.

The globalisation of production processes within a neoliberal framework has restructured northern labour markets around the concept of 'flexibility' within employment relations. With the reduction of the power of unionised labour, many northern workers are unable to protect themselves through nationally based collective bargaining processes. Production has moved from Global North economies, based upon this organised (predominantly) male labour model, to economies in which women and men work with less formal protections in any case but because of the pervasive segregation in employment sectors women generally access the most flexible (seasonal, casual and informal) work across the world, which attracts far fewer entitlements. Thus labour standards are generally under pressure while market-related frameworks for the provision of services and goods are strengthening (Conaghan et al. 2002; Fudge and Owens 2006). Many Global South 'nation states do not have the necessary level of transparency, institutional capacity and autonomy to design and implement the appropriate regulations to keep pace with fast track liberalization schemes and to protect their citizenry from economic shocks' (Beneria et al. 2000: xiv).

However it is important to recognise that the relationship between the market, state and family embodied in the gender contract remains context specific, despite the processes of globalisation. The UK post-industrial economy is able to provide paid, formal work for the majority of the adult population but on the expectation that women will undertake paid work irrespective of any family-based care responsibilities. A universal worker model based on an individual wage and a two-person working household is emerging, although the reality is more one-and-a-half working. Work-related benefits (segment B) such as maternity and paternity leave, requests for flexible hours to care for young children or disabled and elderly family members and so on, which mediate the relationship between work and care, become very important to women workers although state policies are directed towards the maintenance of (gender-neutral) 'parents' and 'carers' within the labour market (Lewis and Giullari 2005). However, much policy discussion in the welfare states of North America, Europe and Australia has tended to be conducted in terms of the less explicitly gendered dyad of work/life balance rather than that of work/care (Conaghan and Rittich 2005; see Purvanneckiene 2009 for discussion of European Union policy).

While the universal worker may be emerging as the dominant model, some communities within the UK are either resistant, or unable, to access this way of relating work with family responsibilities. There are significant numbers of single-parent-headed families, the majority of which are headed by women, for whom paid work may not be a viable option. There are also communities in which women's family care role is given primacy over paid work. In some South Asian communities, for instance, the breadwinner/homemaker family still seems to be the norm although women may undertake paid work within the home (Kabeer 2000).

In Global South contexts the terms of the particular gender contract vary. The size of the formal sector differs but is often very small, offering protected work to the few. Women do not find access easy in these circumstances although state employment as teachers and health workers offers secure jobs for some educated women. The opening up of economies to global markets and the increase in these jobs for women is based upon particular gender contracts and tends to reproduce the 'flexibility' of the informal sector within the formal market offering women seasonal, casual and irregular work. This type of work does not attract the sort of work-related benefits which would enable women to gain access to, and sustain their position within, formal markets. They work in the informal sector and in the most insecure jobs within it (Hassim and Razavi 2006), with few or no employment law protections. They combine these activities with subsistence farming which, in turn, is becoming more precarious (Manji 2006).

Both in the Global North and the Global South, little if any employment-related negotiation takes place in relation to the third sphere (segment C) of responsibility for wider social reproduction issues ('*carer*/citizen/worker'). These are not seen as directly related to specific employment although they are essential to the creation of 'fit for purpose' workers (Pearson 2007). Nonetheless, the market is not only changing working relationships everywhere but also, as we have seen, the way in which care is organised. In most societies caring activities have generally been undertaken within families (however these are constituted) and have been the responsibility of women in particular. As many more activities, including those associated with meeting needs such as caring for children or the provision of food, are being provided through the market place the assumption that these activities are undertaken unpaid by women in the family is becoming less a matter of 'common sense' in some societies (Budlender 2008). In others, particularly in the former state socialist societies, the assumption that the state would take responsibility for many of these activities to enable women and men to undertake paid employment has been disrupted by the post-1989 collapse of the system, leading to a renewed interest in the family as the space for social reproduction. However, there is little evidence to suggest that the terms of gender contracts within families are being renegotiated to take account of the changes in women's roles within labour markets. Men generally seem not to be taking significantly more responsibility for family care even when women migrate to work (Parreñas 2005; Barker 2009).

Because productive work attracts economic value, while socially reproductive labour outside the market does not, this unpaid 'care economy' does not appear in national accounting systems (Hoskyns and Rai 2007) although it is estimated that the value of unpaid work can be the equivalent to up to half of a country's GDP (Elson 1999). There has been until recently little public debate and attention to how such needs are to be met if women's improved life chances are linked primarily with their involvement in paid employment (Fraser 1997: chapter 2). 'Traditional' gender contracts are under pressure across the globe but the terms and conditions for their replacements are contested. If the assumption is that all workers are the same then are all carers also the same? In other words, is the sought-after model one of all individuals combining work and care with lesser or greater degrees of support from their state or is it that care is sufficiently valued and recognised socially to merit parity with work (Fraser 1997: chapter 2)?

To achieve the latter a state would be obliged to organise direct financial support to care-givers outside the market place. Here carers and workers would be different individuals but treated equally. This option does not seem politically feasible in the Global North and is economically impossible in the Global South. Women continue to take disproportionate responsibility for care leading to what is described as the 'triple burden' (paid work, care work in the family and wider caring in the community due to reductions in state provision) and the consequent 'feminisation of poverty'. Nevertheless, the role of the state differs significantly between those states with relatively developed welfare provisions and capacity to cushion some of the vagaries of the market for their citizens and those with little or no such capacity (Razavi 2007; 2009). Therefore, the importance of family-based activities, as distinct from transfer payments from the state, to the well-being of individuals differs significantly between economies.

Women's increased involvement in paid work produces what is increasingly being called a care 'deficit'. Again the way this is filled depends on the particular societal context. In northern welfare states the present response is to encourage 'defamiliarisation' which transfers the provision of care to the market even when the care is undertaken within the home and 'personalisation', which organises service provision around the choices of individual users (Ungerson 2004; Ungerson and Yeandle 2007). In other societies, the care work is purchased by, and provided informally in, families (Razavi 2007). It often involves the purchase of other women's labour, including from migrant women, to care. Thus we see that women from Burma provide domestic work in Thailand so that Thai women can enter the labour market and Polish women are enabled by the opening up of the EU labour market to provide home care services in the UK.

At present there seems to be more policy interest in the demand side – for example how to tackle the 'burden' of ageing in northern economies – rather than the supply side. When the latter is considered the focus tends to be on analyses of the wider economic impact of remittances rather than the care deficit for migrants' families created through the migration of women workers or the 'depletion' in social capital for the society as a whole (Hoskyns and Rai 2007). At an individual level the extent to which the market and/or the state shares responsibility for (unpaid) social reproduction and encourages greater equality through the provision of entitlements within gender contracts and more generally in relation to social reproductive responsibilities (segment C) in these new flexible/precarious working contexts deeply affects women's position within labour markets.

The gender pyramid has been used here to discuss vertical interactions between the state, market and family. We will see how this concept, with its production-focused framework, has been used to understand the ways in which global commodity/value chains, which specifically link production processes across jurisdictions, fail to tackle issues of social reproduction from an employment perspective (the horizontal dimension discussed in part two of this chapter). It has supported policy discussions on ways of capturing more value within the chains in those elements of production which take place in the Global South. As such it has been important in developing 'pro poor' development agency frameworks.

Consuming subjectivities: consumer workers?

> The consumer has become a totem pole around which a multitude of actions and ideologies are dancing. Whether en masse or as an individual, the consumer is no longer a person who merely desires, buys and uses up a commodity. (Gabriel and Lang 2006: 8)

In the Global North, consumerism has become a moral doctrine through which to achieve freedom, power and happiness as well as an ideology of conspicuous consumption: the displays of possessions 'fix the social position and prestige of their owners'. In critiques of these developments, '... style, taste, fantasy and sexuality have come to the forefront; gender makes an intermittent appearance; class has unjustly tended to be obscured' (Gabriel and Lang 2006: 8). Nonetheless, consumption is inextricably linked to production. If paid enough, workers become customers. As Gabriel and Lang point out: 'Ford offered his workforce the carrot of material enjoyment outside the work-place as compensation for the de-skilling, control and alienation that he imposed in the workplace' (2006: 11). Post-Fordist economies have expanded to encompass commodified desires. These 'affects' create personalised 'lifestyles', which mark individuals out as different. Our bodies and arguably identities are constructed through the products we choose to consume. We buy 'affectivity' (nurturing, love and pleasure), 'the real object of production in new industries', which is 'for once and for all liberated from its former, restrictive enclosure in the contexts of intimacy and the family' (Prada 2006).

However, while linked to production, consumerism separates 'glamorised circulation' from the 'at times squalid circumstances of the production of commodities' (Gabriel and Lang 2006: 11). Consumers will usually have little idea where and under what work conditions this production takes place. If we did, we might not feel good and this would undermine post-Fordist economies, which sell satisfaction and well-being. Disassociation is made easier by the spatial distance from the sites of production. However, a wide range of affective services from treatments in spa hotels through nail clinics to lap dancing, are also on offer to enable individuals to carve out a sense of their own identity and to meet their desires (Wolkowitz 2006). In services that require direct contact between provider and consumer, and body work in particular, it is not so easy to separate out the 'messiness' of provision although strenuous efforts are made by providers of 'well-being' services to do so. The messiness is impossible to avoid in the body work associated with physical care of the vulnerable. This work is considered to be menial and undesirable and therefore generally is undertaken by working-class women, including members of minority communities and migrant women, who, because of their social status, can be rendered invisible while they provide the services.

Consumerism is also part of a wider political ideology through which the market place supplies 'increasingly glamorous stylish goods while the state is seen as providing shabby run down services from which proper consumers seek to buy out if they can afford it' (Gabriel and Lang 2006: 9). Thus, market provision becomes the only way of making the satisfaction of needs acceptable, thereby rendering the needs of the poor and the vulnerable invisible in the market. This ideology, which dominates many northern state national policies as well as international development policies, challenges the validity of the state to meet needs through welfare provision (Hassim and Razavi 2006). 'Whereas buying and selling is seen as a natural state of human activity, the very use of the language of needs is to invoke unequal relations in which one party is making a judgment about the other' (White and Tronto 2004: 440). Needs become associated with the 'needy', not with everyone, and then '[t]he majority, the powerful, or the expert, often substitute their own accounts of needs for the voices and views of those who are affected' (White and Tronto 2004: 440). Meeting needs becomes a political issue contested through the language of inequality (Fraser 1989: chapter 7).

In northern welfare states, state provision has become associated with unsustainable 'welfare dependency', which is perceived to be degrading, thus constructing individual recipients as lesser citizens, as failed consumers. The solution is to ensure that as many individuals as possible, irrespective of other responsibilities or vulnerabilities, move into the world of paid work in order to buy their way into the world of consumerism. In the development context, as we shall see, the international financial institutions' structural adjustment policies sought in many countries to reduce sharply the role of states as employers as well as providers of social support and to encourage market forms of provision through reduced direct provision and payment for services.

Body work, solidarity and caring consumers?

Feminism has sought political rather than market recognition of the value of social reproductive activities and care thinking. It has highlighted the way in which lack of valuation affects men and women differently (Badgett and Folbre 1999; White and Tronto 2004; Folbre 2009). Yet as we have seen, some are arguing that affect underpins the world economy and is central to economic value-creation. Can this shift in location of care to the market be seen as a potential gender-based success story? It could be argued that women's position in society will be greatly enhanced by the economic recognition of the attributes or skills 'naturally' associated with them and that they will be able to 'capitalise' on, and organise around, these in the market place.

However, what effect does an affective market have on working relation-ships? Some would distinguish between immaterial labour used to provide an (immaterial) service and material labour, used for (material) goods. Others would seek to identify care within the general service sector with such work defined as 'custodial or maintenance help of services, rendered for the well being of individuals who cannot perform such activities themselves' (K. Waerness 1985 quoted in Yeates 2004: 371). Within care some would distinguish physical labour and emotional labour (Ehrenreich and Hochschild 2003). The latter term relates to the efforts that are necessary to anticipate the non-physical relational needs associated with love and affection. An elderly couple may have a tradition of celebrating one partner's birthday with a particular meal, which represents the continuing love for the other. Now they are incapacitated and need someone else to prepare food for them. A paid care worker's job specification will require her to 'fulfil activities specified in a care plan' which include the preparation of meals. However the worker may recognise that the partner's inability to prepare the meal distresses him and find ways of preparing the food in a way which minimises his sense of loss and retains as much of the significance of the event as possible. The work therefore is more than the preparation of food, the commodity to be produced is love. Can love be provided through the market? Does it expropriate love from the worker while (often) providing it inadequately to the one in receipt of care?

These conceptions in one way or another underplay the importance of the body in the provision of intimate services and separate the mind (emotions) from the body when in fact physical caring is inseparable from emotional labour (Wolkowitz 2006). Body work is defined as 'the paid work that takes the body as its immediate site of labour, involving intimate, messy contact with the (frequently supine or naked) body, its orifices or products through touch or close proximity' (Wolkowitz 2006: 8). Body work or body/work analysis considers 'not only the gender composition of the workforce in various kinds of work, but also [focuses] on the connections between labour processes, gender ideologies and constructions of the bodies of workers and those with whom they interacted, including their patients, customers and clients' (Wolkowitz 2006: 3–4). This conceptualisation is not limited to a particular way or location in which the work is undertaken. It is able to 'capture the feelings of power women especially may feel "flowing out" from themselves as givers of care or intimate services to recipients' while recognising that 'body work occupations and relationships are also structured by the complex, global hierarchies and polarised labour markets in which they are located' (Wolkowitz 2006: 5).

Those who argue that global markets have incorporated in the productive sphere the values and attributes associated with the sphere of social reproduction make reference to feminist analysis, including that relating to the ethics of care, which will be explored in more detail in the next chapter. Such analysis rejects the presumption that human subjectivity is based upon the conception of a wholly autonomous individual with abstract rights. Instead care ethicists argue that a sense of embodied self is moulded through relationships with others. 'The subjective sense of self is formed not by looking inward, but relationally and comparatively, through social interactions' (N. Crossley 2001: 143 quoted in Wolkowitz 2006: 133). Body work involves social relations: a young woman bathing a frail elderly man involves more than applying soap to skin. The self is therefore a 'social body' affected by the way in which power is exercised within a particular social relationship. The exercise of this power is determined not only by the intimate contexts in which the individual body service provider and recipient find themselves but also by wider institutional governance and macroeconomic contexts.

The commodification of sexual desires raises particularly intense issues relating to the separation of labour from product. Consumer-based markets create and seek to satisfy sexualised desires through the provision of myriad products and services, thereby constructing diverse sexualised consumer bodies and individualised sexual identities. There is considerable political contest over the construction and degree of recognition of these sex-based affects which are linked to debates over the appropriate location, whether market, state, family or community, for satisfying them. A number of constituencies would seek to deny the legitimacy of this 'industry' altogether because it is built upon the commodification and exploitation of the bodies of the women providing the labour. The male-focused market culture of sexual entertainment, and entitlement, is the subject of much feminist critique although there are passionate disagreements.

For many Global South activists the family, not the market, has been the focus for critiques of sexual relationships, not only because of the importance of family-based provisioning in the context of a limited state presence but also because of its social and cultural roles. Clan, caste and community assume primary responsibility for the production and reproduction of wider societal norms. The family seeks to regulate its members' behaviour to ensure that the actions of individuals, particularly those of women, do not jeopardise the standing or honour of the group as a whole. In this context women's bodies are constructed more through family/community rather than market identities. Activists, however, challenge the way in which expressions of sexuality tend always to be constructed by 'development' discourse through association with problems (Harcourt 2009). They contend that there are also positive pleasures for women as well as men associated with culturally constructed sexual bodies and that changing contexts for their expression, including through the commercialisation of community-based sexual services, are not necessarily exploitative (Tamale 2006).

Body work analysis helps to diffuse some of the constructed differences between sex and care work and highlights instead the social relationships involved in provision. In this conception the social relations and social interactions are 'written on the body' of the prostitute (O'Connell Davidson 1998, 2002; Sanchez-Taylor 2001; Anderson and O'Connell Davidson 2003; O'Connell Davidson and Anderson 2006). Differing social processes (not simply discourses) will produce different prostitute bodies which are defined less by their sex or gender (the basis of the radical feminist approach), and more by their position within power relations (Wolkowitz 2006: 133). Such power is not just economic but also includes the power that any particular user may be able to exercise in relation to the transaction. The extent to which the 'prostitute is required to relinquish … control over her bodily boundaries, dignity and personal safely' will vary. Therefore the demands made of the sex worker are not 'wrong' because they involve sex but because they reflect the 'prostitute's relative inability to define her bodily boundaries' (Wolkowitz 2006: 133–134). These demands also reflect the client's ability to evade the 'complex web of rules, meanings, obligations and conventions which govern non commercial sexuality' (O'Connell Davidson 1998: 188 quoted in Wolkowitz 2006: 134). While users gain 'recognition of themselves as fully sexual beings, the experience of the sex worker is one of misrecognition' (Wolkowitz 2006: 135). In other words, the power relations involved in the various forms of market provision enable individuals to a greater or lesser extent to avoid the accepted norms relating to sexual relationships that involve mutuality and shared intimacy.

The analysis extends to other forms of body work such as domestic labour wherein the 'employer explicitly seeks a "person who is not a person" to do work the employer considers too dirty or humiliating to put their own hands to (Anderson 2001; Parreñas 2001), work in which connections between disgust, dirt and the transgression of bodily boundaries are also present' (Wolkowitz 2006: 136). Attitudes towards the body are reflected in divisions within the labour market. Proximity to bodily functions is associated with low-status work. The vast majority of care work that is physically tough is also considered menial and not well respected. It makes use of the 'informal skills' (such as nurturing, which women are supposed to possess as a result of social reproduction roles). If men are involved it is usually at the 'high status' end, as far removed from the 'messiness' of bodies as is possible. Where higher status groups provide care for lower status groups, care 'shades into social control' such as in medical and professional nursing provision. Where users have a higher status than those who care for them, workers may experience humiliation or abuse (Wolkowitz 2006: 153). Paid body work also contributes to household and inter-class divisions of labour.

Body work analysis captures the range of the power inequalities that emerge when such work is undertaken in Global North consumer economies by migrants (predominantly women) from poorer economies. These relationships are all work based but take place in a range of contexts and are concerned with different aspects of body work. The varying discourses relating to their governance contribute to the unequal, but often very different, relationships of power between particular groups of body workers and care recipients. Such an analysis exposes the normative framework of the labour contract (see Chapter 3). When it takes place within an institutional setting there are tensions between defined and limited working time and the imperatives of care (caring does not conform to set hours). It is also more likely to take place in spaces defined as private and unregulated, contributing to its invisibility and to potential exploitation. In addition to labour laws there is a wide range of regulatory provisions that contribute to the construction of these different understandings of care. What counts as care and what it includes relates to the context in which it is provided: 'help around the house' for domestic labour; 'offering a helping hand' for a relative providing unpaid care; a live-in migrant worker from the Global South looking after children may be 'a maid', while a European daily worker may be a nanny. There are no longer clear boundaries between paid public, and unpaid private, care due to the expansion and relocation of paid care to private households.

There are problems in the way in which the relationships that underpin social reproduction are incorporated as commodities into the market and into the politics of consumerism. They are being expropriated from the 'social' and the relationship between work and care is reconstructed in ways that tend to reinforce gender injustices and limit the potential for political solidarity. Care work, in particular, often makes substantial demands of the worker's body and involves intimate contact between worker and service recipient or consumer. Complex power relationships are created that do not necessarily lend themselves to traditional forms of labour-based solidarity.

The focus for political activism in relation to contested sexual identities tends to be the state in both Global North and South to secure social sexual citizenship by ensuring women's sexual rights as individual citizens, either by restructuring market provision (to curb a 'free market in sex') or restricting family- and community-based power over women's rights to control their fertility, and to exercise political choice in the expression of their sexuality. Activists also challenge the way in which existing state institutional power contributes to both market and community constructions. There is therefore a growing campaign for erotic justice which 'challenge[s] injustices built into legal systems defining sexuality, culture, gender and sexual minorities' (see also Harcourt 2009: 152; Kapur 2005).

This activism is made politically more complex by the plurality of sexual identities which are increasingly seeking recognition. The differential impact of the dominant form of global production ensures that technologically driven consumer economies can coexist with other forms of production within one state. In countries such as India, China and Brazil, consumer-based identities associated with high-end immaterial production, urban living and access to global markets are emerging alongside those who are working in mass production and those with no access to either of these forms of production who toil away in the agricultural sector. Market cultures interact with socio-cultural contexts in complex ways and contribute to contests over gendered sexual identities. Similarly, contested sexual identities emerge within northern consumer cultures in relation to minority ethnic groups. Communities may seek to maintain cultural and religious identities through transnational family and community links. They may conduct their lives according to norms or laws that are not recognised by the state's legal system. These transposed and trans-formed norms can be pitted against the discourse of women's individual human rights as well as against sexualised market provision.

Can consumer constructed identities form the basis for political solidarity, particularly in relation to gender-based interventions? On the one hand we have seen that consumer markets construct multiple fragmented identities: the focus is on the creation of an individual lifestyle unique to oneself, which is not a propitious starting point for collective action. On the other hand, we care about what we consume, and those who produce goods and services, we are told, are obliged to care about us. Arguably, we understand ourselves and others through what we consume rather than how we labour.

As Gabriel and Lang (2006: chapter 9) point out, a degree of consumer-based solidarity and activism has emerged, which has contributed to the devel-opment of discourses of corporate social responsibility within companies, regional and international bodies and development-focused NGOs but also more radical and utopian initiatives such as those associated with 'deep green' environmental campaigns and ecofeminism, which seek to challenge dominant forms of consumption and involve worldwide alliances. The care discourses associated with some of these initiatives would seem to lend some support to the proposition that affective thinking can be used for more collective social purposes (Hardt and Negri 2000).

However, although a gender-based identity has figured to some extent in consumer-based initiatives on ethical trading and consumer boycotts of products involving the exploitation of women's labour, consumer-constructed identities have as yet generated limited solidarity as we shall see in subsequent chapters.

Social (reproducer) subjectivity: caring and cared-for body

I argue that there is a need to affirm the importance and value of social reproduction in all societies and that lack of recognition leads to unjust benefits being distributed to the Global North. Reformist attempts, therefore, to tackle this unjust distribution within and across societies through a production focus, using the concept of the gender pyramid, are important for women. These can be set within wider policy contexts, which identify and then tackle unequal distribution (Razavi 2009). However, care and social production more generally should be seen as more than a way of creating value for the economy and thereby offering women access to labour markets. We need more utopian visions, which recognise that to be fully human we all need to be nurtured throughout our lives and that our identities are moulded by our relationships with fellow human beings and with the environment around us. The impor-tance attached by the state to policies relating to 'dependency and care [is] a better indicator of the quality of life ... than its Gross Domestic Product' (Razavi 2009: 2).

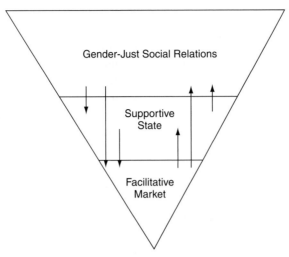

Gender-Just Social Relations

Supportive
State

Facilitative
Market

Figure 3: A care-focused pyramid.

Through incorporation within the market, as affectivity, these values that
shape our identities are being expropriated not socialised. It is important to
imagine ways of wresting caring activity and thinking from the present ideology
of market and use it to further a wider gender justice agenda as represented in
Figure 3. This is not to suggest a return to family-based provision, rather a
transformation of our understanding of a caring world. This vision would
invert the pyramid to privilege social (reproducer)/carer subjectivity. 'A feminist alternative would make social reproduction the dominant domain, with
production and finance acting to serve it. The macroeconomic policy objective
would be decent work for all, with an equal sharing of unpaid work between
women and men, supported by a public policy which recognises the importance
of this work' (Elson 2004: 8). As we shall see in the next chapter, the accom-
panying political vision of this inversion would involve 'a duty to care about
public care, which requires recognition of collective responsibility for all needs'
(White and Tronto 2004: 449).

Introducing global commodity chains

Global commodity chain (GCC) analysis emerged as a way of incorporating
analyses of contemporary forms of globalisation into the study of economic
development (see Bair 2005 for a general overview). 'Take an ultimate con-
sumable item and trace back the set of inputs that culminated in this item – the
prior transformations, the raw materials, the transportation mechanisms, the
labor input into each of the material processes, the food inputs into the labor'
(Hopkins and Wallerstein 1977: 128 quoted in Bair 2005: 155). The original
concept focused on the way in which the productive activities in the chain were
linked with the social reproduction of human labour power and how GCCs

contributed to global inequality. Located within world systems theory, the analysis focused on the way in which capitalist relations had evolved worldwide since the sixteenth century and granted little independence to the role of nation states. It was not a policy-oriented approach.

Subsequently GCCs have been characterised as manifestations of recent internationalisation of production and global integration (Gereffi and Korzeniewicz 1994) and have been development focused. GCCs are defined as 'sets of inter-firm networks which connect manufacturers, suppliers and subcontractors in global industries to each other, and ultimately to international markets, and they are principally concerned with the question of how participation in commodity chains can facilitate industrial upgrading for developing country exporters' (Bair 2005: 156).

Each commodity chain has a number of elements (Bair 2005: 159). The first of these is an 'input-output structure' which involves: 'the full range of activities which are required to bring a product or service from conception, through the intermediary phases of production (involving a combination of physical transformation and the input of various producer services), delivery to final consumers, and final disposal after use' (Kaplinsky 2000: 8). The second requirement is 'territoriality (or geographical scope)': commodity chains are associated with those industries in which large retailers and brand companies play a central role in the organisation of decentralised production networks in a variety of exporting countries, often located in the Global South. The third important element is the governance structure. Gereffi (1994) described two types of chain: producer-driven and buyer-driven global commodity chains. The former is associated with industries in which powerful manufacturers control and often own a number of suppliers. The latter describes how global buyers coordinate production and distribution systems without any direct ownership. Here global buyers (retailers and brand marketers) are key players in these 'globally dispersed and organizationally fragmented production and distribution networks' (Gereffi et al. 2005: 82). Thus the production of a branded sports shirt will involve a complex network of contractors producing, in a variety of settings from home work to large-scale factories and locations, different elements of the garment. Specifications for the products are supplied by the retailer or the company that designs and/or markets the branded products but does not make them (Oxfam 2004). However without owning the factories, they exert substantial control over how, when and where the manufacturing takes place; and largely determine how much profit accrues at each stage in the chain.

More recently analysts and activists have focused on who gains and who loses in the chains. As a result these processes are now more often described within a development discourse as Global Value Chains (GVC). The aim is not just to chart the often complex stages through which a product passes on its way to consumption and disposal but to establish how and where value is added to the product as it passes through these stages. The wider objectives are first to determine how the income is distributed globally and secondly to develop policy measures to ameliorate unequal distribution (Kaplinsky 2000: 9). The aim is to tackle 'immiserising growth': the 'failure of individual firms, groups of firms and national economies to insert themselves appropriately into global markets' which leads to a 'situation where there is increasing economic activity (more output and more employment) but falling economic returns' (Kaplinksy 2000: 7). One key aim is to find ways of 'upgrading' firms, located within the developing world, in the value chains.

The shift to a value-focused analysis has been associated with an increased emphasis on the range of regulatory contexts in which the chains operate. Gereffi and others have identified a range of firm-level governance processes, which depends on the degree of control exercised by the lead firm over the suppliers through specification-setting and monitoring (Gereffi et al. 2005). GCC/GVC analysis also encompasses the way in which globalisation has changed trading and production strategies within both the private realm of firms and the public realm of state economic policies (Gereffi and Korzeniewicz 1994; Kaplinsky 2000; Gereffi et al. 2005). Increasingly the focus has extended beyond what goes on at the 'micro' level of inter-firm relations to incorporate a more institutional analysis.

GCC/GVC analysis now recognises first that the macroeconomic regulatory contexts that contribute to the distribution of value within the chains and that the multilateral trading system, along with regional and bilateral trade agreements, sets the parameters within which specific GVCs operate. An assessment of the impact of trade policies on GVCs therefore becomes important in any discussion of the distribution of benefits (Stevens and Keenan 2000). Do European consumers (via their treasuries) subsidise some African producers via trade preferences, or do African workers subsidise European consumers through the way in which value chains are regulated, or do both processes occur at the same time at different levels?

Secondly, GVCs incorporate the relationship between states and the more generalised private standard-setting (for example industry codes of conduct) that is emerging as governance at firm level (Tallontire 2007). The states in which the original stages of production are located provide the regulatory context in which actors operate: local employers and producers are obliged to comply with their state's employment or health and safety laws and any standards relating to produce quality that may pertain. These will affect the value chain: if there are few labour rights, including health and safety regulations, then labour may be cheaper and crop spraying procedures may be cheaper than in countries with more stringent rights and standards. However, lead firms seek not only to ensure efficient and effective technical management of value chains but also to meet wider consumer market requirements. As we have seen, the value of many products is created by the pleasure they bring to consumers. Quality standards in food, for instance, involve aesthetics as well as lack of contamination. In addition the pressure from those who wish to buy ethically produced commodities (involving no child labour or pesticides) has led to the development of corporate social responsibility policies. Complex and precise specifications must be transferred through the value chain to ensure that these requirements are met.

Suppliers in the South can be faced with a plethora of 'private' standards, which may originate from individual lead firms, from industry-based organisations, or increasingly, from multi-stakeholder groups, which include consumer groups, development-focused NGOs and industry representatives. These developments are prompting organisations in the South to develop their own private standards as a response. Thus these might involve the setting of sector-wide standards for non-traditional agricultural exports to provide the quality standard required in the consuming countries. These private standards may, but this is not necessarily a corollary, be more widely adopted for domestic consumers or prompt the state to enact similar regulations.

These developments raise questions concerning the possibly diminishing power of the state. If national economic policies are increasingly dominated by global and regional trade regimes on the one hand, and governance through private standards on the other, what happens to any wider state-based gender strategy? Activists focus on the state to improve women's position within the labour market by extending rights and benefits down the gender pyramid (increasing entitlements within segment B). States may adopt policies to improve women's property and land rights or their position within the social reproductive sphere, such as within family law (entitlements within segment C). Generally the women's human rights movement has developed a framework for the implementation of increasingly substantive rights for women. If implemented by states, these rights have the potential to improve the lives of all citizens. However, if the state is marginalised in policy development, thereby losing further legitimacy with its citizens, and its capacity is reduced through loss of personnel to private-sector initiatives, efforts to improve women's position within society as a whole may be adversely affected.

The previous section identified potentially different foci for political action based on the gender pyramid. The first focused on women as workers and their need for substantial rights relating to social reproduction to enable them to work in less exploitative ways; the second suggested that action could be more focused around consumer rather than worker identity. Is there therefore trans-ference of 'rights' discourse from the state and incorporation into the market governance of trade and by private standard-setting? Are new 'care' based discourses (connected with corporate social responsibility) developing? While few would point to much that is positive for gender issues within macro trade discussions, some might argue that private standards provide, at least in the workplace, the potential for improvements in the gender pyramid through the incorporation of northern consumer market-inspired 'rights' into these 'soft laws'. It could be argued that the 'care' of northern consumers about food quality and safety is producing care for women workers in the Global South. Civil society-based campaigns involving NGOs and women workers may be able to influence the development of private standards whereas they may have more difficulty finding a voice within male-dominated trade union campaigns that focus on state employment rights. However, women workers may benefit from greater entitlements within the gender pyramid if they work in a global value chain but lose wider and longer-term democratic citizenship rights.

While the original conception of commodity chain analysis placed considerable emphasis on the contribution of labour to the development of global capitalism, the role of labour as *creators* of value has been lost to a large extent in more recent formulations. The focus is still 'on upgrading primarily at the level of the *individual* firm in the context of a *particular* value chain' to achieve a greater share of the benefits (original emphasis) (Bair 2005: 166). Upgrading of firms within the chain can lead to the exclusion of others, particularly those in the Global South. Smaller producers are unable to join the circles where new skills and learning are generated (Bair 2005: 166). Women smallholder farmers or entrepreneurs are, due to wider societal pressures, likely to face particular difficulties in accessing these circles.

While successful participation in GVCs may deliver benefits to upgraded firms, their workers might be adversely affected by this process. If governance through private standards is based upon the dominant concerns of lead firms and set within dominant flexible labour and free trade discourses, these standards may transfer and extend the precarious employment practices which are increasingly being adopted in the Global North and reinforce informalisation within Global South production (Tallontire 2007). Informal work at present is not normally covered by state-based labour regulation and does not attract any state-based employment-related benefits, which are so important for women workers. Much industrial outwork already takes place informally (that is, in an unregulated context) within households. As Yeates argues 'orthodox global commodity chain analysts have neither positioned the household as a site of production within commodity chains nor theorized the relationship between household production and the transformation of commodity chains' (references omitted) (Yeates 2004: 378). Furthermore the emphasis on production fails to recognise the contribution of social reproductive labour to the creation of value within the productive sector. There is a need for a renewed 'emphasis on labour, both productive and reproductive, on material and non-material inputs and on unequal household relations in the production process' (Yeates 2004: 378).

However a productive/worker/consumer perspective for strategies to redistribute benefits will not recapture the value of reproductive labour from the market, as required by our inverted gender pyramid. GVCs that are motivated by profit are highly unlikely to focus on the wider social reproductive contexts in the societies in which they function: governance initiatives, even within the discourse of corporate social responsibility, will not be concerned, for instance, with improvements in women's land ownership rights. These issues are explored further in the agribusiness GVC involving the production of fresh fruit and vegetables in Kenya.

Developing the Global Value Chain analysis: body work chains

Global commodity/value chain analysis is concerned with the production of 'things': commodities. Female (and male) workers contribute to the creation of these things. These chains are products of and produce contemporary forms of globalisation. Capital flows across national borders with ease and enables women workers in the Global South to work at the producer end of the chains. Is it possible to apply this type of analysis to situations where the 'factor of production', that is the worker moves across national borders to provide a service rather than to make a product and in so doing creates a network of relationships? Hochschild (2003) building on work undertaken by Parreñas (2001) first used the concept of a global care chain to capture the relationship between globalisation, migration and care. She refers to the 'series of personal links between people across the globe based on the paid or unpaid work of caring' (Hochschild 2000a: 131). Care chain literature:

> points to the massive and increasing demand for migrant domestic workers throughout wealthier countries of the world, the supply of domestic workers by less wealthy ones, the way in which these transfers are structured by social class, ethnicity and 'race' as well as by gender, and the existence of an international division of reproductive labour. (Yeates 2004: 372, references omitted).

It links a series of care labour suppliers who also consume other women's labour: a daughter within a poor country cares for her siblings while her mother is paid to care for a child by another woman who then emigrates from a poor country to provide care for the children of a woman who works in a richer country in the formal labour market and has caring responsibilities herself. It captures the inequalities involved in this process whereby emotional as well as physical labour is unjustly redistributed. Hochschild argues, therefore, that this chain extracts resources in terms of lost caring capacity from the Third World in order to enrich the First World. '(L)ove and care become the "new gold"' (although it is not extracted forcibly). 'Instead, we see a benign scene of Third World women pushing baby carriages, elder care workers patiently walking, arms linked, with elderly clients on streets or sitting beside them in First World parks' (2003: 26–27).

Hochschild's (2000b) care chains focus on unskilled domestic workers providing care services within private households. Yeates (2004) argues that the GCC/GVC analysis, which was designed for industrial production of goods, is difficult to apply to services, firstly because 'service production requires the proximity of producer and consumer and the immediate consumption of that service', and secondly 'because care involves both productive and reproductive elements (which are not valued by orthodox economists)' (2004: 376–377). She provides an analytical framework which integrates commodity and care chain analysis (2004 and 2009) and in so doing widens the scope of care chain analysis to cover the range of care-based activities from unskilled household domestic work to skilled work within health, education, sexual and social care services. She extends the range of locations in which this care work takes place from the household through to private and public institutions such as residential social care homes and hospitals. She then applies the three key commodity chain characteristics – the structure of inputs and outputs, territoriality and governance – to the range of potential care chains (2004: 380–385). The first of these does not translate directly from commodity to service production. Yeates provides 'a stylized schema indicating the spectrum of skill and remuneration of labour, input intensity, organization and regulation that the care services sector embraces' (2004: 381). Chains will involve activities along this continuum. 'For example the sex trade tends to be unregulated, labour intensive, unskilled and often atomised [provided on an individual basis], while the professional nursing trade involves skilled labour, is regulated and corporatized [provision through commercial services] and supplies capital-intensive production' (2004: 382). While Yeates subsumes sex-related activities within the concept of care, we use the concept of body work discussed above to better capture the social relationships involved in the provision and consumption of intimate services.

Labour is the key element in service production. Therefore considerations of territoriality focus on the importance of transnational labour networks: whence migrant labour can be drawn to supply particular markets. This involves an analysis of the range of migration channels (who can go where) and the agencies involved (such as international nurse recruitment agencies or international sex traffickers). The location of the 'producing' state in the global economic and political hierarchy plays an important part in the construction of particular body workers. Such positioning has a major impact on the degree of 'legality' involved, the potential for exploitation and the distribution of the benefits of her work. Geographical location is therefore linked to governance issues.

We have seen that the focus on internal firm-level chain governance has been extended to cover the influence of external institutional contexts, including those within the macroeconomic trade framework, the state and those involved in private standard-setting. The governance discourse associated with care/body work chains differentiates processes and channels workers into different legal and policy frameworks, including those associated with brain drains (skilled workers), care chains and trafficking (victims of illegal activities). International and state regulation issues are of central importance to body work chains and complex as we shall see in the specific discussion in future chapters. At the macro level, the General Agreement on Trade in Services (GATS) within the World Trade Organization (WTO) is trying to facilitate the restructuring of care activities as commodified services so that they can be traded on the global market. In so doing the services are detached from their specific context and the social relations in which they are embedded (Kelsey 2008: 13). At the same time international crime conventions are creating new categories of migrants. A movement across a border may now be legitimised as a 'market access' commitment on trade in services or subject to criminal sanctions targeted on 'organised crime'. While macroeconomic policymakers may conceivably embrace free movement of people as factors of production, there is considerable political opposition, particularly within those northern states that benefit from migrant labour. Immigration is a highly sensitive issue. Generally, state-level regulation of migration and employment policies within each chain location plays a central role in the structuring of global service chains. Here the discourse of citizen rights can be posed against those of non-citizen migrants.

The original care chain literature focused on the provision of body work within the private sphere of the household and therefore its lack of public regulation. It assumed that the benefit of emotional labour was always unfairly distributed. The literature on trafficking, which is heavily associated with prostitution and criminality (Anker and Doomernick 2006), also focuses specifically on the gender issues involved in labour migration. It is predicated upon an assumption of the extreme immiseration of the women involved who face exploitation and violence in the processes associated with the provision of sexual satisfaction to men in rich countries. The specifically gender-based exploitative potential involved in care and trafficking chains has been separated at both analytical and policy levels. The differing legal regimes contribute to this separation. Body work analysis seeks to reduce the effects of this dichotomy and facilitates a more nuanced understanding of the value distribution involved in migration chains (O'Connell Davidson and Anderson 2006; Agustin 2007). 'Brain drain' literature, involving the migration of health care workers from the Global South, tends not to address the gender aspects involved unless discussing nurses (Connell 2008; Yeates 2009). It focuses on the contrast between the loss of health care benefits within the sending country and the advantages that accrue to individual professional migrants. Legal discussions therefore highlight the conflict between the civil rights of workers and the social and economic rights of health users.

Have these chains led to the creation and spread of governance through private standard-setting? The global framework for the trading of services has contributed to the development of such standard-setting among multinational companies, which has led to a 'blend of international law and private behaviour' involving 'an increasing interdependence in which political, legal and economic governance mechanisms clash and mesh at multiple levels' (Kelsey 2008: 20, quoting Shaffer 2003). There is increasing integration of professional standards, such as nurse and social work qualifications, which facilitate the development of global chains. Providers of nurse education in the Philippines use Global North syllabi to meet 'export standards'. Chains associated with less-skilled care work have not generated this form of governance. Have private standards initiatives provoked the sort of interventions by civil society actors, including consumers associated with concepts of corporate social responsibility, that we saw in relation to commodities? While there have been moves among professional bodies to create ethical codes of recruitment practice, consumers seem to care less about migrant care service providers even though they are more proximate than commodity workers.

The lack of a focus on tackling issues relating to the distribution of benefits within body work chains is associated with the difficulties over determining the economic values involved in service production. The question of who benefits in a care chain is more complex. Activities associated with care cross the boundaries between productive and unpaid reproductive sectors and many care services are also provided in the not-for-profit sectors of economies: for instance in charitable nursing homes and state health services. It is, as we have seen, difficult to disentangle the product or 'affect' from the labour that produces it and to see how value is added. It is possible to chart this process in, say, the transformation of a pineapple grown from seed in Uganda into 'perfectly ripe and super sweet' bite-size chunks, packed in a plastic tray, with a collapsible fork contained in the lid, which are sold from a supermarket in the UK. It is not so easy to apply to the daily tasks of cleaning the same floors and ironing the same clothes undertaken within a household context. The latter involves no profit and is not within the market. Because the care economy does not figure in much national budgeting or international economic development policies, there has been little interest in developing the analytical tools necessary to rework a value analysis.

This has led some to argue that the focus for assessments of value should be on the 'production' of the service provider rather than the product (Lair 2006). Then inputs into the person, such as state education and training, family care and nurture, cultural attributes, such as religious identity, or ascribed characteristics, such as the assumed caring nature of Filipina women, can figure. The extent to which these inputs contribute to valued outputs for the purchaser, for instance, in the form of remuneration for the service, can be assessed. Muslim women are preferred in the Middle East: non-Muslim women must pay more to recruitment agents. Filipina domestic workers who emigrate tend to be educated, middle-class women who can meet the language and cultural standards required by their employers. In the UK they are seen as more natural carers than Indian women (Gordolan and Lalani 2009). They are, however, paid as domestic workers. Their ability to remit money to their families is not commensurate with their 'home' status. Their low wages in the Global North improve production and increase prosperity but reduce the resources available to the Global South. This approach informs Hochschild's (2000a) conception of the transfer of emotional capacity from the Global South to the North. The loss of value may be described as a 'care drain' or depletion in social capital (Hoskyns and Rai 2007).

The development of an institutional focus within GVCs seeks to avoid a narrow focus on firm-level governance. It is even more important to avoid such a focus on the individual characteristics of those involved in body work chains. The effects of the wider institutional contexts, including regulatory frameworks, need to be fully appreciated in order to tackle questions relating to the redistribution of benefits. The macroeconomic policies that have produced contemporary forms of economic globalisation have created the conditions under which female migration from the South now take place, which Sassen (2002) describes as the feminisation of survival. In the Global South, such globalisation has resulted in the 'growth in unemployment, the closing of a large number of typically small and medium-sized enterprises oriented to national rather than export markets, and high, and often increasing government debt' (Sassen 2002: 256–257). These developments have imposed large costs on certain sectors of the economy and created widespread male unemployment and reduced opportunities for male employment generally. 'Alternative means of making a living, making a profit and securing government revenue' (2002: 257) become vital. Families, communities and states become increasingly dependent on poor women's ability to provide these by whatever means possible.

One example of this feminisation of survival is the utilisation of women's unskilled labour in wealthier countries to provide care and sex services. The processes through which women migrate involve different degrees and forms of institutionalisation. They might be facilitated 'legally' by the state, as in the Philippines, which prepares its citizens for the export market; by legitimate recruitment agencies, which market migrant identities to particular purchasers; or 'illegally' through private intermediaries seeking income-creating opportunities, illustrated by traffickers in women from Moldova. Recruitment fees and remittances support families, communities, entrepreneurs and the state, all of which are involved in poor women's migration. These 'counter geographies of globalisation' (Sassen 2002) operate in the shadow of dominant forms of globalisation, structured by regulatory regimes that construct the boundaries of lawfulness. Women's care migration is often valued ambiguously as the work of 'heroines' contributing to national objectives. A low-income woman may be a burden within a state but a resource outside it while the same women are seen as creators of social and family problems because they have migrated.

As we shall see, regulatory regimes associated with care chains are contributing to the wider injustices associated with the processes. They structure legality, which affects the value of women's services and the risks to their well-being. They tend to narrow the focus of the injustice to the perceived harm or benefit to the individuals supplying the service. The wider socio-economic inequalities between 'supplying' and 'receiving' states, which structure the often exploitative processes involved in the chains, are masked. A focus on a production/worker/consumer pyramid needs to be replaced by one that restores the importance of creating positive forms of mutual interdependence within the social relations of caring wherever they take place, rather than relying on inadequately valued transfers of commodified affects. These issues are addressed in the specific body work chains discussed in subsequent chapters.

Usurping the concept of GVCs: transnational family identities and social reproduction

The third 'chain' considered in this book falls outside the terms of the global value or care chain analysis. It considers the creation of South Asian gendered identities, in particular the part played by attempts to define and control women's sexuality. The activities under consideration in these chains involve processes by which individuals move across borders in order to form and maintain families. This is sometimes referred to as chain migration. As we shall see, young men originally arrived in the UK to work, stayed and sub-sequently sent for wives and other family members to join them. The preference for finding marriage partners from within extended families and communities in Pakistan, Bangladesh and India has continued in some sections of the communities. However, more importantly, the chain considers the way in which the norms that underpin these physical movements 'travel' between families and communities located in India, Pakistan, Bangladesh and the UK and how these interact with what could be described as dominant consumer-oriented sexual identities originating in the UK, and with emerging citizen-based identities in South Asia.

The matters under consideration, which are rooted in families and focus on marriage arrangements, are firmly within the sphere of social reproduction, which raises difficulties with GVC analysis. While care analysts have sought to integrate social reproduction within the value framework, the focus is still on a labour market-related activity: the provision of care/body services through the migration of workers. It could be argued in economic terms that there is no value process involved in 'travelling norms' and the question of who benefits is inappropriate. However, there are points of comparison. Care chain analysis assesses the impact of the transnational forms of family life that are created when a women is in one country and her family in another. Women not only continue to care through economic remittances but seek to actively 'mother' their children at a distance in order to maintain their sense of family and community identity (Parreñas 2005). They migrate as part of wider family and community survival strategies (Sassen 2002). Both elements are evident in the South Asian family chains under consideration. Extended families can be used to spread risks through dispersed family locations and mobilise resources across borders through transfer payments. They also root individuals, who may be vulnerable within the dominant culture, within a wider sense of transna-tional or community/religious identity. Normative frameworks within trans-national families are challenged when women become (distant) breadwinners while men may be expected to assume more caring roles. Equally, transnational migration within families presents challenges, albeit different, to family and community-based norms.

Marriages secure community relationships and can enhance family status. Young men and women identified from within often complex networks of social relations in families and communites move from one country to the other. The processes might involve intermediaries acting as brokers. Value may be added to a family in one country by their ability to sponsor the migration of a family member from another country and thereby gain documented entry to a more prosperous state. Women's bodies, associated with honourable behaviour, can become crucial assets in these processes. Family value is affected by dishonourable conduct. In extreme cases, family members may be seen as forcibly selling women's bodies through marriage to men. Governance of the chains takes place within families but also through the state-based regulation of migration and 'trafficking' in forced marriages.

Chain-based concepts of input and output can be used to discover the ways in which norms relating to the construction of women's sexuality are created and transformed through the processes of global family 'production'. Territoriality plays an important role in constructions of the value of these norms: honour may be central to value construction in rural Pakistan but viewed differently within the communities in the UK. Governance frameworks are particularly important to the way in which sexual identities are constructed. At the 'firm' level, governance is through family and community norms. Are the normative frameworks of communities based in the Global North being transferred through these 'private' governance processes or are community norms in the 'sending state' moving north? Are we seeing the development of private standards (community/religious-based laws) which seek to supersede state forms of regulation in the Global North as well as in the Global South through the recognition of community-based family arbitration councils? Are women 'trafficked' between men within majority and minority communities when, in the name of respect for cultural differences, they shield patriarchal controls over women, thus incorporating dominant values in both communities (Mullally 2006: 84)?

These issues are more familiarly associated with the wide-ranging literature on the relationship between multiculturalism and feminism, which includes feminist legal debate on the contribution of universalist rights discourse in culturally pluralist contexts (Mullally 2006). Some of this literature focuses upon the way in which certain manifestations, such as forced marriages, crimes of honour, female genital mutilation and 'cultural defences' are understood generally in criminal law (Welchman and Hossein 2005). The degree of state recognition to be afforded to religious or community-based family/personal laws and the impact of such recognition on gender relations is also much debated (Shachar 2001). Consideration of these issues within an economically inspired chain and 'trading of norms' framework is not intended to deny the insights gained from this literature or to substitute a narrow economistic understanding. It aims to widen the scope for analysis and bring the social and economic relationships that underpin these issues of identity and recognition, and which are moulded by processes of globalisation, more to the fore.

Conclusion

This chapter has used the gender pyramid to stress the importance of linking gendered patterns of social production to women's vulnerabilities within market economies. These vertical contexts are then linked using global commodity/ value chains to demonstrate the ways in which inequalities are distributed across societies. Chain analysis has started to take account not only of immediate, seemingly direct, external factors but also the wider institutional context in which chains operate. However its weakness lies in the tendency to underestimate the importance of labour and the contribution of social reproduction to the creation of value. The gender pyramid shows that it is essential to take account of the interactions between production and social reproduction if women workers are to benefit from global markets.

While women undertake most unpaid care work in societies, the circumstances under which it is undertaken vary according to local contexts. These contexts are set by wider social, economic and political factors, which include the way in which the economy is incorporated within the global market and the interaction between state, civil society and communities. Each affects gender relationships within society and the potential for positive action to address issues of inequality. Recognition of the importance of social reproduction to the creation of value and the distribution of benefits within GCC/GVC analysis requires an assessment of a much wider institutional context than traditionally associated with this form of analysis. However, the strength of the GCC/GVC approach is its recognition of the central role of governance and the importance generally of the wider regulatory context in which global production takes place. It is this aspect of chain analysis that will be developed in relation to gender issues in this book through the discussion of the discourses of trade, rights and care.

While GVC analysis helps to reveal the global inequalities produced through its processes and potentially provides a positive framework for addressing specific production-related gender issues, it may mask the wider effects of this form of global production on gender relations within societies as a whole. It is therefore necessary to address the broader impact of globalisation on gender relations when addressing the issue of the distribution of benefits. This book seeks to provide sufficient understanding of the vertical contexts in order to understand not only the impact of the specific chain on those involved but also to provide an appreciation of the wider implications for gender politics. While recognising the overwhelming need to improve women's position within global markets it is also necessary to pose a more utopian alternative in which waged work is not the sole and ultimate goal. This chapter has introduced its own shadow form, the inverted pyramid, which decentres work to argue for a more utopian vision of the relationship between care and work. From this perspective, life-enhancing activities, including the provision of care, undertaken in contexts of choice, are seen as equally valuable and essential for the well-being of everyone. Is it possible to restructure the market to become more life centred or even to wrest the provision of well-being back from the market in ways that do not reinforce traditional forms of authority but enhance gender justice? Can there be a gender politics of the common good, which creates new forms of caring citizenship and replaces consumerism as the default identity?

2

Globalising feminist legal theory

Introduction

This book seeks to use a feminist analysis to tackle issues of gender justice within a profoundly unequal world. It asks: how do we care about women in a global economy who labour to produce cheap food, clothing and consumer durables? Do we care for the workers recruited in the South who migrate to enable women and men to undertake (relatively well-) paid work in northern economies? What aspects of people's lives do we care about? Can this ethically-based approach to law be used to find ways of tackling global injustices? The previous chapter addressed these questions through analyses of social and economic processes and provided a framework through which to explore them. It argued that global commodity/value chain analysis offers a way of linking the micro- and macroeconomic factors that contribute to the distribution of the benefits of contemporary globalisation. This approach, with its emphasis on the importance of governance to this distribution, assists with a legal analysis. However, the economic focus only provides part of the picture for a gender analysis which requires an understanding of the way in which constructions of sex/gender interact with these processes.

This chapter draws on feminist debates on the relationship between socio-economic processes and the construction of identities to develop and enrich this framework. It considers three accounts of globalisation, which relate to the horizontal linkages in the framework for this book and which are used to understand the nature of global gender injustices. It argues that the market is associated with dominant discourses of trade and consumer identities; the state with rights and citizen identities and the family/community with care and carer (relation-based) identities. Although trade, rights and care discourses are associated with spheres of activity, they are not wholly contained within them. The salience of human rights to trade law is now the subject of much academic and policy debate (Grown et al. 2006; Harrison 2007) while feminist critiques of international law, and in particular human rights activism, have successfully extended coverage beyond the public sphere to family-based issues such as domestic violence. At the same time care thinking, with its origins in feminism, is informing critiques of rights and is being used to challenge national and international public policy formation. In other words, care analysis is not confined to the 'social' world outside politics while that of rights is not contained within the political. In addition, a form of care discourse, as we started to see in the previous chapter, is increasingly underpinning key aspects of consumer economies and thereby extending into economic analysis. Both care and justice approaches are used in the struggle against global injustices.

These differing accounts of the contribution of law to processes of globalisation are best addressed as palimpsests within a legal pluralist framework because they intersect and interact rather than function within a legal hierarchy. The final section therefore sets them within legally pluralist analyses of contemporary globalisation. The chapter concludes with a review of the analytical framework for the chapters that follow.

Who are 'we'? Feminism as neocolonialism?

The chapter recognises the challenges posed by global feminist critiques to the use of 'we' in the earlier questions, which could easily be understood as reinforcing Global North neocolonialist patronage. 'The bond that is necessary for a coalition to evolve within international feminism cannot be created from a romanticized sisterhood that assumes common oppression of all women' (Oloka-Onyango and Tamale 1995: 698). Naffine has described the position of feminists within legal academies as having the 'epistemic privilege of marginality' (2002: 77). What may look natural and right to those at the heart of a community looks very different to those at the margins. Thus 'feminists have been able to identify and articulate the elitism and excluding tendencies of law that promises equality and justice for all'. They perceive the 'deficiencies of law, both from personal experience and from the systematic study of legal doctrine and legal practice' (2002: 78). Global South feminists argue that they often hold this position in relation to feminist scholarship more generally. As Nnaemeka points out:

> Seeing feminist theorizing through the eyes of the 'other', from the 'other' place, through the 'other' world-view has the capacity to defamiliarize feminist theory as we know it and assist it not only in interrogating, understanding, and explaining the unfamiliar but also in defamiliarizing and refamiliarizing the familiar in more productive and enriching ways. (2003: 381)

It is very easy, however, for this enrichment to scholarship to be usurped by 'quarantining "third-world" voices to specific sections [of academic texts] that are marked by predetermined notions of the intellectual and epistemological boundaries of "third-world" knowing subjects'. The '"theory section" excludes the voices of "third-world" women whose work is used to '"rematerialize" or concretise the abstraction of theoretical positions'. Global South women are consigned to case studies or country-specific locations (Nnaemeka 2003: 366.) 'African women (as researchers/scholars and as the researched) are instrumentalized: as researchers/scholars they are the instruments for collecting the raw data with which foreign scholars manufacture knowledge; as the researched they are the instruments through which scholarship is produced and careers built.' (Nnaemeka 2003: 367) Thus feminist theory is itself a commodity chain with a high-value good, marketed and sold in the North, which involves the labour of women in the production zones. However, there is a different way in which the 'we' can be understood, which still retains a focus on the North while maintaining a relationship with the 'others'. As Orford argues in relation to international economic policies: '[t]hose who celebrate the age of globalization "actively forget" the extent to which access to the bodies, labour and resources of people in states subject to monetary intervention is the condition of the prosperous lifestyles of international lawyers and their audiences in industrialised liberal democracies' (2002: 290–291). In other words, it is not only 'local cultures', manifested in family and community norms, which cause injustices to women. Economic globalisation, built on imperial and colonial histories, can be seen as distributing the benefits of development disproportionately, thereby unjustly benefiting a Global Northern 'we' (which includes first-world feminists). As Global South feminists point out, the North does have culture: it is heavily associated with consuming traded goods and services. There is an economics to culture and a culture of economics.

The reader must judge whether this book falls foul of the critiques. While the aim of this book is to address issues of global injustice, there is no return to or reworking of an economism wherein divisions on the basis of 'class' trump those of sex/gender. I would endorse Engle's view that an analysis that refuses to focus 'on *either* gender/culture *or* economics' might provoke feminists across the globe to address how 'committed they are in fact to a radical redistribution of wealth' (Engle 2005: 66).

Global accounts of citizens, consumers and carers

Globalisation at its most general involves 'a historical process which transforms the spatial organization of social relations and transactions, generating trans-continental or interregional networks of interaction and the exercise of power' (Held and McGrew 1999: 1–2). Feminism seems to have figured little in main-stream analyses while within the numerous, competing and overlapping, nar-ratives (Held et al. 1999; Rai 2002), the contribution of law and its relationship to justice differs.

The framework for this book addresses these diverse narratives by adapting Silbey's three 'stories' of globalisation (1997): the first, the enlightenment story, in which reason triumphs over nature (the political); the second, involving the 'historic struggle and triumph of the market economy' in which desire reigns over law (the economic); and third, postmodern colonialism, in which commo-dified cultural symbols triumph (the cultural). Silbey's account, which groups together the economic with free market trading and individual consumer rights; the political with universal rights for citizens within states; and the cultural with the production and consumption of dominant identities, figures prominently in the framework of analysis adopted in this book. However the categories are modified somewhat to reflect a more overtly feminist legal perspective in which 'culture' contributes to the range of narratives relating to globalisation rather than only to the postmodern colonialisation account. It features in the liberal political story, in which law and reason supersede cultural norms and in the economic story, which addresses the commodified consumer identities around which economies are increasingly organised, accommodating aspects of Silbey's neoliberal and postmodern stories to argue that both human rights and economic discourses have cultures. The chapter introduces a 'social' account of globalisation, which recognises its impact on the processes of social reproduction within the family and community. '[F]amilies, households and social communities ... have also been globally restructured, not just the world of corporate profit-seeking and international relations' (Harding 2008: 231). These processes and locations are associated with political accounts, including those associated with some strands of feminism, with 'traditional' or unreasonable (pre-modern) family and community cultures or practices. However, they are presented here as a 'care' story grounded in feminist ethics of care analysis, which challenges the construction of the individual subject that underpins both Silbey's political and economic stories of globalisation. The political engagement between the rights and justice and culture and care 'stories', which lies at the heart of feminist debates, is addressed before turning to the economic narrative, in which care discourse, and carer identity, are being absorbed by processes of commodification.

Justice, citizens and the politics of rights

Within this narrative, science and technology generate progress. '[R]andom and arbitrary activity and the whims of God and nature' are revealed by human reason to be 'highly organized networks and structures governed by laws and procedures' (Silbey 1997: 212). In this story, the rule of law, citizens and now holders of human rights play a significant, and positive, role (Howard-Hassman 2005) and justice is achieved by marginalising those 'still subject to superstition, myth and religion' (Silbey 1997: 213).

Women's rights activists have had long engagement with this political account in their campaigns and networking over the last three decades to gain recognition for women as reasoning human beings (Stewart 2004). The Convention on Elimination of All Forms of Discrimination Against Women (CEDAW), which recognises women's universal rights to equality, dignity and equal worth with men, and which is often described as an international bill of rights for women, is the most obvious outcome (Charlesworth and Chinkin 2000; Buss and Manji 2005; Steiner et al. 2008: 175–223, 541–568). Since then there have been two World Conferences on Women (Nairobi 1985, Beijing 1995), the latter producing the Beijing Platform for Action; the Vienna conference on human rights 1993 (declaring women's rights as human rights); and the development of regional approaches to women's human rights, including the 2003 Protocol to the African Charter on Human and Peoples' rights on the Rights of Women in Africa (Banda 2005). Much of the creative impetus for the rights movement is now located in the Global South (Mehra 2007; APWLD 2008) because, as Williams argues, rights matter to those who have only recently acquired them and to those who hold precarious positions in society (1991). One key focus for action is associated with the institutionalised framework of the UN in particular around the treaty body, the Committee on the Elimination of All Forms of Discrimination Against Women, which is responsible for monitoring the Convention (Byrnes and Connors 2010) although gender has also been 'mainstreamed' into the general UN institutional framework (Kouvo 2005; Merry 2006: chapter 2). Activists continue to develop their approaches, with increasing sophistication, in a wide range of contexts, from localised grassroots campaigns to regional and international networks (Merry 2006) and partnerships with regional governance bodies (see Banda 2005 for the African example).

This positive account of the political project of building international solidarity around gender justice and citizenship has a somewhat uneasy relationship with academic feminist critiques of international law, human rights (Lacey 2004; Mullally 2006) and the contribution of rights to justice (Charlesworth and Chinkin, 2000, Buss and Manji, 2005). Engle (2005) describes an early period in the feminist critique of international law when the Enlightenment philosophical assumption that human rights were an 'indispensable tool in the pursuit of justice and equality' (Mullally 2006: xxix) was not questioned. Instead women were added to the human rights protections guaranteed under international law (the liberal inclusion approach) (Engle 2005: 48). Thereafter, as the limitations of the 'add women in' approach emerged, the focus shifted to a structural bias approach which revealed the way in which international law and its institutions were 'structured to permit, even require, women's subordination' (Engle 2005: 49). Because conventionally international law replicates liberalism's focus on state action and the public realm, it failed to protect women from the actions of non-state actors. Here states must take responsibility for the actions of family or community members who, for instance, perpetrate violence against women, and for cultural assumptions and practices that are oppressive to women. The state is cast in the role of key reformer, particularly in areas that need substantive rights such as women's equal access to family-based assets. Not surprisingly, such demands are often countered with the 'cultural defence', that family, community and religious norms are outside the domain of rights.

This critique moves the locus of women's oppression from the state to the 'private' sphere and 'culture' becomes responsible for women's problems (Engle 2005: 54) and extends state power into the realm of the family and community. Human rights activism opens up the family to legal surveillance, which loses control as an institution, and the patriarchal privileges of males are reduced (or at least transferred to the state). This intervention can be particularly resisted in wealthy and middle-class families including by women. However this reinforcement and extension of state power troubles feminists in post-colonial states whose analyses have focused on the oppressive and patriarchal nature of the state.

Global South feminists critique (Engle's third period of development) both accounts 'for their exclusion or false representation' (Engle 2005: 49). Women in the South become the 'other' suffering from exotic culture (Nnaemeka 2003); secondly, women in the South particularly are constructed as victims lacking agency (Mohanty et al. 1991); and thirdly, structural bias analyses assume a (false) universality of oppression based on private familial sex/gender differences when other divisions such as caste or class are equally important (Kapur 2005; Oloka-Onyango and Tamale 1995). Problematic culture becomes pitted against 'civilised' law (rights) leading to a major fault line between 'universalists' (the same norms apply equally to all) and 'relativists' (norms are culturally specific). Northern women (and men) may assume that in one way or another all women are united by patriarchal oppression, particularly when associated with traditional forms of authority like the family, and that women can be motivated to struggle collectively against its local manifestation if provided with the legal means to overcome these ingrained prejudices. The critique of Global South feminists is that they have been the objects of northern feminism's concern for their oppression within local patriarchies. The objective becomes to rescue women from local traffickers or from those who seek to circumcise them. To echo Spivak, these efforts can seem like white men and women rescuing brown women from brown men (1988: 297; Engle 2005: 62).

This rift, which threatened to derail the consensus necessary for the legitimacy of women's rights, has been tackled through the emergence within human rights policy and practice of what is known as 'culturally sensitive universalism' (Engel 2005: 63). This approach, adopted in the Beijing Declaration from the 1995 World Conference on Women, translates into a duty on states to promote and protect all human rights and fundamental freedoms while bearing in mind national and regional particularities and historical, cultural and religious backgrounds.

Violence against women as culturally sensitive universalism

Politically, understandings of what constitutes culture differ: it can be seen as 'tradition', something which tends to affect the rural poor in the developing world but not cosmopolitan urban elites; as 'national identity or essence', which is inclusive of all citizens; or as 'unbounded, contested, and connected to relations of power, as the product of historical influences rather than evolutionary change' (Merry 2006: 14–15). Violence against women (VAW) is a flashpoint for culturally sensitive universalism not only because such violence is embedded within these contested cultural understandings of gender and sexuality but also because it is heavily associated with the institution of marriage, which supports wider family and community relations. Although states regulate families through laws on formation and dissolution, inheritance and child custody, until recently domestic violence has been constructed as a cultural, not a rights, issue. Its reduction requires the redrawing of the boundary between what is deemed culturally acceptable ('discipline of women') and what is not ('abuse') (Merry 2006). Human rights activists try to recast violent activities as unacceptable abuse that warrants state intervention through criminal sanctions and the granting of specific civil rights to those who experience such violence.

Merry sees the human rights discourse of VAW as a product of transnational modernity, but not as a 'form of global law that imposes rules', rather as 'a cultural practice, as a means of producing new cultural understandings and actions' created through the myriad documents, formal and informal, associated with the system (2006: 228–229). Strategies in relation to VAW are more comfortably aligned to culture as customs (associated with tradition and therefore outdated) than as (national) cultural identity. This alignment can marginalise the poor, rural peoples and immigrants who are associated with traditional culture and risks, replicating colonial discourses, which sought to protect women from the uncivilised behaviour of 'their' men. Human rights 'ideas produced in global settings through international deliberations are being appropriated by national political leaders and NGO activists' and percolate into local communities, 'primarily through the mediation of activists who translate the global language into locally relevant terms' (2006: 218). They are more transformative if they challenge existing assumptions relating to power relationships but more readily adopted if packaged in familiar terms. This 'process of vernacularization' is one of 'appropriation' or extraction of human rights language from the universal and 'translation' or adaptation to national and local communities (Merry 2006: 219), and therefore could be seen as similar to the introduction of imperial law during colonialism.

However, human rights ideas relating to VAW are a result of considerable transnational consensus-building. They are adopted by nation states and local communities, not imposed, although power relations between and within states undoubtedly play a part in these decisions. Poor states, and those with active civil society movements and more democratic politics, have less power to resist. For Merry, the power of human rights ideas has created a political space to rethink gender inequality using a language legitimated by global consensus on standards. They constitute a 'radical challenge to patriarchy' (2006: 221). The price is the acceptance of the norms of individual autonomy, equality, choice and secularism, which might differ from prevailing cultural norms and practices. These norms are creating new cultural practices alongside alternative visions of social justice that are less individualistic and more focused on concepts of communal responsibility. They do not displace other frameworks but add new dimensions. Rights are layered over kinship obligations: at the grass roots, individuals take on human rights discourses through a double subjectivity as rights bearers and as injured kinsfolk and survivors. These two do not merge or blend, they exist as distinct sets of ideas and meanings with translators (including women's rights activists and advocates) bridging the divide.

The individual autonomous abstract legal subject of Western Enlightenment, and the 'cultural' human subject, who is embued with specific and different characteristics such as a sex, religion or a post-colonial history are in effect two 'subjects': one abstract, reflecting the value of individual autonomy for women's emancipation; and the other, with a 'real' body or identity shaped by relationships with others reflecting the importance of solidarity and connection with others for the construction of the human self.

Such an understanding challenges those who argue stridently that human rights are the 'active enemy of women's progress' and that '[r]ights discourse pitch[es] the individual against the community, the universal against the particular, the public against the private' and, reflecting the feminist ethic of care critiques, fails to recognise that 'included amongst the marginalized and excluded are those voices associated with the private, the particular, the affective bases of moral judgement' (Mullally 2006: xxxiv).

Injustice, carers and the ethics of care

Care does not feature in Silbey's narratives on globalisation, although as a moral and political approach, which values difference and 'non justice' thinking, it has presented a major challenge to realist and liberal theories. It has an affinity with the concept of social reproduction discussed in the previous chapter although it has different conceptual origins. It is most associated with the developmental psychologist Carol Gilligan's work (1982) (although see Chodorow 1978) and her empirical study on moral development, in which she heard her male and female subjects speaking with 'different voices' about moral issues. She challenged the orthodox view that human moral thinking developed through stages of increasingly abstract reasoning to arrive at maturity, defined as a 'principled understanding of fairness that rests on the free standing logic of equality and reciprocity' (Robinson 1999: 16). Gilligan's now-famous female subject Amy tackled her moral dilemma through a narrative of relationships that connect people together, which extend over time, rather than through one in which individuals applied systems of rules. She sought to resolve problems through care not justice thinking. Hitherto, this way of moral thinking had been associated with a stage on the way to maturity and therefore inferior. Gilligan presented this way of reasoning as a different but morally mature position, which integrates the needs of both self and others. Gilligan's work has been hugely influential within feminism and beyond (Engster 2004).[1]

---

[1] See Held 2006 for a comprehensive review of the ethic of care: Sevenhuijsen 1998, 2003; Kittay 1999 for social welfare policy; Tronto 1994; White and Tronto 2004; Noddings 1984; Held 2006 for political philosophy and ethics; Robinson 1999. Held 2004 for international relations: West 1997; Drakapoulou 2000 for law.

It has been characterised as a 'morality for women', a feminine way of being, consigned to the 'private sphere' (and therefore outside the sphere of morality) and valuing dependence rather than interdependence. Such an essentialist difference analysis would offer little attraction. However, it is better understood as a form of 'standpoint feminism' (Hartstock 1997, 2006) in which understanding is gained from social experience and the 'concept of the individual, or subject, is seen as an "ensemble" of social relations'. Standpoint theories are 'not about individuals reporting their experience but groups coming to understand the social relations in which they are involved'. It is thus a mediated form of knowledge (experience set within social relations and history) (Hartstock 2006: 179–180 and quoting J. Weeks). The standpoint in this instance is that of persons needing care and attention (Tronto 1994). In contrast to Gilligan's development psychology approach, Joan Tronto provides a social constructivist analysis of the way in which care developed (1994). She traces its origins back to the changes in global and economic society in eighteenth-century Europe. Moral thinking evolved to fit the new circumstances as commercialism and market-based activities moved out of the household and away from local communities to involve distant relationships with others. A 'thinner' universalist morality, to avoid social conflict, based on reason and the assumption that market actors formed the same moral community, developed for commercial and political transactions. At the same time the household became the smaller and separate community of the family into which earlier, and now less important, moral theories of sentiment based upon the local, could be channelled. The rise of the bourgeois family 'contained' woman with the belief that women naturally belonged here and were guardians of the moral sentiments of family life such as sympathy, benevolence and humanity, creating the 'sentimental family' (Okin 1982). Women became associated with family life and care and men with the world of reason in public and economic life.

The central focus of the ethic is 'on the compelling moral salience of attending to and meeting the needs of the particular others for whom we take responsibility' (Held 2006: 10) whether care activities take place in public or private contexts (Tronto 1994; Robinson 1999). Preferential consideration is given for the interests of those with whom there is such a relationship, such as members of family or community, but extends beyond this to those for whom there is solidarity through a care relationship. 'Ethics of care values emotion rather than rejects it . . . empathy, sensitivity, and responsiveness are seen as the kind of moral emotions that need to be cultivated not only to help in the implementation of the dictates of reason but to better ascertain what morality recommends' (Held 2006: 10). Ethical care requires an evaluation of emotions not simply an acceptance of those that prevail.

The ethics of care rejects the moral superiority of abstract reasoning. Rather it 'respects rather than removes itself from the claims of particular others with whom we share actual relationships' and 'calls into question the universalistic and abstract rules of the dominant theories' (Held 2006: 11). Again, the values arising from relationships must be evaluated ethically rather than simply accepted. Like other feminist theories, care ethics does not accept the division within dominant theories between the public and the private. The concept of the person is relational in contrast to the rational, autonomous agent of political liberalism and the self-interested individual of liberal economic theory. Society is not made up of separate autonomous individuals who then agree to form relationships, thereby presuming that human interdependence is somehow optional (Mullally 2006). Rather 'every person starts out as a child dependent on those providing us care, and we remain interdependent with others in thoroughly fundamental ways throughout our lives' (Held 2006: 13–14). We consider ourselves as independent because of the networks of social and economic relations that enable us so to do. As Tronto points out the more independent and powerful we are the more invisible the support systems (1994; White and Tronto 2004). Our relations with others constitute our identity but that does not deny autonomy to individuals. We are not able to choose to whom we are born but we do have the capacity to enter into a range of relationships even if this capability depends on the context in which we find ourselves.

Within care analysis there is no agreed meaning of the term care (see Held 2006: chapter 2). Fisher and Tronto view it as a 'species activity that includes everything that we do to maintain, continue, and repair our "world" so that we can live in it as well as possible. That world includes our bodies, our selves, and our environment . . . (Tronto 1994: 103). Tronto's approach (1994: chapter 4) is adopted in this book. She distinguishes between four elements: 'caring about', which involves recognising that care is necessary and also 'assuming the position of the other person or group to recognise the need'; 'taking care of', which requires the assumption of 'responsibility for an identified need and determining how to respond to it'; 'care giving', which is the 'direct meeting of needs'; and 'care receiving', which involves recognition that 'the object of care will respond to the care it receives' (1994: 106–107). The last is necessary because it is the only way of knowing whether a need has been satisfied. By distinguishing between elements Tronto is able to demonstrate that care relations extend beyond the family and community into the increasingly prevalent social forms of caring offered by the state and market but also that there is a hierarchy involved: the first two elements have been more associated with recognised public activity such as the planning and delivery of services, and traditionally with men; while care-giving involves women and socially marginalised groups such as migrants and is far less valued.

Care is, as Sevenhuijsen (1998) stresses, first and foremost a process and a practice based upon the values identified as central to the ethics of care. These are associated with each of the elements of care described above: attentiveness (caring about); responsibility (taking care of); competence (care-giving); and responsiveness (care-receiving) (Tronto 1994: chapter 5). Care is therefore not a 'naturalized concept' (reducible to existing behaviour) and the ethics of care is not a 'naturalized ethics' which accepts the practices as they have evolved under conditions of 'patriarchy and other domination; it evaluates such practices and recommends what they morally ought to be' (Held 2006: 39).

Dichotomising justice/rights and care thinking carries the danger of reconstituting gender constructs: rights (masculine); care (feminine). Theorists have
therefore sought to inject a relational perspective into the rights approach
while retaining universalism (caring justice) (see Nedelsky 1993, 1997, 2000;
Drakapoulou 2000; Lacey 2004); and to add norms associated with a justice
approach into care while keeping its particularist and practice focus (just caring).
There is no consensus on whether these journeys have led to a satisfactory
meeting (see further Mullally 2006: chapter 1; Robinson 1999: 23–27; Held
2006: chapters 4 and 5; White and Tronto 2004 and the other contributors to
Ratio Juris Vol 17 (4) December 2004).

Caring justice?

Engagements with other schools of feminist thought, including those associated
with Global South scholarship and the difference feminism of care ethics has
provoked a considerable degree of rethinking. The efforts have been motivated
by a desire to retain what are seen as the political power and utility of universalism and rights discourse and a belief that alternative approaches do not provide
the 'resources necessary to build a truly global feminism, global in the sense of
addressing discrimination and inequality in all its complex variety and monotonous similarity' (Mullally 2006: 25).

From justice perspectives, feminists have focused on two areas: the abstract
nature of the subject and the related method of abstract reasoning. They argue
that it is possible to move towards a more relational or embodied form of
subject within liberalism. Okin argues, for instance, that at the centre of Rawls's
work is an implicit voice of responsibility, care and concern for others as well
as for self because without these attributes the parties would not choose the
principles of justice that they do (Robinson 1999: 24). Mullally contends that
through engagement with difference feminisms the theory and practice of
human rights can be transformed rather than abandoned. In particular she
seeks a reconstruction of the way in which rights would be established. She uses
Benhabib's discourse ethics (1992; 1994; 1996, 2002a, 2002b) to move towards
'an interactive universalism, replacing the legislating reason of Enlightenment
traditions with an inter-subjective concept of reason and a discursive mode of
justification' (Mullally 2006: 70). Put very simply, collective decisions undertaken through 'procedures that are radically open and fair to all' (thus through
forms of yet unrealised democratic processes) would form the basis for justice not
principles deduced from abstract reasoning. There would be some procedure-
like 'rules' however. The discussions would be conducted using the 'principles of
universal moral respect and egalitarian reciprocity', which provide the 'pragmatic
rules necessary to keep the moral conversation going' (2006: 71). The reasoning
that produces the rights involved in these dialogues would be undertaken not by

hypothetical abstract subjects but by concrete embodied human selves. In this way the reasoning can be extended to take account of women's lives within the private sphere of the family. Benhabib therefore allows these dialogues to be located within social and cultural contexts but still 'insists upon the right to challenge inherited traditions, in the name of universal principles and as yet "undiscovered communities"', to avoid the reintroduction of reasoning based upon these potentially stronger voices (Mullally 2006: 74).

In what institutional context would these dialogues take place? This question raises the role of the nation state as the locus for human rights. One response is to move from state-centred international law to cosmopolitan law, which 'simultaneously establishes each individual as a world citizen and as a citizen of a state. In this approach, the UN becomes a cosmopolitan democracy. The individual state is then transformed into a "mere agency" for the protection of the rights of individual citizens' (Mullally 2006: 76) and unable to raise nationalistic or patriarchal defences. Gould's project (2004, 2007) is also to rethink democracy and human rights and to open up 'globalized political and economic institutions and trans border communities to democratic participation' because to increase participation radically requires that the 'reach and meaning of human rights ... be more coherently and forcefully articulated' (2004: 1). Functioning in increasingly cosmopolitan ways requires us 'to feel empathy and even solidarity with those at a distance' (2004: 2). Gould's concept of 'intersociative democracy' is based upon relationships and networks, which create trans-border solidarity. She sees care and empathy as essential values in this process and seeks to integrate justice and care (2004: 5).

Fraser, who is rooted in socialist feminism, also seeks political recognition of differences but resists a move to see these as identities originating in 'individual or interpersonal psychology'. Instead she embraces 'the "subjective freedom" that is the hallmark of modernity' that assumes that 'it is up to individuals and groups to define for themselves what counts ... within limits that ensure a like liberty for others' (2001: 27). The moral wrong is the 'denial of the possibility of participating on a par with others in social interaction' (2001: 27). Fraser thus sees lack of recognition (or misrecognition) as an issue of status not identity. Cultural values are institutionalised in ways which differentially affect the respect or esteem granted to individuals. This impedes 'parity of participation' (2001: 27). A reconstituted notion of justice would be based on this universal concept, which would be used both to distribute material resources in a way that would not impede this parity but also to ensure that 'intersubjective' parity of status was achieved.

Just caring?

Justice and rights proponents have a number of problems with care thinking, despite developments in its theory. First, it is a morality for relationships between intimates that does not translate easily into one for distant others, while human rights provide a 'safety net for individuals who are alone and disempowered – those for whom no one cares' (Robinson 1999: 49). Secondly, the preference given to the interests of those with whom one has a special relationship leads to nepotism and favouritism and justifies sectarian or tribal politics: women, in particular, need impartiality to engage fully in society. Thirdly, relational inter-dependency does not provide an adequate degree of agency for women who need individual autonomy and freedom from the responsibilities of relationships. Lastly, it is a morality for interpersonal relationships and is unable to encompass national or transnational institutional relations.

Care theorists have applied themselves to the perceived political weaknesses that emerge when concepts, seemingly designed for personal and social inter-actions, are extended to address the institutional relations associated with globalisation. Some, such as Held, cede ground to keep care and justice concepts distinct. 'At the extremes, [i]n the realm of law, justice and the assurance of rights should have priority, although the humane considerations of care should not be absent' (2006: 17). While not denying a role for justice in the context of caring relations, Held is keen to resist 'the traditional inclination' to expand its reach; instead she would place care thinking at the centre of society because care is the most fundamental value (2006: 17). Care can happen without justice but there is no justice without care. Held argues that promoting care across con-tinents, based on a shared responsibility for meeting need, may be a more promising way to meet desperate needs than through human rights, which require 'mere rational recognition' (2006: 17).

Robinson pursues this last point by developing a 'critical ethic of care' approach to international relations in an era of globalisation that combines relational ethics with a 'critical awareness of the structures of exclusion and oppression which restrict our ability to recognize or relate to others as partic-ular individuals, thwart the development of caring relations, and inhibit the ability of individual persons to speak freely in their own voices' (1999: 47). Critical ethic of care combines the 'is' and the 'ought': it examines the present contexts in which care does, or more frequently does not, take place with the objective of creating more 'humanely responsive institutions' (1999: 48). She stresses that the profound differences and exclusion of an increasingly inter-connected world are not addressed through paternalistic ways of preserving power relations such as charity or 'partnership' based on a false concept of equality. Instead a response requires not a rational act of will but a learned ability, which emerges out of connections and attachments, to focus attention on another and to recognise the other as real (Robinson 1999). Robinson, in moves which take her close to Mullally's position, distinguishes between justice theory's ability 'to recognize that people live in relationships (which involves the ability to treat each other badly as well as well) and justice thinking which centres on the belief that to ensure justice it is necessary to respect the autonomy and individual rights of persons through application of generalizable rules and principles' (1999: 24–25). It is the person as 'generalized' rather than 'concrete' that is the problem with this form of justice rather than 'justice' itself (1999: 25). This is corrected by a care perspective that emphasises the importance of self-esteem and self-respect. A sense of self and an ability to be autonomous is gained through personal relationships because 'an ability to speak in one's own voice ... depends heavily on the approval of others for continued sense of self' (1999: 25). In other words, personhood is constructed through interdependence not independence.

Recognising suffering, revisiting care and needs

Is rights 'talk' more effective in tackling issues of global injustice than care 'talk'? Rights offer a strong, politically empowering message of individual agency and universal coverage. However, justice thinking, argues Sklar, focuses on the justice of normal times and takes little or no account of the persistent experience of injustice or suffering. It 'forgets the irrationality, cupidity, fear, indifference, aggression and inequality that give injustice its power' (1990: 49). Care talk recognises that injustice is felt: it is experienced as personal and social suffering. Its relational, practice methodology focuses on the avoidance of injustice rather than conflict resolution through the application of abstract principles. 'Proclaiming that the poor, the needy and powerless have rights tells us very little about why they are unable to exercise these rights, and about who is responsible for what sort of action to alter their state of poverty or powerlessness' (Robinson 1999: 49). Care, as we have seen, is presently limited to recognition of those who are 'needy', a state of being which is contrasted with autonomous, self-sufficient consumer citizenship (White and Tronto 2004: 434). Care is recast as 'a public value in which the need for care is shared by all members of society, and not just by those who have been defined by their difference as incapable' (White and Tronto 2004: 446). Care talk sees us all as 'citizens in need'.

In consumer-based markets, individual identities are closely linked to the products and services we consume. The powerful can have their 'every need met'. This involves privileged irresponsibility: 'a special kind of personal service in which the recipients of others' caring work presume an entitlement to such care' (White and Tronto 2004 quoting K. Waerness). Those who provide such care through their labour are often relatively powerless. Market place provision avoids any requirement to make judgments on the necessity of these needs but in a political context, need must be defined in order to tackle privileged irresponsibility and to ensure care to those who are less powerful. Gould suggests three elements: materials and sensuous needs to meet such bodily requirements as food and shelter 'which are satisfied by the creation of objects through work'; the need for recognition of the self as an individual and as belonging to a community (both through ascription by others, such as on the basis of family origin, or through self-ascription, such as a gay community); and a need for relationships and connectedness. While the second is predicated on relationships, whether chosen or ascribed to achieve a sense of recognition, the third is an end in itself (2004: 97). White and Tronto, in arguing for a duty to care about public care, make three presumptions: that everyone is entitled to (a) receive adequate care throughout their lives, (b) participate in relationships of care that give meaning to their lives, and (c) participate in the public process that determines the previous two (2004: 449).

Freedom, consumers and trade

In Silbey's second story of globalisation, desire triumphs over law. The 'historic struggle and triumph of the market economy' has swept away the planned and socialised economies and broken free from the confines of national and regional boundaries (Silbey 1997: 213). In this story, a global market creates 'efficiency and controls costs: it also creates justice by empowering consumers' (1997: 214). Consumers, not citizens, are at its core. 'A key feature ... is the fury of [the] critique of legal intervention' (1997: 216). Law, with a differently constructed rule of law to that of the Enlightenment story, is something to be reined in to its core functions of the protection of property and economic rights of private persons and to police a strict boundary between the economy and politics. Law operates in an 'apolitical realm' 'without redistributive consequences' (Silbey 1997: 216 quoting Duncan Kennedy). While in the first story, law has a central role and in the second, a marginal one, the dominant narrative of law in both is one of legal liberalism (Faundez 1997; Silbey 1997). Law is understood as rooted in individual will and agency, whether to serve scientific progress or markets.

The policies of the International Financial Institutions (IFIs) in the heyday of neoliberalism were based on this 'free enterprise' globalisation and a 'grow first, redistribute after' module (Elson 2002: 83). 'Citizens, officials, and politicians must all be disciplined by market forces and bow to the technocratic economic consensus about what will promote growth of GDP and economic efficiency' (Elson 2002: 83). For IFIs, states, particularly in the Global South, were the objects of regulation, not its subjects. State officials became corrupt rent-seekers and state-based social policies were viewed as unaffordable and undeliverable (Rittich 2002). In this model state law facilitates the market and the liberation of consumption by protecting private property and ensuring freedom to trade through the establishment of mechanisms for financial accountability and transparency. The primary purpose of state courts is to protect the interests of property owners and investors (Faundez 1997; Tsuma 2000). Rights support freedom not substantive equality. Article 17 of the Universal Declaration of Human Rights (UDHR) provides that 'Everyone has the right to own property alone as well as in association with others. No one shall be arbitrarily deprived of his property.' Under neoliberalism this entails 'the right to sell your property; and the right to use it to make a profit by employing other people. Under some strands of neoliberal thinking, taxation and government regulations that reduce profits are interpreted as arbitrary deprivation of property' (Elson 2002: 82).

The World Bank, in particular, was persuaded of this institutional economics approach, and because law is constructed as a non-ideological, technical tool, such interventions did not fall foul of its remit of non-involvement in state politics. Generally during the 1990s, IFIs and northern state agencies started to promote 'rule of law projects' to implement this economic narrative (Trubek 2006). Critiques started to emerge in the light of the financial crises in South East Asia and Russia in the last decade of the twentieth century. Dissidents associated with the World Bank contributed, arguing that the policy failed to deliver in its own terms (Stiglitz 2002) and had unexpected and very disturbing results, including fuelling ethnic conflict (Chua 2003). Consequently, states have been rehabilitated to an extent, under neoliberalism with a human face, to play a wider role by limiting market excesses and providing 'safety nets' for those impoverished by these processes, including 'poor women' who are encouraged to attach themselves to markets (Wolfensohn 1999). A more expansive 'rule of law' has re-emerged (Trubek 2009; APJRF 2009).

Macroeconomic policy generally is not fertile territory for feminist analysis with its strongly entrenched discourse of technocratic neutrality although feminist economists, development specialists and activists continue to toil in it (Beneria et al. 2000; Elson and Cagatay 2000; Elson 2002; Pearson 2003; Williams 2003). There are signs of significant progress in the recognition of gender issues within some institutions as a result (Beveridge 2005). The World Bank, in particular, has recognised the relationship between gender relations and economic efficiency (the business case) and has mainstreamed gender throughout its operations (Beveridge 2005: 194; Zucherman and Qing 2005; Schech and Dev 2007). This greater awareness of gender issues has coincided with and contributed to an increased engagement with human rights and the discourse of empowerment for women (see Sarfaty 2007).

Gendered economic entitlement

Feminist engagements with justice and rights theories and practices have been provoked more by political contests over recognition of cultural diversity than by the profoundly unequal global distribution of wealth (Fraser 1995, 2000). From a southern perspective, dominant feminist approaches tended to replicate the importance granted to law and its role in 'civilising' less rational beings in the Enlightenment narrative of globalisation: rights aim to protect them against the institutionalised culture of family and community, and men. However, these rights do not challenge the dominant power relations associated with an expanding neoliberal market economy and its institutions, which reconstruct hierarchies in society and impact negatively on many women's lives (Otto 1999). This market benefits from a construction of women as fully acting, unencumbered subjects. In this way, arguably feminism has been a fellow traveller in the triumph of the economic narrative where desire reigns supreme (Fraser 2009).

Southern scholars highlight the need for a substantive, contextualised approach to rights that is rooted in an understanding of all aspects of globalisation and focuses on substantive social and economic rights (Oloka-Onyango and Tamale 1995; Banda 2005: 247, 263–279):

> women's rights to an adequate standard of living, to freedom from hunger, to work with fair wages and fair conditions of service, to mental and physical health including reproductive health care, to education and training, . . . outlined in the ICESCR and CEDAW, are violated *systematically and on a daily basis*' (original emphasis). (Ilumoka, 1994: 318)

She speaks for many (Kuenyehia 1994; Oloka-Onyango and Tamale 1995; Wengi, 1997) when she argues that 'African women's struggle for human dignity and well-being are located . . .. within an unjust international system of allocation of resources' and that 'poverty is a priority human rights issue' (Ilumoka 1994: 321). These calls for a substantive approach to rights were addressed to the split within international women's activism around the 1995 Fourth World Conference on Women in Beijing between women's rights as culturally sensitive universalism and the 'women and development' policy approach which focused on women's social and economic vulnerability. The Platform for Action that emerged called on UN members to analyse macroeconomic policy from a gender perspective and to pay particular regard to its impact on women's poverty. However, the focus shifted to civil and political rights as a way of tackling the effects of globalisation on women and men in the South. This shift resulted in women being recognised as holders of more substantial political rights, but not to the development of social and economic rights.

A 'rights approach to development' subsequently emerged in the policy community as an alternative conceptual amalgam to mirror that of culturally sensitive universalism and has been adopted enthusiastically by a wide range of institutions including international development agencies, NGOs and government departments. It has proven particularly popular in relation to the pursuit of gender-focused policies and practices because of its perceived advantage of linking development policies to the legitimate claims of individuals (women's empowerment) rather than an externally imposed assumption about their needs. Its focus is not clear beyond this use of rights talk and feminists within the development community are sceptical about the use and effectiveness of presently constituted rights, reflecting in part the critiques discussed in previous sections (Cornwall and Nyamu 2005; Cornwall and Molyneux 2006; *Third World Quarterly* 2006: 27 (7)).

Critiques of liberalism frequently refer to its inadequacies in addressing inequalities in global power relations. Ideal theories of social justice such as that of Rawls (1971, 1999) have not been particularly addressed to the processes for resolving pressing real world injustices although there are notable attempts to apply other strands of Enlightenment thinking to the reduction of global inequality (Pogge 2001, 2002; Sen (Amartya) 1999, 2009). The economist,

Amartya Sen has presented a strong challenge to the orthodoxy of wealth creation as the goal of development with his argument that human development is an end (the freedom) in itself rather than a by-product (Sen (Amartya) 1999). Working with the UN Development Programme (not the World Bank) he contributed to the development of a Human Development Index, which measures development through indices of human well-being rather than purely economic indicators. The UN Human Development Programme has also used its flagship reports to challenge the neoliberal paradigm through concern for both the creation and distribution of wealth (McNeill and St Clair 2009).

The various bodies of the UN attempted to reclaim for states their regulatory autonomy by stressing their legal obligations under international treaties to protect social and economic rights. Supporters of a justice and rights approach emphasise the indivisibility of rights which, unlike economic discourse, does not focus on priorities and trades-offs (Elson 2002: 79). The state is expected to act as the potential protector of women's well-being against the predations of the global market although in practice the trade-off happens, with priority given to the 'imperatives' of the market even when they will have significant detrimental effect on gender equality.

Applying and developing Sen's approach to development, Nussbaum (2002; Nussbaum and Glover 1995) has explicitly addressed the issue of women's poverty in the Global South through her capabilities approach. Her work is firmly rooted within liberalism but has nonetheless disrupted the boundaries of liberal thinking. She has drawn up a list of central functional capabilities that she sees as essential for a human existence: life, bodily health and integrity, senses, imagination and thought, emotions, practical reason, affiliation, being able to live with other species, play and control over one's environment, which has two aspects, political and material (2002: 60–62). She expects this list not only to be the basis for development policies but also for actionable rights claims. Her approach draws upon the strand of liberalism that insists on an active role for the state in creating the material and institutional prerequisites of positive freedom. She uses the concept of combined capabilities to link an individual's internal capability with the external conditions necessary to facilitate this capability. She sees the distribution of resources and opportunities to each person as of primary importance. She is adamant that what women need is more individualism, to be seen and see themselves as autonomous, free human beings, capable of making their own choices. Nussbaum insists that '[c]apability not functioning, is the appropriate political goal' (2002: 64) but that it is also necessary 'to prepare the material and institutional environment so that people are actually able to function' (2002: 65).

The capabilities approach offers an approach that valorises the role of the state while recognising individual agency, which is grounded within specific social and cultural contexts. Gender issues are central to its analysis. Nussbaum tackles head on the objections to her entitlements, which provide a set of universal norms in relation to women's equality, by arguing that her cross-cultural normative account leaves plenty of space for people to determine their life courses once opportunities are secured to them (2002: 51–53). Treating women as 'members of an organic unit such as the family or the community' may ensure that 'the impressive economic growth of a region means nothing to women whose husbands deprive them of control over household income' (2002: 55). She focuses on well-being and includes material considerations such as the right to a life free of poverty, thus seeming to move her close to the responsibilities assigned to the state by the care ethicists. However, her approach does not tackle distributional injustice, which results in economic impoverishment. It does not recognise the relationship between equality and inequality. In the end it is the freedom to develop the capacity to choose what matters rather than what resources any woman or man may have (Phillips 2002b). Nussbaum's capabilities approach cannot capture the interdependence involved in the concept of care (Lewis and Guillari 2005).

Gender and the subject of trade

The contested approach to, and constructions of the subject within, these international macroeconomic development policies underpin the more specific global trade discourse discussed here, which has been the subject of limited but developing gender analyses (Rittich 2002; Beveridge 2005; Kelsey 2008).

Neoliberal trade ideology is based on the notion of comparative advantage: expanding global trade is beneficial to all countries and all citizens although there will be winners and losers. The gains allow the losers to be compensated. Trade theories are gender blind and 'have such dominance that other perspectives are routinely excluded' (Beveridge 2005: 178). Trade policies tend, therefore, to be constructed as gender neutral. Those wishing to contribute to debates within the WTO must speak their language of '"imbalances", "technical assistance" and an already outmoded and increasingly irrelevant "special and differential treatment"' (Beveridge 2005: 178 quoting F. Williams). International trade policy is also founded on the gendered hierarchical dichotomy between economic and social priorities. International trade law replicates this division between the public and the private: the international trade law (public) comprises a set of gender-neutral rules, while women's issues can be tackled in the 'private' domain of the state as long as they do not challenge the trade rules. The 1995 Uruguay Round Agreements are binding obligations between states that require adjustments of non-compliant state laws. Domestic laws are no excuse. 'Core provisions of WTO agreements, though far from uniform, generally reflect the economic objectives of the WTO, including non-discrimination and market liberalisation. "Social" objectives usually fall to be justified as exceptions or exclusions' (Beveridge 2005: 182). 'Thus quantitative restrictions to trade which are contrary to the General Agreement on Tariffs and Trade (GATT)

Article XI might be justified under GATT Article XX as "necessary to protect human life or health" or "public policy"' (2005: 182). This provision probably justifies national laws that prohibit trafficking in women and children and regulate the importation and distribution of pornographic materials. If such a measure were challenged before a WTO panel it would need to satisfy the 'necessity' test and not be simply arbitrary discrimination or a disguised restriction on trade (2005: 183).

Each WTO member is free to set its own level of protection in areas covered by Article XX. The level can be high. So service providers under GATS Article XVI can be subject to local wage regulations, employment rights and policies relating to welfare and training as long as the treatment is no less favourable than that enjoyed by other foreign or domestic service providers. Thus measures to protect women's position might be framed to ensure that they are below the WTO radar. If there are negative impacts of (neutral) trade obligations then it is up to the state to find (gendered) ways of pursuing social objectives. Social protection is thus constructed as an exception to trade law.

One way, therefore, of injecting a gender dimension is to use the orthodox legal analysis, which focuses on developing WTO jurisprudence in the Dispute Settlement Body to include gender objectives as a valid exception. This is based on the increased recognition of environmental legislation as a valid policy objective, justifying accommodation (Beveridge 2005: 185). So the existence of Article XX, it is argued, legitimates the values and policies of state members. Therefore omission of any explicit reference to gender-based concerns in the WTO can be remedied by adding it into Article XX (as women's rights were added into other areas of international law). Feminist legal scholars are sceptical. Such an approach is obliged to rely on judicial balancing by trade law judges of claims in a context where there is no explicit endorsement of equality laws and policies in the Preamble (2005: 186).

If this positivist perspective on law is replaced by one that concentrates on law as a discourse, then the focus shifts to the impact of this construction of international law on the actors who are involved with its processes. Law is seen as privileging certain claims and voices over others. So the absence of a gender perspective reinforces the dominant construction of gender neutrality and institutionalises existing inequalities and disadvantages. It operates as a 'chilling' effect, whereby only national laws or policies that can be 'defended' within the dominant discourse are adopted. This hardly encourages officials in a sector in which women are underrepresented to take risks and to think imaginatively about tackling gender injustices although the 2004 UN InterAgency Task Force on gender and trade is a step in the direction of positive engagement with trade officials (UNCTAD 2004a). Santos and Rodriguez-Gavarito would argue that those doing the imagining are elites with economic and cultural capital and that we should take the lead from the myriad local groups and actors pursuing anti-hegemonic globalisation in search of an alternative 'bottom up', cosmopolitan legality (2005; Merry 2006).

Transforming care and rights economically?

In Silbey's third narrative, globalisation is a form of postmodern colonialism 'where the worldwide distribution and consumption of cultural products removed from the contexts of their production and interpretation is organized through legal devices to constitute a form of domination' (Silbey, 1997: 219). Here power over 'consciousness and consumption' becomes more important than 'control of land or political organization or nation states' (219). 'People live in worlds in which their emotions, desires, and rationalities may be produced independently of their experience' (219). It is not only local products that can be supplanted by globally produced commodities (coconut juice by Coca-Cola) but also local interactions can be overlaid by remote, globally produced and consumed substitutes. The manufacturer, L'Oréal, constructs the image of an economically independent, publicly confident, sexualised 'woman who is worth it' to sell its cosmetics to women in consumer markets across the world. This may not match the constructions of female embodiment in any particular context, which may value more relational identities based upon status as a daughter or wife. Law plays a key part in the symbolic communicative aspect of this form of globalisation. As we have seen, it is possible to view the national laws and policies relating to violence against women adopted in individual states as standardised products of global women's activism, distilled into norms and 'good practices' and distributed through international human rights governance processes (Merry 2006).

Optimists would argue that within postmodern cultural globalisation capital and culture circulate, rather than simply dominate, and therefore can be captured by new groupings (Silbey 1997: 217; Santos 2002). New communication systems enable formally disenfranchised groups not only to join global networks but also to create emancipatory movements, new forms of people's law, and new global concepts of justice (Santos and Rodriguez-Garvito 2005). While some see the emancipatory potential in hybrid identities and pluralist conceptions of justice, others see the erosion of cultural identities (Silbey 1997: 218). For some, the possible decline in sovereignty of the nation state undermines citizenship, for others it opens up the possibility of cosmopolitan democracy (Turner 2001: 11).

Diverse discourses and legal pluralism

Within the political Enlightenment narrative of globalisation, women are constructed through holding rights as autonomous, independent citizens, while the economic liberal market narrative assumes that women are self-sufficient (unencumbered), self-interested agents, able to sell their labour freely and to satisfy their desires through the consumption of goods and services. Within dominant narratives on culture and community, women's identities are constructed through social relationships within family and community. A woman is a (political) citizen rights holder, a (social) kinswoman carer and an (economic) consuming worker simultaneously. Each construction is presently associated with a different institutional context: rights with the state; care with family and community; and desire and freedom with the market. Each context has its own governance process: human rights norms and law; family, religious and community norms and laws; and international economic/trade norms and law. These contexts overlap and interact. Globalisation affects power relations between the institutions and the locations of the discourses: international human rights are used to challenge both state economic practices and community social norms; economic actors use (private) governance standards to regulate their relationships and to avoid national and international regulation; and community actors use religious and community norms to regulate 'public' as well as private relations. These multiple and interacting normative frameworks point to the need for a pluralist legal analysis.

As Anne Griffiths points out, there is considerable confusion over the meaning of legal pluralism (see Merry 1988; Tamanaha 2000, 2008; Griffiths 2002; Melissaris 2004): 'The term and the concepts it encompasses cover diverse and often contested perspectives on law, ranging from the recognition of differing legal orders within nation-states, to a more far reaching and open-ended concept of law that does not necessarily depend on state recognition for its validity' (2002: 289). It has been a Cinderella subject within legal theory until recently with interest limited to anthropologists of law, folk law specialists and those working in the area of law in development particularly in post-colonial societies (Falk Moore 1978; Griffiths 1986; Merry 1988, 1991; Woodman 1998). New life has been injected by gender analysis, primarily from those working in southern contexts (Griffiths 1997; Bentzon et al. 1998; Hellum 1999b; Hellum et al. 2007); debates on pluralism and multiculturalism within post-industrialised-societies (Menski 1993; Yilmaz 2001, 2002; Shah 2005; Menski and Shah 2006); considerations of the legal effects of political and economic globalisation (Teubner 1992; Snyder 1999; Twining 2000; Santos 2002; Berman 2007) and, finally and more generally, through the influence of discourse theories, to law (Teubner 1992; Melissaris 2004).

John Griffiths distinguished (1986) between 'weak', 'juristic' or 'classic' and 'strong', 'deep' or 'new' legal pluralism. In weak pluralism, which is closely associated with Enlightenment thinking and colonialism, law is seen as a product of the development of rationality whereby rule by self-interest or force was replaced by the rule of law. The ideology of state law, whereby the state becomes the sole source of legal authority, is associated with the rise and consolidation of state power in the eighteenth and nineteenth centuries. The processes of state-building in Europe replaced the constellation of laws drawn from a wide range of sources that has prevailed for much of its history (Tamanaha 2008). European states tried to impose versions of European law in the colonies while recognising those local, customary or religious regulative frameworks (in the area of family and community matters) that were not 'uncivilised' ('repugnant' or 'contrary to public morals'). The colonial state defined 'the parameters that mark the territories of legal systems within its domain, such as customary and Islamic law, in ways that depict them as separate and autonomous spheres' (Griffiths 2002: 291). While European states were consolidating their power through legal centralism at home, they were contributing to the creation of pluralism in the areas under colonialisation. Many post-colonial states are in social reality weakly pluralistic as a result. As we shall see, colonial engagement with local power structures moulded, rather than merely reflected, local customary laws in ways which altered and still affect gender power relations (Bujra 1982; Chanock 1982; White 1987; Mbilinyi 1988).

'Strong' legal pluralism assumes that there are 'multiple forms of ordering that pertain to members of society that are not necessarily dependent upon the state for recognition of their authority' in all societies (Griffiths 2002: 302). Law is not self-referential but 'porous' (Santos 2002); it interacts with, using Falk Moore's terminology, the many and various 'semi autonomous social fields' (such as a factory, a lineage group or a family) which constitute daily lives. Such a field 'can generate rules and customs and symbols internally, but ... is also vulnerable to rules and decisions and other forces emanating from the larger world by which it is surrounded. ... [It] has rule-making capacities, and the means to induce or coerce compliance; but it is simultaneously set in a larger social matrix which can, and does, affect and invade it ...'(1978: 720).

State laws, therefore, may or may not supplant the rules within any field. Some radical pluralists would not give state law this level of weight while others recognise the significance of its coercive power and authority (see Tamanaha 2008). Such 'strong' pluralist analyses are criticised for creating an unworkably indeterminate concept of law, which cannot be distinguished from other forms of social control (Tamanaha 2000, 2008). Whatever position is adopted, legal pluralism is a social fact, not a characteristic of a particular form of society (Tamanaha 2008). State legal systems in many developing countries are estimated to resolve only 20 per cent of disputes (DFID 2002). Customary law remains the most important source of law for the majority of Africans (An Na'im 1999).

If law is seen as a system of thought, a discourse, rather than as a system of rules, then the task for legal pluralists involves distinguishing legal from other discourses (Melissaris 2004). For instance, De Sousa Santos imagines legal pluralism 'as a cluster of interpenetrating legalities, which regulate all instances of our whole lives and correspond to our knowledge of the world. As this knowledge changes, so do the forms of regulation we experience' (Melissaris 2004: 65).

While the focus for much legal pluralist analysis has historically been the transposition of laws from one society to another or the determination of various legal regimes within one society, the processes of globalisation are leading to new transnational forms of pluralism. Global legal pluralism seeks to understand the ways in which the diverse effects of globalisation affect relations within and across state boundaries. It is no longer satisfactory to analyse global economic networks in terms of 'contracts between nominally equal parties, such as individuals, companies, or states' or 'in hierarchical terms, for example, as constituting various regional or international forms of multi-level governance' (Snyder 1999: 339). Instead, Snyder develops Teubner's concept of *lex mercatoria* (which consists of 'invisible' markets, branches, specialised professional communities and highly technical social networks all of which transcend territorial boundaries) in his analysis of the European toy industry (1999: 340). This perspective takes seriously 'the economically and socially significant norms that operate across national borders and, to a large extent, independently of states' and also soft law rules of conduct (1999: 341). The focus is not limited to contractually inspired relationships but also includes the role of nation states, regional organisations such as the EU and international organisations such as the World Trade Organization (1999: 341–342). 'Global legal pluralism does more, however, than simply provide the rules of the game. It also constitutes the game itself, including the players' (1999: 343).

Concluding the framework

Although contemporary feminist legal studies are a product of both *'analytical and political-ethical claims'* (Lacey 2004: 16), they have not recognised sufficiently the impact that the various processes of globalisation are having on gender relations both within and between societies. There has been far more energy devoted in Global North scholarship relating to the cultural differences in plural societies than to global economic and social inequalities. Those working in post-colonial contexts have taken advantage of their positions at the margins to critique feminist legal scholarship originating in the North. If we place understandings of law and injustice from the Global South at the centre of an analysis that nevertheless is aware of the relationships and structures which bind 'us' together, the importance of the political-ethical focus of feminist thought comes to the fore. From this perspective the impact of globalisation on gender relations and distributional aspects of gender justice becomes far more prominent. If we are trapped within languages or thought patterns that produce 'gender', as post-structuralist feminists argue, can we 'think the unthinkable' to produce a new language for gender and for law? Can 'normative terms' such as 'rights, justice, equality' be re-imagined, reconstructed in different ways' (Lacey 2004: 45)? We need to find a language that relates 'critique' to a 'utopianism' (Lacey 2004: 43) that seeks to reduce injustices in an era of globalisation.

The previous chapter introduced a framework which placed social and economic relations at its centre and as such, owes much to the work of socialist feminists. It focused on the specific activities associated with caring and the 'care economy' and the ways in which social reproduction is being integrated within an increasingly global market. It argued that commodity chain analysis assists with an understanding of the way in which the unrecognised value of socially reproductive labour, whether incorporated in the market or undertaken in the family and community, can be distributed unjustly. The marginalised 'standpoint' of social reproduction enables us to see the impact of globalisation on gender relations and to consider the way in which governance structures contribute to the injustices. It also enables us to start to imagine alternatives if social reproductive activities were the centre of concern for national and international economic as well as social policy.

The economically inspired chain analysis by definition focuses on markets but more recently has developed to assess the impact of institutional relationships on market relations. The critiques by feminists of this approach have demonstrated some of its weaknesses. In this chapter the focus has shifted to the way in which feminist legal scholarship has engaged with analyses of globalisation. Within this scholarship much attention has involved an assessment of the ability of universalist liberal justice theories, and human rights in particular, to tackle contemporary global gender injustices. The discourse of human rights has considerable political power but is based upon a construction of personhood which is built around an abstract individual's capacity for rational autonomous action. It seeks to ignore real differences between women and men and between women. In contrast, care is a moral philosophy which sees personhood formed through relationships. We gain a sense of self and self-esteem through interactions with others. Its critics would confine it to 'private' interactions, such as within the family or community, where values of love and trust are appropriate for carers but not the basis for a moral or political theory for citizens. Its proponents see its huge potential for providing an alternative, and better, understanding of all aspects of human interaction, whether public or private, than justice thinking.

While its origins associated it with familial relationships, and even with a feminine (and essentialist) way of thinking, care theorists have developed the concept through engagement with other strands of feminism and justice theorists. It remains a theory based upon the particular but is no longer confined to the familial. It focuses on relationships between individuals but has gained a critical dimension which recognises the way in which institutional structures create unequal power relationships and deny care. It shares with socialist feminism a critique of capitalist individualism and rights-based ethics. Care ethics also has at its core a socially constructed relational self but it does not see morality as an expression of class interests alone but as emanating from particular and diverse social and personal care relationships (Robinson 1999: 130–131). Care thinking is process thinking: awareness of relationships (outside the obvious familial) is learned. It requires individuals to recognise and understand relationships and to respond to them with attentiveness. However, care processes are not limited to the actions of individuals but form the basis for institutional involvement. Learning how to respond involves taking full account of the position of the recipient.

The care approach has the potential, although this is yet to be realised, through its process-based method, to recognise more fully the way in which social and economic relations create injustice unlike justice and rights approaches. Feminist justice thinking has had little impact on the dominant forms of macroeconomic theory or the practice of international trade where the concept of the rational economic man pursuing his own self-interest reigns supreme and altruism is literally inconceivable outside of the family. As critics have suggested, the women's human rights approach has paid little attention to the effects of the globalisation of capital and suggests fellow travelling with (Fraser 2009) or co-option by (Otto 1999) global capital. 'The equality paradigm silences women's diversities by confining rights entitlements to those who fit the model of woman of legal discourse.' 'The woman of international human rights law' is a 'woman living in a heterosexual family but increasingly committed to employing her skills to promote market-driven development' (Merry 2006: 231 referring to Otto 1999).

The chapters that follow use caring as the process through which to examine particular relationships. These relationships involve different degrees of proximity: from familial and community to distant strangers. Thus their nature is not necessarily self-evident or presently understood. The range of such relationships in each context is revealed through the application of care thinking to commodity chain analysis. Through attentiveness, the consequences of these unequal relationships are incorporated. Because self is revealed through relationship with others, we can consider the impact of the relationships on the persons in the chain, both those who may presently be considered to benefit and those who do not. We can consider the way in which the relationships construct consumers, carers and citizens, and the contribution of regulatory frameworks to this process. Such an approach facilitates an assessment of how to change these relationships both individually, but also through institutions, to avoid injustice. Morally this process involves more than the application of abstract rights to others, although it does not preclude it, and moves towards a 'thicker' concept of responsibility. However responsibility is not to be confused with obligation: care is not an imposition.

The different discourses, political, economic and cultural, told in relation to globalisation are not mutually exclusive but compete and overlap. They are associated with governance of different aspects and within different spheres. Trade discourse absorbs that of human rights, while the relational discourse associated with families and communities adapts to women's rights discourse. The extent of the effect of one upon the other depends upon contexts and power relationships. One discourse in a pluralist legal world does not eliminate another. It is important to examine the interactions between discourses within global governance contexts. In this way an exclusive discussion of women's rights that considers the ways in which all women across the world are linked together to promote justice is avoided. Instead, the focus shifts to an exploration of the ways in which some women in different contexts across the world, in different geographical spaces, are linked through global economic, political and social governance processes with the consequent effect on the construction of their identities. It becomes possible to understand a set of unequal relationships among and between peoples rather than to dwell on a set of traits embodied in 'others' (Alexander and Mohanty 1997: xix). Differences and specificities are recognised (Otto 1999).

Care thinking involves a combination of the 'is' and the 'ought'. It allows us to discover the relationships in which we are involved and to understand how they work. It then requires us to respond in ways which seek to produce better care. It is possible to use care processes to rethink far more radically to place care and caring relationships at the heart of our world. While recognising the existing salience of analyses grounded in concepts of democracy, justice and equality, I explore the possibility of an ethical reconstructive analysis based upon concepts of responsibility, accountability, engagement and solidarity (Alexander and Mohanty 1997).

This book provides a contextual understanding of the 'we' in the questions posed at the beginning. It considers the ways in which gender issues relating to work, the family and sexuality have been constructed within a number of specific 'domestic' legal contexts including Kenya, Moldova, India and the UK. The aim is to provide sufficient knowledge of gender relations within these jurisdictions as a foundation from which to build more detailed discussions of the particular 'case study'. Thus it is important to understand the way in which a colonial history affects legal relationships in family and work settings in Africa to situate the case study on gender relations within agribusiness. The 'we' in 'do we care about women working in the Kenyan agribusiness sector?' looks at the issue from a Kenyan gender and labour law perspective; the transnational labour and trade discourses associated with networking among activists; the interventions of gender policy makers; the various international trade and 'rights' bodies; and UK gender and labour law debates.

The case study on 'trading' norms/laws in transnational families concentrates on the South Asian community debates in the UK and the construction of gendered concepts of culture within law, particularly in family and immigration law. It explores the developing debates on multiculturalism and legal pluralism from the perspective of women within the communities. South Asia 'produced' the communities in the UK and there is a continuing and complex relationship that is constructed through family laws as well as activism on violence against women, which is 'traded' across the jurisdictions. The different ways in which the normative frameworks of religious norms and state law interact in specific legal contexts in South Asia and the UK become clearer and offer wider insights. A consideration of the way in which Indian, Pakistani, Bangladeshi and English family laws construct a 'South Asian Muslim or Hindu woman' reveals the way in which laws contribute to the construction of fragmented identities while simultaneously fixing certain facets of such identities.

3

State, market and family in a Global North consumer society

Introduction

Globalisation is affecting gender relations in complex ways. This book explores the connections created between a Global North multicultural consumer society and a range of Global South jurisdictions when needs that are associated with social reproduction are, to differing degrees, reconstructed through global market processes as desirable goods and services. These processes create gender-based inequalities within and across societies. Within the overall framework of this book set out in Figure 1 in the Introduction, this chapter is represented by the Global North pyramid. It is concerned with socio-economic and regulatory contexts (the vertical relationships between market, state and family/households).

The UK occupies a particular place within the global market as the producer of desires and demands. It has a strong national economy and a relatively powerful position within a dominant regional trading body, the EU. Most of its citizens have access to formal paid employment and enjoy relatively affluent lifestyles based upon the consumption of a wide range of goods and services. The state is also able to provide a reasonable social safety net to most of its citizens. Britain's colonial history has structured its economic and social history and this legacy continues to play a significant role in the organisation of society although the realignment of interests within the European regional trading bloc has had an increasingly important impact on social and economic relations. Thus Britain is a prosperous, multicultural, consumer-based society, which nevertheless is built on major social and economic inequalities. In 2008–2009 there were 2.8 million children (proportionately more than most rich countries), 5.8 million working-age adults and 2.3 million pensioners living in relative poverty (proportion living in households with below 60 per cent of contemporary median net disposable household income) (Department for Work and Pensions 2010).

All the activities in our chains are concerned with social reproduction and involve care. The first is based upon the need for food to sustain life; the second on the need for nurture (including sexual satisfaction) and to care for everyone, but particularly for the vulnerable (the young, sick, disabled and infirm elderly); and the third on the need for an identity and sense of belonging. In the UK global consumer society there are relentless pressures to shift these needs from provision through familial relationships where they have, to a greater or lesser extent, been provided through unpaid labour. Since its inception, the welfare state has, in a variety of ways, shared this responsibility so that needs are met both through relationships among family members but also through citizenship. This state role has been under pressure, not only within recent neoliberal economic discourse that champions market-met desires rather than state-provided needs-satisfaction, but also within 'third way' social democracy.

Needs are transformed and expand when provided as desirable products and services to individuals acting as consumers within the market. Within the structure of this book, the UK functions as the demand end of the specific chain: namely the purchase by individuals of luxury pre-prepared fruit and vegetables; the purchase by individuals, or by the state on their behalf, of a range of forms of 'body work' services relating to care and sex; and the arrangement of marriages by family groups. Each chain meets a constructed 'deficit' in local supply. The deficit is not simply related to the shortage of an essential need, such as a staple food, but to a market-constructed desire for, for instance, a fair trade pineapple, which contributes to its consumer's sense of identity as a caring person. The 'supply' jurisdictions (the Global South vertical pyramids) are discussed in the following chapters.

These constructed deficits are a product of the wider socio-economic and political context of the UK, including significant changes in gender relations within the labour market and within the family. So, for instance, a deficit in childcare or in care for the elderly is understood as a withdrawal of women's labour from the family as they have joined the labour market, a process which has been encouraged by a range of recent state policies. Each 'demand' is constructed within a regulatory framework, which itself contributes to the understanding of its composition and normative validity. Thus we see legislative interventions in labour law to encourage 'work/life balance' or 'work/family reconciliation' and social welfare interventions to address the 'care deficit' by reconstructing 'carers' as 'caring/carer workers'. Each constructed demand is based upon assumptions relating to gender roles. There is far more consensus, reflected in regulation, on the validity (and practicality) of purchasing prepared food rather than growing or preparing it 'at home' than there is to purchasing sex in the market or alternatively confining sexual activities to a family unit consisting of two heterosexual married persons.

The UK state also contributes to the production of dominant international and transnational regulatory discourses via its membership of international and regional bodies such as the WTO, the UN and its specialist agencies such as the International Labour Organization (ILO), and the EU. The resulting 'hard' and 'soft' laws also impact upon the domestic regulatory frameworks for our chains contributing to the global legal pluralism introduced in the previous chapter. In each case the perceived deficit is met through particular forms of engagement with the global market and as a result international and transnational regulation contributes to the construction of the trade, rights and care discourses represented by the ellipses that link the two lower pyramids in Figure 1.

This chapter concentrates primarily on the constructed deficits for food and body work. The demands for care and sex, both of which involve body work, are discussed separately because of their very different regulatory contexts. The discussion focuses particularly on the demand for social care and sex work because the changing relationships between production and social reproduction are at their most complex in these two areas. Subsequent chapters add detail in relation to nursing and domestic work.

The transnational marriage context, which addresses the perceived deficit in 'suitable' local partners and a demand for belonging, is presented in outline only. Detailed discussion takes place in Chapter 9. Transnational marriages are a product of, and create relationships between, family members living in the UK, Pakistan, Bangladesh and India. The actors are members of British Asian (BrAsian) communities with economic, social and political histories within British colonialism but whose identities are also moulded by contemporary global relationships. They are affected by the increasingly politically heated debates over multiculturalism and legal pluralism in the UK, in which transnational marriages are associated with illegality and force. These debates take place within, and are affected by, the global market place of ideas, in particular the contested constructions of sexuality and gendered identity, which involve trading honour and rights discourses.

Consuming global food – the demand for fresh fruit and vegetables from Kenya

The first chain involves the demand and supply of imported fresh fruits and vegetables (FFV) from Kenya, which are bought in UK supermarkets by women and men as consumers. Although fruit and vegetables are produced domestically, there is a perceived demand for a range of FFV that cannot be grown in the UK or only during specific seasons. Consumers want these items to be available throughout the year, to be of consistently high quality and, where appropriate, to be offered ready prepared and packaged for convenience of use. Women and men work to grow, prepare and supply these items in Kenya. There is therefore a constructed deficit of particular forms of non-essential food products, which is being satisfied by methods of production associated with global agribusiness. The relationships created by these processes link individuals in the Global North as consumers to distant producers (farmers) and workers in agribusiness, who process the FFV in the Global South. The chain under discussion here is not directly concerned with the relationships between customers and those who are engaged as workers (including European migrant labour) in agribusiness in the UK.

The development of consumer capitalism means that immense resources and efforts are deployed, both within the market but also by the state, to engage with and manage the population as consumers (Gabriel and Lang 2006). The national 'contract' has been constructed as: work and you can consume; consume and you will have work. Citizens have a duty to consume to keep the economy going and in exchange they will be rewarded with increasing living standards. The domestic form of this contract has been challenged by developments in the global market, which have broken the link between national industrialised production and consumption of goods and the development of new forms of consumption based around services, particularly in northern states.

The UK market in food

Food is big business: spending on food was estimated to be worth £129 billion in 2006 in the UK. The food and drink sector accounts for 7 per cent of GDP and is the single largest manufacturing sector although its manufacture is increasingly spread across Europe. There has also been considerable consolidation in the UK: in 2004, 4 per cent of food and drink manufacturing enterprises (259 companies) generated 77 per cent of the sector's output (Strategy Unit 2008: 8, 20, 25). Within the retail sector there were estimated to be 59,200 food and drink retailers with over 99,000 outlets in 2007. However the 'big four' supermarkets (Tesco, Sainsbury's, ASDA and Morrisons) account for an estimated three-quarters of all food retail sales. It is argued that their size produces economies of scale that are passed on to the consumer (and the economy more broadly) as lower prices. The intense competition between them puts immense pressure on their supply chains to ensure efficient delivery, producing consolidation not only within the UK industry but at all points in their global supply chains as we shall see (Strategy Unit 2008: 18).

The food and drink sector of the economy employs 3.7 million people, a significant proportion of whom work part time indicating the presence of many women. The government argues that the 'flexibilities of the UK labour market are important to agriculture and the rest of the food chain', which is also more dependent on migrant labour (well beyond traditional seasonal agricultural work) than other sectors. In 2006, 17 per cent of workers in the food chain were foreign born (compared to 11 per cent of the UK workforce as a whole) (Strategy Unit 2008: 25).

The UK population generally does not consume food to meet basic subsistence. In 2007, only (on average) 9 per cent of household expenditure was spent on food although the poorest 10 per cent of households set aside 15 per cent of their income for food in 2006. This contrasts starkly with the estimated 50 to 80 per cent or more spent on food in developing countries. The recent rise in global commodity prices, which has brought to an end the long-term decline in the price of food (which fell for twenty years between 1985 and 2005), differentially affects purchasers in the UK and the developing world. For instance, the price of wheat (a global commodity) accounts for only 13 per cent of the final price of a loaf of bread in the UK (Strategy Unit 2008: 26, 28).

While the firms consolidate their products proliferate. The average number of items (food and non-food) for sale in the big four supermarkets rose from 30,000 in 2000/1 to 41,500 in 2004/5 (Strategy Unit 2008: 19). Because food amounts to a small share of household expenditure, retailers encourage consumers to trade up to higher-value products: to pay for attributes such as 'convenience, quality and provenance' (Strategy Unit 2008: 19). Generally, the supermarket shelves are stacked with items rich in meanings for consumers, offering pleasure, solace, love and affection. Retailers make use of highly sophisticated data analysis to categorise their customers. 'Using the 2001 Census figures and data on such things as county court judgments, credit ratings, qualifications, car ownership, age and background, and working on this data with geo-demographic software, Mosaic UK (a consumer classification system) divides the country into eleven groups, each of which is given an evocative name and a stereotypical – and determinedly heterosexual – couple to match' (Jeffries 2004: 2). Products identify consumers as affluent or thrifty; environmentally sensitive or impetuously indulgent; short of time but health conscious; and so on. 'Consumers are increasingly making statements of personal principles when shopping by choosing to buy products that are organic, fairly traded, free range or "local"' (Strategy Unit 2008: 9). Purchasing imported, out-of-season, carefully prepared, packaged and perishable baby green beans at a premium price says much more about a consumer than that he or she likes green vegetables.

Food security in the UK is not based upon self-sufficiency but on trading in the market. In 2006, 49 per cent of the food consumed in the UK was produced locally: £24.8 billion of food, feed and water products were imported although products worth £10 billion were exported. A single market in food operates throughout the EU under the auspices of the European Common Agricultural Policy (CAP). As a result, over two-thirds of the imports originated in the EU. The import of FFV (£6 billion in 2006) (including from Africa) accounts for much of the UK's food trade deficit (Strategy Unit 2008: 26, 33).

Triumph of desire? Consumers in the market

There seems to be a general consensus that food is provided by the market. The consumer reigns supreme although this supremacy is mediated through the market strength of the large retailers. There is little public debate relating to over supply although there is a growing concern about waste with an estimated 30 per cent of food sold in supermarkets 'grown, processed, packaged, distributed, sold and taken home only to be thrown away uneaten' (Strategy Unit 2008: 2). The environmental impact of the way in which food is supplied and consumed is moving up the wider political agenda, sometimes replicating the contest between local and overseas producers (a preference for locally bought produce) that is seen in relation to the labour market (a preference for local workers).

Public debate over the 'gender contract' in relation to responsibility for food provision within families and households is muted even though women still devote more time to this activity than men. 'Home cooking' still carries a value, but food products that are 'conveniently provided' are seen as a corollary to women's entry into the labour market and necessary for 'hard working families'. Retailers aim to provide a huge choice in food that is cheap and convenient but they must also ensure that it is safe because consumer confidence depends upon this.

Consuming citizens? The regulatory context of trade, rights and care

The non-ministerial government department, the Food Standards Agency was established in 2000 under the Food Standards Act 1999, in response to a number of high-profile outbreaks of illness and deaths resulting from unsafe food. Until then, one government department had been responsible for both the health of the farming and food processing industries and also food safety. The Agency's national oversight role is 'to protect public health from risks which may arise in connection with the consumption of food (including risks caused by the way in which it is produced or supplied) and otherwise to protect the interests of consumers in relation to food' (Food Standards Act 1999 section 1(2)). It has the statutory right, which it has exercised routinely, to publish the advice it gives to government. The Agency, which employs 2,000 people and has an annual budget of £135 million a year, has been involved in a regulatory battle between the large food companies and consumers and public health professionals over proposals to introduce a mandatory European-wide food labelling system on products to denote the amounts of fat, saturated fat, salt and sugar contained per serving. The food industry spent an estimated £830 million on lobbying to stop this traffic lights scheme and substitute its preferred alternative. The future of the Agency was in doubt in 2010 when the government considered transferring its regulatory powers back to the Department for Environment, Food and Rural Affairs and its responsibilities for nutrition, diet and public health to the Department of Health (Ramesh 2010).

The state's food policy, which focuses on support for the consumer, seeks to 'build a system to meet the demand for safe, low environmental impact food and healthy diets' (Strategy Unit 2008: 5), although as the vulnerability of the Food Standards Agency indicates, the nature of the regulatory intervention is not so clear:

> (t)here is still a significant gap between what people say that they believe, as citizens, should be done and how they behave as consumers. ... Surveys suggest that many expect retailers, manufacturers or the Government to act on their behalf and to 'edit' problems out of the system rather than ask them to choose. (2008:3)

While the way in which citizens consume food has become the subject of increasing state concern, the macroeconomic context is provided by the activities of the supermarkets, which are hugely powerful actors within the global market, and the UK's membership of the WTO and the EU. In practice, there

are relatively few areas in which the UK national government has a direct
regulatory role in relation to the food chain. Responsibility for product safety is
undertaken at the EU level. Over 90 per cent of the legislative interventions that
relate to food safety and standards are set at regional EU level and implemented
through devolved governments in Wales, Scotland and Northern Ireland. The
Westminster government is only responsible for implementation in England.

The wider regulatory framework relating to global agribusiness is discussed
in Chapter 5. However, it is important to note that the European CAP directly
affects the food chain in the UK through its system of agricultural subsidies and
programmes. In 2007 UK farming received about £3 billion a year in direct
subsidies while total income from farming amounted to £2.5 billion (Strategy
Unit 2008: 22). In 2006 the CAP cost £557 to every household of four people in
the EU through higher consumer food prices and in tax (Strategy Unit 2008:
29). There is also an international governance framework made up of internationally recognised guidelines, codes and standards, which operates not only
through multilateral institutions such as the WTO, via the Agreement on
Agriculture, GATT and GATS, but also through the 'private' standard-setting
associated with the GVC. Both the regional and global governance contexts
contribute to the discourse of trade relating to the consumption of food. The
move away from protectionism for producers within Europe to more open
competition (freer trade) within a global market for food products and related
commodities is based upon the assumption that consumers will generate
demand for forms of regulation that meet their perceived anxieties. We have
seen that consumers want convenience and are concerned about the quality and
safety of their food, particularly when it is sourced through international supply
chains. Increasingly consumers also want to know its provenance – where it
comes from – which leads to demands for traceability. This is also a related
public concern for animal welfare and a growing environmental awareness.

A desire to know more about production presents challenges for consumerism, which is based upon the separation of these definitely unglamorous and
often squalid processes from the pristine displays of desirable consumables on
supermarket shelves. To maintain their position in a fiercely competitive
market, retailers will prioritise not only price but also quality and safety controls
through the imposition of exacting standards in their supply chain governance
and will be joined by other interested parties, including governments, in
international standard-setting in areas such as phytosanitary requirements.

What is consumer care?

Within this narrative on the supremacy of market-driven desire leading to
generalised self-interested standard-setting, we can ask: to what extent do
consumers care about the welfare of those who work to produce the food? It
seems that individuals constructed as consumers care more about the conditions of the chickens whose carcasses they eat than those of the workers who

kill, gut and process them, particularly if these processes are carried out in remote locations. At present the UK demand for fresh produce grown in Africa supports over 700,000 workers and their dependents (Strategy Unit 2008: 15). Are consumers aware of the relationships involved in meeting the constructed deficit in FFV through imports from Kenya? Can discourses associated with corporate social responsibility, such as ethical trading, or with wider concepts of care, such as fair trade, extend to workers? Can consumers, rather than states on behalf of their citizens, generate a discourse of universal rights for workers that recognises the way in which labour markets often operate to disadvantage women? Can relationships constructed through markets be transformed into relationships of care? Future chapters take up these questions.

The demand for global body work: purchasing care labour

The perceived deficit that creates the demand for the second chain involves a variety of care relationships: nursing; care for the young, vulnerable and elderly; and domestic labour in the home. Nursing care is professionalised and generally involves formal employment relationships either within the socialised National Health Service or the private sector. As a result of the increased political priority given to the NHS to improve its services, there has been a shortage of nurses. Those who perceive themselves as unable or unwilling to meet socially determined (and varying) domestic standards in households can use the labour of others to tackle this deficit in 'housework'. The relationships created are private and usually informal. Consumer societies generate high levels of socially required investment in children while simultaneously requiring parents to work in the formal labour market. There is a deficit in childcare that can be met through social or commercial provision.

There are also rising expectations among and in relation to other groups, such as the elderly, which result in demand for care that substitutes and supplements unpaid family forms because family carers are increasingly expected to work. Although the deficit has emerged as one of 'social' (non-familial) care involving paid labour, there is less political consensus on the relative role of the family, state and market. The ideological assumption that state-provided services which meet need are second best (to the market) has gained political ground although the degree to which this assumption holds good varies: state provision of most health services, including nursing, is still valued. So care services may be purchased by individuals as consumers in the market or provided by the state to a recipient who is increasingly constructed as an independent citizen with choices rather than as needful. Such care may be consumed within domestic environments through personalised services or within institutional settings. By repositioning this form of care work within the 'social' and in increasingly regulated labour relationships, care work is increasingly differentiated from domestic work. Care generally has an economic value once it is transferred to the market, although this value is limited by its origins in female familial labour and through its association with bodies. This must be paid for by individuals and/or by the state. Consequently, there is a perceived, but nevertheless politically contested, shortage in the local supply of appropriate (cheap but quality caring) labour, which is outsourced in part to migrant workers, the vast majority of whom are women, whose working relationships range from the highly informal 'private' to the 'public' formally regulated.

These deficits are a product of the major socio-economic and demographic changes involving the relationship between productive and social reproductive activities, which were described in outline through the work-related gender pyramid in Chapter 1, but which are set into the UK context here. The debate over the relationship between production and social reproduction takes place in two related contexts. The first relates to the employment relationship (production), which involves the relationship between the market and the state represented in segments A (formal employment conditions and entitlements) and B (employment-related benefits and entitlements) and a move towards a household model that contains universal caring (paid) workers rather than one that contains an unpaid carer and a paid worker.

Women's entry in large numbers into the paid labour market and the changing nature of the labour contract limits their capacity to undertake care although slower changes in the societal norms underpinning the gender contract ensure that much responsibility still rests with them. The second context therefore involves the relationship between the state and families and relates to the greater commodification of social reproduction within segment C (social responsibilities and entitlements). A relationship between a care purchaser and a care worker substitutes for and reconstructs familial caring relationships. Women's socially reproductive labour is not appropriately valued in either context. It is not the touchstone of labour or social welfare policies. As a result, these changes reconstruct gender-based inequalities.

The women in the body work chains whose labour is used to meet the deficits share these consequences but as we shall see in subsequent chapters, their position as particularly constructed migrant workers often adds to the injustices they experience.

Markets and families

New Labour's 'third way' sought to re-orientate UK economic strategy to meet new circumstances:

> To survive and prosper in the new context of a global economy, businesses constantly have to improve the quality and design of their products, invest in new technologies, and reduce costs. A key ingredient of competitiveness is to use the workforce efficiently and effectively. For this purpose the workforce has to be properly trained and prepared to work flexibly and to co-operate with all innovations. (Collins 2002: 450–451)

The objective of the welfare state moves away from the redistribution of wealth and the promotion of egalitarianism to the creation of the 'conditions for equality of opportunity by opening up the market mechanism for the production of wealth for everyone' (Collins 2002: 452). Its role in underpinning and supporting the 'traditional' labour contract with social benefits and public services is redesigned. Poverty, redefined as social exclusion, is tackled through ensuring access to the market. Individuals are expected to avail themselves of these opportunities. If they do not, the welfare state (through the social security and welfare systems) limits its responsibilities to subsistence support. Women are expected to be within the labour market, contributing to the formal economy irrespective of their wider social reproductive contributions. A single parent should work: if she chooses to care at home she cannot expect the state to fund her 'lifestyle' beyond the bare minimum (Collins 2002: 452).

These policy changes are set within longer-term socio-economic changes. Since 1970, there have been two converging trends in labour market participation. The overall male employment rate for sixteen to sixty-four-year-olds has fallen from 92 per cent to approximately 79 per cent in 2006, while the proportion of women working has increased from 56 per cent to 70 per cent. Women now form around 45 per cent of the economically active workforce. The employment rate of women with children under five doubled from 28 per cent to 56 per cent between 1980 and 2005. The general employment rate is higher for mothers with dependent children living with a partner (71 per cent: 29 per cent in full-time work and 42 per cent in part-time work – defined as fewer than thirty hours a week) than for lone parents where the rate is 54 per cent (28 per cent in full-time and 26 per cent in part-time work). Women are far more likely to work part time between the ages of twenty-five and forty-five (10 per cent of men work part time in these key twenty years) (Moffat 2007: 137–138). Employment patterns have shifted away from the dominance of manufacturing: between June 1985 and March 2008 the percentage of employee jobs held by men in manufacturing dropped from 28 per cent to 16 per cent; the equivalent figures for women were 15 to 5 per cent. In marked contrast, the services sector, which accounts for 63.5 per cent of total employment (OECD 2000), accounted for 74 per cent of male employee jobs and 92 per cent of female employee jobs in March 2008 (ONS 2008). Almost 75 per cent of the 3.8 million self-employed people are men.

Regulating precarious work: trading or caring rights?

Women have entered a changed labour market in which the bargaining power of organised labour has been reduced by the forces of the global market. The normative model for the standard European employment relationship (segment A), which involves a full-time and year-round employment relationship for an indefinite duration with a single employer, is associated with a model of the breadwinner/homemaker household, into which the majority of older retired households would still fall (Fudge and Owens 2006: 3). There has been a significant increase in 'precarious' work which departs from this normative model. It is associated with 'part time employment, self employment, fixed term work, temporary work, on-call work, home working, and telecommuting . . . all [of which] tend to be distinguished by low wages, few benefits, the absence of collective representation, and little job security' (Fudge and Owens 2006: 12). Such work is incapable of sustaining a household (Fudge and Owens 2006: 3). As a consequence, both men and women are obliged to engage in the paid labour market as individual workers to support households although such conditions are closely associated with women's work.

The European Union provides 'transnational binding labour regulation via pre-emptive legislation, which includes treaty provisions and EU regulations, and harmonisation' which guarantees a variety of legal protections for workers within standard labour contracts (within segment A) (Fudge and Owens 2006: 17; Ashiagbor 2006). These protections, which relate to security, uniform working hours, non-discrimination and relatively free collective bargaining, cover those who work in standard ways in recognised places of work. Neither these regional EU protections nor the standards set internationally through the ILO (Vosko 2006) have extended to work undertaken in different contexts (relating to time, place or status) until relatively recently. Now, 'atypical' work (associated with precariousness) attracts much more attention within the European Employment Strategy and also legal intervention via the Part-time Work (97/81, [1997] OJ L 14/9) and Fixed-term Work Directives (99/70, [1999] OJ L 175/43) and also through the Agency Working Directive (2008/104/EC) (Ashiagbor 2006).

The UK state has underpinned women's labour market participation since the 1970s through anti-discrimination legislation. The provisions relating to anti-discrimination apply to a wide range of workers but do not extend to those working in private households. Equal pay rights have been applied to more limited categories (Fredman 2006: 195–197). In the last decade of the twentieth century, the Labour government introduced a substantial legislative programme to strengthen employment rights primarily associated with Segment B: longer maternity leave, with better income replacement measures (Employment Relations Act 1999; Maternity and Parental Leave etc Regulations 1999 SI 1999/3312 amending the Employment Rights Act 1996 Part VIII; Work and Families Act 2006; dismissal when pregnant is now automatically unfair (Employment Relations Act 1999 section 34 (4)); rights to leave and time off for parents (unpaid) and for carers (Parental Leave Directive 96/34 [1996] OJ L145/4; The Work and Families Act 2006 section 12); time off (unpaid and reasonable) to deal with family emergencies (Employment Rights Act 1996 (as amended) section 57A); and rights for part-time workers (The Part-Time Workers (Prevention of Less Favourable Treatment) Regulations SI 2000/155).

However entitlement is often confined to workers, legally defined as employees, which, as a category, can exclude many non-standard workers who,

Fredman argues, 'pose particular challenges for contract-based labour law because their services are not wholly at the disposal of the employer' (2006: 187). Employment law has been built around a 'strictly bipartisan notion of contract' between a worker and a specific employer (2006: 188). The 'independence' of non-standard workers limits an employer's wider social responsibilities (segment B) towards them, particularly if such workers undertake tasks for more than one employer or limit their availability to an employer because of family responsibilities. The arrangement starts to bear the 'hallmarks of the independent entrepreneur or micro-enterprise'. Both women and their employers gain flexibility. 'In this model, the worker/entrepreneur bears the risks and benefits of the market' but in reality the flexibility adds to the 'vulnerability and precarious status of the worker' (2006: 187). While the courts tend to deny employment protection to those who have more fragmented or multiple relationships, the flexible labour market requires a new conception in which all employers share responsibility for the labour market as a whole, through an ideology of corporate civic responsibility (Fredman 2006: 188, 189).

The Labour government's 'Third Way' regarded employment rights as assets for productive, committed non-standard workers who then improved the competitive advantage of their employer. It extended rights, including minimum wage laws, working-time and part-time workers' rights, to a wider range of workers: both minimum wages and maximum working-time legislation extends to agency workers, home workers and contract workers. However, contracts for the supply of services provided through a commercial relationship are not covered. The aim is to distinguish between 'two distinct sets of power relationships: one between employer and worker, where the former is clearly dominant, and one between a service provider and a client or customer, where relationships are on the basis of market equality' (Fredman 2006: 189).

This new flexible labour market also required a 'radically new approach to the provision of childcare, reconceiving it as a public policy issue requiring a nationally coordinated strategy [the National Childcare Strategy] and enhancing both public and private provision' (Conaghan 2002: 59). The government invested substantially in policy initiatives with employers to encourage positive attitudes to work/life balance, through 'family friendly policies' (Conaghan 2002; Fredman 2006; Lewis and Campbell 2008). These measures are directed, within policy and legal discourses, to workers as parents and carers and emphasise the advantages of offering choices to all workers and their employers. While constructed in gender-neutral terms of parent and carer, it is assumed that women workers will take advantage of them (Conaghan 2002) although the government is 'reluctant to intervene to promote any particular change in the gendered division of labour at the household level, stressing that this remains a matter for private decision-making' (Lewis and Campbell 2008: 534). Neither construction of work/family (which focuses on mothers' involvement in the labour market) nor work/life (which focuses on parents/carers) explicitly recognises the 'asymmetrical changes in men's and women's contribution to households' (Lewis and Campbell 2008: 534). 'The UK Time Use Survey 2000/ 2001 indicates that mothers carry out three-quarters of childcare during the week and two-thirds at the weekends' (Moffat 2007: 137). The Royal Commission on Long Term Care (Sutherland 1999) saw no evidence of working women being less willing to provide unpaid care. They continue to take far more responsibility for the care of the elderly and disabled relatives than men (Buckner and Yeandle 2005: chapter 10).

We see here a complex contest over the construction of relationships within a consumer economy based primarily upon the provision of service work. The discourse of service providers in a flexible market who are able to exercise choice over the manner in which they provide their labour to a client is associated with that of global trade rather than with the rights of employees under 'traditional' contractual employment law. It constructs a world devoid of gender divisions and inequalities of power. At the same time, this construction of the worker is built upon an assumption relating to changing relationships between work and care: workers are embodied as parents and carers who need state rights to support them. In this respect we see pressures to develop a more expansive concept of workers' rights on the one hand, to tackle precarious working, but on the other, to support the development of a competitive labour market. These provisions have been developed primarily through gender-neutral language of work/life balance. Here again the specific gender inequalities associated with unpaid social reproduction within the family are masked.

Carers and caring workers

Labour-related interventions that enable women to 'choose to work flexibly' (within segments A and B of the pyramid) have not tackled the social reproductive issues associated with segment C. Demographic changes are affecting needs. There are now more people over sixty-five than under sixteen in England. The number of people over sixty-five is expected to rise over the next five decades from 9.3 million to 16.8 million and 'the number of people over eighty five, the age group most likely to need nursing, residential or home care, is now expected to rise from 1.1 million in 2000 to 4 million in 2051' (DH 2005: 22). 5 per cent of the total population aged sixty-five and over have dementia, rising to 20 per cent of the population aged eighty and over. By 2050 it is estimated that there will be 1.2 million people with dementia (DH 2007a).

However, the normative framework of the flexible consumer economy presents challenges in the way in which these needs are to be met:

> Most families rely on two incomes, or longer working hours, to maintain an adequate standard of living. Many families find it difficult to balance work with the care needs of friends and relatives *without significantly impacting on their own standard of living, esteem and independence- the lifestyle to which the family has become accustomed* (my emphasis). (DH 2008: para 1.61)

Despite these fears relating to the consumer economy culture, it is estimated by Carers UK that the 6 million carers save the economy £57 billion per year, the equivalent of the NHS budget (Buckner and Yeandle 2007). The 2001 Census identified about 1.25 million people who provided more than fifty hours of care per week (Herring 2009: 97). Roughly three million carers also work (although 21 per cent of those of working age defined as economically inactive are carers); 13 per cent of full-time and 17 per cent of part-time workers are carers (Himmelweit and Land 2007). For those in the same household, 54 per cent of carers were women, 40 per cent were aged between forty-five and sixty-four, and 29 per cent were aged sixty-five or over. 60 per cent of those two-thirds who care for someone living elsewhere were women, 48 per cent were aged between forty-five and sixty-four and 16 per cent were aged sixty-five or over. In sum, almost half of married or cohabiting women between forty-five and sixty-four are carers for elderly parents and/or spouses or partners (ONS 2002). It is obvious that without 'carers', social care would collapse. It is only recently, however, that carers have gained formal recognition within social policy and legal discourse (Carers (Recognition and Services) Act 1995; the Carers and Disabled Children Act 2000 and the Carers (Equal Opportunities) Act 2004; Herring 2009: chapter 4).

Carers are not care workers within welfare law and policy because they are family members. However, their identification as a group is associated with the increasing commodification of care as an often personalised service to recipients. 'Care' is becoming less integrated into 'normal' relationships within the family and community and is now identified in terms of time spent and tasks undertaken (DH 2009a). It is therefore associated with an economic value and suggests that care-giving requires skills apart from those associated with 'natural' affection and nurture. Carers therefore need to have access to training and support to improve the quality of care for recipients but 'it might also offer the carer who has left employment a longer-term route into education and training, and into more formal paid employment once their immediate caring responsibilities cease' (DH 2005: 38). In this way, carers with significant levels of caring responsibilities can be 'trained' for the formal labour market and avoid the financial penalties of withdrawal, including loss of pensions.

Demanding care: taking responsibility

Social care for vulnerable adults, including the elderly, has also undergone substantial policy changes in recent years (Stewart 2005, 2007; Herring 2009). The 1970 Local Authority (Social Services) Act established local government social services departments to provide an organisational focus for a range of duties and responsibilities owed to, among others, children, the disabled and the elderly. The NHS continued to provide health as opposed to social care. Although the activity of caring for the elderly is contained within a policy framework of 'social care', the legal framework is widely recognised as fragmented, even chaotic (Mandelstam 2001; McDonald 2001; Clements and Thompson 2007). There is no single originating statute to provide legal clarity or to encapsulate the values which might inform any policy or procedures (Clements and Thompson 2007; see now recommendations in the Law Commission report 2011). Since 1948, the politics of the welfare state has created a palimpsest of approaches: post-war state collectivist paternalism; neoliberal marketised provision; and the 'third way' positive welfare approach (Williams 2001). The evolution of the consumer economy is 'decasualising' care for the elderly. There is a growing demand for social welfare services to be available as of right to individuals who then choose the way in which care is provided to meet self-determined needs and aspirations (DH 2009b). Recent policy has continued to develop a mixed market approach by focusing on the care recipient as the service purchaser: '[S]ervices should be 'person-centred, seamless and proactive. They should support independence, not dependence and allow everyone to enjoy a good quality of life, including the ability to contribute fully to our communities' (DH 2005: 16). This ethos of personalisation also implies that the elderly take increasing responsibility for their own care rather than relying on family, community or the state. Those in receipt of care are now encouraged to purchase their care directly with funds either provided by the state, if they meet means-tested criteria (Clements and Thompson 2007: chapter 12; Ungerson and Yeandle 2007; Herring 2009: 105–107), or by themselves. Citizen purchasers of services in a social care market will stimulate the development of innovative and cost-efficient care products (DH 2009a: 40). A well-trained social care workforce will provide the bulk of the care but will be supported by working carers (DH 2009a).

These proposals contribute to a relatively well-developed but under-resourced care economy, which provides a range of services to those in need of care. In total about 1.75 million adults use social care. A small proportion of elderly people live in residential care homes (421,000 in 2006; one in twenty of all elderly). 60 per cent of those living in the independent sector (private and charitable) are wholly or partly funded through local authority funding (public) funds. 32 per cent (118,000) of UK care home residents are self-funded, while the rest (30,000) are funded by the NHS (public funds). The trend is away from residential to domiciliary services; 600,000 individuals receive this care support in their own homes (Clements and Thompson 2007).

The allocation of resources and distribution of costs involved in preserving a family intact in later life is a source of considerable political tension. As infirmity increases it becomes very costly to provide adequate quality care in the community and policymakers recognise that 'the current care and support system is unsustainable' but there is no consensus on how to move forward (DH 2009a: 9). 45 per cent of the NHS and Social Services budget is consumed by those over sixty-five. The way in which these costs are distributed is highly confused and considered to be unfair. Well over 50 per cent of older people presently partially or completely fund their own care if they cannot or do not want to rely on unpaid family support and many more will do so in the future.

Those in need of care, or the state on their behalf, purchase services in a market characterised by large numbers of small (87 per cent) and a tiny number (1 per cent) of large employers (DH 2009a). There are at present about 1.5 million people in the social care workforce in England who work in people's own homes, care homes, day care, hospitals, and in the wider community. There are huge difficulties in the supply of labour in this sector, reflecting the menial status associated with body work. In a recession the vacancy rates for the statutory sector remain at well over 10 per cent (Community Care 2009). Its workforce tends to be constituted by marginal groups. There is a very high turnover rate (25 per cent for domiciliary work) costing an estimated loss to the social care sector of £78 million per year (Care Council 2007). The present care workforce, which is primarily constituted of female workers, is generally poorly trained and poorly paid. Those working for private companies receive much lower wages than those working for other employers. Jobs in residential or nursing homes are the lowest paid. 62 per cent have no occupational pension scheme. Most have basic qualification levels only although younger workers have more. While the majority of care workers interviewed in 2007 expressed satisfaction with their job, they also thought that their work was not highly valued or understood by society more generally (Skills for Care 2007).

Regulating uncaring workers

As care becomes a contract for services rather than a familial relationship, the nature of the provision becomes more visible. Domestic environments become places of work: an elderly person in need of care becomes an employer (probably for the first time in their lives) if they buy services directly. If these are provided through the state, they are not parties to the contract of service between the public commissioner and the private provider of the care workers. So in theory in these two situations, the elderly person has either total control or none over the workers. If the care is provided in an institutional context of a residential care home they may be direct purchasers of the care service provided but most likely they are 'placed' there as a result of local authority funding for their care. The contract for services again lies between the commissioner and provider, the care home owner and employer of labour.

The lack of recognition of the value of care is reflected in the under-developed care market, with the underinvestment in its workforce and infra-structure more generally. This form of care is not at the cutting edge of the new flexible consumer market economy. The quality of the services provided both in the residential sector and at home is as a result very variable. While the elderly are increasingly constructed as independent empowered service purchasers, elder abuse is emerging as a major issue for social policymakers as well as anguished family members (Herring 2009: chapter 5). Poor treatment of the elderly has been normalised and institutionalised into market-based provision, with the added dimension that there can be no expectation of love and affection in these relationships. However, such treatment of older citizens is increasingly being seen as no longer acceptable. They have a right to services, which through the affective labour of workers, provides both emotional and physical care.

The market provision of care is therefore subject to regulation of care providers which extends to care workers specifically. Care homes are regulated under the Health and Social Care Act 2008. They must be registered with the Care Quality Commission and meet a range of quality standards including ensuring the human rights of the residents. Since 2003, professional social workers must be registered and are subject to public regulation by the General Social Care Council. The requirement to meet minimum standards for registration and abide by a code of conduct is extending to home care workers and their managers (DH 2009a: chapter 8). It will not cover 'personal assistants, or family members and friends who may offer personal care or assistance' thus maintaining the distinction between carer and care worker for the time being (DH 2009a: 49).

However, care relationships are complex as much feminist scholarship has pointed out (Lewis and Guillari 2005). The power relationships involved in these contexts are not always one way. There is also evidence of abuse of care workers (as well as carers) by those for whom they care. The 2007 survey of care workers referred to above found that half of respondents said that:

> they had suffered some kind of verbal abuse (49%) such as insults, name calling, being sworn at, or having racist or sexist comments made about them. A third had suffered some physical abuse from a client or their family (35%), including being hit, punched, slapped, kicked or poked. 13% had a false allegation made against them, and 9% had been bullied or harassed. 7% had not been paid correctly by their client or their family, and 5% had suffered sexual abuse at the hands of their client or their family (Skills for Care 2007: 26).

Domestic goddesses

We have been discussing relationships of care that involve primarily intimate body work (Wolkowitz 2006). However, those women and men who are in households that are 'cash rich/time poor' due to their high dual-earning capacity are in a position to buy in services to replace their own social reproductive activities in the maintenance of the domestic environment and also personal care services. Here the services required involve domestic work. Domestic work is not only about maintaining the basic cleanliness necessary for existence but also about reproducing life styles and status: the cultural reproduction of life (Anderson 2001: 6). It is not finite but definable: ironing bed linen, preparing 'homemade' meals or holding dinner parties may be deemed essential in some households but not in others. The service can be provided in a variety of ways, ranging from the formal contracts for services provided through a company to informal and 'invisible' work within the home, provided without the benefit of a formal contract of employment and subject to no formal state regulation. It is then truly precarious work. In general, this is an area that the state considers purely a matter for private and market relationships although recent statutory protections relating to minimum wages and working time can apply.

Caring in a market?

The way in which many women (and increasingly men) engage with the labour market involves precarious work, which may provide the flexibility for women to seek to 'balance' work with care responsibilities, but offers, in relative terms, poor conditions of work and low earnings. Despite seeking to balance work/ care in this way, women's involvement in the labour market is generating demand for care work because there has not been significant renegotiation of the wider gender contract within the family and society, which would value and distribute care more equally. Those who meet the demand for care face particular hardships in the labour market because those who need to purchase the care often have limited resources and need flexibilities in their 'employees' due to their own precarious situation. In a differentiated labour market, clearly high-earning women and men have more resources at their disposal to meet their care needs. There is much discussion within popular culture about 'cash rich/time poor' households, which is reflected in the development of luxury convenience food discussed above. All care purchasers desire high-quality care for their loved ones and, for those who can afford it, to achieve high standards of home-making from workers whose labour is regarded generally as unskilled and undervalued. Social investment in, and concern for the welfare, and now rights of children and increasingly of the vulnerable and elderly, has led to additional public regulation of the institutional providers of care but also of care working itself.

The reorganisation of relationships of care through their defamiliarisation and commodification with the associated move towards 'professionalisation' of family carers (without the protection of employment status) and the increased use of paid domiciliary care workers presents particular challenges to contractual concepts of labour law. Care workers, themselves often in precarious working contexts, are expected to meet the rising expectations, generated through discourses of choice and rights, in relation to care services. These legitimate demands raise questions for employers and workers over the control and management of working time, which has been the subject of much struggle between employers, organised labour and the state (Conaghan 2006). Care generally is task- not time-governed: it happens at all times of the day with degrees of intensity depending on the particular circumstances. Workers are exposed to unplanned 'overtime' when care cannot be slotted into the agreed time. They are also exposed to potential new forms of exploitation. To what extent is a worker's emotional capacity available to employers and their clients?

Issues arise as to how to specify the service required and how to produce labour market conditions as more forms of work move away from traditional public locations. Many more people may become private employers of care workers or many more workers may become small-scale entrepreneurs, providing a contract for services to their clients. The power relations of providing care in a domestic environment are, as we have seen, complex. The public regulatory framework concentrates on the abuse of care recipients while the harassment of workers is contained within the private sphere of employment relations.

These broad consequences of the undervaluing of women's social reproductive roles in society generally not only disadvantage women workers and carers in the UK but also provide the context for further injustices for those to whom the work is outsourced. We shall see that migrant women workers, who contribute to meeting the perceived deficits in care produced in part by the asymmetrical changes in the provision of care within the household, are themselves primarily constructed within the service/trade discourse and enter this confused and precarious regulatory context with the added disadvantages associated with the regulation of migration, which channels individuals into a variety of insecure statuses.

Who takes responsibility for the quality of care relationships? Is this increasingly becoming a matter for private contractual discourse even though it takes place often within a setting associated with familial solidarity? To what extent is it a responsibility of individuals in need of care to care about the context in which their workers work? How can a legitimate demand for good carers be separated from a perception of being good at the job because of ascribed characteristics such as ethnicity, gender, or sexual orientation? Can social care be provided ethically in ways that do not lead to exploitation of migrant workers?

The demand for global body work: trading trafficked bodies or consuming pleasure?

Historically women's bodies have been seen as the property of their husbands and exclusively available to meet male sexual needs, with little recognition of women's sexual satisfaction, thus such satisfaction has only had a recognised value for one sex. These perceptions of responsibilities and the values attached to them have been challenged, not least by women's movements. A satisfying self-defined sexual life is beginning to be recognised as a human right although there is still considerable resistance to this development and there is little consensus on how to provide sexual well-being (Cornwall et al. 2008; Harcourt 2009). Nonetheless, there is now in the UK a huge demand for a range of differentiated sexually related goods and services. We have seen that the consumer economy has developed in such a way that many households have more disposable income available for the purchase of 'non-essential' goods and services that give pleasure and a sense of identity to the consumer. Many aspects of the highly lucrative and diverse market in products offering sexualised pleasure and services have been 'normalised' into the majority consumer culture. It has expanded exponentially with the development of new communications and information technologies, which provide access to goods and services and enable customers easily to buy, sell and exchange millions of images and videos (Hughes 2002: 129). Such material is affordable to a mass audience and provided anonymously. It can be consumed publicly, in working time, or privately, within the domestic environment.

Many of the body work products and services are marketed to gendered bodies. Women, who are recognised as active sexual beings, are offered 'special treatments' such as massage, aromatherapy, nail therapy or body waxing, while men are offered sexualised pleasure in the entertainment industry (pole, lap and table dancing and the services provided in 'gentleman's clubs' and 'stag' weekends). The commercial exchanges of direct sexual services take place within a range of market-differentiated contexts: in 'high-end' escort agencies and down-market massage parlours; in off-street brothels to on-street sex working. Purchasers also seek wide choice in their services based on bodily identities. These involve a range of erotic constructions that are often based on 'race' and ethnicity: hot latin lovers; beautiful Russian women; skilled oriental temptresses and so on.

The global sex industry is estimated to generate profits amounting to US$ 33.9 billion, with almost half – US$ 15.4 billion – realised in industrial countries (Belsar 2005). However, there are limits to normalisation. It is generally not acceptable to involve children in the provision of either goods or services (the Sexual Offences Act 2003 sections 47–51). Although sexual activity has never been 'contained' within family relationships, there is far less public consensus when commercial services move towards the direct provision of sexual intercourse. Unlike food and care services, there is no political support for an expansion in these aspects of the sex industry. This is the unacceptable face of sexual capitalism for many. Economically, the ways in which market sex services, particularly those associated with 'prostitution', are valued complicates analyses. While prostitution is considered an economic activity, however provided (Belsar 2005:13) and women survive on the money they earn, the activity itself (satisfaction of sexual desires) has value for the client alone. Much of the sex industry is not valued in national accounting mechanisms because it is derived from activities that take place within the informal economy or are registered incorrectly as nightclubs or massage parlours.

Such services are socially and legally constructed through the discourse of prostitution and now trafficking. The focus for public policy is shifting away from the providers to the male consumers/clients with the express aim of suppressing demand for these forms of commercial sexual services. The regulatory framework denies the status of worker to service providers and criminalises the context for the transaction. As such the work is both highly precarious for women workers, and associated with high levels of abuse and violence, but also potentially very lucrative for those who are in a position to benefit from the illicitness of the trade. These conditions generate considerable demand for differentiated services, based often on ascribed characteristics of the workers involved, which are perceived to be unmet in the home market.

Locating 'prostitution'

The primary consumers of commercial sexual services are men from all backgrounds, while the primary providers are women, the majority of whom are generally poor and, particularly in the case of street-level services, from vulnerable groups. However, there is a paucity of reliable evidence on all aspects of this activity. There are studies that consider 'prevalence' of use (that is demand) that point to a drop from 25 per cent of the population in 1949 to about 6 to 7 per cent in the 1990s and one study suggesting a further reduction to about 4 per cent in 2001 (Brooks-Gordon 2006: 84–86). There are also no reliable figures relating to the size of the workforce. Matthews (2005) sought to establish some clarity on levels of on-street prostitution in his research in 1994 but found it very difficult. The police provided three different figures: those based on total numbers that they were aware of in the last twelve months; the number currently active (last three weeks or so); and those on the street on any one night. These figures varied widely although the relationship between them was more consistent. To give two examples: the three figures for Bradford were 150, 50, 10 (population 468,000); for Sheffield 200, 100, 25 (population 530,000).

Research studies relating to sex working, particularly concerning street prostitution, show a link with family problems. The Home Office analysis suggests that many of the sex workers on the streets are young people who have left deeply troubled homes or institutional care. Many have experienced sexual abuse and now have drug addictions (Home Office 2004). Matthews cautions against a popular myth that the majority of women are driven into prostitution to service a drug habit. He points to research that found that half of street workers did not have a drug habit when they started (2005: 890). Generally there has been a reduction in the level of 'on-street' sex work and a substantial rise in 'off-street' provision. A growing number of those working in these establishments are foreign nationals. Police in London estimated that about 5 per cent could be described as trafficked although more may be involved in 'debt bondage' whereby the woman had to pay off the expenses associated with her travel to the UK before she could earn money for herself. London police found 730 flats, saunas and massage parlours with between 3,000 and 6,000 women working in them, only 19 per cent of whom were UK nationals. One in four of the women were from Eastern Europe. They also identified 164 escort agencies, involving about 2,000 women (Matthews 2005: 891–892).

Trade, rights or care?

There are many, contested, constructions of prostitution but these can be simplified into three policy approaches in England and Wales (Walkowitz

1980; Brooks-Gordon 2006: chapter 1; Wolkowitz 2006: chapter 6). The first argues that prostitution involves work. A trade-related discourse in this context would emphasise the freedom to contract to provide and purchase sex. The growth and diversification of the market in sexual desires and the emergence of a consumer discourse would not distinguish the purchase of sexualised products and services from any other form of purchase. In this construction, workers have the right to sell their labour unhindered by inappropriate state interference in private activities.

However, some advocates who conceptualise sex as work would not accept this trade-related understanding, which ignores the network of power relations in which such work is undertaken. While accepting the market, they focus on strengthening the rights of workers. They call for the abolition of all crimes specifically relating to prostitution and a move to the regularisation of employment status so that workers would be eligible for 'normal' employment-related benefits. Women would then be entitled to protection from work-related harassment and abuse as employees or as service providers as well as protection from violence as citizens. (Since 2003 the largest trade union in the UK, the GMB, has accepted women working as prostitutes as members (Westmarland 2006: 26).) Others would accept that there is a market but would not wish to 'normalise' it in this way because the power relations that underpin the transaction enable the client/purchaser to make demands that encroach too heavily on the bodily integrity of the worker for it to be considered work (which is more akin to bonded labour). Prostitution as body work is discussed further in Chapter 6.

Constructions based on sex as work are vigorously opposed by some activists and not supported by state policymakers who deny the existence of a potentially legitimate trade. They associate it with an unacceptable norm of a male entitlement to sex. The second approach therefore sees prostitution as the abuse of women, as an act of violence against women rather than a product of a contextually specific form of provision. Women within this approach need to be seen as holders of human rights, as exploited sex victims not as exploited workers. The discourse of rights is therefore invoked by the various constituencies but to different ends. Are women exercising a right to contract or do they have a human right not to be degraded and sexually violated? Are these mutually exclusive? Does the right to act as an independent economic agent take priority over a right to physical integrity?

The third approach, which is to a large extent still reflected in the present laws, sees prostitution as a nuisance to the public. The aim is to protect communities from the effects of commercial sex provision. Inner city communities are blighted by prospective clients and general voyeurs cruising around the neighbourhood and by the drug culture that tends to be associated with 'on-street' sex working. It leads to a sense of insecurity, which particularly affects local women. In this approach, the state has responsibility to take care of citizens whose lives are affected by inappropriate public behaviour. The Street

Offences Act 1959 which increased control over the activities that produced offensive public behaviour, provides the origins of the 'negative regulationist approach' that still prevails (Brooks-Gordon 2006: 10). The nuisance approach is reflected now in the Human Rights Act 1998, which provides for direct applicability of the European Convention on Human Rights. Article 8(1) of the Convention, which provides a right to respect for private life, has been interpreted in case law to include a sex life (*Niemietz* v. *Germany* (1992) 16 EHRR 97) and Article 8(2), which limits state interference with such a right inter alia to the 'prevention of disorder or crime' or the 'protection of health or morals'.

Regulating 'prostitutes'

The twentieth century saw significant changes in the acceptability of paying for sex as the concept of conjugal, companionate and romantic love was progressively promoted (Brooks-Gordon 2006: chapter 1). Although the male use of prostitution has been seen as inevitable, it has been met with increasing social disapproval, with the men involved seen more as deviant and dangerous. The status of the person (who can be a woman or a man: Sexual Offences Act 2003 section 56) providing paid sexual services is not clear although the European Court of Justice (ECJ) seems to consider that prostitutes are workers. Even though the issue of status was not addressed explicitly, the Court upheld the right to freedom of movement for two French prostitutes working in Belgium. The women therefore successfully invoked rights associated with work (Joined Cases 115 and 116/81 *Adoui and Cornuaille* v. *Belgium* [1982] ECR 1665; see Kraamwinkel 2002: 327–328). The criminal laws have focused on women who are constructed within a specific category of 'prostitute': 'a person who on at least one occasion offers or provides sexual services to another person in exchange for payment or the promise of payment (Sexual Offences Act (SOA) 2003 section 51). Prostitution is not defined directly but is 'to be interpreted accordingly' (SOA section 51(2)). The transaction is not illegal although the associated activities are subject to criminal sanctions: persistently loitering or soliciting on the street or public place for the purposes of prostitution is a criminal activity (Street Offences Act 1959 as amended section 1).

Since 1982 courts can only fine, not imprison, prostitutes for the offence although three or more convictions can lead to a community sentence. A prostitute who has been caught soliciting can now receive a 'rehabilitative' order to attend three meetings to discuss ending their involvement with prostitution (The Policing and Crime Act 2009 section 17 and Schedule 1). Failing to meet a magistrate's summons to attend can lead to arrest and imprisonment for up to seventy-two hours. The term 'common prostitute' (which arose after two police cautions for soliciting,) was removed in 2009. However, the concept has been reconstructed in the discourse relating to anti-social behaviour. Civil orders introduced under the 1998 Crime and Disorder Act relating to such behaviour

(ASBOs) attract a criminal penalty, including imprisonment if breached. This updated public nuisance offence enables local authorities to tackle behaviour that causes harassment, alarm or distress to people not in the same household. ASBOs, which can contain an exclusion requirement preventing a person entering a particular place or area, have been used in relation to women involved in prostitution. They have also been used against clients who cause a nuisance through soliciting (Westmarland 2006: 28). These developments reflect a shift in the regulatory context for prostitution with a reduction in the activities of police vice squads targeting women and an increase in multi-agency working (including the police) with women. The 'problem' therefore is increasingly constructed as an issue of disorder and quasi-criminality (Matthews 2005).

Purchasers of on-street services have not until relatively recently attracted criminal sanctions. The changing attitude of policymakers towards the management of prostitution has led to an increasing focus on purchasers. Much more police attention is paid to their behaviour with the aim of disrupting and reducing demand. They can now commit an offence if they solicit once (in a public place including from a vehicle, known as kerb crawling) for the purpose of prostitution (Sexual Offences Act 2003 section 51A inserted by Policing and Crime Act 2009 section 19 removing the need for persistency). The offence attracts a fine. In 2002 it became an arrestable offence, with punishment extended to possible disqualification from driving in 2004. The potential for further criminalisation of purchasers is discussed below.

These legislative measures focus on 'street' prostitution. They are widely thought not to have worked (Westmarland 2006; Brooks-Gordon 2006) and have provoked much policy debate over appropriate forms of intervention. Some have advocated the use of official tolerance zones (red light districts), situated away from residential areas and managed by police and public welfare bodies in an attempt to reduce violence and harm to the women involved and to protect inner city communities. The Coordinated Prostitution Strategy 2006 rejected this approach, reinforcing a move away from viewing prostitution as work or a nuisance to seeing this form of prostitution as abuse (see Westmarland 2006).

There are also offences that relate to 'off-street' sex provision. It is an offence for a person to keep or to manage or act or assist in the management of a brothel to which people resort for practices involving prostitution (Sexual Offences Act 1956 sections 33 and 33A). 'Brothel' is defined in case law as premises from which more than one person is involved in prostitution. (Recent proposals to increase safety by enabling two or three people (two prostitutes and a 'maid') to share premises have not materialised.) Landlords and tenants can be prosecuted for letting premises for use as a brothel (sections 34 and 35). Generally a woman cannot legitimately rent premises, thereby increasing her vulnerability to unscrupulous landlords. There are offences relating to causing or inciting prostitution for gain (anywhere in the world) and controlling prostitution for gain (anywhere in the world) (Sexual Offences Act 2003 sections 52 and 53). Both can lead to imprisonment. These offences are targeted at the exploitative practices of those who are often described as 'pimps' but not at landlords who supply premises.

The enormous profits to be made in off-street sexual service provision have encouraged entrepreneurs to invest in this market. A small massage parlour or sauna employing three or four women can make profits in excess of £1 million a year (S. Devi quoted in Matthews 2005: 892); according to the Serious Organised Crime Agency a trafficked woman is estimated to be 'worth' £93,000 per year. As in street provision the regulatory focus has increasingly been targeted on those who run, and more recently use the services of, brothels with the aim of disputing and reducing demand (Matthews 2005). The Proceeds of Crime Act 2002 has enabled the Assets Recovery Agency to take goods and property that have been obtained or bought with the proceeds of criminal conduct. These powers, subsequently enhanced by the Proceeds of Crime Act 2005, have been used by the police against brothels and have proven a lucrative source of income for the state: £2.5 million in cash was seized from the sex industry in 2004/5 (Brooks-Gordon 2006). The powers to close such premises have been tightened recently (Policing and Crime Act 2009 section 21, Schedule 2).

Many aspects of the 'off-street' sex industry are not singled out for special treatment in England and Wales. If appropriately licensed, 'sex establishments' selling sex products are legal (Local Government (Miscellaneous Provisions) Act 1982 Part 2 and Schedule III). Venues that offer erotic entertainment and special treatments rather than 'off-street' sexual intercourse have recently been reclassified as 'sexual entertainment venues' to place them within the more stringent licensing framework for the control of sex establishments (Policing and Crime Act 2009 section 27). The policy aim is again to suppress demand in spite of considerable opposition from those involved in the industry.

Reconstructing prostitutes: victims of trafficking

While the feminist movement has viewed pornography and prostitution as problematic, there are very deep divisions over the appropriate response to the issues raised (Barnett 1998: chapter 12). These heated debates have, to a large extent, been refocused on the issues relating to trafficking, which has become the pivot of substantial international policy activity (Kelly 2003). The trafficking of women and children for exploitation within the sex industry has caught the imagination of the world's media and brought to wider attention the suffering of those involved. It has led to an elision between the construction of 'prostitutes' and 'trafficked women'. Market expansion has also raised new grounds for concern rooted in the discourses of national security. Demand in the growing global sex market is met by the ready supply of migrant labour, which keeps labour costs down and profits up. The supply of this labour is not provided through 'legal' migration channels but through processes thought to be associated with organised crime networks, which pose wider threats to states. Trafficking is understood through a legal discourse of international criminality, which distinguishes between trafficking (which involves no agency by the victim) and smuggling (which does). This transnational discourse is discussed in Chapter 7.

Within England and Wales, the 2000 International Protocol on Trafficking has been implemented via the Sexual Offences Act 2003 (sections 57–60). These measures cover both adults and children and deal with recruiting, harbouring or facilitating the movement of another person for the purposes of sexual exploitation. (In 2008/9 eighty defendants were prosecuted for trafficking.) Offences incur punishment of fourteen years' imprisonment. They are based upon the assumption that these activities involve the use of force, coercion, deception, or abuse of vulnerability. Sexual exploitation is not defined, which leaves open the range of interpretations discussed above. Is all sex work exploitation or only that which is carried out in circumstances that amount to exploitation? The UK government now has an Action Plan (Home Office 2007) and funds the multi-agency UK Human Trafficking Centre which coordinates actions in relation to this Plan. The UK contributes to the EU framework for trafficking and ratified the Council of Europe Convention on Trafficking in 2008.

Responsible clients? Dangerous offenders?

There is now a strict liability offence relating to the client who pays for the sexual services of a prostitute subjected by a third person 'to force, deception or threats of a kind likely to induce or encourage [the prostitute] to provide the sexual services' where that third person acts 'in the expectation of gain' (Sexual Offence Act 2003 section 53A inserted by Policing and Crime Act 2009 section 14). It can be committed anywhere in the world. This controversial provision reflects the Swedish model of criminalising the client while treating women as victims of exploitation, in contrast to the German model, which adopted a normalisation policy to provide women with full employment status and rights (Brooks-Gordon 2006: 50–54). While policymakers have been influenced by the discourse on trafficking, many fear that increasing the illegality associated with men's actions will result in further losses in the rights of the sex worker.

Until recently, there have been few reliable profiles of the users of sexual services (see Brooks-Gordon 2006 chapters 3 and 4). There is recognition of the need to gain understanding (Anderson and O'Connell Davidson 2003). 'Market research' on customers seeks to establish the characteristics of those who purchase sex and their motivations although unlike other consumer research, it aims to disrupt rather than expand the market and to gauge the malleability of public attitudes to approaches that would seek to create a discourse of customer responsibility for potential exploitation of prostitutes (Coy et al. 2007; Home Office 2008; Government Equalities Office 2009). The evidence suggests that the men who buy sex are not necessarily either sick or sad (while never forgetting that sex work is dangerous, involving much violence, including death). Such men work and have 'normal' relationships.

Can these consumers be encouraged to take more responsibility to care for the service provider? Is it possible to force/criminalise a caring client into being? Would clients take more care and be persuaded to consider the position of the service provider if these services were constructed through normal employment relationships? Does the responsibility for tackling trafficking lie with the individual consumer of the service?

Securing transnational identities: the demand for embodied kinsfolk from South Asia

The broader contextual detail relating to the BrAsian communities is not presented here because it is discussed within Chapter 9. The desires contained within this last chain are firmly located within the sphere of unpaid social reproduction although not unaffected by the global economic context and the rise in the discourse of individual choice. In this chain, 'consumers' take a far more active part in initiating and managing the processes involved. It is therefore more 'bottom up' than our other chains. It concerns the methods of family formation associated with, but not limited to, particular communities in the UK. For some, the UK 'pool' from which to choose seems not to provide what they are seeking in a spouse or life partner. This constructed deficit is met by sourcing an appropriate person overseas. Home Office immigration statistics report that there were 102,685 grants of settlement in 2008 of which 69 per cent were for spouses and their dependents. These included 23,220 husbands, of which 37 per cent were from the Indian subcontinent and 34,170 wives, of which 30 per cent were from the Indian subcontinent. Children constituted the bulk of the rest (38,945) with 26 per cent from the Indian subcontinent (Home Office 2009b: 36). The chain can involve the use of market-related processes, such as formal advertising for a partner and intermediaries of varying degrees of formality including commercial agencies, but also family members. There is also increasing use of internet-based services. Described in this way, the transactions involved could cover 'mail order brides', whereby mainly men are introduced to an overseas partner through the use of a commercial agency in exchange for a fee and where the initiative is taken by an individual. However, the focus here is on the variety of community-based arranged marriages in which there may be direct transfer payments (a dowry) within the families (Charsley and Shaw 2006).

A transnational union can be based upon the processes associated with the discourse of romantic love: mutual identification of attraction with no necessary involvement of wider family members or commercial intermediaries. This free market in relationship formation is in part a product of the hard-fought struggles to gain recognition of the right of all persons to sexual fulfilment and to freedom from coercion, discrimination and violence relating to sexuality, irrespective of sexual orientation or sexual identity (Harcourt 2009: 146). These rights add to those which protect the family, as a fundamental unit of society, and which have enabled heterosexual marriage based on the consent of the individuals involved (UDHR Article 16; Convention on Consent to Marriage (1962); Minimum Age for Marriage and Registration of Marriages (1964); ICCPR Article 23; ICESCR Article 10; CEDAW Article 16). This discourse is firmly rooted in concepts of choice and autonomy. Unions with the romantic love discourse even when commercially arranged, do not challenge dominant normative assumptions that inform the relationship between families and the market and are generally presumed to be 'genuine'. They only become 'suspicious' where there seems to be an explicit purpose of gaining access to European labour markets.

However, the pursuit of a free market in arranged marriage formation is more normatively contested. Pursuing a desire for economic redistribution of resources and recognition of identity primarily through family relationships sits uneasily within a northern consumer economy. There may be a suspicion that the transnational activities within the families of some communities in the UK involve too much agency by kinsfolk in the pursuit of security for the wider family network. While much political rhetoric extols the virtues of 'decent hard working families', the assumption is that hard work will secure the position of UK citizens (as family members) and contribute to economic and social prosperity. Families that use the state's global market positioning and potential citizenship as an asset (hard won by present and previous generations of family migrants) to negotiate an economically or socially advantageous marriage for a UK-based son or daughter is not so easily recognised. The perceived demand is contested in these circumstances. A desire for a union with an individual to meet the need for an intimate relationship is recast as an inappropriate desire.

As we have seen, a gender contract allocates responsibilities for different types of activities between men and women although its content is changing. Both women and men are expected to contribute to funding the household directly through the labour market. Some marriages may result in households that involve gender contracts which are resistant to these 'third way' economic policies and therefore not seen as entering into the national contract of work and consumption. This may be because there is a preference for the breadwinner/homemaker gender contract or because the spouse faces particular barriers to entry to the labour market.

State-recognised family law provides the regulatory framework for intimate relationships within the UK. It prescribes the requirements of a valid marriage or civil partnership. The UK is a legal centralist state, which generally does not recognise other forms of law such as those based on customs or religion. There are concessions to, and accommodations with, different normative systems but no legal recognition, for instance, of 'personal laws' such as those pertaining to Muslims or Hindus. However, in practice, the UK is legally pluralistic: different communities arrange their affairs in the light of their understanding of such

personal laws. Thus the personal relationships of some citizens may be regulated by two systems, as kinsfolk, through largely unrecognised but normatively
powerful personal laws that operate within the sphere of the family and
community, and as UK nationals/citizens, through state-based laws.

Because a state-sanctioned personal relationship such as marriage or civil
partnership can be a route to wider economic and social entitlements for
non-EU nationals, these assets, which result from a relationship between
marriage and markets, are increasingly subject to protectionist discourse relating to suspicious or 'bogus' arrangements. The actions of families who seek to
arrange marriages transnationally become enmeshed in these wider regulatory
discourses around migration control. There is, however, another strand to the
protectionist discourse, which relates to the risks to individuals who are coerced
against their wishes into marriages arranged by family members, which has led
to the Forced Marriage (Civil Protection) Act 2007 and a range of national
policy interventions to try to prevent such marriages taking place. Young
women are particularly vulnerable to attempts by powerful members of families
who seek to constrain their wish to express choice in the construction of their
sexual identities. Feminist activism has long campaigned for state recognition
of the danger of violence within family relationships. As a result there is a
relatively extensive legislative and policy framework in place to seek to protect
violence against women. The measures on forced marriages add to the rights of
(female) citizens.

The construction of this demand is challenged for its perceived reliance on a
particular 'cultural' understanding of identity and belonging which undervalues
potential 'local' UK partners. This is seen as potentially affecting a sense of
belonging (and loyalty) to the UK state. It also suggests an understanding that
insufficiently recognises individual agency of women in particular, but also
young men. Is it the wider family or the individual who wishes to meet this
need? Is it a need to secure a sense of belonging to a wider network of family
relationships or a need for an intimate and nurturing relationship? Are the two
wishes mutually exclusive? Who decides that this need can best be met
transnationally?

Conclusion

This chapter has considered the changing relationship between production and
social reproduction in the UK's consumer economy which provides the
'demand' context for the chains. The increased involvement of the market in
activities that were once more contained within family relationships, supplemented by provision through the state, is reshaping the nature of the relationships involved (vertical relationships in the pyramid). The UK governance
contexts affect not only the construction of the domestic desire for the goods
and services in our chains but also form part of the governance of them (the
horizontal relationships linking Global North and Global South). Domestic

forms of provision and governance contribute to the ways in which the gains and losses are distributed among the networks of social relations within the chains and have a differential effect on the Global South women who contribute to meeting the desires.

Trade

Individuals in the UK are expected to satisfy their needs and desires through the market place through the goods and services they buy. The increasing transformation of many aspects of unpaid social reproductive activities, which have been associated with family relationships, albeit never fully sustained by them, into services is both a result of, but also produces, changes in norms relating to gender relationships. There is an economic assumption that the demands for goods and services can be met from 'anywhere'. The international trade regime seeks to support this assumption through the objective of facilitating the free movement of goods and services. The various multilateral agreements including those relating to goods (GATTS), agriculture (AOA) and services (GATS) all play their part in this trade discourse. As a party to these and other regional and bilateral agreements, the UK state fashions its domestic economic and social policies accordingly. However, involvement in global market places brings risks and imported goods compete with local suppliers. UK farmers' share of the 'retail basket' has changed little in recent years. It is lower than in the early 1990s and predicted to shrink further. UK food security policy is predicated on global markets. Increasingly, food is subject to value added processing: an apple is a ready-sliced, vacuum-sealed, child's healthy lunch pack apple. Such value-adding is met through supply chains, which can pare down costs through managing local and distant labour and regulatory processes efficiently and effectively. These processes present enormous challenges to UK food processors who require maximum flexibility in local labour markets to compete but also to the Kenyan producers who supply exotic fruit and vegetables to large retailers. They meet what often seem like punishing delivery deadlines and the exacting quality and safety standards required to enter the European market and to satisfy consumer expectations.

There is less support for the free movement of labour than for that of the goods produced. The IFIs argue that economic migration can be a 'win win' situation, providing a supply of appropriate labour to sectors with shortages, thereby keeping wage levels down and providing financial resources to workers who can support themselves and contribute to their home economies through remittances. The IFIs make this argument in relation to less skilled labour, particularly in relation to women involved in the care sector, but migration is a very politically sensitive issue in northern welfare states, particularly in relation to low-skilled work. The UK, which has access to labour markets within Europe as a result of membership of the EU, increasingly meets demands for such work from this source. The flow of European workers into the UK still raises political tensions, which justify greater restrictions on those from outside of this regional market.

The economic discourse of overcoming a shortage in the market for services through the provision of competitively priced overseas service providers falters in relation to the provision of sex services. While there may be covert commercial estimates of unmet demand disguised as hospitality or entertainment services, there are no Confederation of British Industry estimates of shortages or UK government targets for workers within certain sectors of the economy; instead there are police statistics on numbers of raids on illegal brothels, trafficked women rescued and criminals prosecuted.

Trade discourse is not interested in issues of social reproduction and the family and so there are no trade treaties relating to such matters. Nevertheless, there is a discourse, even though it is taking place in a different context to economic migrants, whereby local 'suppliers' are seen as losing out to those from overseas in the heated debates that surround family formation involving a transnational partner. 'Local' BrAsian young women and men are constructed as losing out to foreign cousins. Here the tension lies between the objectives of families and state policies. The spectre of the economy remains in that families can be seen as acting in the interests of their distant members by gaining access to northern labour markets and welfare systems but also through the creation of community solidarities which are at odds with dominant consumer identities. The state at the same time sees a supply of people who add after an initial period of dependence on family resources, to a pool of unskilled labour and are a drain on social capital.

Economic pressures to meet consumer demands clash with political imperatives to protect livelihoods and social resources and result in vulnerability for those caught up in the regulatory frameworks associated with immigration, including trafficking provisions, which seek to manage these tensions. Such individuals become precarious and migrant workers if they are defined as workers at all or precarious kinsfolk (partners/spouses). They become trafficked sex workers and victims of forced marriages.

Rights

While the trade discourse would tend to champion the meeting of desires, the international human rights framework, in response to sustained pressure from activists, has developed its own discourse on protecting those who are adversely affected by the growth in the consumer markets. The ILO has sought to extend its remit to cover aspects of precarious/flexible work that particularly affect women and has developed its decent work campaign. The CEDAW reinforces the rights of women to equal opportunities within employment (Article 11). The ICCPR recognises a human right to form families and to choose marriage partners. The European Convention on Human Rights (ECHR) provides a qualified right to respect for private and home life (Article 8) and to freedom of expression (Article 10) and a right (if of marriageable age) to marry and to found a family (according to the national laws) (Article 12). The right to equality between men and women in family and marriage laws is enshrined in Article 16 of CEDAW. The protocol to the International Convention on International Crime on trafficking tackles forms of coerced migration, Article 6 of CEDAW seeks to protect women against trafficking. The UK is a signatory to all these measures.

The trade and rights discourses offer different ways of seeing the globalisation of needs: trade as the provision of services involving independent entrepreneurs and human rights as protecting vulnerable workers or family members. Both discourses miss or fail to take full account of the changing social relations upon which the present work-related regulatory framework is built. Caring relationships within the family are based upon a norm of solidarity. When care moves to the market and becomes an 'affect', it is undertaken within contract-based labour law, which is based upon a norm of exchange and does not 'fit' easily (Conaghan and Rittich: 2005).

These changes challenge many aspects of the UK labour market. They 'cast doubt on regulatory provisions premised on sharp distinctions between paid and unpaid work, between "employed" and "self-employed" workers, between employment and unemployment, and between "work" and other life-activities' (Conaghan et al. 2002: xxvi). The interactions between market and welfare state constructions of work and care reflected in labour and welfare law seem at the same time to destabilise and reinforce the work/family dichotomy (Conaghan 2002: 72). Economic value is attributed to paid work for the market while it is denied to unpaid family/caring work. A woman can work unpaid as a carer for a family member but usually cannot be paid as a care worker for this person. She can be paid to provide care for someone else's family member. The way in which these distinctions are constructed legally are reflected more broadly in the EU case law on equal treatment in relation to state social security, which requires a relationship with the labour market for eligibility, thus excluding 'housewives' (see Kraamwinkel 2002: 332–333). Those that provide unpaid care are dependents consuming resources they have not earned (Conaghan 2002: 72). Yet adults in receipt of care are constructed increasingly in terms of independence. They are encouraged to purchase care via the market rather than through 'dependence' on the state or the family. The status of workers providing paid sexual services is ambiguous within ECJ case law and heavily associated with illegality and immorality constructed through the discourse of criminal law.

We see here applications of the justice and care distinction within shifting socio-economic contexts. Is there therefore a need to introduce market norms of promise and exchange (concepts of justice) into the sphere of the family? Is there a need to reassess the categories of labour law to think, as Conaghan and Rittich (2005) suggest, not about the workplace but work's place: to move the basis of labour law from an employer/employee relationship to that of the labour market, to include all forms of access to paid work, to protect all precarious workers, particularly those who have increased vulnerability due to their immigration status? Does this lose the relational aspect that binds the employee and employer together and upon which labour law is premised? If so, is it preferable to consider interventions based upon citizenship?

Care

Service provision in the market to meet the desires associated with social reproduction raises new questions relating to bodies. The 'desires' in this chapter involve 'body work' (Wolkowitz 2006) and 'body politics' (Harcourt 2009). Body 'work' takes place now in different political and economic contexts as it becomes less associated with solidaristic familial relationships and poses challenges to existing regulatory frameworks. The move to meet more desires in the market place deals with what seem to be very different issues: the demand for market-based sexual services and the desires associated with diasporic family solidarity, which focus on family formation. Both, in different ways, involve the politics of sexualised bodies. The first is set within the heated political debates on how to analyse gendered power relations within the sex industry and the demand for market-based sexual services. The second addresses the politics of 'multicultural sexualities'. They take place within different analytical and institutional contexts. The first is more obviously related to an economic analysis of the impact of consumerism and the global market on the construction of sexualised bodies. In the UK, the second has been tackled primarily through the lens of politics and issues relating to the recognition of groups and individual agency.

Both issues are contested through gender discourses because both, in different ways, challenge male entitlements: either through loss of male control within the family or loss of male entitlements in the market. Both are products, in part, of contemporary globalisation and both are fought out over women's bodies. However, it is important not to lose sight of the economic context in which these issues emerge. Globalisation and the development of northern consumer markets are clearly influencing the way in which each of the 'problems' relating to needs and desires is understood.

Can the conceptual frameworks relating to trade rights and care be reconstructed in ways that would start to address the recast gender inequalities which this move to the market seems to entail? Care analysis is built upon the way in which relationships shape our understandings of ourselves. Bodies therefore matter to care ethics. Are there ways of caring about those involved in these evolving relationships associated with aspects of social reproduction without reproducing market-based concepts or reconstructing an outmoded gender contract? Is it possible to utilise a discourse of care for those involved in the purchase of goods, which emphasises the responsibilities (not duties) that are a consequence of good caring? Can caring relationships form the heart of a 'service economy' rather than be an unfortunate side effect of consumerism? Is it possible to consider responsible relationships in the area of sex working without denying employment status to women and criminalising men? Is it possible to consider responsible relationships within families without denying agency to whole categories of women because of the way in which some family relationships have responded to senses of identity and belonging? These questions are explored in the chapters that follow.

4

Gender justice in Africa: politics of culture or culture of economics?

I find my loyalty to my cultural identity wrestling with my loyalty to gender identity. My culture is misunderstood and slighted, and I feel that unless I defend it, I am guilty of betraying it. And yet . . . I cannot deny that my culture betrays me qua woman . . . What I need is a stand-point that allows me to speak *as a woman of this cultural grouping. . ..* [Women] do not know themselves outside that cultural framework; it provides their social bearings. Women might also have a legal self-understanding, but it is one that conflicts with their cultural being, one which is largely alien and peripheral to the context within which their lives are lived. (Maboreke 2000: 110, original italics)

Introduction

This chapter sets the wider context for the global value chain which, involves the consumption in the UK of FFV products grown and prepared in Kenya. While women employed in export-focused agribusiness, the most economically successful area of agriculture, can be viewed as 'modern' formal sector workers, their working lives are shaped by the macroeconomic position of their states within the global market and also by the prevailing socio-cultural norms.

Using Silbey's narratives of globalisation, women and men (from the majority communities) in the Global North have no group or national culture. They are freed from such constraint by their economic position as consumers/workers. They create their own cultures through the exercise of choice, which is guaranteed by the rights they hold as individuals. The culture of economics is positive; freedom from culture. In practice, many women and men in the UK do not experience this freedom. Their lives involve a daily struggle against the depredations of relative poverty, the effects of violence or other forms of exclusion from the perceived benefits of the consumer market.

By the same narrative, African women are constituted by culture; they embody it as victims of violence, which is perpetrated through family and community institutions within a framework of a national culture. The culture of economics is negative; women are victims of poverty, which results from woeful state mismanagement of the economy and the prejudices against women within family and community institutions. Women are denied the right to freedom from culture. The politics of rights are set against the constraints of culture. In practice, some women and men have this freedom because they are part of the elite and/or are able to access the global market, however precariously. There is a shared discourse of rights but in the Global North this is associated with the culture of economics while in the Global South it is constructed through the politics of culture.

Rights and culture take a particular legal form in post-colonial Africa. Culture is heavily identified with the socially reproductive sphere, associated with the family and local communities. Women are seen as the conduits for, and repositories of, culture with family and community relations regulated to a large extent through customary laws. Public life is organised through state law, which is associated with, although not necessarily functioning within, liberal rule-of-law values. This construction of the relationship between productive and socially reproductive spheres as a hierarchical distinction between two legal domains is a legacy of colonialism and imperialism. Culture is constructed through customary laws and rights through state law: in public women are individual abstract citizens, in private legally constructed embodied kinspersons.

The first half of this chapter analyses the way in which productive and social reproductive spheres have been separated out and regulated under colonialism, nationalism and now contemporary globalisation and their contribution to the gendered construction of cultural and legal identities in sub-Saharan Africa. The present culturally positive approaches to socio-legal analysis in Africa have considerable similarities to the analyses associated with the feminist ethic of care in which the individual is constructed through relationships rather than based on the liberal concept of the abstract individual. Previous chapters discussed the impact on the construction of concepts of care when many socially reproductive needs transfer from the sphere of the family to that of the market and the way in which 'care' is incorporated within market-based discourses. In Africa we see incorporations of 'care', understood as the culture of customary laws, into the market relationships that result from contemporary social and economic development policies.

Work in the agribusiness sector provides an alternative means of livelihood for a tiny number of the women involved in agriculture, the majority of whom seek to survive as small-scale farmers. Much macroeconomic policymaking has been directed towards improving productivity within agriculture in recent decades. The state has become the focus for a range of power struggles involving the relationship between communities and the development of markets in Africa. Land reform is one area of intense conflict. These developments raise further challenges for those seeking to pursue gender justice for women. Do women give up on, or at least relegate, 'top down' rights struggles focused on the state and concentrate on positive, 'bottom up' entitlements within communities set within a market context? The second half of the chapter considers the struggles over access to, and regulation of, land which, along with the discussion of effects of legal pluralism on gender relations, lay the foundations for the more specific discussion of the impact of these processes on the women who are involved in the FFV chain as workers and potential producers of FFV. These factors contribute to the external governance of the chains and contribute to the distribution of the benefits. The discussion is limited to countries in sub-Saharan Africa formerly colonised by Britain particularly in Eastern and Southern Africa.

The politics of culture

The imperial legacy

In pre-colonial Africa, '[m]en generally built houses, hunted, herded and milked, fished, and fought. Women cultivated, processed, and marketed crops; collected fuel and water; cared for children, the sick, and the elderly; made pottery, cooked, cleaned, and washed' (Tamale 1999: 7, describing the position in what is now Uganda). Within this sexual division of labour, roles were complementary rather than hierarchically ordered and women's work was valued by society (Mama 1997; Tamale 1999 quoting Jack H. Driberg). Nonetheless, societies were patriarchal even where matrilineal, with men holding positions of political, economic and social power supported by belief systems.

The introduction of capitalism into Africa changed the nature of these relationships. Africa's economic role under colonialism was primarily to render up raw materials to enrich its imperial masters. Men were obliged, under varying degrees of compulsion, to work as employees in mines, on commercial farms and in the construction of infrastructure to pay the taxes imposed upon them. Women were excluded from these activities. More collective agricultural societies became divided into separate households and women took on responsibility for the maintenance of the family, growing its food and selling any surplus to acquire goods. In Uganda women became the primary producers, constituting 60 per cent of the labour force in the agricultural sector and accounting for 80 per cent in food production (Economic Commission for Africa, quoted in Tamale 1999: 9). Thus households became economic units with wives controlling agricultural produce. At the same time the value of women's labour changed as it was transformed into non-valued reproductive labour in the reconstituted 'private' sphere of the family.

Waged and unwaged labour now took place in different locations. Colonialists did not want the indigenous populations settling in towns or in the mining areas so men tended to work as migrants, occasionally returning to their villages where their wives, family and community were located. Women were expected to remain within the indigenous systems of social relations, under the control of elders in the villages. However, some women took advantage of the new opportunities that emerged to escape male control by 'running away' from their villages to the mining settlements and to the urbanised areas to join men or, in other instances, to earn a living in the new economies by selling brewed beer or providing domestic services such as food and sex (Bujra 1982; White 1987, 1990; Mbilinyi 1988; Stewart 1993).

White's work on prostitution in colonial Kenya (1987; 1990) suggests that rather than being victims of sexual exploitation, women were urban pioneers, understanding their activities as providing services to men working in the colonial economy. They were some of the first to live all year around in Nairobi and used the money they earned to buy their own homes and cattle. They were independent heads of households and avoided constraints by not remitting funds back to the villages. In some cases they reinforced their position by converting to Islam, which provided a more favourable property ownership system (Stewart 1993).

The British brought their own constructions of sexuality. In particular the middle classes, who made up the colonial administrative cadre, had established an identity in late-Victorian Britain that separated them from the aristocracy and the working class. This was based on sexual restraint (monogamy) and economic moderation (thrift) although monogamy was only for women and accumulation of property for men (McClintock 1992: 78). Women were regarded as naturally inferior to men, a distinction that was extended to other races. 'The invention of *imperial nature* [original emphasis] ... would guarantee that the "universal" quintessence of Enlightenment individualism would belong only to propertied men of European descent' (McClintock 1992: 80). Women who ignored the ideology of heterosexual marriage and unpaid domesticity by becoming sex workers were seen as less human.

The domestication of women was reinforced through the ideology of missionary education. While offering some elite women a better education than otherwise available, it was not equivalent to the education of men. Reflecting the times, girls were educated to be wives of educated men, to operate within the domestic sphere of the family, not to work in either the paid or subsistence sector. Women's existing economic roles and the relative independence these roles provided were deemed inappropriate and devalued. Christian constructions of sexuality reinforced its containment within heterosexual, monogamous relationships. Women who did not conform were seen as uncontrolled and a threat to both indigenous and colonial ideologies. There was a common interest between patriarchs in the indigenous communities and colonial administrators to rein in women who transgressed.

The colonialists supported economic processes through political administration. They imported substantive and procedural laws that were generally referred to as general or received laws to cover public order and criminality. Other 'native affairs' were regulated through local customary laws as long as they were not 'repugnant to the morality or public policy' of the colonialists. In addition to women's labour being recast under the colonial market and devalued, their position was reinforced by the location of their activities as being within the family and therefore the private sphere. Matters relating to marriage, divorce, inheritance and other property were regulated through the now separate domain of customary laws.

A repugnancy clause in one guise or another was written into each colonial state's system. Ideologically this clause, heavily influenced by Christian doctrine and missionary practices, imposed a construction of morality on indigenous practices that particularly affected gender relations. Various marriage practices were found to be repugnant. In Ghana 'the wrong African approach was seen in such practices as betrothals, "forced marriages" and the "inheritance of wives"' (Bennett quoted in Banda 2005: 16). In pre-colonial Uganda customary marriages were all potentially polygynous, recognised through the payment of bridewealth, and constituted a contract between the families of the bride and groom (Tamale 1999). Bridewealth consisted of marriage gifts offered by the groom to the bride's family before, at, or after the marriage. It provided a social and political link between clans, secured relationships between families and stability to the marriage and sought to ensure the good treatment of a wife in her new home (Tamale 1999: 7). The parties were active participants within the context of 'societies that emphasised communitarian ideals in contrast to individual autonomy' (Tamale 1999: 7). A woman could leave an abusive marriage and return to her parents. It was not a commercial transaction. However in *R* v. *Amkeyo* [1917] EAPLR 14, Chief Justice Hamilton referred to the practice as wife purchasing: 'having regard to the vital difference in the relationship of the parties to the union by native custom from that of the parties to a legal marriage, I do not think it can be said that the native custom approximates in any way the legal idea of marriage' (Tamale 1999: n 18).

Bridewealth/price is still a very important social institution in Uganda (Odonga Mwaka 1998). It has been the subject of a recent challenge in the Ugandan constitutional court by a coalition of NGOs headed by Mifumi on grounds that in its contemporary commercial form it violates women's right to equality and demands for its repayment on the breakdown of marriage in particular encourages domestic violence (*Mifumi(U) ltd & 12 others* v. *Attorney General, Kenneth Kakuru* [2010] UGCC 2). The Court rejected the petition. The majority of the judges did not find proof that the diverse manifestations of the practice violated constitutional rights and found no direct causal link with violence against women. They did, however, find that the requirement to repay brideprice on divorce was unconstitutional. They were reluctant to interfere with feelings of identity, dignity and self-worth held by the variety of ethnic groups (Justice A.E.N. Mpagi-Bahigeine). In the lead judgment, the Deputy Chief Justice L.E.M. Mukasa-Kikonyogo stated that '[t]his practice arises out of the value society attaches to virginity as the fountain of life that is valued as the proper form for any marriageable woman to be in'.

Ideologically public interests were separated from 'private' in two different systems, one constructed through a colonial interpretation of the rule of law, the other as customary (or cultural) practices. In fact they were interwoven because the customary, in most instances, was presided over by colonial administrators. In this way, the colonial state recognised customary practices as law and thus legitimised them. Women used the colonial courts set up in part to regulate indigenous marriages to increase their bargaining power within marriage and on divorce by using arguments that would be recognised by the colonialists (Parpart 1988). This led to a reaction from male elders who, it is argued, redefined 'custom' to bring women back under clan control (Bentzon et al. 1998: 102).

Legal historians and anthropologists have questioned the existence of a separate customary law that embodied traditional culture and argue that customary law was a product of the relationships between male clan elders and the colonial state anxious to prevent social unrest (Chanock 1982, 1985; Ranger 1983). Customary land law, in particular, was a product of resistance and negotiation with the colonial state as Africans argued that customs dictated what could legitimately be done with it (Chanock 1991: 72). The custom of inalienability of land was pitted against the white land grab. As a result, colonial administrators enabled clan leaders/chiefs to distribute land on an individual basis within the clan, not through the construction of rights but rather through administrative discretion. Customary practices were reconstructed and then interpreted by colonial administrators to become 'traditional', creating new power relations including between men and women (Chanock 1985; Parpart 1988; Rwezaura 1989). Customary practices hardened into traditions and law when they interacted with the general law system (Chanock 1991: 82).

Therefore, under colonialism law contributed significantly to the construction of gender relations. It reinforced a market that operated to differentiate male and female labour to the detriment of women by increasing their labour but reducing and recasting its value. Men, albeit in conditions of exploitation, joined the public sphere. The African agricultural unit was remoulded as a household or family unit and uneasily assigned to the private sphere. Women were relegated ideologically to this sphere. Although the legal construction of public and private did not 'fit' women's wider economic role as main family provisioners, within the private sphere women became more vulnerable to wider power relations as their labour became less valued. Social relations, particularly the treatment of women, were recast within a moral framework of repugnancy. Women became victims of male immoral customs. The role of the missionaries and the subsequent spread of Christianity (and Islam) reinforced dominant perspectives on the need to control women's sexuality within marriages. As women strove to take advantage of new opportunities, those with greater power redefined customary law to try to control their behaviour.

Colonial gender constructions continue to resonate in the post-colonial era (Merry 2001). Constructed divisions between rural traditional and modern urban women persist. The legacy of the power battles between the colonial powers and indigenous leaders continues to affect women's access to land (Manji 2006).

Nationalism and the post-colonial context

It is important not to generalise too much. The nations of Africa gained their independence at different times and in different contexts. Ghana, Nigeria and

Kenya have been independent states for around fifty years, while it took Zimbabweans until 1982 to dislodge the white settler government of Ian Smith, and Namibia and South Africa struggled under apartheid until 1990 and 1994. The first states therefore emerged at the height of the Cold War and were influenced by the competing economic and political ideologies while the last became black majority democracies after the fall of the Soviet bloc.

Nationalism was linked to economic modernisation and growth. However, those who obtained state power on independence had 'an insecure base in the economy, which was dominated by foreigners or immigrants' (Ghai 1993: 68). The regimes were made more vulnerable by external factors. Early international development policies encouraged states to develop their markets within international trading blocs thereby making them contingent on the 'outside world for economic and military aid, trade and technology' (Ghai 1993: 71). Corruption became integral to this economic system, 'woven into the very fabric of the state apparatus' (Ghai 1993: 69). As it became clear that governments were not producing the results through such modernisation, some sought answers in the practical application of underdevelopment theory, which limited the exposure of national economies to international markets and substituted internal commodities wherever possible. For women, the division of labour did not change much. They were still responsible for food production while men migrated in southern Africa to work in the mines or worked on the commercial farms, which were still owned by the minority white population in Zimbabwe and Kenya.

The relationship between feminism and nationalism was initially complementary but, as in other regions, became increasingly uneasy (Jayawardena 1986; Obbo 1989; Gaidzanwa 1992: 101–113; Tamale 1999). African activists have had to negotiate ways through the suspicion, even hostility, of nationalists to perceived external imposed feminist approaches. However, influenced by women's contributions to anti-colonial struggles and supported by an enlightenment ideology, the nationalist project recognised women as fully fledged African political citizens of the new countries being created. Restoring the dignity of the people was a very important element within the nationalist agenda (although it has been argued that much of the focus was directed at overcoming male humiliation and reinforcing African masculinity (Enloe 1989)). So, for instance, one of the first Acts to be introduced in Zimbabwe was the Legal Age of Majority Act 1982, which established women (and men) as adults at eighteen. Women became legal subjects rather than 'jural minors', obliged to act legally through men.

Nationalist movements also saw women as 'the bearers and upholders of traditions and customs, as reservoirs of culture' (Mama 1997: 54). Motherhood was valued as a way of creating the integrity of the new state, particularly by missionary-educated male leaders who held conservative views on sexual politics. '[T]he domestic roles of mother, wife and homemaker become the key constructions of women's identity in Africa' (Tamale quoted in Banda 2005: 92). Nationalists, including the women who took part politically, had no wish to perpetuate a view of African culture that demeaned women. Women valued, and continue to value, motherhood (Hellum 1999b) and sought recognition of their role in a productive family, which had been devalued under colonialism. Family values and motherhood feature strongly in Afrikaner and Zulu nationalism in South Africa, which is reflected in the African National Congress support for motherhood (Hassim 1993; McClintock 1993). The family was fashioned into a positive institution (McClintock 1993: 75).

The twin objectives of recognising women as political citizens and kinswomen at the heart of a communitarian value system are reflected within the post-colonial legal discourse of constitutionalism. Constitution-making played a significant role in the processes of nation-building although the degree to which each post-colonial constitution was imposed or negotiated internally varies considerably. Women's political rights as equal citizens figure in most constitutions. Constitutions also recognise the role and value of customary practices that regulate family relations. The constitutional relationship between liberal concepts of equality on the basis of sex and/or gender and customary laws (understood as embodying African cultural values) varies (Banda 2005: 34–40). 'Strong cultural relativism' allows customary law to exist unfettered by considerations of non-discrimination or equality before the law provisions (Zimbabwe); 'weak cultural relativism', which recognises customary law and also provides for equality before the law without making explicit the hierarchy between the two (Tanzania); and 'universalism' wherein customary law and a right to culture are recognised but are made subject to the test of non-discrimination and equality before the law (Namibia, Ethiopia, Uganda (Tamale 1999; Matembe 2002: ch 4) and South Africa (Goetz and Hassim 2002)). Under universalism, the concept of equality becomes a fundamental value within the constitution.

On independence, although some states embarked on programmes of law reform, often supported by external agencies, much of the colonial general/received law was retained but deracialised to apply to everyone where appropriate. The division between customary and received law was constructed partly as one of choice and lifestyle. Thus 'modern' urban dwellers regulate their lives via state laws, including family matters in some instances, when previously these would have been organised through customary laws. A 'traditional' rural person can regulate their family and community life through customary laws but, if they work in the formal economy, this aspect of their life would be regulated by state laws.

African politics of culture in a global context

Women's human rights: more state less community?

The division between women's public rights and customary law, the latter being synonymous with culture, continues to be an area of considerable difficulty for women legal activists. Banda (2003, 2005) argues that to posit universal rights against local values is, first, to underestimate the flexibility within the 'universal' (now recognised by adding 'culturally sensitive' to universal) and secondly, to fail to notice the way in which the African regional approach to the issue of women's rights has emerged based upon a 'flexible' or grounded universalism that seeks to dissolve this dichotomy. Africa has developed its own regional approach to human rights through the African Charter on Human and Peoples' Rights 1981 (Banjul Charter) which is characterised as capturing positive African values (Onoria 2002). Any international human rights instrument, ratified by a state, will be applicable within this regional approach, thereby interlinking the two systems. Women's identity is constructed through the prism of the African family:

(1) The family shall be the natural unit and basis of society. It shall be protected by the State which shall take care of its physical health and moral.
(2) The State shall have the duty to assist the family which is the custodian of morals and traditional values recognized by the community.
(3) The State shall ensure the elimination of every discrimination against women and also ensure the protection of the rights of the woman and the child as stipulated in international declarations and conventions.

(Article 18; (4) omitted)

While some are sceptical about this location (Banda 2003), which constructs women as responsible for the social reproduction of culture, others argue that it can be interpreted positively and in a liberating way as evidenced by the presence of Article 18(3), which offers a positive way of tackling discrimination (Tamale 2008: 55). The Charter has, in any case, been strengthened by the adoption of the 2003 Optional Protocol on the Rights of Women in Africa, which has its origins in collaboration between an African women's NGO (Women Law and Development Africa affiliated to Women Law and Development International, with headquarters in the USA) and the African Commission. It follows CEDAW by encompassing civil, political and social, economic and cultural rights. It includes measures relating to violence against women, prohibiting all forms whether they take place in the private sphere or in society and public life (Articles 1(j), 4 and 11). Article 5 covers harmful practices, which states must take all necessary legislative and other measures to eliminate. Monogamy is encouraged as the 'preferred form of marriage' but the rights of women in polygamous marital relationships are 'promoted and protected' (Articles 6 and 7). Importantly, 'women shall have the right to live in a positive cultural context and to participate at all levels in the determination of cultural policies' (Article 17). This right is reinforced by Article 2(2) which commits States Parties to modify practices that are harmful to women or create gender stereo-types. By recognising a positive cultural context (as well as seeking to tackle the negative) and women's role in moulding cultures, the drafters have attempted to resolve the constructed dichotomy between culture and rights. Banda argues that it marks 'at the normative level, the end of the "culture debate"' (2003: 130; 2005: chapter 7). It remains to be seen whether this optimistic claim will be borne out. The Protocol has not been ratified by many African states as yet (twenty-seven in February 2009). The Optional Protocol does replicate in many ways a 'top down' rights approach and a reaffirmation of the value of universalism. Although drafted by 'Africans for Africans', there is still a strong suspicion that the women's rights discourse reflects a neocolonial version of the repugnancy clause.

The debates over the appropriate relationship between custom and law, particularly in relation to matters relating to social reproduction, continue with some arguing that customs 'trump' human rights while others argue the reverse (Banda 2003). In between these extremes are those who focus on the interactions between plural and malleable cultural practices and rights norms and recognise the complex power relations that exist. The 'evolutionists' suggest that it is impossible to will away deep-rooted norms through laws that have limited legitimacy but there is a potential for customary norms to evolve through interaction with wider societal changes, including human rights norms (Stewart 1996; Hellum 1999a). An Na'im (1990; An Na'im and Hammond 2002) represents a growing source of inspiration with his view that international human rights must be legitimated through 'explicit local negotiations' with local communities to achieve a mandate. This process values local cultural identities but in exchange local cultures must be reviewed and stripped of undesirable values. It is very much a 'bottom up' approach (with echoes of the deliberative democracy approach discussed in Chapter 2) that seeks internal 'cultural' transformation, which top down/state-centric human rights approaches cannot achieve (Banda 2003: 13 -14; Tamale 2008: 56).

Contemporary political globalisation

Rule of law projects – less state more community?

The discourse on positive cultural strategies that tempers the more dominant orthodoxy on state rights-based strategies does find resonance in another global political discourse relating to rule in Africa: the rule of law project.

A key legacy from colonialism and the political economy of post-colonialism is the nature of state law. Colonialism imposed authoritarian laws to achieve economic aims and to keep order. These laws, and the administrative fiats associated with them, attempted to spread their tentacles into all aspects of people's lives. Such law had little legitimacy, and in many instances, efficacy. On independence the new administrations assumed these powers. Their economic vulnerability and reliance upon corrupt exercise of power for political survival in many cases further undermined the legitimacy of state laws. Shivji argues that states that are 'extra legal' rather than 'intra legal' (within the rule of law) still use law: they rule '*through* law but not *within* it' (Shivji 1993: 83).

Increasing the legitimacy and the efficacy of the rule of law ideology in African states has played a significant part in development discourse since independence. Early enthusiasm to use law to implement the progressive development objectives of newly emerged independent states manifested itself in the Law and Development movement (Trubek and Galanter 1974; Trubek 2006). Based on the modernist paradigm, this movement showed little interest in 'non-state' forms of social or legal ordering. The movement's aspirations were swept away by the neoliberal orthodoxy that came to dominate macroeconomic and political development discourse in the 1980s and 1990s. Now the rule of law was seen as offering a technical tool with a limited role in the development of free markets. 'Rule of law' projects proliferated throughout Africa, funded by both multilateral and bilateral development agencies (Faundez et al. 2000; Trubek 2006). State rules and institutions were assessed against the imperatives of the market to see whether they contributed to good governance, as understood by international financial and development institutions (Faundez et al. 2000; Rittich 2002: 3). Thus the World Bank blamed the failures of Structural Adjustment Policies to produce growth in sub-Saharan Africa on the corruption within ruling elites in sub-Saharan Africa (World Bank 1997b). The rule of law in Africa did not emerge from local circumstances but from the rules and institutions derived from the 'normal' markets of the industrialised world and the law books of the Global North. Within this framework customary law was seen, if it was seen at all, as lacking in rationality, complex and hindering integration into the wider world economy.

Rule of law and good governance projects have not ignored gender issues because women have made their mark on development thinking and policies, although the extent to which such issues matter varies by agency (Rai 2002; Beveridge 2005). Most gender projects in Africa are supported by external funds and subject to the understanding of the particular agency (see Banda 2005: 286–294). Generally, international agencies require states to demonstrate, at least at a formal level, a commitment to gender justice in order to access international capital. This results in the ratification of human rights instruments, including those specifically relating to women, although many have also listed reservations (Banda 2003: 5). There is often little will or ability to implement much beyond those rights associated with political citizenship. Despite the efforts of some gender policymakers, mainstream development practice more generally therefore tends to focus on the public political sphere, which assumes that women need more rights to ensure the freedom to participate in economic markets or act as citizens.

The assumption of the rule of law project-funders that they were involved with a modern state that was sufficiently strong and organised to apply a monopoly of law proved to be flawed. Not only have proposals been resisted by groups with entrenched power within communities, but the limits of state law have been revealed. When development agencies discovered that in Africa state legal systems resolve only 20 per cent of disputes (DFID 2002), their attentions turned in the last decade or so to the location for the other 80 per cent and therefore to the 'non-state' legal systems and the workings of legal pluralism, particularly in order to pursue gender policies.

Discovering bottom up (positive) culture

Until relatively recently very little was known about the effects of complex normative regimes on the construction of gender relations, precisely because the study of law is a 'modern' discipline, rooted in the ideology of the rule of law. To understand the relationship of women to law in a post-colonial Africa requires a methodology to implement an understanding of plural legal systems or to use Falk Moore's (1978) terminology, semi-autonomous social fields. Yet '[a]lmost universally, legal education remains conservative and confined within relatively narrow parameters of form and content' (Bentzon et al. 1998: 23). Since the late 1980s a number of scholars and activists have sought to create a body of socio-legal knowledge on gender and law.[1] It has not been an easy climate in which to do this. Universities, as state institutions, experienced the same predations as other state institutions under international economic policies. They have been marginalised and under-funded. However, the IFIs and development bodies have funds, which sometimes support academics working on projects while located within the university but more often are channelled through NGOs. Many of Africa's NGOs are therefore foreign funded and are treated with suspicion by both governments and local populations (Shivji 1993; Banda 2005: 291–292). Nonetheless, the activities of these organisations and also the work of a number of individual academic researchers have generated a substantial body of socio-legal literature relating to women's relationship with law, which finds considerable interaction and overlap between normative orders and signs of rapid change in some. Thus it is quite possible to have a range of competing understandings of the same issue within the customary domain depending on the institutional context in which it is claimed and by whom. To these must be added the effect of state laws, which may cover the same issue but adopt a different understanding of the legal subject. These regulatory contexts must then be set within the wider choice-of-law rules, which determine which legal system, state or customary, governs a particular dispute.

Research within six southern African countries (excluding South Africa) found that marriage laws under general law were similar (Armstrong 1992). Conforming to the common law, marriage is a contract between two consenting parties of the opposite sex who are competent to marry generally and to marry each other. A surviving spouse is generally entitled to an intestate inheritance from the estate of the deceased spouse. Contrarily customary marriage involves families as well as individuals and does not require registration for recognition. On death the surviving children and spouse are the main beneficiaries of property in Botswana, Lesotho and the Ndebele in Zimbabwe, but not in Swaziland and Shona in Zimbabwe. Inheritance practices differ but within the

---

[1] Women in Law and Development in Africa (WILDAF); Women and Law in Southern Africa; Women and Law in East Africa; research at the Southern and Eastern Africa Regional Centre for Women's Law, based at the University of Harare.

traditional customary law applied by the higher courts, a woman is deemed unable to inherit property although the family is expected to maintain her.

Land is increasingly scarce in many areas due to marketisation, which encourages consolidation. The AIDS pandemic has led to the early death of men leaving many female-headed households on land that is 'grabbed' by the deceased husband's relatives because of the assumption, under some understandings of customary law, that women cannot inherit from husbands. The death of a husband can be devastating for rural women in Zimbabwe, involving loss of protection, including from her husband's family. They are now socially disabled despite their substantial roles in running farms and maintaining the household before the husband's death. Some urban widows do not view their situation – 'my shade is gone' – in this way. They are able to exert their rights and defend themselves where necessary (Aphane et al. 1995: chapter 5; contra Parpart 2000).

An heir has a variety of meanings. Under general law it relates to the person who takes over the residue of the deceased's estate. Customary law separates out a 'composite of three different functions: rights, obligations and status. When reduced to an heir the rights become emphasised and the obligations and status de-emphasised' (Armstrong 1992: 156). The eldest male steps into his father's shoes and assumes the obligations of his father and is granted a right to property to enable him to fulfil his obligations but he does not acquire the individual rights exclusive to the rest of the family. Property is distributed to other males and females in the family. Women have access to and some levels of control over property and could inherit these.

Thus 'when deconstructed [customary law] reveals that women had rights they have been assumed not to have' although researchers found a deterioration of the obligation aspect in favour of the rights aspect. 'Customary law is also being constructed in practice as it evolves to meet the demands of individualised ownership, cash economies, moveable consumer goods, the break up of subsistence economies, and modern conditions in general' (Armstrong 1992: 156). The problems that emerged were associated with adapting a communitarian-based system to the conditions of the market and to nuclear forms of families. The researchers concluded that it is necessary not only to create an enabling environment within the extended family for a woman to use her formal legal rights but also to stress obligations as well as rights. The discourse of obligation is better understood by women who feel value-connectedness rather than autonomy as constructed within the dominant discourse of legal rights (Armstrong 1992: 162).

The value of connectedness

What are the wider implications of this form of research? First it reveals the fluidity of the concepts of 'custom' and 'culture', reinforcing similar anthropological perspectives (Merry 2006). It reveals the agency of women, even if constrained by wider factors and that women are not necessarily or uniformly disadvantaged in the customary domain. Subsequent research on cultural approaches to the construction of women's sexuality comes to similar conclusions (Tamale 2006, 2008). Secondly, the research focuses on women and their perceived interests. The researchers do struggle with what Molyneux (1985) would classify as practical interests (the immediate and context constrained) and strategic (enabled by wider opportunities) interests. The political task is to identify the incentive structures that will lead to gender-progressive change within cultural practices (Tripp 2002; Tamale 2008). It involves finding ways of affirming cultural values while changing gender-based inequalities. This 'bottom up' cultural change can be done by building on the indigenous, which refers to whatever the people consider important to their lives, whatever they regard as an authentic expression of themselves, and taking 'African societies seriously as they are, not as they ought to be or even as they might be' (Nnaemeka 2003: 376, quoting Claurd Ake).

Nnaemeka argues that it is possible to establish this despite the accumulated effects of externally imposed norms because there is a foundation of shared values, attitudes and institutions that binds together the nations south of the Sahara (Nnaemeka 2003). These values are identified with the concept of *ubuntu*, a southern African Zulu word, which is seen as one of the founding principles of the post-apartheid South African state. A similar term is used widely across local African languages. It embodies the essence of being human as connectedness to others. A human being cannot exist in isolation but is understood through an individual's connectedness to others. *Ubuntu* seeks, therefore, to capture the communitarian, solidaristic values of African societies and respects African values of negotiation, give and take, compromise and balance. It views human life from a total, rather than dichotomous and exclusive, perspective; the male is not other but part of the human same.

Maboreke is less optimistic about finding these shared values but considers it essential to return to 'the authorising and legitimating traditional framework' to 'carve out a discursive practice for the gender discourse' (2000: 112) while Tamale recognises that the power relations through which these values are expressed are not unaffected by wider socio-economic changes associated with the development of market cultures in Africa (Tamale 2008). Nyamu (2000; Nyamu-Musembi 2002) argues for a critical pragmatic approach to law-related activism in plural legal contexts. Sometimes this will involve support for what is defined as a culturally based approach – using customary law or practices to support women's interests. At other times it may require the use of more formal legal discourse to pursue justice for women. At all times it involves a close understanding of the overlapping plural normative orders that structure gender relations.

Armstrong (2000) suggests that the communitarian values in customary laws reflect the values that feminists developing the ethic of care would support: a relational approach to issues, non-adversarial, more rooted in care rather than rights. While the methodology is explicitly focused on valuing women's lives and improving their position within a wider framework of the shared value of relationships, this approach to the politics of culture is not a resort to utopianism or a lost past. It is fully aware of the power structures associated with cultural representations forged in colonial and post-colonial economic and political contexts. Values are set within deeply patriarchal and hierarchical institutional structures. Some values support women's interests and some do not. The value of family connectedness and supportiveness is positive; the value of freedom from responsibility is not. Is it possible to dislodge these structures to develop a discourse of positive cultural values? As we have seen, the ethic of care has been posed against an ethic of justice in northern scholarship. If we accept that community-based practices embody some of these values, will further erosion of customary values through the increase in market relations reduce the positive power of this discourse or will new alliances between communities and the market strengthen women's position?

Culture of economics/economic globalisation

Introduction

Agriculture provides, either directly or indirectly, the livelihoods for millions of people around the world (see UNRISD 2005: chapter 6) for the effect of agricultural liberalisation policies on gender relations in rural areas). The Food and Agriculture Organization (FAO) estimates that farming is the 'only source of income for an estimated 70 per cent of the world's rural poor, many of whom are small farmers' (Garcia 2005: 5). The following sections focus on the ways in which developments in the agricultural markets, state policies and community norms relating to land interact and impact on gender relations in ways which disadvantage many women within rural areas in sub-Saharan Africa. There is a particular emphasis on the position within Kenya, which provides the context for the external governance of the food chain discussed in the next chapter.

Trading local food

There has been a long history of cross-border trade in agriculture, which has brought benefits to some economies both in terms of the foods on offer but also as sources of employment. Although agriculture only became the subject of global trade rules in 1994 with the adoption of the Agreement on Agriculture, it has been subjected to the rigours of the structural adjustment programmes, which sought to 'impose a neo-liberal agenda of fiscal restraint, open trade and capital accounts, and privatisation on indebted developing countries' (Razavi 2003: 2). Subsequently, under the multilateral trading system, agricultural trade liberalisation continues with the aim of reducing or eliminating 'traditional pillars of agricultural protection' (Williams 2003: 48). The focus for development has been on input-intensive commercial agriculture and agribusiness organisations. These policy interventions in Africa have been of unparalleled range and depth (Razavi 2003: 5).

In theory, agricultural trade liberalisation should increase growth and income in each country and result in a wide range of assorted benefits. These include increased employment, lower food prices and enhanced access to technology (Williams 2003: 48). Women can share this positive outcome if they are able to either transform their farming activities through commercialisation and diversification, the key policy objectives, or have access to, and then command, a higher income by working as employees in an expanding agribusiness sector. Women then share in the potential gains associated with non-traditional agricultural exports (NTAE) in one way or another through purchasing, rather than producing, cheaper food and thereby ease their burdens.

However, agriculture in many parts of the developing world is struggling. 'Estimates of per capita agricultural production for domestic and export markets showed it to be declining throughout the 1990s. In particular, LDCs continue to be marginalized from world agricultural markets: they accounted for only 1 per cent of global agricultural exports in the late 1990s' (Garcia 2005: 5). In sub-Saharan Africa there has been a steady decline in agricultural exports as a share of the world's agricultural trade (Razavi 2003: 14). The evidence to date suggests, therefore, that the benefits of global agricultural trade are not materialising for small farmers, particularly women.

The bulk of farming is undertaken on small farms to provide food for family consumption and for local markets. Community-based assumptions determine use, control and ownership of land and in sub-Saharan Africa women produce as much as 80 per cent of basic foods while 'commercial or industrial crops, cultivated on a much larger scale either for direct export or for further processing ... are more frequently the economic domain of men' (Garcia 2005: 5). For instance 'In Tanzania ... while men tend to dominate in maize, wholesale and intermediate trade, women are to be found in retail, where there are small margins and the volume of trade is lower ... Women also tend to produce vegetables and fruits while men produce grains (which have a higher value and are more durable)' (Williams 2003: 67). Women work on marginal land with simple or no tools and with very little access to fertiliser or extension training to improve their chances of competing in the market (Williams 2003: 48). Until the early 1990s most were able to make a decent living in subsistence agriculture. Not any more. Smallholder agriculture was transformed into feminised agriculture in entire areas of many African countries as men sought non-farm employment away from villages, often migrating to urban areas, and the size of family landholdings decreased. Women took more responsibility for the family farm but also for producing cash crops and participating in food processing activities in order to increase family incomes at a time of growing insecurity (14; Garcia 2005: 14; Williams 2003: chapter 3). Most rural households now rely on a range of sources of income, which may include informal trading or providing services. Therefore women are not only own-account food producers but they are also involved in agricultural production, often as informal workers. 'Two thirds of the female labour force in developing economies is engaged in agricultural services' (FAO quoted in Garcia 2005: 20).

Cheap imports compete with food that smallholders produce, thereby destroy-ing their income base. 'In practice, reducing trade barriers has not been sufficient to generate new demand for developing country exports' (Williams 2003: 49). Small and family-scale farmers traditionally have been able to produce staples (such as coffee, cocoa, palm oil and sugar) for bulk commodity markets, which are marketed at arm's length at central spot markets. This trade is anonymous and based on standard assumptions. However, these markets are 'characterized by instability, structural oversupply, stiff global competition, historic downward price trends and declining terms of trade for producing countries and regions' (Fox and Vorley 2006: 164). Policies of privatisation and liberalisation of com-modity exports have made it more difficult for countries to control the flow of exports and therefore world prices. The gap between world prices and retail prices widens. While retail prices for coffee remain the same, 'producer prices have dropped to less than one third of their 1960s level' (Fox and Vorley 2006: 164). The trade is no longer covered by international commodity agreements and the states in producer countries have had to abandon their role as inter-mediaries (through the provision of safety nets of credit and trading institutions) in the market due to pressure from international fiscal policies. Risk is passed to individual farmers (Fox and Vorley 2006: 165).

Small farmers generally are particularly vulnerable to these changes in global agricultural markets but the impact on men and women can be very different due to the gender division of labour. Not only are women often obliged to combine their roles as farmers and workers but they must undertake their roles as carers for their families' well-being and also contribute to the welfare of their communities. This social reproductive role has become more burdensome in recent years due to the cutbacks in state-based social safety nets while the AIDS pandemic has greatly intensified care responsibilities by orphaning millions of children. It has also created social tensions, which often require the investment of women's time and emotional energy to assuage. Commercialisation affects rural livelihoods more generally as families rely more on insecure wages from off-farm activities and migration. It seems generally to be associated with an increase in household workloads. There may be a gain in financial capital (income) if farmers adapt successfully but there is a loss of social capital (time for childcare, education, leisure).

State-engendered trade policies

What role does the state play in agricultural trade liberalisation? To what extent do state policies contribute to or counter gender divisions and injustices in the developing global agricultural market? Do such policies enable women to gain access to and control over the resources needed to benefit from this market either as farmers or employees?

Developing world states have been seen as obstacles to the development of markets (see UNRISD 2005: section 1). As a result, African marketing boards and parastatals 'which had serviced small holders' input requirements, provided marketing channels to geographically dispersed and under-capitalized farmers, and enforced commodity standards' (Razavi 2003: 14) were dismantled to be replaced by private traders. State policies are now reoriented to support trade liberalisation, which can have the effect of dislocating agricultural smallholders from their land because they do not have access to resources such as credit facilities, adequate fertiliser allocation and equipment and technology. Women tend to fare less well than men, not only because men usually own the medium- and large-scale commercial farms and are consequently in a better position to capitalise on state policies, but also because agricultural extension services and training in Africa are significantly biased against women (Williams 2003: 65 quoting the World Bank). Other policies, such as the privatisation of key utilities, including water, for irrigation and electricity, reinforce the difficulties that women with few resources face. Small farmers are therefore excluded from the emerging and globalising food economies. They tend to abandon or sell their farms, leading to land concentration and the increase in commercial crop production, but without growth in the sector as a whole.

Government incentives to shift both land and labour to export-oriented crop production may oblige women to seek employment in this sector, reducing the time they are able to spend tending farm plots. Yet the produce cultivated on these plots is the basis for national food security and is not being substituted by the newer forms of production. Subsistence farming is often neglected within state policies and women's contribution, characterised as unpaid work on family farms, is not reflected in national accounts. Women's contribution to the wider economy, as well as their livelihoods, is marginalised.

Although the focus for gender and development studies has been to gain recognition for the role women play in development and for development policies to take account of the realities of gender power relations, there is still a lack of understanding within state policies of (or willingness to act upon) the importance of the relationship between reproductive and productive activities and the impact that policies of agricultural liberalisation may have on women. These issues emerge in land reform policies, which affect women in their role as farmers.

Plural and gendered access to land

Inadequate land tenure systems have been seen as a key obstacle to successful agrarian development in Africa from the colonial era. Land tenure reform has been a highly politicised issue since the colonial era with post-colonial states reflecting various ideological positions from a commitment to modernist regis-tration of individual ownership to support for state allocative and community-based systems (Manji 2006). It has therefore been on the agenda for over forty years but at the height of neoliberal orthodoxy in the 1980s and early 1990s, the IFIs and many bilateral development agencies exerted considerable pressure on

African states to reform land laws to create free markets in land based on a 'presumption that there was a direct causal link between formalisation of property rights and economic productivity' (Nyamu-Musembi 2006). The orthodoxy has been that formal titling is essential for growth because investment is based on certainty. A number of African states therefore enacted new Land Acts using development-funded technical assistance (McAuslan 1998, 2003). The process usually involves establishing individual ownership; translating this understanding into some form of official mapping; and then the official registration of title. The system establishes an institutional framework for maintaining the register.

The poor, and women in particular, were thought by policymakers and many women's organisations to benefit from formal land rights. The gender case for state-based formalisation of land rights depends on the constituency seeking it. The 'economic efficiency' case, favoured by the World Bank, is linked to the development of land markets. For the majority of the population, particularly those living in rural areas, customary law regulates family and allied property relations, including land distribution and inheritance issues. Therefore, for the majority of women, access to resources is structured via customary law, which is based upon communal and reciprocal, rather than individual, values (Stewart 1996, 2000b; Hellum et al. 2007). Customary systems are also primarily based on status and stage in life cycles, so women's access to resources is derived from their relationship with men. Women rarely own land outright and access typically terminates upon divorce or death of their husband. Access to land is conditional and uncertain and women cannot use land titles as a basis for accessing formal credit markets and therefore to upgrade their farming activities to take advantage of any of the benefits of agricultural trade liberalisation. Thus women's contribution is not translated into potential property accumulation.

This case constructs land as very much part of the public domain of production. Customary practices are seen as blocks on economic development and oppressive to women because they reflect patriarchal power relations and do not treat women as fully acting subjects in their own right. There is some recognition of the broader analysis that links women's productive role with social reproduction (women's labour on the land to provide food is crucial to the survival of the family) in the World Bank's more recent report on land policies but the emphasis is still very much on economic growth (World Bank 2003: 58; Ikdahl et al. 2005).

Another constituency more associated with gender-based analyses stresses the socially reproductive importance of land by focusing more directly on the 'private' context of customary laws in which women's access and control over land is mediated through men (Ikdahl et al. 2005). The inequalities and injustices faced by women through marriage, divorce and inheritance norms are highlighted along with the conflicts thereby created. This group also stresses the importance of land to a wider sense of belonging (Bassett 2007). The advantages of formal rights are seen as providing women with social assets that improve their bargaining position within the family and community.

These two constituencies highlight the way in which entitlement to land can value either its productive/public or its socially reproductive/private value, the relationship of which is shifting with pressures to create land markets. However, there is growing recognition, partly as result of successful women's activism, of the need to combine these two perspectives both within the policy community (see World Bank 2003: 57–60) but also within state law reform initiatives. More generally, human rights activists argue that as citizens of countries with constitutional commitments and international legal obligations to ensure equality, women have the same rights as men, including those associated with land and property (and the assumption is that these are state based).

Enthusiasm for formalisation faltered in the late 1990s at an international policy level (World Bank 2003) although it has since revived through the adoption of De Soto's work (2000), which advocates a system for formalising the property rights of slum dwellers to enable them to use these assets to lift them out of poverty (Nyamu-Musembi 2006). This 'business case' for formal titling of rural land now appeared overly simplistic (Nyamu-Musembi 2006; Hunt 2005). There was precious little evidence of efficiency gains; instead wealthy, powerful men had taken advantage of the opportunities at the expense of women and the poor.

State-based systems of formalisation failed to recognise the vibrancy of local custom-based systems and the plurality of legal norms that operate. The state would see the registered title holder, the male head of household or eldest son, as holding all the ownership rights (unless 'subsidiary' claims were also registered) while he would be seen in customary law as holding the same rights on trusteeship for a range of family members. The register does not necessarily reflect the existing social reality while enabling the title holder to transform trusteeship into outright ownership. Challenging titles within the formal legal system is not an option for the majority of women for whom it is remote, costly and hostile. Official records of titles can become quickly outdated if transactions are not officially notified, or irrelevant if transactions continue to be conducted according to customary norms in areas covered by titling schemes. Furthermore, states have been unable, due to lack of resources or enthusiasm, to extend the reach of these schemes to cover more than a tiny proportion of the total land area.

As a result policymakers started to consider the ways in which transactions took place at the local community level. In relation to land, two possibilities emerge in relation to women's position: the first suggests that customary systems are not so bad for women; the second that they are better for women than the state system (Whitehead and Tsikata 2003). Development specialists increasingly recognise that the main constraints on female farming result from the absence of capital; an inability to command labour; and difficulties accessing markets rather than lack of outright ownership. This insight leads them to reconsider the potential support offered by customary systems. Some gender and law scholars support the first of these two positions. They have demonstrated through empirical research that in sub-Saharan Africa not only are women able to make claims to land independent of fathers or husbands but also that women have relatively strong claims through their husbands and fathers although these claims are not the same as men's. Unlike the modernist state systems, flexible customary claims can take account of shifting wider social and economic circumstances. Although this flexibility may disadvantage women who are less powerful than men, there is evidence to suggest that women are able to press their claims in these circumstances (Nyamu 2000, Nyamu-Musembi 2002).

In order to understand the way in which customary norms operate, it is essential to move away from the 'bundle of rights' understanding of property, which is drummed into the heads of first year students in property law courses. This liberal law concept enables property to be subject to multiple co-existing but *separate* rights, which encompass both ownership and use rights: a piece of land can be held freehold but be the subject of a lease and a mortgage. In the context of Africa these concepts falsely translate into the clan or men holding ownership and control rights, while women have weaker use rights. Thus the rights become hierarchical and gendered. The alternative view is that customary property norms are far more fluid and negotiated. They are not based on abstract hierarchies of rights but on embedded systems of social obligations. They therefore overlap. For instance, Odgaard and Bentzon's local area study on Tanzania (2007) shows that women do have recognised claims on land in their natal home (which they seek to exercise on divorce or widowhood). These claims are often backed by their fathers but resisted by their brothers. Fathers reconstruct women's historically recognised claim as one based upon women's present care responsibilities for the elderly in the absence of state welfare provision. Sons, in an increasingly competitive land market, are making claims on the basis of productive rather than socially reproductive activities (see also Whitehead and Tsikata 2003; Nyamu-Musembi 2006; Stewart and Tsanga 2007).

These arguments are used by those described as proponents of an 'evolutionary theory of land rights' (ETLR)(Hunt 2005) to argue that customary law systems are better for women than state law (Whitehead and Tsikata 2003). The World Bank now argues that what is needed for growth is land security, which involves building on customary tenures and existing institutions rather than replacing them although their economists expect that communal engagement with the market will lead to the development of individual property rights (2003: 62–64; Bassett 2007). This route of collaboration with communities bypasses the heavily contested, slow, and therefore costly processes of state law reform. Some supporters of ETLR root their analysis in support for local community-based forms of social and economic relations that stand in opposition to the state and its alliance with international capital. They seek to wrest control away from those pursuing the commercialisation of land and to restore it to local communities. They would want also to make community allocation more positive for women.

Many gender activists are uneasy about these denials of the role of the state despite all the gendered limitations associated with liberal law (Stewart 1996). Constructed dichotomies, this time between formalisation and ETLR, once again fail to recognise the interactions between state, family and market. Women, due to wider assumptions about gender roles, often lack power to negotiate within communities, particularly over scarce assets such as land, and are not well represented within local institutions. The HIV pandemic has placed huge strains on the practices associated with land in rural Africa such as loss of land rights including inheritance claims; changes in use and tenure of land; distress sales; in some areas decreases in the amount of land cultivated or changes in types of crop cultivated with a move to more labour intensive crops (Villarreal 2006: 5). These developments have led to the breakdown of traditional methods of support. In particular, the early death of large numbers of prime-age men challenges assumptions over women's entitlements to land. Women access clan land and other productive resources through marriage. Traditionally on the death of a husband a widow would be 'inherited' by a brother of her deceased husband, thereby enabling her to continue to live in the community and access their land. This arrangement was both a social safety net for widows but also a way of preserving male property entitlements. This system of levirate marriage, which was already dying out under changing norms relating to gender relationships, cannot absorb the social and economic consequences of mass deaths. Widows, however, are left in a very vulnerable position if they are not able to establish an alternative social basis for their continuing use of land (Villarreal 2006).

It is in this context that women's human rights advocates argue for a rights-based approach to development. They argue strongly that land policy and law reform, whether customary or state based, must be subjected to human rights norms, which infuse concepts of equality, and possibly justice, into these processes (Ikdahl et al. 2005). The rights contained within Conventions such as CEDAW and the African Charter on Women's Rights provide a way of increasing women's voice and negotiating powers if they form the basis for policy development and, crucially, implementation. Here the state can play a pivotal role in opening up a space for women to pursue their claims backed by wider norms of equality and justice.

Can a rights discourse be used to ensure that reconstruction of the productive and reproductive aspects of land-based property claims do not adversely affect women's ability to access resources generally? The aim of much policy reform has been to increase efficiency in agricultural production by enabling it to be used as security in a market. Loans secured against land can provide the capital for investment. If land is more firmly located within the public sphere of production, women in theory may take equal advantage of the benefits. However, in general, women access land more through socially reproductive related activities associated with family provisioning. The normative framework assumes that these entitlements are derived through women's social status within communities. If women lose these through processes of securitisation, they must be replaced by increased recognition either within the productive discourse, for instance through co-ownership rights or within the redefined reproductive sphere associated with family laws, such as through equal rights in matrimonial property and to inherited wealth.

Within state law reform policies issues relating to marital property ownership and inheritance rights (involving customary laws and constructed as family law) have been separated from land law reform as was demonstrated very clearly by the political struggles over land reform in Uganda (Matembe 2002; Tripp 2002). Thus some provisions relating to access to land are constructed as commercial/productive while other provisions also relating to access, but involving potentially increased benefits for women, are constructed as unproductive. As Manji (2006) points out, credit institutions opposed co-ownership provisions in the Land Bill in Uganda on the basis that such a measure would threaten their securities. There is often considerable resistance to family law reforms from a number of constituencies, not only from those representing lineage groups, who see a further reduction in their power, but also from increasingly vocal religious groups who challenge the values, relating to liberal rights and women's human rights more specifically, upon which these reforms are based (Tamale 2008). States have not had the will or the capacity to push through proposals, and this area, deemed private, is of much less concern to mainstream international policymakers. The value of women's labour within the socially reproductive sphere and its underpinning not only of household but national security is not recognised.

Women and Kenyan land ownership

Kenya has a population of around 39.5 million. The rural–urban balance stands at 78 per cent and 22 per cent respectively. Land is a major cause of political and ethnic conflict in Kenya. Only 20 per cent of the land area can be classified as medium- to high-potential land; the rest is mainly arid or semi-arid. Approximately 75 per cent of the country's population lives within the medium- to high-potential-land areas and the rest in the vast arid and semi-arid lands. There are four distinct zones with different patterns of land use: the coastal plain (used for fishing, horticulture and tourism); the arid low plateau (over 60 per cent of the country's land mass) on which pastoralists raise 50 per cent of the country's livestock and which is used for safari tourism); the highlands (which consist of rich agricultural land for food production by large and small-scale farmers and contain the largest concentration of human settlements); and the Lake Victoria basin (used for crop and animal production and containing medium-density human settlements) (Ministry of Lands 2007). Colonial land policies concentrated ownership of the best land to serve commercial interests.

Generally in Kenya, the vast majority of women eke out an existence as small farmers. 92 per cent of women farmers use only hand cultivation, compared to 62 per cent of men (Williams 2003: 65), providing food for their households. Women constitute 64 per cent of subsistence farmers and produce approximately 60 per cent of farm-derived income. 96 per cent of rural women work on family farms in addition to performing household tasks such as cooking, cleaning, caring for children and other family members, and fetching water and fuel wood. Women also constitute 80 per cent of Kenya's agricultural labour force (Ministry of Lands and Housing 2005a, 2005b). Output from smallholding farms contributes about 75 per cent to total agricultural output, which accounts for about 30 per cent of Kenya's GDP overall. However, very few women are able to grow cash crops for the domestic market or for export. As elsewhere in Africa, the international economic policies pursued in the 1980s increased both food imports, including the dumping of products, and the price of farm inputs. Women were worse off at the end of the decade than they had been at its start. Under the same SAP that sought to produce diversification in smallholders' livelihoods, some rural women were 'integrated into micro and small enterprise in village markets where they bought and sold farm products like milk, maize, beans and vegetables' (Williams 2003: 63). Others were obliged to migrate to find other sources of work in the informal economy.

Kenya, like other developing countries, has a small formal and large informal economy. In Kenya 83 per cent of women are engaged in informal working (including casual work on other small holdings or seasonal work not necessarily in agriculture) compared to 48 per cent of men. 42 per cent of this informal working in Kenya is own-account working in the non-agricultural sector, including the provision of services such as sex work or beer brewing; 58 per cent is waged labour. Men constitute the majority (56 per cent) in the first category and women, 67 per cent in the latter, informal, waged category (UNRISD 2005: 76–78). The number of women working for wages outside the agricultural sector has risen significantly in Kenya to about 38 per cent of the total in 2002 (UNRISD 2005: 53).

The land tenure system in Kenya is extremely complex. There are forty-two ethnic communities, all of which have customary land tenure systems. In addition, the state system, which was introduced to provide a basis for economic development, is widely recognised as being inefficient, subject to widespread corrupt practices and generally incoherent. National land policy has recently been the subject of major policy review (the National Land Policy Formulation Process, funded principally by the UK Department for International Development. The move away from land distribution policies to land law reforms has led to deep political conflicts between those seeking to retain traditional power bases in land and those who have been intent on market development (Manji 2006). Land issues have been at the heart of recent ethnic violence in Kenya.

Written land policy in Kenya started in 1888 when the Imperial British East Africa Company was granted a Royal Charter to trade. Between 1897 and 1902, laws that enabled the creation of leases and licences were enacted to support the colonial government and settlers who sought to develop the agricultural production for European markets. These interventions marginalised and displaced the native peoples and introduced an alien system of property concepts based upon British law. Subsequently, native reserves – areas designated for African occupation – were established under the trusteeship of Native Land Authorities. The Swynnerton Committee, set up in response to African demands for land rights, recommended the introduction of a system of formalisation of land tenure, which involved adjudication of land rights; the consolidation of scattered holdings under African customary law; and registration of interests in land. This led to three distinct categories of land rights' holding: government (public) land; trust land, which comprised the former native reserves; and private land derived from grants to individuals of government land and by the process of adjudication and consolidation in the native reserves (Ministry of Lands and Housing 2005a).

The transfer of power from colonial administrators to Africans did not lead to a change in policies. Colonial land policies, laws and administrative infrastructures were maintained, enabling the new power elites to have continued access to the European economy. An incremental process of formalisation, which confers upon the owner a fee simple estate in the land, has been in operation ever since. This legislation was intended to provide a comprehensive system for the public registration of formal land rights and to enable the use and disposal of land with the minimum of restrictions (Ikdahl et al. 2005: 93). Section 30 of the Registered Land Act lists the rights that are capable of overriding the rights of an absolute proprietor. Customary rights are excluded. Such rights are not capable, therefore, of qualifying the absolute proprietor's rights unless they are recorded on the register against his/her interests.

Land owned by the government (in theory, due to colonialism, all land) is governed by the Government Land Act Chapter 280 of the Laws of Kenya. This Act grants powers to the President to make grants or dispositions of any estates, interests or rights in or over unalienated government lands. Much government land has been converted to private ownership in recent years. Finally, the Trust Lands Act Chapter 288 of the Laws of Kenya recognises group rights in areas occupied in the colonial period by native peoples. Such trust land, which is not registered under the Registered Land Act, makes up 63 per cent of the total land area although this land is increasingly being transferred into private or state ownership.

It is estimated that only 5 per cent of registered owners are women for the reasons discussed in the previous section. The formalisation exercise establishes the interests in the land. The power to allocate is considered to be the registrable interest, which is constructed as an absolute right to own. Thus a power more associated with trusteeship is reconstructed as an individual, not joint, right to own. A hierarchy of entitlements is constructed: allocative power is separated from use rights and privileged. Use rights are in effect downgraded: women's position as holders of derivative rights is solidified. 'Families designated one of themselves, usually the eldest son or the male head of household, to be registered as the absolute owner without realising the latitude that such person would have to deal with the land once so registered' (Ikdahl et al. 2005: 91). The Act does allow rights of occupation, derived from customary law, to be noted on the register but 'many families did not bother to do [this] for they saw no possibility of a piece of paper vesting any more rights in the family representative than he would have had at custom' (Ikdahl et al. 2005: 91).

Customary rights of use are not recognised under the Registered Land Act: they are not included as overriding interests in section 30. The separation between customary and state law is confirmed in case law in *Obiero* v. *Opiyo* (1972) East African Law Reports 227 and *Esiroyo* v. *Esiroyo* (1973) East African Law Reports 388. Registration therefore frees the new owner from interference by parties whose interests are not shown on the register, including the right of use, which is not registrable. Formalisation weakens a woman's capacity to mobilise social support to a claim to property within the family or kinship network. It also reduces the possibilities for supervision by traditional social institutions while not providing her access to state-based regulatory frameworks.

The system itself commands little legitimacy, simply providing a 'formal' backdrop to transactions relating to land in registered areas while local customary practices of adjudication provide the immediate framework (Nyamu-Musembi 2006). Customary understandings of multiple, coexisting uses for land prevail. There is little evidence that the formal system has facilitated access to markets. Small farmer owners have not been able to use their title to access formal credit although they do make use of informal credit arrangements. Some farmers with greater access to resources have managed to scale up their production but this process does not seem to depend upon formalisation of title. However, when it comes to issues of security, then this process, formerly gender-neutral, has strengthened the position of the title holder to the detriment of others. As Nyamu-Musembi points out, this insecurity affects not only women but all those who hold entitlements based upon customary rights that they cannot protect against the absolute title holder even though in reality their property relations continue to be based on custom (2006: 19–20).

The detrimental impact for women can be greater because property law interacts with problematic family law provisions. The vast majority of married women derive interests in family land through their marriages, which are regulated through customary law. The non-recognition of their interests in the formal state legal system renders them particularly vulnerable. Unmarried daughters living on land registered in their fathers' or brothers' names are equally so. Their security depends on their relationship with the titleholder. Once a husband becomes the registered owner, a wife's interests under customary law cease to exist. On his death, she cannot rely on her customary law entitlements when faced with the competing registered claims of third parties (*Elizabeth Wangari Wanjohi and Elizabeth Wambui Wanjohi* v. *Official Receiver and Interim Liquidator (Continental Credit Finance Ltd)*, Civil Application NAI No 140 of 1988, Nairobi Law Monthly, 14 February 1989 at 42; Nyamu-Musembi 2006: 21).

The regulation of marital property is still covered by the English Married Women's Property Act 1882 in the absence of a specific Kenyan statute. In *Karanja* v. *Karanja* 1976 KLR 307 the Act was extended to parties married under customary law. 'The statute follows the common law doctrine of separate property – each spouse retains as personal property whatever he or she owned before the marriage as well as what he or she acquired during the marriage'

(*I* v. *I* (1971) East African Law Reports 278). On one level this can be seen as a positive step to recognise women as having equal rights to ownership of property. However, the property unit is the individual not the family unit. Marriage does not confer any proprietary interest on the other spouse. In a dispute the starting point is to establish legal ownership over property. In the case of land this is evidenced by title. The courts follow the common law system of recognising beneficial interests so a woman can seek to claim that she has made a substantial contribution in the form of money or labour but this is an uphill task (see Ikdahl et al. 2005: 87–88). The interaction between formal titling and a separate property regime reinforces women's exclusion from property and increases her (in)security.

It is important to note that the Kenya Land Alliance has campaigned hard, and with some success, to include principles of gender equality in the land reform process (Kenya Land Alliance 2004). The draft Land Policy was finally adopted by the cabinet in 2009 (but not yet enacted in November 2010) and includes under a heading 'cross cutting issues requiring special intervention' a section on 'gender and equity principles'. It contains wide-ranging commitments by the state to put in place effective measures to ensure equality and non-discrimination. There is a commitment to joint spousal registration and for joint spousal consent to land disposals (Ministry of Lands 2007: 45).

Kenya has been involved in a protracted and highly conflictual process of constitutional reform in recent years. The new constitution was finally promulgated in August 2010 after a national referendum. It highlights principles of democracy, accountability, people's participation, human rights and social justice (Ikdahl et al. 2005: 98). Chapter 7, which deals with the development of a national land law policy, inserts a commitment to gender equality in relation to access, ownership and control of benefits of land and other resources, including those that are inherited. It may offer a basis for protecting women's rights to agricultural and other land when they occupy without ownership rights (Ikdahl et al. 2005: 99).

Formalisation of property rights constructs a distinct dichotomy and hierarchy between customary-based use, socially understood as accessible to women, and ownership rights. Women's position is therefore weakened not only because they are not recognised as owning land but also because traditional use-based 'rights' cannot compete with formal rights. The gender consequences of these changes are reinforced through family law provisions which tend to be within the domain of the customary. Formalisation of property rights without the development of family laws based upon similar presumptions makes women particularly vulnerable.

Conclusion

The politics of culture focuses on the relative merits of a location within the public sphere of the state or within the 'private' sphere of the community. The discourse of human rights requires states to take responsibility for violations of women's rights perpetrated through cultural practices within the family and community. Feminists, who adopt the perspective that culture is malleable and open to political change, focus on the positive potential for reconstruction of relations of power based on gender within communities and families. They draw on the communitarian African values that have gained recognition within regional rights frameworks and state constitutions. They also assess the effects of wider social and economic changes on community relationships.

Customary law was forged in the power struggles between the colonial state and local clans over land. As the distinction between the public and private spheres hardened, women were assigned roles within the 'non-productive' sphere of the family although they remained responsible for the provisioning of the family, including growing and securing food. Often their work constituted unpaid family labour. Access to land was derived through lineage group members, usually fathers, husbands or sons, and regulated through wider customary practices. Newly independent state government did not develop and implement policies, backed by the necessary legal provisions, to redistribute land back to local Africans. For the last quarter of a century macroeconomic policies have been geared towards greater integration of African agriculture into the world market with the aim of increasing productivity and stimulating growth in the economies. These activities were underpinned by land reform policies that have sought to create more asset value in land (securitisation) and to commercialise and diversify agricultural production. The focus for state attention moved from land distribution policies to land law reforms and has led to deep political conflicts between those seeking to retain traditional power bases in land and those who have been intent on market development (Manji 2006).

The legally constructed dichotomy between rights and culture is a product of colonial legal values and practices, which recast customary practices into a private sphere of customary law while public relationships were conducted through 'civilised' laws. The value of women's economic activities was reassessed as they moved into the sphere of regulation associated with community and family relationships. Nationalism maintained women's association with the family while revaluing the contribution of the family and community to national identity and women's role as conduits for social reproducers of African values. Post-colonial states adopted the ideology of the rule of law, and maintained, albeit with different emphases, the imposed legal pluralist systems. Externally imposed policies associated with development and economic liberalisation sought to strengthen and extend the rule of law to enable women to 'exit' customary practices and enter a reformed market-oriented framework of rights, which would enable them to access the market as individuals. There has been a marked reluctance, nonetheless, to overhaul state family-related laws even though they reflect the values of nineteenth- and early twentieth-century colonialism. Although these policies were based on a much more limited role for the state than those associated with a rights approach to development, both shared a state focus.

However, the pursuit of macroeconomic policies has ensured a change of perspective which has started to acknowledge the role of community regulation in constructing power relations. Women's identities and access to resources are moulded through their status within families and communities. While not necessarily viewing such 'cultures' as positive, economic policymakers have been increasingly willing to recognise that the prerequisites for economic woman or man may not be a full range of individual state rights. It may be possible to align market with community relationships, which bypasses or reduces the significance of state rights and creates a culture of economics. Although these policies are based on different values to that of women activists championing positive cultural approaches, they share a more 'bottom up' approach, which tends to reduce the role of the state.

Those intent on developing markets in rural Africa have recognised culture in the sense of not necessarily requiring a formal rule of law framework to underpin their activities. The orthodoxy that markets require individual property rights and formal dispute resolution fora has been challenged, partly because it has not proven possible to establish 'rule of law' states. Other normative systems, including corruption, and operating at the community level, still form the basis for many activities. Feminists working with 'law' in Africa are not necessarily operating with legitimate state law systems, which represent the cultural values of at least the dominant communities. In societies where the state resorts to the rhetoric of law, including support for women's international human rights, to bolster legitimacy with external agencies but relies on other sources of legitimacy with its population, such as African nationalism and tradition, the pursuit of justice for women is complex. While the political rights of women as citizens are enshrined within constitutions and external agencies seek reassurance on the way in which the states are implementing international human rights in relation to women, there is precious little discourse of economic justice to counter the effects of global economic policies (Banda 2005).

Can the discourse of care/*ubuntu* be transferred to the market and retain its value? Or does the expansion of the market and market relations (the productive) relegate the socially reproductive to the margins? Given that few women in Africa access the market on positive terms, what impact does this have on the constructions of identity?

5

From anonymity to attribution: producing food in a global value chain

Introduction

This chapter explores the supply end of the fresh fruit and vegetables (FFV) chain. It looks at the way in which the production of FFV in Kenya is integrated within the global market and the various regulatory regimes that orchestrate the process. It argues that unequal gender relations in relation to social reproduction within the community and family are replicated within labour laws and built into the global trading regime. It questions whether, as a consequence, women's labour in Africa is subsidising consumption in the Global North.

Global North consumer culture enables consumers who want to buy at any time in the year a wide range of high quality, 'good value', sometimes 'exotic' or luxury, FFV. Customers want to take pleasure in eating a ripe mango, unmarked because it has been protected in a plastic container although packaging is not only or primarily for the convenience of customers: fruit needs to be bagged to obtain a barcode for stock control; vegetables need to be packaged because they are transported over hundreds of miles (once in the UK) from centralised supermarket distribution centres (Lawrence 2004). To meet demand, retailers scour the globe to source products, which they then display at the entrance of their stores, thereby encouraging their customers to purchase items that usually provide, through the added value elements, a considerable profit.

These activities take place a long way from the fields and pack houses in Kenya in the Global South where women and men labour to grow and prepare these products for export. We saw in the last chapter that colonialism provided the context for the relationship between much of Africa and the Global North until the latter part of the twentieth century. While tea and coffee grown on farms and plantations using colonial labour have long since been enjoyed by northern consumers, more recent macroeconomic policies have been geared towards the wider integration of African agriculture into the market. Land reform policies have sought to create asset value in land held previously more for its use (socially reproductive) value. The aim has been to commercialise and diversify agricultural production to increase productivity and to stimulate growth in economies more generally. These developments have affected all forms of agricultural production.

This chapter explores the way in which global economic policies are bringing the relationships between Global North consumers and African producers closer together. Some African women (and men) working in agriculture are now more transparently linked with northern consumers. A picture of a named African woman, smiling and looking healthy, appears above a rack of grapefruit in a leading UK supermarket. The label on a pack of pre-prepared mangetout beans states that it is a product of Kenya or Uganda. As individuals, UK consumers are seemingly encouraged to know about the origins of their products, including who produces them. More generally 'trade' not 'aid' is seen as a way of improving the lot of the poor.

The development of GVC and 'social labelling' are creating relationships between individual consumers and producers. As a result of knowing more about the relationships that result in the product being on the shelf, the consumer may be willing to pay more for it. FFV value chains utilised by the dominant food retailers in the UK have stimulated civil society campaigns based on concepts of fairness and justice and led to interventions that recognise the unequal relationships associated with the chains. These campaigns have involved new alliances, including with women's organisations, outside the trade union movement, the traditional focus for such activities. They have also contributed to the development of private standard-setting, a process that shifts the locus for regulation from the state to the market.

Trading relationships are constructed within various governance contexts, from the global economic framework of the WTO Agreement on Agriculture, through state-focused labour and human rights, to the transnational civil society-focused ethical/care initiatives. Certain discourses are associated with each of these contexts: trade with freedom; labour with rights; and civil society with care. There are considerable crossovers and the discourse of justice merges with that of care, leading to a plurality of approaches which, to a lesser or greater extent, recognise the interdependence of those involved in producing and consuming these products. However, despite these developments, the gender relationships that underpin agribusiness are far from transparent to either consumers or policymakers. Women's contributions, through combinations of formal, informal and subsistence work, to the caring for and provisioning of their families and communities, are not quantified by their states or by the international policy communities. The value of women's labour does not inform agricultural trade policy development sufficiently at community, national or international levels. The differential impact of global agricultural trade which can cause varying forms of injustices for women in the South, is not recognised.

Women who work on the farms and in the packing houses of the commercial enterprises that export FFV through GVCs to European supermarkets are the main focus for this chapter. While the agribusiness sector is clearly very important to Kenya's economy, it does not provide the income for the vast majority of women who are involved in agriculture. The last chapter showed the way in which local land systems as well as state land policies have marginalised most women farmers. Despite the development of individual entitlements through land law reforms, women's access is still predominantly derived from their social relationships within lineage groups and rooted, therefore, in the normative frameworks associated with customary systems of land distribution.

GVC and Kenyan agribusiness

We saw the origins and development of the concept of the value chain in Chapter 1. To recap: it is used to describe and analyse the way in which globalisation has changed trading and production strategies both within firms and also within the public realm of state economic policies (Gereffi and Korzeniewicz 1994; Kaplinsky 2000; Gereffi et al. 2005). The descriptive framework covers three main elements: how the activities associated with the particular process are organised (input/output); where the activities take place (the territorial aspect); and the governance structure. The analytical task involves charting where and how value is created and added in the chain in order to assess the distribution of benefits. Within recent value chain analysis, although not within the original commodity chain approach, the aim is to use the findings for development policy purposes: to increase the potential for value creation and retention in the Global South. GVC analysis now seeks to assess the impact of the macroeconomic context on particular chains, thereby recognising wider institutional effects. However, its economic focus has led to the underdevelopment of a gendered understanding of the relationship between social reproduction and production. The next sections consider each of these elements in the specific context of FFV chains originating in Kenya.

Input/output – what happens

Kenyan FFV chains are relatively simple (Barrientos et al. 2001; Lawrence 2003; Kritzinger et al. 2004; Women Working World Wide 2007). The vast majority of the vegetables (such as green beans, mangetout, corn, carrots and leeks) are grown on large intensive farms in the fertile areas around Lake Naivasha. Workers on the commercial farms plant, weed, spray and then harvest the crops daily. Commercial firms also contract smallholders to grow produce for them with seeds they supply. The commercial grower will tell the smallholder when to plant and when and how often to spray the crops. The vegetables harvested daily by smallholders are taken to growers' cooperatives where they are assessed. The vegetables grown specifically for export must meet the same exacting supermarket-supplied specifications in relation to length, diameter and straightness as those required of the commercial farmers. Many fail to meet the standard required: for instance about 35 per cent of the green beans are rejected. There are few alternative outlets (cattle feed or local markets) so most are wasted.

All farmers must meet the daily orders, emailed about midday, specifying the requirements of their supermarket buyers. There are no written contracts specifying quantities so orders can fluctuate widely depending on sales logged from supermarket tills the day before. Orders are flown out the same night. Once harvested the crops must be trucked to the highly supervised cutting and packing sheds or factories where they are washed, sorted, topped and tailed, sliced, mixed and so on and then packaged, probably using imported materials. These processes often require considerable manual dexterity. Once the orders are complete (usually on the same night as the order is placed), the containers will be air freighted to the UK (8,500 miles away). They will be trucked to the central distribution points for further distribution to individual supermarkets. Products will be bought by consumers who discard the packaging. Approximately 40 per cent of UK household rubbish in landfills is packaging from supermarkets. About 30 per cent of the produce will be thrown away, uneaten.

Territoriality – where it happens

Production, and increasingly preparation, occurs in Kenya both in the farming areas but also on the outskirts of Nairobi where the pack houses or factories are located, while design, marketing, distribution and consumption takes place in the UK. Export of horticultural products, in particular FFV and flowers, now constitutes a large and growing part of the Kenyan economy (Barrientos et al. 2003: 1513). By 2003 these exports were worth approximately US$ 460 million and accounted for roughly a quarter of all Kenyan exports (EPZA 2005). Many products can only be grown in certain geographical areas and they are also labour intensive to grow, sort and pack so profits depend on a supply of cheap, relatively unskilled labour. Both factors provide comparative advantage to countries such as Kenya, which is the largest supplier into the UK and fifth largest into the EU as a whole (see Dolan et al. 1999). Producers in Kenya rely heavily on European markets: 85 per cent of all horticultural exports and 99 per cent of all cut flowers are supplied to the EU. The UK (34 per cent) and the Netherlands (31 per cent) import the majority of Kenya's horticultural exports; the UK and France are the biggest importers of Kenya's fresh vegetable exports; and the UK imports 25 per cent of the cut flowers (EPZA 2005).

Britons spend over £1.5 billion a year on cut flowers as a whole (Conn 2007). Consumers will change stores to buy flowers and FFV (few items have this value); they are 'income elastic products' (shoppers' per capita income can be gauged from the proportion of FFVs in their trolleys); and they are largely unbranded (supermarkets do not have to share their profits with branded suppliers) (Kaplinsky 2000: 19). Major retailers in Europe and in the UK in particular now dominate the market. The top four supermarkets (Tesco, Sainsbury's, ASDA and Safeway) account for over three-quarters of all UK FFV sales and between 70 and 90 per cent of fresh produce from Africa (Dolan et al. 1999: 9).

The majority of the workers in the fields and the pack houses are women. On the farms they harvest the crops under pressure to work until the orders are met, however long that may be, although formally working shifts. In the pack houses, women also work in shifts but must meet the orders.

Governance

Until the mid 1980s, '[t]raders in Kenya bought produce in wholesale markets or at the farm gate and exported it to the UK, where it was sold in wholesale markets' (Gereffi et al. 2005: 93). At that time price and seasonal availability dictated market share. In order to expand and increase their share of the FFV market, large UK retailers started to impose new requirements in relation to quality, consistency of product, reliability of supply (through year round global sourcing) and price. Retailers sought new varieties and introduced the concept of 'pre-prepared' vegetables and fruit. As public concern over food safety increased, retailers were also obliged to comply with externally imposed health and environmental standards. They developed closer relationships with UK importers and African exporters, adopted renewable annual contracts with suppliers whose activities were regularly monitored and audited. They started to check all stages of the processes through to the fields. To meet requirements growers had to change their practices substantially. Wholesalers were replaced with two new parties: 'export agents in the producing countries [who] assured and monitored supplies and 'category managers' (that is, importers) in the buying countries [who] liaised with retailers and export agents' (Kaplinsky 2000: 21).

Arm's-length relationships have been replaced by buyer-driven value chains, which coordinate global production and distribution systems without any direct ownership (Gereffi et al. 2005: 83). Key actors in the chain use three forms of governance to ensure that inter-firm division of labour works efficiently and effectively: legislative governance (the conditions (rules) for participation in the chain); judicial governance (the auditing of performance and checking compliance with the rules); and executive governance (proactive, assisting participants in the value chain to meet the operating rules) (Kaplinsky 2000). Different parties, private and public, can be responsible for these. In the FFV chains, the retailers set the 'legislative' standards and demand compliance audits from category managers who pass these 'judicial' demands on to export agents in producing countries. 'Executive' governance is exercised by a 'combination of developing country-based exporters, and the category-managers based in final markets' (Kaplinsky 2000: 21). These forms of governance require a strong presence in both final product markets and at the sorting and packaging points in the growing countries. Work practices along with worker health checks to avoid any risks to the products, require regular audit.

Supermarkets therefore tend to work with a limited number of UK suppliers/ importers for each product range and pass responsibility to suppliers for management, product development and even consumer research (Gereffi et al. 2005: 93). 'A Kenyan exporter will only deal with one UK importer, although it may sell to other markets through other channels, and a UK importer will only have one Kenyan supplier'(Gereffi et al. 2005: 94). We will return to the issue of the governance of the chains to consider the growing role of private legislative standard-setting on women's ability to protect themselves against exploitation while working in this sector. First we need to consider how governance contributes to the distribution of benefits in the chain.

Who gains and who takes the risks?

There has been a significant growth in the proportion of African production that is traded: within sub-Saharan Africa the proportion of GDP attributable to trade (imports and exports) rose from 47 per cent in 1960 to 56 per cent in 1995. This liberalised regime should increase growth, increase the numbers employed and improve living standards. Sub-Saharan Africa has increased its participation in global exchange but seen a decline in its relative income share. One explanation is that this region concentrates on trading primary commodities (such as coffee) that have been badly affected by fluctuations in world commodity prices in the last twenty years. Agricultural liberalisation, as we have seen, encourages more diversification but does not seem to have led generally to rising returns for local producers delivering '"immiserising growth": increasing economic activity but falling economic returns' (Kaplinsky 2000: 7). GVC analysis seeks to explain why this occurs and also to provide a framework for both public and private policy interventions to tackle issues of inequality.

The FFV export trade has provided significant economic benefits to the Kenyan economy and employment opportunities for individual Kenyans. However, in general, the benefits have not been distributed equally. At the inter-country level, the value chain delivers the bulk of the gain to the marketing and retailing end of the chain as seen in Table 1 below: the supermarkets account for roughly 46 per cent of the final price of the product while the producer in Kenya obtains 14 per cent.

This system places a premium on product development, value chain coordination and marketing: growing the crops does not provide substantial rewards. However, the capacity to sort, pre-prepare and package products in large quantities can retain more added value within producing countries like Kenya although these activities require substantial facilities with refrigeration. These post-harvest activities require major investment. Smallholder farmers have found it impossible to scale up. In 1992, almost 75 per cent of FFV were grown by smallholders (Dolan et al. 1999: 23). By the end of the 1990s, '. . . the ten leading exporters accounted for seventy percent of Kenya's FFV exports and the four largest bought less than twenty percent of their supplies from small farms' (Kaplinsky 2000: 23). Exporters have moved into farm ownership to source their products (Gereffi et al. 2005: 94). While Kenya has about 5,000

Table 1 Cost structure of Kenyan FFV exports to the UK

Price per tonne (£)		*Export of fresh vegetables from Kenya (one tonne)*
		% of final price
Producer	630	14.1
Exporter	291 ⎫	13.1
Packaging	274 ⎭	
Air freight and handling	1036	21.2
Total CIF from Africa	*2230*	*48.4*
Importer charges and commission	624	6.1
Supermarket stockout	714 ⎫	
Other costs	285 ⎬	45.5
Mark-up	1427 ⎭	
Total price	5281	100

Adapted from Dolan et al. 1999

flower firms, 75 per cent of total exports are supplied by twenty-four large- or medium-scale operations (Barrientos et al. 2001:7). Within Kenya, value is retained through consolidation of commercial interests and adding value through undertaking more judicial as well as executive governance such as providing the traceability necessary to guarantee phytosanitary standards.

In this context most women will not access the potential benefits of non-traditional agricultural exports through their small-scale farming activities. They may benefit through working as employees in a sector that commands higher wages.

Flexible and precarious women workers

The demands of consumers define the risks involved for the retailers who manage these through very tightly drawn governance processes, which keep costs pared down to a minimum while passing the risks along the chain to the sites of production. Fluctuations in demand are managed through just-in-time delivery and by producers using their workforce flexibly. Women with their wider social reproductive responsibilities constitute the bulk of this flexible, widely available and therefore cheap workforce. They absorb the risks while gaining few of the benefits.

The production-focused gender pyramid, introduced in Chapter 1, is represented in Figure 4. The model distinguishes the provision and regulation of formal relations of employment (freedom of association, collective bargaining, safety and hygiene, equal and living wages, work hours, contracts and discrimination) (segment A) from the regulation and provision of

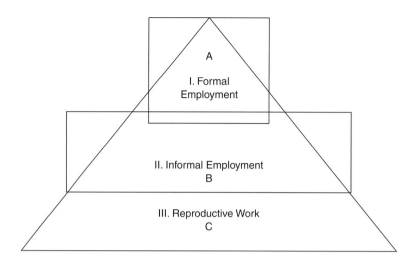

(A) Regulation and provision of formal conditions of employment

(B) Regulation and provision of employment related benefits

(C) Non-employment related benefits and social provision
      suporting reproductive work

Figure 4: Gendered employment.
Source: Barrientos *et al.* (2003: 1516)

employment-related benefits (provision of housing, training, workplace childcare, reproductive rights, maternity and paternity leave, transport and occupational health) (segment B) and non-employment-related benefits and social
provision supporting reproductive work (social norms and practice, education,
domestic responsibilities and gender relations) (segment C). The pyramid
becomes more gender differentiated as it broadens to its base.

   Formal employment is characterised by a contractual relationship between
an employer and the employee underpinned by state-based labour laws, which
provide whatever work-related benefits are available. Temporary, seasonal and
casual work is usually classified as informal work, and as such the worker is not
an employee for the purposes of state-based labour laws and has limited or no
work-related benefits. Due to wider assumptions and responsibilities relating to
social reproduction, women constitute the core of the temporary, seasonal and
casual workforce, while men generally undertake the fewer permanent jobs.
Women have less protection from state labour laws even though access to these
benefits would often provide them with more assistance precisely because of
their wider social responsibilities.

   This division of labour between formal and informal work is reproduced in
sub-Saharan horticultural value chains (see Barrientos et al. 2001, 2003). There
are few official statistics but it is estimated that between 40,000 and 70,000
workers are involved in the Kenyan flower industry, 75 per cent of whom are

women. 65 per cent of women are temporary or seasonal workers. It is estimated that about another 70,000 work in the FFV sector, most of whom are women (EPZA 2005). Women are concentrated in the value-added stages in the export production process associated with the quality of the final product, such as picking and packing, and processing activities. 'Companies see women as more productive, with nimble fingers and a capacity to perform the delicate and tedious work to fulfil the quality imperatives of overseas buyers' (Barrientos et al. 2003: 1514).

Women face many difficulties at work (see research findings of Smith et al. (2004). These include unequal pay relative to men because women perform tasks generally associated with lower pay rates, despite their importance to the export trade, reflecting wider social assumptions that women's incomes are supplementary to those of men (Barrientos et al. 2001: 8). Because of their precarious position as informal workers, women were particularly vulnerable to sexual harassment. Supervisors were able to exercise informal power within inoperative formal procedures and with lines of people waiting outside the gates hoping for work. While rates were generally higher than the low statutory minimum, many workers reported that their wages did not cover their basic needs.

The value chain processes place huge pressures on producers to meet not only quality but time deadlines. Orders vary and often require overtime at little or no notice. While workers were not required to work more than forty-eight hours a week, the reality, particularly for women in the pack houses, was that overtime was obligatory and excessive (up to eight hours a day). This caused huge problems for women who were often heads of households with childcare responsibilities. Many women were frightened of becoming pregnant because they risked losing their jobs. The provision of benefits such as sick pay, maternity leave, housing allowance, funeral grants, health care and childcare can provide a safety net to workers but were only available to permanent workers, although some of these benefits had been extended to seasonal workers on a pro rata basis. Casual, migrant and contract workers in general were not eligible. Women workers wanted on-farm housing and also health- and death-related benefits because of the high incidence of HIV/AIDS.

Women had less access to training than men (often because employers associated women with higher turnover and absentee rates), limiting women's ability to develop skills and upgrade their status. In general, women held few supervisory or managerial positions. Promotion tended to be based on social relationships (friend or kinsperson) rather than on merit. Although health and safety measures had improved considerably particularly in relation to the safe use of chemicals (for spraying flowers in greenhouses) and for pesticides (for spraying crops), due to social activism, researchers still found serious problems. Non-permanent workers were less likely to be provided with protective clothing and regular occupational health and safety training was not widespread in Kenya.

Unionisation is generally low among agricultural workers and is a relatively recent phenomenon in the agricultural sector in Kenya although it is attributed with some success in improving conditions for workers. Membership was much lower among non-permanent workers: few casual, seasonal and migrant workers have knowledge of unions. Most companies have workers' committees, but again there was limited knowledge of these bodies among non-permanent workers. Women were under-represented, both in unions and on workers' committees, despite being the majority of the workforce. Both women and men thought that women would not be good leaders.

Broader social norms therefore structure women's position within the labour force and contribute to their vulnerability as workers within a system that seeks to transfer much of the risk of the enterprise to those closest to the point of production. Women are clustered within the insecure areas of employment, which provide employers with flexibility but which attract fewer work-related benefits. Poor-quality accommodation where provided, inadequate or non-existent child care provision, inadequate health care facilities and lack of transport all affect women more than men, particularly in isolated rural areas (Barrientos et al. 2001: 9). The unequal distribution of social provision and entitlements that constitute the 'gender contract' in Kenyan society more generally further contribute to women's vulnerability as workers.

Legislating decent work?

Subsequent research by Women Working World Wide in association with a number of workers' organisations in East Africa in 2007 suggests that in Kenya, although not in other East African countries, the large companies, responding in part to external pressure, have moved away from the use of casual workers, thereby offering their regular workforce greater security. This employer-led initiative coincides with the modernisation of Kenya's labour laws.[1] Undertaken with ILO sponsorship, this project aimed, among other things, to harmonise labour laws within the East African Community as part of the East African Economic Partnership Agreement.

A casual employee is defined now as a person 'the terms of whose engagement provide for his payment at the end of each day and who is not engaged for a longer period than twenty four hours at a time' (Employment Act 2007 section 2). Section 37 provides for the conversion of casual employment if continuous for one month or an aggregated period of three months into a contract of service for which the employee is entitled to a 28 days' period of notice of termination in writing (section 35(1)(c)). If, after conversion, the person is employed for two months he/she is entitled to the same rights as

---

[1] Employment Act 2007; Labour Relations Act 2007; Occupational Safety and Health Act 2007; Work Injury Benefits Act 2007; and Labour Institutions Act 2007.

someone initially employed on a contract of service (section 37(3)). All workers with a contract of service of three months or more must have a written contract stating the particulars of employment, including one day off in seven; reasonable housing accommodation or housing allowance; and access to drinking water and medicines. In addition workers accumulate paid sick and annual leave through length of service. The Labour Relations Act 2007 guarantees rights to form and belong to a trade union and to collective bargaining. There is a new duty on the state, Labour Court and employers to promote equality of opportunities (including specifically for migrant workers) and for employers to strive to eliminate discrimination in employment policy and practice and to pay equal remuneration for work of equal value (Employment Act 2007 section 5(1) (a), (b), (2) and (5)). There is a specific requirement not to discriminate or harass employees or potential employees on grounds of sex, and sexual harassment is specifically recognised and defined (Employment Act 2007 sections 5 and 6). Importantly, women employees with a contract of service are entitled to three months' paid maternity leave and job security, and men to two weeks' paid paternity leave (sections 5(3)(a) and 29). No minimum wage is set in the new framework. Instead the Kenyan Minister for Labour continues to set wage guidelines for employers (Dwasi 1999: 365). The level is very low and largely ignored.

While the 2007 Act provisions seem to draw their normative framework from work contexts far removed from those pertaining for most women in Kenya, if fully implemented, these provisions could improve the rights of more workers and, in particular, offer access to more work-related benefits to women covered by their provisions. The legislation maintains the distinction between casual workers and those with contracts of service. As we saw in the previous chapter, the institutional framework, including gender-focused policies that would promote the normative changes within the community necessary for effective implementation of this legislation is yet to develop within the state. There is also likely to be considerable resistance to provisions such as increased maternity benefits, which are perceived to threaten comparative advantage in a highly competitive global market.

The construction of gender within global governance discourses

Introduction

The discussion now moves away from the interaction of the GVC governance on the 'vertical' gender relationships within Kenya to the 'horizontal' macroeconomic and institutional governance discourses associated with agricultural trade (see Matsushita et al. 2006: chapter 9; Williams 2003: chapter 3). These global discourses are creating new forms of legal pluralism, which affect the construction of gender relations. They offer both challenges and opportunities for gender activism, which seeks to expose and counter injustice. Is it possible to care about Kenyan women working very long hours, on low wages, in possibly unsafe conditions to produce a 'convenient' tray of pre-cut beans or a romantic bunch of cut flowers for Valentine's Day? To what extent does a rights discourse tackle unjust distribution? Can a discourse rooted in the relational concept of care be used to develop redistributional strategies?

From SAP to the WTO Agreement on Agriculture and Economic Partnership Agreements

Kenya, like much of sub-Saharan Africa, has faced huge economic and political difficulties in the last decades and has been subject to the interventions of the IFIs as well as various forms of international development assistance. Stabilisation and SAP were used to tackle hyper-inflation in the 1980s at the expense of incomes, wages and employment levels. When the harshness of this regime proved unacceptable, the policies were toned down by both Washington-based financial institutions and governments. However trade and financial liberalisation policies designed to open up developing countries to world markets remain the dominant ideological approach. While Kenya's export horticulture is successful in generating increased employment and foreign trade, its economy is now tied to changes in European agricultural policies as well as trends in consumerism (Stevens 2005a, 2005b).

Agriculture was not subjected to the 'disciplines' of the multilateral trading system under the GATT 1947 because the contracting parties could not agree to reduce protection. From 1947 to 1994 key GATT contracting parties erected additional barriers to trade in farm products. Spearheaded by the US, Article XI was transformed into 'a mechanism favouring farm protectionism' (Matsushita et al. 2006: 291). The US freely subsidised their farm production unchallenged and were joined by Japan and European states. The European Community (EC, now EU) developed its own system of protectionism under the Common Agricultural Policy (CAP), which was based on imposing a variable levy on any farm good about to be imported, which was equivalent to the price of that good in the EU. 'As a result, exports rarely if at all, occurred and EC farmers for years operated completely insulated from the competitive pressures of the world market' (Matsushita et al. 2006: 291). While the CAP was inconsistent with GATT, the US at first did not challenge it, recognising its importance to the process of European integration, but when it did seek to use the GATT dispute settlement procedures, it found they were of little use. Export subsidy wars between the US and the EC broke out in the 1980s and provided some impetus for liberalisation through multilateralism. However, domestic politics stalled such an initiative. While this protectionism was in full force in the key northern markets, the same states, represented within other institutions, such as the World Bank and the International Monetary Fund (IMF), were imposing agricultural liberalisation policies on developing countries through SAPs.

The present multilateral trading system is based upon agreements negotiated and signed by a large majority of the world's trading nations, and ratified by member states and overseen by the WTO. These agreements guarantee member states trade rights on the basis of national treatment and most favoured nation treatment. While the agreements are negotiated and signed by governments, their purpose is to help producers of goods and services, exporters, and importers conduct their business. The fifteen agreements of the Uruguay Round of GATT negotiation were drawn up at the height of the enthusiasm for free market economics. The stimulus for change in relation to farm products was provided by the CAIRNS group, consisting of farm product exporting states, which forced worldwide agricultural liberalisation on to the agenda of the Uruguay Round. The result was the 1994 AOA, which was seen as merely a start, a point reflected in Article 20.

The Agreement focuses on reducing the 'so-called three pillars of trade protection: (1) market access; (2) export support; and (3) domestic support' (Williams 2003: 52). Developed and developing countries (with subcategories of least developed countries (LDCs) (twenty-nine WTO members) and net food importing countries) operate within somewhat different parameters, with the latter granted more latitude on implementation timescales and quantity reductions. The key measure (Article 4.2) to promote market access relates to the restriction of domestic subsidies and is described as 'tariffication' (the conversion of non-tariff market access barriers into tariffs and therefore provision of a common language for negotiators). Once set (at no more than the previous level of protection), the aim is then to achieve reductions. Developing countries had high average tariff rates, which they were required to reduce by 24 per cent over a ten-year period by the AOA (Least Developed Countries are exempted) while developed countries were required to reduce by 35 per cent over six years. Where full tariffication would lead to prohibitively high tariffs then tariff rate quotas are deployed. Under this scheme a fixed minimum quantity of imports is allowed in but quantities above a threshold are taxed at a higher rate. Through various 'ploys' some (in particular the US and the EU) have been able to keep roughly the same levels of protection as before (Williams 2003: 53). The EU and the US are also the heaviest users (out of thirty-eight WTO members) of the special agricultural safeguard mechanism (Article 5), an emergency measure that protects certain products from a flood of imports by raising tariffs.

Domestic support has generally involved direct payments to farmers for crops that are exported or consumed domestically. These 'amber box' programmes are considered trade distorting and are required to be reduced. Under Article 6.5 'blue box' programmes, designed to keep farmers on the land, are exempted. They include crop set aside payments or payments to enhance environmental quality. The EU has been a big user while very few developing countries have developed such programmes. Other programmes, deemed minimal or non-trade distorting schemes are put in the exempt 'green box' (Annex 2). These include publicly funded government programmes relating to research, training, food security programmes, environmental programmes and decoupled income payments (those not related to production but to 'social goods'). Because of domestic political sensitivities, countries still provide high levels of tariff protection to their domestic producers although the EU has started to move towards some rationalisation of its CAP for domestic reasons (the CAP budget currently consumes about 55 billion of the European Union's 130 billion Euro annual budget) with a slow but steady trend towards supporting 'social goods' associated with land.

Export subsidies in agriculture (defined in Article 1e) are used to cover the difference between the world price for a product and an amount paid to domestic farmers. Other forms of export support involve export credit and food aid. These distort world commodity prices and are subject to the disciplines of the AOA. 'About twenty five countries have been allowed to subsidise exports, though developing countries were largely restricted to subsidies for marketing and transportation' (Williams 2003: 54). However, as Williams points out, existing export support payments were maintained through the use of the 'green box' (payments to farmers not related to production; domestic food aid programmes; support for environmental protection; research; and disaster relief) (Matsushita et al. 2006: 234–235).

The special and differential treatment (S&DT) framework within the AOA recognises the importance of agriculture to developing countries' economies and also to their food security generally by granting special time frames, different target reductions and exemptions. Presently, around 71 per cent of the EU's agricultural imports originate from developing countries. Although there is much debate over their usefulness, preferences are important to Kenya's horticulture and floriculture trade with the EU (Stevens and Keenan 2004). The Doha Development Round in principle addresses the difficulties faced by developing countries in implementing these agreements although there are doubts about the practice.

Although the WTO system is democratic in that it offers each member state a vote, the realities of global power result in block negotiations (the EU negotiates for its members) and bargaining among groups of states:

> ... developing countries usually find that they have accepted commitments to reduce their own market access barriers ... but in return do not receive significant changes in the market access barriers of the major players. .... By the end of the 1990s, many developing countries' economies were already being inundated with cheap heavily subsidised agricultural imports from the North. (Williams 2003: 58)

Regulatory regimes such as those relating to Sanitary and Phytosanitary Standards (for instance on the traceability of products or control of pesticide residues) are not included in European trade preferences for particular countries, yet they can have a huge impact on smallholders who do not have the resources to ensure that their produce meets these requirements, contributing, as in Kenya, to the concentration of supply of products from a few large suppliers (Stevens and Keenan 2004).

Economic Partnership Agreements and gender policy

Powerful economies such as the US are increasingly making use of bilateral agreements to circumvent some of the disciplines and complexities of the multilateral system with its formal democratic base. The EU has been obliged to negotiate Economic Partnership Agreements (EPAs) with seventy-nine countries, known collectively as the ACP (African, Caribbean and Pacific), including all but one of Africa's sub-Saharan states, under the Cotonou Agreement 2000. As the EU is the biggest export market for most ACP countries, changes in these agreements have major impacts on the economies of many of the world's least developed countries.

The Agreement has three aspects: trade, development and political 'dialogue' with states and non-state actors. It aims to reduce poverty through sustainable development and integrate ACP countries into the world economy (Article 1). The trade-related EPAs are based on reciprocal access and the phased removal of all trade preferences and trade barriers between all partners. They replace the preferential trading arrangements, within the Lome Conventions (1975–1995), between European countries and former colonies, which allowed ACP countries access to European markets for their specific commodities without the need for reciprocal arrangements so Kenya's agricultural exports had found some protections from the rigours of international trade law as a consequence of its colonial past.

The Cotonou Agreement is underpinned by a number of fundamental principles, including differentiation and regionalisation. As a result, ACP countries have been encouraged to create and negotiate EPAs as regional trading blocs. (ACP countries that are also LDCs have preferential trading relations: the 'Everything But Arms' programme, grants duty-free and quota-free access to the EU market.) A number of interim EPAs were negotiated, including one with the East African Community. Under this agreement (pending a comprehensive EPA) Kenya is able to maintain WTO-compatible access to EU markets (Ong'wen 2008).

Article 31 requires that systematic account be taken of the situation of women and gender in all areas covered by the agreement, including macroeconomic policies and political participation. It encourages the adoption of positive policies to increase women's access to basic social services and productive resources such as land credit and labour markets. The agreement also commits all parties to respect the ILO convention on core labour standards (which include equal pay and the elimination of discrimination) (Hoskyns 2006). These provisions are the backdrop to the harmonisation of East African labour laws discussed earlier.

Just trade discourse?

We can use Tronto's (1994) fourfold categorisation of care discussed in Chapter 2: caring about; taking care of; care giving; and receiving care to consider the way in which the discourses associated with the market (trade), state (rights) and civil society/family (care) are understood. How is 'care' about economic inequality and unequal gender relations understood in the discourse of trade? Is trade theory capable of caring about the effects of the relationships described in the FFV chain? Is it attentive to Kenyan women's well-being?

Macroeconomic discourse is detached, concerned with modelling economic flows and measuring indicators (Beveridge 2005). The assumption is that trade liberalisation is beneficial, that it creates growth and new jobs in both Global South and North economies. The processes involved are recognised as creating negative impacts but these will be short term. For liberal trade theorists the goal is generally to develop mechanisms that will deliver economic growth, which will provide the basis for political discussions over distribution. The political is constructed as outside the boundaries of the discourse, as a problem for states to sort out. It is therefore not necessary to be attentive to any need to care for the specific effects of trade theory on individuals and their relationships.

Trade policy and law take care through implementation. Policy is responsible for identifying economic objectives and determining how to respond. It is associated with negotiation and is based upon the outcome of bargaining between organised interests as represented by state-based trade negotiators. It does, therefore, include political interests within its boundaries but to be recognised these needs, understood here as interests, must be powerful and 'fit' trade discourse. The legal constructions embodied in the AOA and EPAs reflect often obtusely, a combination of theory and policy discourses. The legal framework of the trading system is based upon liberal values such as freedom of contract: no government is forced to join the WTO or to sign an EPA. The system is based upon reciprocity between governments as legal entities. The WTO governance standard is based on fulfilling agreed terms and liability for non-compliance. It can recognise inequality in power at the margins, through special treatment for developing countries or exceptions within Article XX. It contains within it concepts of formal and embryonic substantive equality (Beveridge 2005). However, the wider context of power inequalities is not recognised. ACP countries consider that they must participate in the EPA negotiations because they want legally binding agreements. The EU is not only their trading 'partner' but also, for LDCs, their major aid donor. Such funds are discretionary and can be withdrawn (Hoskyns 2006).

The dominant construction of trade law is gender neutrality: the actors are not embodied social beings but self-interested economic individuals. Existing inequalities and structural disadvantages are institutionalised within, rather than addressed through, the discourse. Thus while the Cotonou Agreement has an article that directly addresses the need to take care of gender issues and to act with responsibility to incorporate this perspective into all aspects of the Agreement, including the EPAs, this provision has little or no resonance. The conceptual framework of trade operates as a 'chilling' effect. The improved Kenyan labour laws can be justified within the dominant discourse as harmonising provisions within East Africa and therefore avoiding unfair advantage. However, tackling the structural inequalities that result in women's highly precarious position within the GVC and distributing the benefit of their labour to a small number of southern producers and northern retailers requires more than some improvements in formal rights. It requires measures that shift the responsibilities for social reproduction from women and encourage changes in gender relationships, in effect a new gender contract, within family and community as well as within the public sphere. Such measures would meet the objective of Article 31 and implement EU gender policies but could not be 'defended' within the present dominant discourse. It would require both EU and Kenyan trade negotiators to take responsibility for the pursuit of gender justice and to think imaginatively about ways of developing trade law and policy to achieve this. Given Kenya's vulnerability in the global market, far more responsibility rests with the EU.

While trade negotiators inhabit a world of abstract economic exigencies, development activist discourse is often fuelled by understandings gained from specific care-giving activities such as aid projects with women who experience the consequences of global trade policies. It is based upon understandings of the effects of global trade policies on women's lives and often involves relationships at the 'grassroots'. Frustration in meeting the norm of competence associated with this care-giving has propelled many NGO activists into 'upgrading' their focus to taking care of trade policy and caring for trade theory. Their discourse is concerned explicitly with power imbalances between countries, the lack of transparency over the powerful role of private actors such as the UK supermarkets and multinational companies, the double standards of northern countries' practices of protectionism while requiring liberalisation in the south, and the dire effect on, and lack of voice of, the poorest (CAFOD 2003a, 2003b; Oxfam 2004; Christian Aid undated). Some oppose the present trade system altogether, others try to 'rebalance' through interventions such as attempting to add a 'development' box to the AOA or incorporating gender indicators into EPAs.

Gender activist discourse cares about the effects of trading on women's overall well-being because women have a variety of roles in society, of which paid work is only one, albeit important, element. The problem is that this gender discourse is not 'heard' by trade negotiators. It is 'relegated' to impact studies or ameliorative policies, which form part of care-giving and care-receiving rather than used imaginatively and positively.

Multilateral, regional and bilateral trading provisions constitute the framework in which the specific GVC discussed above operates. We can see from the discussion that a gender- and care-based understanding of the position of women working in the Kenyan pack houses seems very distant from trade theory or the negotiations around EPAs or the Doha Development Round of WTO negotiations. Yet the 'push' (the increased economic vulnerability of small farmers due to liberalisation) and 'pull' factors (the demand for cheap flexible labour in the GVC) contribute to the reconstruction of gender relations and impact directly on Kenyan women's lives. When women work many hours overtime to meet 'just in time' supply orders, the market, as represented by UK consumer demands for particular imported products, affects Kenyan women's ability to care for their children.

Trading rights – rights approaches to trade and development

Can a discourse of women's rights counter trade rights and provide a way of reducing women's vulnerabilities as they are both integrated and marginalised within the global economy? There are two ways in which the discourse of rights plays a part here. The first uses international women's rights while the second focuses more specifically on international labour rights. These are not separate conceptual categories but they have been used in different ways in global governance contexts. The human rights of women focus is more associated with the wider policy framework known as a 'rights based approach to development' and used to challenge the macroeconomic and social policies of the development bodies (see Chapter 2). The engagement with labour rights concentrates more narrowly on the challenges presented by the effects of globalisation on labour relations and involves the regulatory framework for global trade.

Ideologically, trade law and human rights have developed in parallel conceptual frameworks. An attempt to introduce a rights discourse via a 'social clause' containing minimum labour standards directly into the WTO framework has largely failed (Braithwaite and Drahos 2000: 236; Steiner et al. 2008). It was opposed by the majority of states, particularly in the developing world, and business lobbies. 'Territoriality is . . . a fundamental principle of labor law, which has ostensibly not been affected by the intensification of globalization. It is based on the assumption that labor law is community-based . . .' (Mundlak 2009: 191). Moving the locus for discussion of labour rights challenges these assumptions. It is not surprising that this initiative was rejected by the WTO in 1996 at the Singapore Ministerial Conference and that labour rights were placed firmly in the separate domain of the ILO (Braithwaite and Drahos 2000: 235).

Alternative strategies are emerging. One such, which does not disrupt the ideological base of labour law in states, is based upon a 'compliance and co-operation approach' (Harrison 2007), which would introduce a system for auditing the impact of the trading system on human rights (including gender and labour rights). Where negative effects were identified, states would have clear grounds on which to introduce re-distributional policies to counter them. This would enable states to develop a more socially grounded, evidence-based approach to trade policy, which could extend to its effects on the socially reproductive sector, and use this evidence to substantiate claims to violations of social and economic rights.

This approach requires the development and acceptance, at both international and state levels, of a robust feminist development law analysis that would remould present understandings of rights to ensure that they encompass issues relating to care. The fault lines within the women's human rights movement, discussed in Chapter 2, are revealed here. Analysis is not strong in the areas of social and economic rights although Nussbaum's capabilities approach is recognised as providing a good starting point because of its focus on the need to provide resources to substantiate women's capabilities, whether they choose to exercise them or not. It can be used to focus the spotlight on state economic and social welfare policies. The developing jurisprudence associated with CEDAW is beginning to integrate issues of production and social reproduction through its concepts of indirect discrimination and substantive equality. For instance the CEDAW Committee in 2006 used these concepts to critique Kenya's lack of data on women's employment, the weakness of its (pre-reform) labour laws and inadequacies in family and land laws (CEDAW Committee 2006).

Caring rights – the ILO and transnational rights talk

In 2007 the ILO reported that more women than ever before are participating in labour markets worldwide although the participation rate has stopped growing (ILO 2007). It divides work into three categories: unpaid contributing family members (for example working on a family owned farm); own-account working (for example cultivating a plot and selling the produce or selling eggs in a market); and paid employment. 'The poorer the region, the greater the likelihood that women work as unpaid contributing family members or low income own account workers. Female contributing family workers, in particular, are not likely to be economically independent' (ILO 2007: 1–2). In the two poorest regions in the world, sub-Saharan Africa and South Asia, more women than men work as own-account workers than as waged and salaried workers. Nonetheless, 48 per cent of women are engaged in paid employment worldwide, although rates of pay vary dramatically.

As far as the ILO is concerned 'the move from being an unpaid contributing family worker or a low paid own-account worker into wage and salaried employment is a major step forward in terms of freedom and self determination for many women – even though it does not always entail getting a decent job right away' (2007: 10). Globally, since 2005 agriculture no longer provides the main source of employment for women: it has been replaced by the service sector (ILO 2007: 11). The ILO associates this move out of agriculture with progress, a view confirmed in the UN Millennium Development Goal 3 (Promote gender equality and empower women), which uses the share of women in wage employment in the non-agricultural sector as an indictor of progress (ILO 2007: 10).

Precarious or Decent Work?

While the dominant market discourse relating to work is one of flexibility for competitiveness, that of the international labour movement is based upon concepts of worker solidarity and protection. Has the ILO provided a framework to support its enthusiasm for women's empowerment through productive labour? Has it recognised the interaction between social reproduction and production? Who does it care about and take care of?

An international discourse on labour rights emerged in the twentieth century within the development of an international trade union movement which lobbied successfully for the establishment of the ILO at the peace negotiations at the end of World War 1. The international labour movement philosophy for most of the century was heavily influenced by state socialism. However, the collapse of most of the communist regimes in 1989 opened the way for the new politics of labour market deregulation, which was championed by the USA (and the UK) and promulgated by the IFIs in their dealings with the former Soviet Bloc and many developing countries. The weakening of unions within northern states has also led to new relationships between workers and employers. Now 'good' employers are engaged by the state to secure the productivity of their best workers through the provision of decent labour standards, thereby reducing the role of the unions. This corporatist approach to labour relations is mirrored in the international arena in the initiatives that encourage leading-edge transnational corporations to take over responsibility for labour standards.

The ILO, now a specialist agency within the UN, has a tripartisan constitution that encourages consensus decision-making, which does not disturb the principle of territoriality within labour law. Its Conventions (over 180) and recommendations have developed global labour standards rooted in a social democratic, Keynesian welfarist ideology reflecting its Western European membership (Braithwaite and Drahos 2000: 233). However, this consensus was challenged by new waves of membership from the Soviet Union in 1954, the Soviet Bloc countries and finally the newly independent developing countries.

As Braithwaite and Drahos point out, 'free' labour in the colonies was repressed by imported northern master and servant laws, which enabled employers to impose summary justice on workers (2000: chapter 11). Colonialism as a global force 'exploited and accentuated distinctively local forms of labour regulation' (2000: 227–228). In the North, the rise of trade unions ensured that labour contracts were transformed from 'free liberal contracts' into 'hybridized distinctive forms of regulatory law' located within a framework set by state laws and wider social welfare policies (2000: 227). New post-colonial member states could not meet the standards set by these 'modern' European contexts. Recognising these difficulties, ILO standards tend now to avoid specificity and build in flexibility through such terms as 'adequate or appropriate measures' (Braithwaite and Drahos 2000: 234) to enable the principle of territoriality to prevail. 'While many domains of standard-setting ... underwent a ratcheting-up process during the second half of the twentieth century, this was not the case with labour standards' (2000: 234).

The ILO has also been obliged to retrench and reposition itself as the relationship between capital and labour changed with neoliberal globalisation. It has done this through the promulgation of the Declaration on Fundamental Principles and Rights at Work 1998 (the Social Declaration), which involves the repackaging of a limited number of existing provisions and a revival of a rights-based approach to international labour regulation' (Vosko 2006: 57) and the Decent Work campaign which involves some rethinking of the norms that underpin labour rights.

At an international level, the ILO works by exhortation and encouragement. Some Conventions, including those of particular importance to women, such as equal pay, do have considerable international recognition. However, the responsibility of taking care of these rights lies with states, which must ensure that they are implemented effectively. Few states ratify many Conventions. Of those that do, many do not take responsibility for their 'domestification' (although most states do enshrine in their constitutions and domestic legislation measures prohibiting discrimination in employment). This lack of responsibility has led the ILO to attempt to elevate certain standards contained within core Conventions into fundamental principles that apply within member states, irrespective of ratification, and which require states to monitor. Thus the Social Declaration covers a limited number of fundamental international rights (freedom of association and the right to collective bargaining; the elimination of all forms of forced or compulsory labour; the abolition of child labour; and the elimination of discrimination in respect of employment and occupation). Standards become rights and are loosened somewhat from the hold of territoriality.

The international labour framework has traditionally seemed to care little for women: there has been a lack of attentiveness to the position of women workers. Partly because women have not figured strongly in domestic or international trade union movements, ILO conventions have taken care of their constituents' interests and adopted the breadwinner/homemaker model that underscored the work patterns of men: full-time permanent employment, with access to additional social benefits and entitlements, located within defined workplaces, and membership of trade unions. This model is particularly unsuited to protecting the interests of women who work primarily in informal, casual and temporary contexts, and does not 'fit' contemporary conditions of precarious working more generally.

Women within the international labour movement have challenged received understandings of rights, including the early protectionist Conventions, which constructed women explicitly as different, vulnerable and justifiably excluded from certain activities or workplaces. More recently, more attention has been paid to the issues necessary to incorporate a gender perspective[2] and to underpin

---

[2] The four key equality Conventions are: Discrimination (Employment and Occupation) Convention, 1958 (No. 111); Equal Remuneration Convention, 1951 (No. 100); Workers with Family Responsibilities Convention, 1981 (No. 156); and Maternity Protection Convention, 2000 (No. 183).

women's ability to work given their social commitments (Homework Convention no. 177 1996; Part-time Work Convention no. 175 1994; Workers with Family Responsibilities Convention no. 156 1981 (Vosko 2006). However, Vosko argues that the ILO has only sporadically recognised the 'erosion of the standard employment relationship and the gendered character of precarious work' and that it is hampered by its liberal equal treatment approach 'where the male norm continues to function as a benchmark for women's and men's labour force activity and the issue of care giving remains marginal' (2006: 53–54).

The ILO's Decent Work Agenda is not pursued through Conventions and Declarations; instead the ILO works 'in partnership with the principal institutions and actors of the multilateral system and the global economy' and supports 'integrated decent work country programmes which aim to tackle major decent work deficits through efficient programmes'. It is designed to improve the conditions of all people, waged and unwaged, working in the formal and informal economy, through the expansion of labour and social protections. It therefore moves the ILO 'beyond employment' into the realms of the social but the 'vision for the gender contract is underdeveloped'. While covering more employment situations it does not displace the male norm. Instead it seems to shift to a 'dual-earner/female caregiver contract' in which women achieve greater equality with men at work but remain responsible for care-giving (Vosko 2006: 74–75).

Kenya is a member of the ILO and has ratified Conventions of particular relevance to our discussion, including Convention number 111 (1958) on Discrimination and number 100 (1951) on Equal Remuneration. It has also ratified the CEDAW, with its broad concept of non-discrimination, covering employment and family life. However, most of these provisions have not been incorporated into Kenyan domestic legislation and therefore do not form part of the law and cannot be relied upon in court although they have hortatory value. Kenya has not ratified the newer Conventions that take more account of gendered divisions of labour.

In any case, effective rights depend on states to implement them and one of the effects of the liberalised trading system has been to limit the ability of states to care for their vulnerable citizens, and the existence of high levels of corruption undermines any such commitment. Additionally, the capacity of the Kenyan state to provide more extensive employment-related and welfare-focused benefits to larger constituencies of workers, or indeed all citizens, is limited by the wider economic and ideological context, which seeks labour flexibility as the key to economic progress. One of the comparative advantages offered by developing world states to the global market is the easy availability of a large pool of labour that is not as constrained by employment protection measures because of the colonial legacy of underdeveloped 'modern' labour laws or the establishment of Economic Priority

Zones (EPZs), which offer much lighter regulation to foreign businesses located there. While Kenya has recently reformed its labour laws, it makes use of EPZs as part of its industrialisation strategy (Dwasi 1999; EPZA 2005).

Transnational consumer care

Introducing 'soft laws'

States have become just one 'player' in the global market, with reduced influence over the activities of corporations nominally located within their jurisdictions but wielding huge power. In an age of deregulation, states, through international bodies and the labour movement have sought to incorporate Transnational Corporations (TNCs) into the governance of labour laws, through the adoption of 'soft law' measures.

The formal lack of accountability of TNCs other than to shareholders has led to attempts to widen responsibilities through exhortation, which are routed through the international institutions. The UN has developed its Norms on the Responsibility of TNCs and other Business Enterprises in relation to Human Rights as models for use by TNCs and states and has constructed a voluntary Global Compact, which encourages TNCs and others to comply with ILO minimum labour standards and basic human rights. The Organisation for Economic Co-operation and Development (OECD) established guidelines for Multinational Enterprises in 1976 and the ILO adopted a Tripartite Declaration of Principles concerning Multinational Enterprises and Social Policy in 1977.

Multilateral Framework Agreements result from the efforts of the labour movement to regroup after the shocks of 'economic liberalisation, deregulation, privatisation and the emergence of new and vast labour, manufacturing and consumer markets' and have involved 'forms of organising and campaigning that pick up historic fragments of international trade union work and adapt them innovatively, often in new alliances, to the contemporary context of a global economy dominated by multinational corporations (MNCs)' (Hammer 2005: 512). They attempt to capture some of the corporate social responsibility terrain through the voluntary adoption by MNCs of fundamental labour rights (as defined by the ILO) across their spheres of activity, including their suppliers. They seek to tie such company-level agreements not only to core labour rights but also to the institutional framework of social dialogue, to encourage governments to enforce the rights of workers to join trade unions and to bargain collectively (Hammer 2005: 514). Linking MNCs to state-based process rights, is seen as a way of overcoming the weaknesses of initiatives such as the one discussed below involving voluntary codes of conduct. However, they are of little use to most women workers because they are primarily concerned with industrial production, the traditional base of the organised labour movement, not with the service or agricultural sectors in which the majority of women work.

As we have seen, the development of the global market has produced changes in the way in which food is produced and sold. The governance of GVC have produced new transnational networks of actors. At the same time, the importance of consumers in the Global North economies has led to the rise in consumer power. Coalitions of civil society organisations, made up of consumer groups, trade union activists, women's groups, development NGOs and charities, which loosely share a concern with the way in which the global trading environment works, now play a role in constructing transnational discourses of trade. They care about working conditions and often combine this concern with a wider sense of the injustices produced by an unequal world. The focus for their attention tends to be the private actors in the GVC. The aim is to increase their responsibility; to oblige TNCs to trade ethically and to act with corporate social responsibility. A particular target has been the retailers and companies that set the terms for governance of the GVC. Food retailing is a highly competitive business. Supermarkets are very sensitive to the wishes of their consumers and vulnerable to loss of reputation. Campaigners use this vulnerability to organise boycotts or 'name and shame' projects, particularly on high-value-added products such as flowers, stressing the connection between women's working conditions and the luxury nature of the product (Klein: 2000). Women's organisations networking between Kenya and the UK have been able to publicise the impact on women's health of spraying in greenhouses in Kenya in this way. This led to rapid responses by supermarket managers to tackle the problems, keen not to lose a lucrative market.

The major initiatives, however, involve ethical trading and fair trade. While there are similarities and overlaps between these two discourses, they do have different origins (Barrientos and Dolan 2006). Ethical trading, as expressed through corporate codes of practice, is explicitly associated with the rise of the corporate social responsibility agenda in the 1990s and with value chains in particular. It involves collaboration between varieties of interested parties and has not been particularly concerned with changing the wider trading and production relations that underpin the chain. It is targeted on the conditions experienced by employees involved in production. Fair trade, which has a longer history and origins in charitable and development movements, seeks to ensure better trading conditions for small producers of food products and is therefore more explicitly focused on changing relations of production. Thus, ethical trading primarily relates to women working as employees while fair trade relates more to women working as small farmers, although these distinctions are becoming blurred with the move into fair trade by mainstream producers.

Purchasing social justice or private standard setting

> In African horticulture, codes have been introduced from three different origins:
> by dominant buyers such as supermarkets, importers and/or individual exporters
> within the chain (company codes); sectoral trade associations linked to the
> horticultural value chain (sectoral codes); and independent bodies comprising
> companies and a range of civil society organizations (independent codes).
> (Barrientos et al. 2003: 1518)

Company codes initially were developed to cope with increased requirements
of food safety and pesticides legislation and governed food safety, hygiene
and quality assurance throughout the supply chain. They apply to all horticultural producers. Retailers have no direct employment relationship with
workers in Kenya and therefore are not legally responsible for the implementation of the labour rights to which these workers are entitled under
state and international law. However, they have responded to civil society
concern over the conditions under which workers produce their food by
agreeing to incorporate specific provisions within their company codes.
Sectoral codes have been developed at an industry-wide level or by trade
associations (for instance by the Kenya Flower Council and the Fresh
Produce Exporters Association of Kenya). Many now contain employment-
related provisions.

Two independent social codes have emerged from partnerships between
retailers, trade unions, NGOs and companies: the US-based SA8000 and the
UK Ethical Trading Initiative Base Code (ETI Base Code), which has been
adopted by seven of the UK's largest supermarkets (see www.ethicaltrade.org/).
These multi-stakeholder social codes tend to be the most comprehensive in
their coverage of core UN and ILO Conventions relating to minimum labour
standards. The ETI Base Code covers process rights (freedom of association,
collective bargaining, forced labour, discrimination) and outcome rights
(safety/hygiene, living wages, work hours, regular employment and work contracts). It does not extend to employment-related issues such as maternity or
paternity leave, protection for pregnant women or childcare.

A number of issues are raised by these voluntary codes. First, do they have the
potential to recognise gender issues that are not covered by trade and rights
discourses? Barrientos and her colleagues have researched the impact of such
codes on women's work conditions in our chain (Barrientos et al. 2001;
Barrientos et al. 2003 and Barrientos and Smith 2007). They asked first, whether
the gender sensitivity of codes is sufficient to give women in employment the
same coverage as men and secondly, whether the codes are sufficiently broad in
their scope to cover related non-employment issues that affect the different
forms and conditions of employment of men and women (2001: 9). In other
words, can such codes tackle not only segment A and B of the pyramid but
also segment C, which covers the broader socio-economic circumstances that
affect women's ability to access particular types of employment (social norms

and practice, education, domestic responsibilities and gender relations)? Their answer was no.

Most codes of conduct are based on ILO Conventions, which form the foundation of segment A. Without incorporation into domestic laws such Conventions are voluntary agreements with no direct mechanism of enforcement. Conventions presume full-time and permanent employment (men's work) and their coverage of temporary employment (women's work) is limited. The Conventions also presume that employees are represented in a collective bargaining agreement. If women are working on a permanent basis with collective bargaining they will be well covered by codes based on these Conventions. Women, however, often do not work under these conditions. So codes need to extend beyond the formal Convention 'rights' and include the issues covered in segments B and C.

Codes require adherence to national legislation. As the authors point out, if national legislation promotes and protects 'decent work' then it will provide the framework for specific clauses in the code. Where state protection is limited, then the specific clauses in the codes must stand alone. Thus codes interact with national legislation and can mutually reinforce. The authors conclude that where there is good legislation but poor enforcement codes of conduct can become an important mechanism of enforcement. Where legislation is weak it is the code and relevant international Conventions that set the standard for segment A, and the provisions of the code alone that set the standards for segment B. There is little or no coverage of segment C.

Barrientos and Dolan (2006) found that codes had had an effect on outcome rights – in particular on health and safety and on hours of working, but not on process rights – to enable workers to organise for the improvement of their own rights. This reflected the 'inherent tension between the corporate and civil society perspectives on how to achieve international labour standards' generally (Barrientos and Dolan 2006: 714). The former prioritise technical or outcome standards while the latter prioritise universal or process rights. In other words, civil society actors wish to use these codes to empower workers to fight for access to decent work (a more bottom up model), while the corporate stakeholders want to contain the process within existing technical compliance systems (a top down model). It remains debateable whether women would fare much better in the empowerment model unless there was far more extensive coverage of issues within segment C, which would enable them to tackle the gendered assumptions about women's wider social position and access to trade unions. Existing auditing procedures in any case tend to be unsystematic in relation to gender issues. Few recognised the need for local knowledge and language or for the participation of local stakeholders. Most auditors from the northern companies were men.

Codes concentrate on one element of GVC governance and use a form of privatised rights discourse, without recognising the disciplines imposed by the market. The governance system allows dominant buyers to offset many of the risks of production and distribution on to producers, such as accepting falling competitive market prices and working to tight just-in-time production schedules. Producers cope with these risks and volatility of supply through flexible production and employment methods. Many of the risks are moved even further down the chain to women workers. Codes do little to redistribute value towards women in these chains (see Kabeer 2004; Luce 2005). The separation of trade and rights discourse is reproduced with the former maintaining its power.

What effect do these 'soft law' private standard initiatives, which are emerging as a significant feature in transnational labour market regulation, have on global governance more generally (Arthurs 2002: 487)? This self-regulatory approach has been the subject of considerable criticism from labour lawyers for being discretionary, unenforceable and, unlike the public standards of rights, specific rather than universal in its effects (Arthurs 2002; Muchlinski 2007). Macroeconomic policies have led to the withdrawal of states from intervention in agricultural markets in the Global South. Within the EU, responsibility for implementing food safety legislation has moved to the private sector. Instead standards are being set through alliances of corporations, NGOs and civil society groups. As Tallontire points out, although private standards initiatives (PSIs) originated in the Global North, they are emerging, with enthusiastic support of the IFIs, in the Global South. More positively 'private sector provision of services and activities previously the domain of government is being actively promoted'. PSIs may be 'more effective and efficient than state bodies, having greater capacity and resources'. They may also support 'new forms of cooperation between the private sector, the public sector and civil society to achieve development goals' (Tallontire 2007: 778) and 'allow new voices such as those of women to be heard in the establishment of norms . . . such that working conditions are improved and rights, particularly labour rights, are recognised and business becomes more socially, and environmentally, responsible' (Tallontire 2007: 788).

So initiatives born out of a combination of northern consumer concern for women exploited in the production of FFV, southern women activists working with women in Kenya, development agencies keen to support women's empowerment through better employment, the supermarkets and organisations of producers in Kenya could develop a regulatory framework that is more sensitive to the needs of women. These alliances would be a result of the increased sense of responsibility and connectedness engendered by the global value chain. This is corporate social responsibility transformed into care for development.

An alternative perspective would see these developments as marking a further shift in power away from state-based rights and solidarity based upon organised labour within trade unions. They marginalise or 'override states bodies that "ought" to take responsibility for regulation'. Not only is state capacity reduced but the private sector is enabled to 'reorganize aspects of the market to better suit its needs' (Tallontire 2007: 778). While business is interested in the nature of labour markets, it is not concerned about issues of high unemployment or poverty. It is not interested in the redistribution of wealth. Corporate social responsibility does not concern itself with general social welfare. Women's activism has led to the development, however patchy, of state-based gender policies and a rights framework. Women seek to engender responsibility within the state to implement these policies widely in order to tackle the divisions constructed between 'private' social reproductive family and community norms and 'public' work contexts. Reliance on production-focused PSIs creates a new division between these spheres.

These developments return us to the wider question relating to the territoriality of labour laws. Mundlak (2009) argues that trade law is premised on the free movement of capital while labour law is premised on sovereignty. Labour laws are regulated within states by states. They do not 'travel' well across borders: UK labour law will not cover workers 'outsourced' in India who provide services solely for a UK company. Can labour laws adapt to meet the challenges raised by the dismantling of key aspects of the traditional labour contract such as the proximity between those who employ and those who supply the labour? It is interesting to note that it was the ETI (a PSI-related institution) that made a connection between conditions for agricultural production and processing in the UK and those in East Africa. It found that all the leading UK suppliers to the supermarkets were using labour from gangmasters who were acting illegally (Lawrence 2004). In order to compete globally, they were operating under the same conditions as prevailed in the Global South (Lawrence 2004). If the UK law can be used to tackle the conditions of these workers in the same relationship with producers and retailers as those in the South why cannot southern workers use the same laws?[3] If state-based labour laws fail to offer this possibility, perhaps PSI can.

Fair trade and women farmers

Fair trade has its roots in the solidarity and charity movements of the mid twentieth century and focuses on providing support for small producers marginalised by the global trading system. Unlike ethical trading initiatives, it offers an alternative to conventional trade relations. Fair trade is distinct from the 'Fairtrade' mark which refers to the specific labelling system controlled by Fairtrade Labelling Organizations International and its member organisations (Barrientos and Dolan 2006: 4–6). It is defined as '. . . a trading partnership based on dialogue, transparency and respect that seeks greater equity in international trade. It contributes to sustainable developments by offering better

---

[3] The Gangmasters Licensing Act 2004 defines a gangmaster as anyone employing, supplying and/or supervising a worker to do work inter alia in agricultural and horticultural work and processing or packaging of any products derived therefrom. The Act establishes a Gangmasters Licensing Authority.

trading conditions to, and securing the rights of, marginalized producers and workers – especially in the South' (EFTA quoted in Barrientos and Dolan 2006: 6). Fair trade schemes now involve over one million small-scale producers and workers in over fifty countries in the South. Their products are sold in specialist shops and increasingly in supermarkets. In 2004, sales of labelled fair trade products generated an additional US$ 100 billion for producers and workers in developing countries (Barrientos and Dolan 2006: 7). The fairness comes from a model of equal partnership between producers and purchasers. 'Fair trade from the farmers' perspective is about a quality exchange – the best quality product, grown taking environmental care, delivered on time, in return for a better quality of life for the farmers and their families, including better opportunities for women' (Nicaraguan fair trade coffee cooperative reported in Hoskyns 2006: 7). Thus the discourse is one of trade not aid to lift disadvantaged producers out of poverty by redistributing (a little of) the value added of trade back to them.

Fairtrade labelling involves certification of products rather than their production. It acts as a conduit for products, ensuring that producers receive a fair price and a premium paid to invest in producer organisations and/or community improvements in health care, education, housing and local infrastructure. It provides an identifiable label for consumers. It has facilitated a rapid expansion in fair trade labelled products since 2000 (Barrientos and Dolan 2006: 9). Niche markets such as for organic fair trade goods are popular with donor agencies as well as civil society organisations because they seems to provide 'win-win-win' – environmental protection, poverty alleviation and economic growth (Fox and Vorley 2006). Fair trade discourse is not directly concerned with governing the supply chain. It links consumers with producers through understandings of unequal marketing relations. The discourse is focused more on equitable processes than outcomes. Fair trade does not necessarily mean gender-equitable trade. The impact of fair trading on gender relations within cooperatives and among producers varies although there are examples of empowerment for women (Hoskyns 2006).

Conclusions

The interactions between the market, state and community/family within agriculture in Kenya work to construct women's labour as less valuable than men's and to marginalise them in policy development. Community norms, which in themselves have been affected by colonial policies, distribute access to land in complex ways, reflecting the understanding of the different roles and contributions of men and women to social reproduction. Women use land both to produce family food but also where possible to contribute to family income; men use land 'productively'. The policies of the IFIs and the international trading system value productive use and are directed towards increasing this sector. The distinction between use and exchange is thereby accentuated and gendered. State land policies of formalisation and securitisation construct another dichotomy between ownership and use, with the former being given recognition in the state legal system and the latter relegated to the customary. This distinction and hierarchy is also gendered. It has enhanced men's negotiating power as legal owners to the detriment of women's claims to use. Women small farmers are disadvantaged within a disadvantaged group.

The market creates new opportunities for trade in agricultural products through diversification and access to the export market. It also produces new sources of paid employment. Kenyan horticultural producers have taken advantage of the new context. The growth in this export industry has offered women access to employment in more numbers than men. This provides an income but also potentially contributes to the strengthening of their position within the community and family as valued wage earners. This potential is, however, affected by the way in which women access this labour market, which is mediated through wider social values, which ensure that women must balance their care responsibilities with their paid work. Received understandings of what women are good at are reproduced in the workplace. As a result, women are concentrated in the casual, seasonal, most flexible, sector of the labour market. Men tend to be permanent and formal employees. Labour laws reinforce a gendered work hierarchy.

The governance of the global market in agriculture through the WTO and also through the value chains ensures that women working in Kenya are integral to the system. The UK, through its membership of the EU, is a member of the WTO. Workers in both countries face the disciplines imposed. In the opening up of the market in land and also horticultural exports to encourage competitiveness in a global context, we see the reconstruction of concepts. Informal working allows producers to shift the risks of production on to workers: elasticity of labour is seen as a competitive asset (Barrientos et al. 2003: 1515). Formal and informal forms of working are no longer denoted by distinct sectors, rather they are situated within these broader flexible production strategies, both within the small farmer sector and the horticultural value chains. These forms are gendered. Men tend to hold permanent jobs with higher wages while women are concentrated in the 'twilight' zone between the two types of work, increasingly engaged in 'informal' types of employment, moving 'flexibly' between productive and reproductive economy as required by the dictates of work and the wider societal values reflected within family structures. The plural legal frameworks reinforce divisions between gendered access to family-based resources and formal employment. The regulatory frameworks, which are based more broadly on gendered concepts relating to work, are being reconstructed by global markets.

Both Kenya and the UK are members of the ILO. Women workers in both countries experience the limitations of rights based upon male work patterns and assumptions. However, their legal positions are very different in that women within the UK have the benefit of EU labour protection as well as domestic labour law which is far more extensive than the minimum offered by Kenya. There is as yet little opportunity within the legal framework of Kenya to develop a deeper understanding of concepts of indirect discrimination and substantive equality, which we have seen in Europe in relation to the workplace. Even though women's labour is not valued in either the formal or informal sector, it is essential both for domestic food security and also for export development.

Can the global discourse of rights challenge the discourse of trade disciplines and enhance women's bargaining position within community and family contexts? We have seen the attempts to permeate trade discourses with labour standards using a trade-related discourse of agreement – a voluntary adoption of core labour standards by TNCs. The governance of GVC reveals the links involved and the inequalities generated. It has focused civil society action on to ethical trading initiatives, which attempt to reinforce state and international labour standards through codes of labour practice. We have seen that the inherent weaknesses in these legally constructed labour laws are reproduced within the codes, which fail to tackle the gendered context for labour markets – segment C. They are also moulded into the existing governance systems and do little to redistribute the value in these chains.

Impositions of labour standards are not popular with developing states. They were resisted in WTO discussions when attempts were made by some Global North states to make them a condition of trading. In the Global South they are seen often as neocolonial attempts to 'improve' but also further disadvantage the one asset that such states have – a supply of flexible labour. There is also cynicism over motives, given the same states' championing in the last twenty years of the fiscal and trade policies that have created this flexibility. Civil society discourse of caring champions fairness and justice through these measures. However, who is cared about and for what reason (see the debate between Kabeer 2004 and Luce 2005)? The focus is on the traded sector not women's position more generally in any particular society. This represents the most beneficial sector for women in many ways even if the benefits are not great. There are few other opportunities to work in paid employment in economies that have a tiny formal sector (10 per cent). The alternatives are eking out an existence in the informal, unregulated sector or struggling along as a small farmer. Core labour standards are predicated on a model of labour organisation developed in different times and different economies. They are process based, facilitating workers to join trade unions and to bargain collectively. Kabeer points out that women are very unlikely to join unions, which in any case are highly vulnerable in economies where there are queues of unemployed workers standing at the gates of commercial farms waiting for any opportunity to take up a job (Kabeer 2004).

The caring has to extend beyond this group of (women) workers, who become visible precisely because they are linked clearly to the global market via the governance of supply chains, to women who work as small farmers and in informal trading contexts both of whom are equally tied to the global market but less visible. How? One limited possibility is to use the discourse associated with fair trade (direct purchase, guaranteed minimum price and price premiums, credit allowances and long-term relationships) to 'reregulate' the GVC – to attempt to exert more control over supermarket retailers and redistribute value within the chain – to associate fairness with modest economic redistribution.

Should corporations care about the wider social responsibilities faced by their workers at any time – to refer back to segment C? Clearly they profit

> from the system of social reproduction which organises both the daily reproduction of the labour force (ie the processes which ensure that workers replenish their labour power between the end of one working period (day) and the next, and the generational reproduction of the labour force (the ongoing production and nurturing of working people who over time grow and develop into workers who supply labour power to the corporation). (Pearson 2007: 745)

This could be achieved through the payment of a local hypothecated 'Maria tax' based on the Tobin tax (0.1 per cent levied on every amount exchanged from one currency into another (Sandbu 2009; Tett 2009), which would provide services that complement the productive role of women such as transport systems, childcare, education and training and health services (Pearson 2007: 746). Kabeer also argues for redistribution through wider taxation:

> a global economy that is becoming increasingly interdependent and increasingly unequal, a struggle for some degree of redistribution from North to South, from rich to poor, from capital to labor, and from more to less privileged forms of labor can be the only basis on which claims to international solidarity on workers' rights can have any moral force. Such redistribution, moreover, has to be a matter of right rather than gift, welfare, charity or 'aid'. (Kabeer 2004: 30)

She focuses on a discourse of citizenship, not work, as the basis for this caring responsibility and argues for a universal citizen benefit that would provide a floor for everyone funded by some redistribution of the values created by global trade.

So we can care as individuals by buying fair trade grapefruits, which give a woman small farmer a little more and may facilitate her girl children going to school. We can care by only buying our cut flowers from retailers covered by the ETI code of practice. We can care through ensuring that employment rights internationally are developed to recognise women's gendered access to labour markets and cover the wider entitlements that make paid work possible. We can use the wider women's human rights framework to do this. We can ensure that land laws are equally gender sensitive by seeking to use CEDAW to develop a gendered understanding of a right to food.

To tackle the wider injustices, however, we need to find ways of moving from individual ethical actions and rights campaigns to tackling the trade value system. One way may be by imagining the impact of a universal citizen's social benefit – a social rather than labour minimum wage, funded by our consumption, which would combine concepts of individual entitlements with a wider understanding of relational justice. To quote Felicity Lawrence:

> Food that is produced in a way that degrades the environment is invariably the product of human degradation too. Food grown without a thought for judicious use of the world's resources is nearly always food that is nutritionally depleted too; food industrially processed without recognition of labour rights or equitable distribution is often food stripped of its goodness. The way we eat today is not just ecologically unsustainable, but also morally, socially and even biologically unsustainable. (Lawrence 2004).

6

Constructing body work

Introduction

'Moldovan sex slaves rescued in raid on UK brothels' (Tiraspol Times 2008); 'Young Polish care worker murdered in cross fire in South London' (Taylor (M) 2007); 'Filipino maid held in virtual slavery in Saudi home in London' (Taylor (R) 2007); 'Ghanaian nurses lose out in NHS pay restructuring' (Henry 2008).

Each headline constructs a particular identity for migrant women who undertake body work in the UK. The reasons why they have left their home countries, the conditions under which they have migrated, and the contexts in which they find themselves vary considerably. However they are all contributing to meeting the demand in the UK for services that are associated with aspects of social reproduction. These services are predominantly, although not exclusively, undertaken by women. In contrast to the production and consumption of commodities such as FFV discussed in the previous chapter, these forms of services require proximity and, in many instances, an intimate relationship between the provider and recipient consumer.

The increased commodification of body work is at the centre of the development of an international market in services. It has resulted in the global migration of women workers to meet the deficits created by increased demand. Economists relate the 'push' (reasons for leaving a home country) to the 'pull' (opportunities in the destination countries) in market terms and have until recently not paid much attention to the gender issues involved because the assumption has been that men migrate for work and women migrate as family members. The significant increase in primary migration by women challenges this assumption.

The next two chapters explore the network of relationships involved in the movement of people from more marginal economies to fill the perceived deficits in the provision of care in the Global North through various body work chains. This chapter is represented by the 'vertical' Global South pyramid and concentrates on 'push' factors in the migrants' home jurisdictions to explain why there has been such a huge increase in women migrating from the Global South and transitional economies. It considers how different identities of migrant women are constructed within countries and how macroeconomic, social and political processes contribute to the social and economic relationships that result in women's migration. In countries on the margins of the global economy, the majority of women live in households that have been described as 'semi prole-tarianised' (Wallerstein and Smith 1992) and so must 'diversify' into a range of activities to survive. Such households (and the wider economy) also rely heavily on women's unvalued (and unpaid) reproductive labour in nurturing and provisioning. One way of surviving in such a household is through migration of a household member either internally to urban areas, away from the reduced opportunities available in rural areas due to restructuring, or internationally. Women who migrate often use their hitherto unpaid household capabilities to provide them with 'adaptive social reproduction strategies' (Yeates 2009: 16). The demand for labour in the Global North results from changed ways of providing for social reproduction. The gendered relationship between social reproduction and production is central therefore to any analysis of body work chains and to an assessment of the distribution of benefits.

This chapter constructs four archetypes: a Moldovan woman associated with sex work; a female Polish social care worker; a Filipina female domestic/care worker; and a Ghanaian female nurse. In reality there are male Ghanaian care workers, Filipina nurses and Polish sex workers but the archetypes enable us to explore specific body work relationships and their regulation in specific social and economic contexts to better illustrate the range of factors at play and also to reinforce one of the main arguments in this book that attentiveness to gender relations within the Global South and, in these chapters, transitional societies, is essential. The chapter concentrates on the four source countries. Moldova is discussed in more detail than the other three countries because it has received little attention in gender literature other than through its association with 'trafficking'. It introduces the changes in the relationships between production and social reproduction in post-Communist societies, which apply also to Poland. The aim overall is to provide a more rounded review of the social and economic processes that pertain and contribute to the construction of gender relations.

The chapter makes use of the three commodity/value chain elements – the structure of inputs and outputs, territoriality, and governance – to understand the processes involved and also the distribution of value. It considers the local application of these elements in the specific context of the four 'sending' countries but broadens the discussion to understand how gender relations, such as differential access to local labour markets and levels of unchecked domestic violence, are constructed through the institutions of the market, state and family in the countries that produce the identities of migrant body workers and impact on women's decisions to migrate. The location of the 'producing' state in the global economic and political hierarchy plays an important part in the construction of particular body workers. Such positioning will have a major impact on the degree of 'legality' involved, the potential for exploitation and the distribution of the benefits of their work. Geographical location is therefore linked to local governance issues. Horizontal governance issues, which include the wider 'macro' institutional context of the world trade system, immigration, labour and social welfare laws and policies, professional regulations and informal social norms, are discussed in the next chapter. However, it is important to note here that each form of body work tends to be at least partially located within a different regulatory discourse, which contributes to the way in which body work is understood and valued in both sending and receiving countries.

Understanding how benefits (and value) are distributed within any body work chain is central to the theme of this book. Underpinning the discussion in these two linked chapters is the question: who is cared about? For instance, are those who migrate to provide the body work associated with care more cared about than those who provide sex, or do the regulatory frameworks associated with body work migration suggest otherwise? By integrating the body work approach within the Yeates extended care chain analysis within our four examples, we can begin to understand who gains and who bears the risks even if such an assessment would not satisfy the requirements of ortho-dox economists.

States of migration

The identity of a migrant woman is constructed partly through the level of anxiety that migration from a particular state arouses in the international policy community and within the 'receiving' state. The economic, social and political conditions in the home state affect and are affected by the governance of the body work chains. Are workers from a particular country seen as filling a specific gap in the labour market and thereby reducing pressure on labour costs or simply determined to leave in order to 'take advantage' of opportunities offered in a more prosperous state? Does their desire to leave spawn a network of dangerous entrepreneurial gangs or is it facilitated by legitimate commercial enterprises?

Moldovan 'sex slaves': market, state and family

Moldovan women, in the UK, are seen through the lens of trafficking. The suffering of those who are trafficked is well known. Women (and some men) are deceived by false promises of a job abroad and find themselves trapped in brothels with no documents, working in slave-like conditions. Vulnerable children and young people are abducted and subjected to violence as they are passed through a number of intermediaries to a final employer. While Moldovan citizens undoubtedly are trafficked, and into the UK, using this legally con-structed perspective to define the 'problem' is to empower a shakily constructed concept rather than Moldovan women. While the discourse of trafficking con-centrates on the benefits to the entrepreneurs who manage the chain and the losses to the women involved in this trade, it obscures the wider context, which affects relations of power in Moldova and contributes to women's decisions to migrate as a survival strategy.

Restructuring women's work for the market

The Federal Republic of Moldova is situated in Eastern Europe between the Ukraine and Romania. It has a population of approximately 4.3 million. Formerly part of the Union of Soviet Socialist Republics, it gained political independence in 1991 with the collapse of the Soviet Union. Because its economy was heavily integrated into the soviet system, it experienced huge economic and social upheavals as a result of this separation and also due to the 1998 Russian economic crisis (Pantiru et al. 2007). The economic restructuring, instigated under IFI structural adjustment policies, has not proceeded at the same pace or to the same degree as in many of the other countries in the region. It is the poorest country in Europe despite some evidence of economic growth recently (UNIFEM 2006). In 2005, 30 per cent of the population were estimated to be living below the poverty line, particularly concentrated in the south in the small rural towns (Abiala 2006: 92). It remains an agrarian economy despite the growth in the service sector. Its small industrial base is mainly located in the separatist region of Transnistria, which is effectively autonomous. It imports almost all of its energy from Russia and is therefore vulnerable to the politics of the region. Moldova has tried to focus more on its Western markets, with the EU being its main trading partner since 2003, but there is little interest from foreign investors (Burca 2006). The longer-term objective of joining the EU, supported by EU trade preferences in 2008, may encourage more market-oriented measures. Remittances (estimated at US$ 300 million per year) of the estimated 25 per cent of its economically active population working abroad accounted for one-third of its GDP in 2006 (IOM 2007a). It is deeply affected by corruption (Carasciuc 2007). Moldova is ranked as 111 out of 177 countries in the UN Human Development Index for 2007/2008: it would be ranked lower but for its very high adult literacy level. This legacy (and that of the higher educational achievement of women than men) of the soviet system is also evident in the gender-related development indices (55 out of 93 on the gender empowerment measure).

During the 'transition' from a planned to a market economy, millions of men and women in Eastern Europe and the former Soviet Union lost their jobs. In many respects there was an equal opportunity for impoverishment (see Fodor 2002 and the other contributions to *Communist and Post Communist Studies* 35 (4)). However, applying the 'gender pyramid' analysis to the context of transitional economies reveals differences in the ways in which segments A (formal contract terms) and B (work-related benefits) interrelate with C (wider social and economic entitlements) and have particular gender consequences. Employment among young women, in particular, declined with overall unemployment rates for women increasing to 'double-digit numbers in most transition countries' (UNIFEM 2006: 9). The familiar gender segmentation of the labour market pertains: men in manufacturing, construction and transport; women in education, health and social assistance and hospitality services (Burca 2006: 32 Table 4), with lower pay associated with the latter. In the transition economies, women increasingly constitute the public-sector workforce, which is now much smaller (UNIFEM 2006: 41), and men, the private sector. The two sectors are changing their relative economic advantages. The private sector commands potentially higher wage levels and work-related benefits such as contributions to pension funds, access to higher-quality medical and childcare and travel allowances (segments A and B) but 'few women can take advantage of the new opportunities (which come with higher risks) offered by international companies or domestic private sector firms' (UNIFEM 2006: 9).

'Women are increasingly crowded into less prestigious, underpaid public sector jobs' and have 'become active participants in the growing informal economy, where many receive minimum wages in unstable jobs that offer no benefits at all'. The consequences of these structural changes 'are strikingly different in a market economy than they are in a centrally-planned economy'. In the state socialist period, income differences were relatively small and people could survive on average wages. A '30% gender wage gap is more tolerable than when inequalities are large and women's wages do not meet a family's or even a single person's needs' (UNIFEM 2006: 9). Despite their better education, women are paid less than men wherever they are located, leading UNIFEM to conclude that 'the position of most women has undoubtedly deteriorated across Eastern Europe' (UNIFEM 2006: 9).

These structural changes are less marked in Moldova due to the slower pace of privatisation than in most other countries. Moldova's agricultural sector provided 42 per cent of women's employment (44 per cent of men's) in 2003. The growing service sectors in the wider region attract female workers although in Moldova this sector remains relatively small. Women are spread relatively evenly across both sectors (58 per cent in public-sector employment, 45 per cent in the 'private sector'). The private sector in Moldova, unlike other transitional economies, is not generally characterised by good-quality employment: 'it involves petty trading or providing personal services in an informal, underpaid and insecure setting'. Women feature strongly in 'own account' informal enterprises (UNIFEM 2006: 42–44). 'Reliance on informal networks and the informal economy often become the only available strategies left for survival' (Abiala 2006: 93).

Repositioning state and family: women as working mothers

The restructuring of the soviet system profoundly affected the role of the state in society, the relationship between production and social reproduction and the gender division of labour. Women's emancipation formed a central feature of the ideology of state socialism. Women were guaranteed equality in society and marriage but expected to be productive citizens (undertaking paid work and participating in politics). Unlike the nationalist ideologies of Africa and South Asia, socially reproductive values were not located primarily within the family, rather women were expected to learn the values of the system, which they were then to pass on to the next generation, in the public sphere. The family wage structure was abolished, women's access to benefits was in the main no longer derived through men but directly from the state: male rule was replaced by state rule (Fodor 2005: 2). The care of children was socialised and domestic labour communalised. Women were encouraged to acquire education leading to a highly educated female labour force.

Although in areas heavily dependent on agricultural production women remained much more closely tied to family-based farms, women's participation in the formal labour market was far higher than in Western Europe during this period. However the ideological project was resisted not only by men but also by women, who were obliged to do three jobs: productive work, political work and domestic labour at home given that the system did not reconstruct 'private' gender relations (Fodor 2002). The birth rate dropped sharply at a time when more workers were needed and governments recognised that they had under-valued the cost of providing domestic labour publicly rather than through women's unpaid family labour.

The states began to recognise women's roles as mothers within the work environment by providing employment-related social benefits such as maternity and paid family commitment leave (segment B-related benefits) much earlier again than in Western Europe. The Soviet constitution in Moldova granted women equality officially but in practice women were not treated as equals: 'Soviet law always regarded women as a "specific labour force" because of their maternal function' (citation removed) (Abiala 2006: 93). For instance, the Moldovan labour code contains a wide range of protective measures (See ABA/ CEELI 2006: 68–96) exempting women from inter alia hard physical labour, night work, overtime, and any requirement to engage in business trips while pregnant or with a child under three. As a consequence women were relegated to lower quality jobs (UNIFEM 2006:12).

The neoliberal market restructuring introduced in the 1990s severely cur-tailed this role of the state as mediator between family and market. State welfare benefits have been restructured and reduced in value. Women's ability to access the labour market is now more closely tied to their reproductive role, with the reduction in social support, and less to educational attainment. This context of deep social and economic disruption affects relationships and entitlements within the socially reproductive segment C of the pyramid. Under the soviet system, families continued to be based upon patriarchal relationships: the gender contract was not redefined (Abiala 2006: 93). The effects of the wider changes have resulted in a significant rise in alcoholism, ill health and early deaths among men. Women experience the consequences of this despair through substantially increased levels of domestic violence (Minnesota Advocates for Human Rights 2000) and the responsibilities associated with caring for sick men and the loss of income (if there was one) on death. Family breakdown increases the alienation of young men and women. There is also a backlash against what is perceived as the earlier regime's state-based imposition of women's emancipation in both the economy but also within politics. With the disintegration of the political project, and power relations within families unregulated, traditional patriarchal values more generally resurface (Ungureanu 2006; La Strada 2008a).

Reconstructing citizenship: women and men as equal citizens

Within the soviet system, regulation took place through state policy, administered bureaucratically. Women's (and men's) 'rights' to work and to social protection were understood as social and economic entitlements/obligations rather than civil rights. The introduction of market economics with the restructuring of state power provided the focus for policy development in the early period of transition. For instance, in Moldova, land was privatised. However since 1990 international and regional organisations have been heavily involved in the processes of binding countries into their frameworks and remoulding existing laws to provide an appropriate framework for 'democratisation' and accession to the EU. The gender area has been no exception. There is a complex network of organisations reporting on aspects of women's lives to various bodies. They recommend new laws and policies, produced with funds and 'technical' assistance, to ensure that Moldova becomes CEDAW or EU 'gender compliant'; meets the US or the EU trafficking standards; or civil rights organisations standards in the area of domestic violence laws. (See for example the complex role of different actors involved in the CEDAW Assessment Tool Report for Moldova (ABA/CEELI 2006).)

In 1994, Moldova adopted its new constitution which establishes a liberal democratic framework guaranteeing equality before the law (Article 16(2) and protection for private and family life (Article 48). Article 49 protects motherhood and under Article 50 mothers and children have the right to receive special protection and care. Article 43 provides citizens with a right to work and to be protected at work. Article 44 protects against forced labour. The Republic of Moldova became a State Party to CEDAW in 1994. Its initial country report submitted in 1998 recognised the difficulties women faced. The responses from the CEDAW committee strongly reinforced this perception, highlighting the lack of effective measure relating to domestic violence and introducing trafficking as a problem to be tackled. These points were reiterated in the second and third periodic reviews in 2006. The Shadow NGO report in 2006, which concentrated on discrimination in the area of employment (Burca 2006), and the 2007 implementation review, point to the continuing deep problems women face in economy and society. Moldova also signed the ILO Conventions on Discrimination in Employment and Occupation (1995), Equal Remuneration between men and women (1999) and the Revised European Social Charter (2001). All international Conventions are directly applicable in the domestic law (see ABA/CEELI 2006). The ECHR has also been deemed directly applicable by the Supreme Court.

Recent years have seen a number of domestic attempts to tackle gender issues. The key measure has been the introduction of the Law to Ensure Opportunities between Women and Men in 2006 along with the establishment of a Governmental Commission for Equality between Women and Men to oversee its implementation. This Act is seen as a major step forward by women's NGO and other bodies. It covers both direct and indirect discrimination in the workplace and outlaws unequal remuneration for work of equal value on the basis of sex. It covers sexual harassment in the workplace (until recently a very unfamiliar concept within Moldova). However the definition of unlawful discrimination is confined to sex not gender discrimination. Family relations are excluded from its provisions, thereby constructing a public/private divide.

Women's organisations struggle to argue for this liberal democratic conception of women's civil rights within the discredited and weakened state institutions where the 'rule of law' has very little legitimacy and little institutional backing (Bugaric 2008). Women have gained individual rights in the formal sector of employment but lost access to these jobs and social protection. The special measures to protect women as mothers in the labour market are now seen as barriers in a 'flexible' (and riskier) market economy, justifying discrimination against women. There are no specific enforcement mechanisms nor earmarked funds to change generally held perceptions that 'discrimination' against women is 'too harsh' a way of describing gender relations (ABA/CEELI 2006).

Domestic violence is common (see Winrock International 2005) but until recently the government has taken little responsibility for it. The Criminal Code has no specific provisions relating to domestic assault and prosecutions for domestic assaults are few (Minnesota Advocates for Human Rights 2000) and penalties low. The police continue to view such violence as a personal and social problem to be resolved within the family not through the state. This context of unchecked violence is seen as contributing to the trafficking of women with a 2003 UN Development Programme report recording that 80 per cent of trafficked women experienced domestic violence before they were trafficked (Abiala 2006: 94) and the International Organization for Migration (IOM) reporting between 50 and 100 per cent of those they assist in repatriation being previously subjected to domestic violence (ABA 2006/CEELI: 50).

This link with trafficking is probably the key to the recent legislative initiative (rather than the campaigning efforts of women's non-governmental organisations) that resulted in the adoption of the Law on Prevention and Combating of Domestic Violence, which came into force in 2008. It adopts the internationally recognised definition of violence, covering physical, psychological, economic and emotional duress (Article 2).

'Prostitution' and trafficking

Ideologically the socialist project of emancipation for women removed the need for women to be involved in prostitution. There were no laws and no 'prostitutes' just 'women with impudent behaviour or with light-minded behaviour' (Abiala 2006: 95). Prostitution was not 'abolished', and there is anecdotal evidence to suggest that it is increasing, but 'prostitution is currently not an issue of much debate' (Abiala 2006: 95).

A 2003 survey (reported in Abiala 2006) established that three-quarters of the population thought that prostitution was not justified; almost 60 per cent thought it was not a legitimate way of gaining independence or providing for a family. Conversely many connected 'trafficking' with unemployment: three-quarters thought that young women moved abroad to find work and 53 per cent suspected that women who migrated voluntarily knew they might be engaged in prostitution. However over 70 per cent thought that women were deceived by traffickers over the type of work they were going to do. One international organisation suggested that many young women glamorise prostitution, seeing it as an adventure and do not realise the harsh conditions under which women are often forced to work. They wanted to be 'hard currency prostitutes' with fancy clothes and cars (Minnesota Advocates for Human Rights 2000: 13).

The Moldovan government's initial CEDAW report linked the exploitation of prostitution with trafficking in women and described it as a new problem of social weakness (echoing the Soviet perception) that had spread rapidly, although the figures presented were low. The Criminal Code 2002 contains provisions relating to prostitution and trafficking. Activities associated with the prostitution transaction are punished by a fine or term of imprisonment of between two and five years with a heavier sentence if the crime is committed against a minor, by an organised criminal group, or results in grave consequences. Keeping a 'brothel' is no longer a criminal offence under Article 220. The transaction itself is covered by Article 171 of the Code on Administrative Offences and attracts lower fines and administrative arrest of up to twenty days unless the transactions are repeated within one year of the administrative offence. Advertising for prostitution is punished under the Administrative Code with a larger fine. Soliciting the services of a prostitute attracts no penalties. Thus the familiar binary, whereby male customers retain respectability while women are disdained and policed, is reinforced. The legal discourse constructs women as immoral others who are also naïve victims of 'pimps' and 'organised crime' (Abiala 2006: 101).

The Council of Europe and the CEDAW committee both recommend that Moldova criminalise soliciting to stigmatise customers and reduce demand. The alternative of further decriminalising prostitution to legitimate and tax it as a business was discussed in Parliament and by NGOs but, under heavy pressure from European countries and the US in 2004, was not pursued (Abiala 2006: 101). Trafficking, however, has become a matter of overwhelming policy interest and activity. Trafficking is covered by Articles 165 (adults) and 166 (minors) of the Criminal Code 2002 and attracts severe punishments. Article 362, amended by Law No. 376-XVI, covers the organisation of illegal migration. The Law on the Prevention and Combating of Trafficking in Human Beings 2005 is the outcome of a National Plan to combat trafficking first set up in 2001 (updated in 2005) in conjunction with international organisations. The Act brings domestic law more into conformity with the International Protocol to Prevent, Suppress and

Punish Trafficking in Persons, especially Women and Children (the Palermo Anti-Trafficking Protocol) (ratified 2005) and also the Council of Europe Convention on Action against Trafficking in Human Beings (ratified 2006). Moldova also has obligations relating to its treatment of this issue as a member of the Stability Pact for South Eastern Europe and the Organization for Security and Co-operation in Europe (OSCE). The domestic Act provides the first explicit definition of anti-discrimination on grounds of sex in Moldovan law, thus associating sex discrimination with trafficking. In addition to the legislation the National Plan covers a host of measures to strengthen both state and civil society responses to all aspects of trafficking. Since 2005 there has been an EU–Moldova Action Plan containing seven chapters (requiring some 300 actions) to be implemented in three years. Tackling trafficking effectively, while addressing the problems of the trafficked, figures in the objectives of the plan. Moldova has established a National Committee to Combat Trafficking in Human Beings to coordinate this plethora of provisions, plans and stakeholders, including a range of NGOs.

There are no reliable figures on trafficking from Moldova or elsewhere (see Wylie 2006 for a detailed discussion of the unreliability of the figures on trafficking in popular circulation). However, Moldova was 'relegated' to Tier 3 (the bottom, 'most at risk') of the US Department of State Trafficking in Persons Report in 2008, which estimates that over 1 per cent of approximately 750,000 Moldovans working abroad are victims of human trafficking. The number of women actually reported to the police is very low (364 in 2001, 235 in 2003 and 464 in 2005) but it is generally considered that only 10 per cent are identified and assisted (RCP 2003). Moldova is considered a major 'source' state within the South-East European (SEE) region. Research identifies young women who are poor from geographically isolated areas (rural/small towns) and poor regions within their countries, as at risk (in Moldova, the southern region of Cahul along the border with Romania). The Moldovan government is castigated internationally for not doing enough and urged to demonstrate vigorous efforts in relation to the detection and prosecution of traffickers (La Strada 2008b). At the same time, organisations working on rescue and repatriation record dropping numbers and identify, among other factors, the attitude of government officials who regularly refer to the victims of trafficking as 'prostitutes'.

Prostitution has been reconstructed in state legal discourse under the influence of external actors from a social vice to a problem of trafficking in women. Patriarchal values are reproduced in domestic laws, which see individual men as entitled to purchase sex while the women who provide it as immoral. Within the discourse of trafficking women may fall into the hands of organised criminals who deceive them, in which case women are not prostitutes but naïve victims of crime and sexual exploitation. This perception is not necessarily held by those responsible within the state for the implementation of the anti-trafficking measures. Thus, if women extricate themselves from the control of the traffickers, they are likely to be seen as prostitutes on return although the assumption behind much of the trafficking discourse is that women were not engaged in prostitution before they left.

There are wider problems over the use of law to tackle gender issues in Moldova. In a context where '[g]ender discrimination is rampant, unchecked and often unquestioned' (UNIFEM 2006: 18), laws are essentially declaratory, a result of collaboration between a weak, corrupt state and a range of international bodies intent on binding Moldova into wider frameworks to ensure its stability and a move towards democratisation. NGOs, themselves reliant on external funds, who argued for better laws to tackle gender injustice, now take responsibility for their implementation. While governments within SEE have accepted little responsibility for those who are subjected to trafficking, too much is expected of NGOs. Without denying the commitment of local civil society organisations to tackling trafficking, 'these initiatives make little real difference to the fates of those actually trapped in this trade' (Abiala 2006: 100 quoting the British Helsinki Human Rights Group).

This chasm between 'theory and practice' is characterised as the gap between de jure and de facto equality, an approach reminiscent of early liberal feminist analysis of UK and US legal systems (ABA/CEELI 2006). Few identify the lack of legitimacy of the rule of law itself, which is treated with considerable scepticism by Moldovans, not only because of the very high levels of corruption, which links government officials with organised crime (Abiala 2006: 99), but also because of the wider limitations of liberal democratic 'rights' to tackle the economic and social injustices that have resulted from the structural changes associated with globalisation. They seem oblivious to critiques of 'law and development' strategies, now transformed into 'rule of law' projects (Trubek and Galanter 1974; Faundez 1997; Carothers 1998, 2006; Trubek 2006, 2009).

Threatening migration: protecting state interests?

Given the dire economic and social circumstance in Moldova, it is not surprising that 71 per cent of Moldovan young people expressed a wish to move abroad in 2003 (Abiala 2006: 93). According to the Department of Migration of the Ministry of Labour and Social Affairs, 1 million passports were issued between 1996 and 2000 although there are conflicting estimates of the numbers of actual migrants ranging in 2004 from 265,000 to 650,000 (Pantiru et al. 2007: 9) with some suggesting 25 per cent or thereabouts of the population. Moldovans leave to work within the Commonwealth of Independent States (CIS), with roughly 60 per cent heading for Russia, often for seasonal and construction work, while others cross into the countries now within the EU for longer-term jobs. Female migrants are estimated to constitute roughly half of the total (Limanowska 2005: 113; Pantiru et al. 2007:10) with many heading for Italy because jobs are available in the services/ social care sector (Pantiru et al. 2007: 11; Limanowska 2005: 113). Migrants to Europe are generally more educated and from better-off families but their jobs in destination countries do not match their qualifications (Pantiru et al. 2007: 12).

It is estimated that over 40 per cent of the population lives in a household that receives remittances ((IOM 2007a; Pantiru et al. 2007). One survey found that remittances accounted for on average 87 per cent of the household budgets of interviewees, and in 66 per cent of migrant households they constituted the main or only source of income (Pantiru et al. 2007). About 30 per cent of families had managed to accumulate some savings, although the sums involved are relatively small, with women saving more than men (IOM 2008a). The 2006 survey found that remittances from EU migrants were significantly more than from the CIS because EU migrants tend to earn more, despite working in jobs below their qualification levels, and are expected to remit considerably more ((IOM 2007a: 9).

'[B]y 2006 the incidence of poverty fell to just over 20% for migrant households while it decreased only slightly to 32% for non-migrant households' with EU migrants faring the best (IOM 2007a: 11). However, there are costs. Households report emotional stress caused by separation and lack of parental care (IOM 2007a). Migration is perceived in Moldova to cause a breakdown in families with young children, abandoned when parents migrate. Although there are significant numbers of children in households where both parents migrate (Elena Prohnitchi quoted in Pantiru et al. 2007: 20), care chains are in operation and children benefit financially from high levels of remittances and are better off than their counterparts (Pantiru et al. 2007: 20). Very little of the migrants' savings finds its way into bank accounts and less than 7 per cent overall goes towards business development. Even so, on official figures, remittances amounted to one-third of Moldova's GDP in 2006, making it the most highly remittance-dependent economy in the world (IOM 2007a). Given that almost half of all remittances are sent informally, this level is likely to be higher.

Migration is therefore at the core of economy and society in Moldova. However, the legal channels of migration into the EU for persons living outside its boundaries who are simply fleeing poverty or generalised violence are very limited. Often to avoid being deemed 'illegal', migrants must claim political asylum, whatever the reason for their presence (Vachudova 2000), or be victims of trafficking. Otherwise people make their own often costly arrangements, with the assistance of a range of entrepreneurs, to leave without the appropriate documents. However, it would be wholly inappropriate to equate illegal or undocumented work with trafficking. Moldovan migration involves degrees of legality. In 2003, it was estimated that 36 per cent of Moldovan migrants were 'fully legal'; 13 per cent entered illegally but now have legal residence and a work permit; 14 per cent entered legally with legal residence but worked illegally; 21 per cent entered legally but now live and work illegally; and 15 per cent are 'fully illegal' (Pantiru et al. 2007 quoting Ghencea and Gudumac 2004: 12).

The large numbers of migrants seeking opportunities in more prosperous states, particularly those within the EU, or seeking refuge or asylum is seen as a major political and social problem for the EU member states. Moldova's economic and political position changed with the accession of Romania to the EU on 1 January 2007 because it is now situated on the border of the EU, stimulating roughly 750,000 requests from Moldovan citizens for Romanian citizenship. Citizens in the EU bordering countries face barriers to entry into this market as producers of goods and services and restrictions on their ability to move to be legal workers. Both exclusions provide an environment in which criminality and exploitation can flourish. Their governments, seeking membership of the EU in order to improve their position, must demonstrate that they are able to police their borders effectively and tackle 'illegal' migration and criminality, which involves policing their populations for these purposes. The EU foreign policy exports crime prevention strategies to strengthen the abilities of governments to control their borders; in effect to keep their citizens and their products out of the EU until such time as the country is permitted to join the club. Economic and social development policies that seek to improve the conditions of Moldovan citizens have received less finance and policy attention (Lindstrom 2004: 49; Limanowska 2005).

The EU's policy is to tie the countries on its eastern borders into networks of cooperation to foster economic growth but also to combat organised crime. There are a bewildering number of networks and partnerships weaving a web around these states (Lindstrom 2004: 50). Moldova is gradually harmonising its national legislation with European laws, particularly in the field of trade and commerce. It is also required to tackle unemployment among young people to stem the tide of migrants and to find ways of attracting migrants home. The National Migration Bureau (established under the 2002 Law on Migration), which oversees emigration and immigration, has entered into a range of bilateral labour agreements with third countries (Pantiru et al. 2007). Since 2001 'tourist' agencies used by migrants to handle their exit arrangements have been brought under state regulation with a consequent drop in number from 750 to 250 (Limanowska 2005: 113).

Controlling trafficking: protecting victims' interests?

The regional context for policy intervention around trafficking can be summed up as protecting the interests of the state (in this case primarily the states in the EU but also in other 'receiving' countries). In this 'repressive approach', supported by states and international organisations, measures concentrate on preventing migration and tackling organised crime within the home state using the framework provided by the UN Convention on Transnational Crime 2000 with its two protocols, one on smuggling and the other on trafficking (Limanowska 2005: 2). Anti-trafficking is heavily associated with measures to tackle criminality around migration, and victims of trafficking become instruments in the battle to beat organised crime.

Since 2003 there has been a growing disquiet with this approach, which has shown no noticeable results. On the contrary, Limanowska argues that the strategy has contributed to a growing acceptability of sexual exploitation and use of women's bodies for the profit of the community (2005). While the image of the 'trafficker' is a member of an organised criminal gang, in fact the most likely recruiter is an acquaintance or friend (RCP 2003). Lindstrom describes the expanding sex trafficking trade in the Balkans, which ties together traffickers, trafficked women and opponents of trafficking in the regional economy:

> Traffickers capitalize on permeable borders, political and military instability, economic dislocation, and rampant corruption to create efficient supply chains to satisfy the lucrative market for sex workers in Western Europe and the Balkans. Many of the methods and routes used to smuggle contraband and escape international sanctions during the wars of the early 1990s are now used to traffic persons ... trafficked women are viewed as commodities ... (Lindstrom, 2004: 45)

Many women's organisations have been incorporated into this market and have contributed to the construction of women as 'passive objects of interventions', persuaded by international organisations to cooperate with state institutions on their anti-trafficking initiatives (Djordjevic 2008: 167). This approach 'closed the door' against exploring who else, beyond 'vulnerable' women, might experience exploitation in the process of migration' (Djordjevic 2008: 167). Such strategies to tackle the exploitation of women migrating into sex work based on the legal constructions of trafficking obscure wider causes of injustice. 'Traffickers and trafficked women can be viewed as two complementary social forces participating in the trafficking economy. Both forces impair the licit channels of neoliberal restructuring, democratisation, and – the ultimate aim – EU accession' (Lindstrom 2004: 52).

Traffickers regularly outperform law enforcement agencies: after 'rescue' raids on bars and brothels, traffickers shift women to private locations, driving the trade more underground (Lindstrom 2004: 47). Law enforcement difficulties relating to the distinction between smuggling and trafficking compound problems. Trafficking defines Moldovan women who migrate, although the vast majority move under conditions of varying degrees of legality and exploitation, to work in a range of body work occupations (such as care workers in informal contexts in Italy (Caruso 2002)) only a small proportion of which involve sexual services. The construction of trafficked woman disassociates her from the activity with which she has been involved while trafficked (selling sex services) but she does not escape the status associated with prostitution if she returns home (after being rescued or escaping). Women sex workers who seek to migrate are particularly vulnerable to the traffickers but very unlikely to be seen as victims of trafficking (Djordjevic 2008: 173).

An alternative approach advocated by human rights organisations and some women's organisations involves 'empowerment', which would focus on the interests of the victims of human rights violations. Women would be able to protect themselves from trafficking if the causes of crime – poverty, discrimination and marginalisation in employment and the conditions under which women migrate – were addressed. They argue for a move away from anti-trafficking measures to a domestic economic development and empowerment strategy (RCP 2003; Limanowska 2005; Pantiru et al. 2007). Migrant women need incentives to stay. This involves the provision of decent local jobs, social protection and anti-discrimination measures, all of which are unlikely in the present economic and political context. It involves taking violence against women seriously in Moldova, which, despite recent legislation, is unlikely given the weakness of the state institutions and severe lack of legitimacy of law.

Remittances from migrants contribute significantly to state coffers yet the state is required to stem irregular migration by the very states whose policies have contributed to this form of migration. As we shall see in the next chapter, immigration policies of receiving states define the legal status of the migrants. Moldovan women need the prosperous states of Western Europe to grant quotas for migrant workers to enable them to leave legally. They also need to be able to work in jobs abroad that attract employment protection laws and policies. This requires receiving states to regularise the informal sectors of their economies in ways that do not further punish those who presently undertake these activities 'irregularly'. Many would argue that it also requires the decriminalisation of sex work to bring it within the formal market and labour regulation, thereby reducing the potential for criminal exploitation.

Polish social care workers: market, state and family

Polish women are not so heavily identified with one form of body work as Moldovans. However, those who migrate to the UK work primarily in the services sector and are increasingly identified with care work (Coyle 2007). They are seen as possessing positive attributes that make them very desirable care workers: reliable, skilled/educated but willing to work in care, holding appropriate (Christian/Catholic) values and, because of their country's position within the EU, available but unlikely to wish to stay permanently, and able to work legally within both public and private spheres. For example, a review of a specific recruitment initiative involving Polish care workers for an organisation providing social care reported a 'big success with both AG Care's service users and the commissioners of the contract that had been awarded in Bromley' (www.agcare. co.uk). Another social care organisation recruited in Poland when its UK campaign failed 'to attract the right calibre of people'. The organisation saw the pool of Polish labour as a 'dream come true'. They are 'all English speaking', 'very well qualified and some were over-qualified', have 'the right kind of values and caring values, but also have leadership characteristics to become managers within the care sector' (Jackson 2006).

Polish citizens share a common recent history with Moldova and others in the former state socialist countries. All experienced the enormous impact of the restructuring that followed the political collapse of the regimes, which is set out in detail above. The economic collapse and initial restructuring had devastating effects on the labour market position of both women and men within the region but while these events have produced differential gender impacts, these have not been as significant as some would have predicted in countries such as Poland (Fodor 2005; UNIFEM 2006). The positive legacy of the state socialist system of high levels of education for women and an expectation of work in a formal economy have meant that women have remained, and seek to remain, in the workplace despite very high levels of enduring unemployment. While state support for working mothers has been reduced it still provides rights to social support. Nevertheless women take primary responsibility for the management of 'work/family life' balance under the new circumstances. We have seen that in the UK there has been relatively strong political support under the recent Labour governments for positive measures to support those with caring responsibilities (mainly women) to remain in the labour market. There are institutional structures in place through which to implement and monitor these measures and a strong civil society sector to keep up the pressure. In contrast, in the former socialist states, women have reduced political representation in multi-party politics and there is a backlash against the emancipation project (Fuszara 2005). There is therefore limited enthusiasm to support women's position within the workplace and to tackle inherited, but also emerging, gender inequalities. The necessity of earning a living in the absence of jobs coupled with an inability to live on available state benefits, encourages educated women, as well as men, to consider migration.

Poland, however, is very differently placed to Moldova, not only in its physical location in Central Europe rather than in the western CIS. It has one of the highest levels of economic prosperity in the region with a high UN human development index of 37 (out of 177 in 2007–2008). The gender development score places it at twenty-third although the gender empowerment measure (relating to political involvement) places it at thirty-ninth. Poland adopted a 'shock therapy' approach to liberalisation rather than the unenthusiastic approach of Moldova and the economy recovered sooner. Crucially for overall prosperity, it has had a smooth transition into the EU to which it acceded in May 2004. This has facilitated inward investment and trade within the market and an increase in the private sector. Poland, however, has the highest unemployment rate in the EU although the rate has fallen considerably over the last decade to around 10 per cent in 2009. There was a sharp increase in long-term unemployment, particularly for women, after accession to the EU (UNIFEM 2006). Polish women already had a lower level of involvement in the labour market than most of the former state socialist societies. This dropped to 48 per cent because many older women (aged fifty-five plus) have withdrawn from the labour market altogether (UNIFEM 2006; Coyle 2007). The segregation of the labour market follows familiar lines with women clustered in service occupations, although due to their educational levels, women constitute 63 per cent of the professional and semi-professional occupations. There are significant wage gaps between men and women.

Liberal democracy has taken root and has grown quickly so that Polish citizens do not experience the same problems with governance as citizens of

Moldova. Poland has ratified six of the seven major international human rights instruments although, like many others, it has not ratified the International Migrant Workers Convention. Poland joined the Council of Europe in 1991 after it met the 'rule of law' entry requirements and adopted the ECHR. It is therefore integrated into the European human rights regime. Poland ratified CEDAW in 1980 and withdrew all reservations in 1997. Its 4th, 5th and 6th periodic reports under CEDAW were considered by the Committee in 2007. In its concluding remarks the Committee expressed concern over a number of aspects relating to state action to tackle discrimination against women and to promote gender equality (CEDAW 2007). It noted amendments to the Labour Code of 2001 and 2002, which introduced a chapter on equal treatment for men and women and provided a definition of direct and indirect discrimination; the Social Welfare Act 2004, which introduced crisis support including shelter provision for pregnant women and those with small children who face violence; and the Law on Combating Domestic Violence in 2005. However, it clearly considered that there was a lack of commitment to institutional development to implement these measures, which reflects a wider reluctance for more gender equality in society. Despite the 1997 Constitution commitment to equality before the law (Article 32) and equality between men and women 'in family, political, social and economic life' (Article 33), Parliament has consistently rejected attempts to introduce a comprehensive law on gender equality. Domestic violence continues to be viewed as a gender-neutral phenomenon. There are 'deep-rooted prejudice and stereotypical attitudes regarding the traditional division of roles and responsibilities of women and men in the family and in society at large' (CEDAW 2007). However membership of the EU, with its Social Charter, is now binding Poland into the normative social policy frameworks, including gender equality, and numerous projects aimed at encouraging gender justice, funded by the EU, are underway. There has been encouragement for the development of civil society organisations and there are now over 300 women's organisations (Coyle 2003; Fuszara 2005).

There has been considerable realignment of state welfare provisions in Poland, which affect both women's relationships with the state and their position within the family. Poland is now seen as a familial welfare state with women as the primary carers of children (Fodor 2005; UNIFEM 2006). There is little childcare provision for children under three so women are expected to leave the labour market. They no longer have automatic rights of support for their role as mothers directly from the state, derived from their role as individual workers. Women have become petitioners. Benefits to women are channelled through the family, which is now expected to take primary responsibility for dependents. Women must rely on husbands rather than the state. As in Moldova, a study of the effects on gender relations intra-household of these policies suggests that women in the transition period became the managers of poverty and experienced the consequences of men's response to despair which involved high levels of spending on alcohol (Tarkowska 2002). Women's pension rights are also differentially affected by reforms that reduce the value of 'caring credits' (Fodor 2005). Generally it is impossible to subsist on state unemployment benefits.

In these circumstances, migration within the EU is a very positive option for Polish workers generally, and young women in particular. 'Mobility, not employment, is the new opportunity created by transformation' (Coyle 2007). At any moment it is estimated that there are about two million Poles, mostly in their twenties and thirties, working abroad, about half of whom are women (Coyle 2007). Accession ensures that such migration is legal as long as requirements relating to employment registration are complied with in the UK, which is outside the Shengen zone. In contrast to Moldovan citizens, EU citizens are not affected by recent clampdowns on work visas in UK immigration policies. The transport infrastructure, including cheap flights, makes the journey and visits home relatively easy. Educated women, who have traditionally worked in the professional and semi-professional caring services sector, find their labour much in demand in the expanding social care market in the UK, while there is far less demand in the reduced public sector in Poland. Consequently migrants from Poland have constituted by far the largest group of accession country workers to move to the UK for work (constituting 447,000 of the 600,000 workers from the eight countries that applied for registration to work in the UK in 2006). The numbers have decreased significantly since, with workers returning due to the increasing strength of the Polish economy and the recession in the UK. However, it is estimated that there are about 600,000 Polish workers in the UK at any one time.

While the Polish economy is stronger than that of Moldova, the inflow of remittances from its workers abroad is still important. About £4.3 billion was remitted to Poland, amounting to 3 per cent of GDP in 2007. Polish women may increase their earning capacity substantially and be able to acquire some capital or remit funds home but they are often 'deskilled' in the process because they are not working in jobs commensurate with their educational qualifications. The care sector is associated with low skills, poor working conditions and low wages in both public and private domestic provision. The potential for exploitation is substantial in a poorly regulated market, which nonetheless expects its workers to provide forms of caring that are often not quantifiable or adequately valued in the market.

Filipina domestic workers: market, state and family

Filipina women are seen as the world's migrants: providing domestic and caring labour in households across the globe. Their attributed characteristics make them attractive to prospective employers. The export of their labour is central to state economic and political policy. The state markets its citizens' attributes actively in the international arena supported by flourishing migration support services. The state, however, seeks through its relatively well-developed governance processes to keep costs down by regulating the commercial market and seeking to ensure that its citizens are received as legitimate migrants. In return the state expects a direct share in remittances.

The Philippines is located in South East Asia and along with its neighbours within the region, it was subjected to colonialism by the European powers. It experienced 300 years of Spanish rule until the late nineteenth century, when the war between Spain and the US led to the latter taking control of the Philippines, which was resisted, and a civilian government was established in 1902. Formal independence came in 1946 at the end of World War 2, during which it was occupied by Japan. Two groups of countries emerged in South East Asia in the post-war era: those under Communist/Socialist rule that were not integrated into the developing international economy (Vietnam, Cambodia and Laos who traded with the Eastern bloc) and the others (excluding Burma). These latter five countries adopted market economics and pursued policies of industrialisation based on the export of labour-intensive manufactured goods (Kaur 2006). As the newly-industrialising countries of Southeast Asia (within the now expanded Association of Southeast Asian Nations ASEAN) they sustained economic growth until hit by the Asian economic and financial crisis of 1997–98. Singapore, Malaysia and Thailand have largely recovered; Indonesia and the Philippines, with a weaker economic base and continuing political instability, struggle. Within Asia, the Philippines economy is far weaker than that of Hong Kong or Japan. The Philippines is considered by the UN to fall into the category of a medium human development country and ranked ninetieth. Its gender development score places it higher at twentieth (UNDP 2007–8), forty-fifth on the gender empowerment measure.

The Asian Development Bank (ADB) reports that overall the Philippines economy has been improving in recent years: '[g]rowth and investment are increasingly concentrated in non-labor-intensive services, and there is little evidence of growth of a dynamic industry sector' (2008a). The 2008 Philippines Labour Force statistics record an unemployment rate of 7 per cent overall but with big differences between the national capital region (13 per cent) and elsewhere where it is lower. However, they also reveal an underemployment rate of 19 per cent, which is much lower in the capital region than elsewhere but very high in the agriculture sector (49 per cent) (Government of Philippines 2008). Women's participation in the labour force is low (37 per cent compared to men at 64 per cent in 2007). There are more unemployed men than women but more Filipina women work in low paid jobs (26 per cent compared with 11 per cent for men) (ADB 2008a; ILOa 2008). Jobs that offer a decent income for either men or women are scarce. The incidence of families living in poverty has increased to 27 per cent so that about 27.6 million people lived in poverty in 2006 (ADB 2008a).

Given these conditions the incentives for labour migration are considerable. The Philippines, like Moldova, is a major exporter of its labour. There were 8.23 million Filipinos abroad at the end of 2006, equivalent to 9.5 per cent of the resident population. Of the total, 3.56 million are permanent emigrants (ADB

2008a). The close association with the US enabled Filipino men to emigrate to work there or in its Pacific territories during the first part of the twentieth century. Hawaii became the major destination after restrictions were introduced in relation to the US (which were subsequently relaxed in the 1960s). Large numbers of Filipino men and later women emigrated (as family members) permanently to the US.

Almost four million Filipinos are overseas contract workers (with an estimated further 0.88 million irregular migrants (ADB 2008a). Temporary labour migration only emerged in the 1970s as a way of dealing with the shortage of local work because the economy could not keep up with population growth and there were severe balance of payments problems. The oil crisis in 1973, which exacerbated problems in the Philippines, fuelled massive infrastructural development in the Gulf States, which required large numbers of construction workers. The Overseas Foreign Workers (OFW) programme was intended to be a temporary measure but the demand for labour from the Middle East, East Asia and the other countries in South East Asia increased while the local conditions of low rates of foreign investment, instability, high unemployment, low wages and poverty continued. The number of OFWs increased rapidly and continues to do so. The majority of land-based OFWs continue to go to the Middle East (50 per cent) and Asia (38 per cent) while small numbers of workers (8 per cent) come to Europe (Asis 2006) (2004 figures)).

The enactment of the 1974 Labour Code which still governs all employment practices relating to Philippine workers and their employers provided the institutional framework for the development of the Overseas Foreign Workers (OFW) programme. It coverage is extensive ranging from pre deployment to obligations relating to remittances (Presidential Decree 442 as amended) (Asis 2006). The Philippines Overseas Employment Administration (POEA) is the government agency responsible for overseeing the processing of OFW contracts and the mandatory pre-deployment procedures. It is also responsible for licensing, regulating and monitoring private recruitment agencies, which, since 1976, have taken over the vast bulk of the recruitment and manning of workers (the term used for the recruitment of seafarers who constitute 20 per cent of OFWs) and placement with employers. There are now over 1,000 government-licensed agencies (with unknown numbers of unlicensed ones). Agencies are entitled to charge a standard fee for recruiting land-based OFWs. Excessive fees are often charged. POEA is responsible for all procedures up until the departure of the OFW. The Overseas Workers Welfare Association (OWWA) assumes responsibility for the workers once they are employed overseas, which involves the provision of support and welfare services to workers and their families. The Commission on Filipinos Overseas in the Office of the President oversees the welfare of permanent emigrants (Asis 2006).

A policy in relation to labour has been transformed into the state's economic and political development strategy. It provides a way by which the Philippines seeks to become internationally competitive in the global marketplace as a broker between its national 'stock' and those that wish to purchase it. As a result, a range of government agencies are actively involved in the process. POEA has a marketing branch engaged in extensive global market research, providing market matrices (intelligence) on a wide range of countries. These include data on markets and specific immigration rules and visa policies. The International Labour Affairs Service of the Department for Labour and Employment has labour attachés in host countries. Embassy and consular staff use diplomatic relations to improve country-specific awareness and to market Filipino labour (Rodriguez 2003).

The return on this investment is seen not only in the reduction of political pressure relating to unemployment but also in terms of remittance inflows, which more than doubled from US$ 6.2 billion to US$ 15.3 billion during the period 2000–2006 and now account for 13 per cent of GDP (ADB 2008a) making it the fifth largest recipient of remittances worldwide. Unlike in Moldova, 80 per cent of OFWs send these remittances through banks. Families spend them on fulfilling basic needs and there is evidence that increasing the proportion of remittances relative to the household income raises the likelihood of a household climbing out of poverty (ADB 2008a).

Filipina women migrate in roughly equal numbers to men but their destinations and jobs differ. Many men work as seafarers and construction workers in the Gulf and elsewhere while women constitute 90 per cent (150,000) of those who migrate to Hong Kong where they work primarily as domestic workers or 'maids' in private households. They also constitute a specific workforce in Japan where they work in the entertainment industry. Generally the vast majority of Filipina women work in these two sectors although the number of nurses is growing. Women migrant domestic workers, and their vulnerabilities, have become far more visible as their numbers have increased but also because of two high-profile tragedies, which highlighted the gendered nature of migration and its consequences. The first involved the death in 1991 of Maricris Sioson, an entertainer in Japan, and the second, the hanging in 1995 of a domestic worker, Flor Contemplacion, in Singapore after what most believed was the wrongful conviction for the murder of a fellow Filipina domestic worker and the child she looked after. Both exposed the limitations of the state to protect its citizens abroad.

Internationally the state seems to have been successful in branding its workers as the world's favourites while seeking to market this export commodity to its citizens as 'heroes of the nation'. However, these constructions are contested: Filipino migrant workers are more likely to describe themselves as 'forced labour'. The protests over the two deaths highlighted the contests over the 'domestic' and gendered identities of Filipina women. The gendered role of women within the family becomes problematic for two reasons: at home they can be seen as neglectful of their private domestic roles, not caring for the families and seeking to further their own interests through work overseas; once overseas the transfer of their labour from the private to the public domain of paid work can be seen as shaming their country because they fulfil low status jobs associated with the domestic sphere or the provision of sexualised services (Rodriguez 2005). Filipina women are seen as valuing their productive role (caring about money) instead of undertaking unpaid socially reproductive work for the good of their family and society, while at the same time, their state values its position as a world class exporter of maids and entertainers. The remittances of women working abroad finance a country that continues to discriminate against them. Until recently the government required female domestic workers to remit 50 per cent of their earnings. Now, they will receive letters from the state reminding them of their obligations under legislation to remit to their families. Non-migrant husbands, to whom the remittances are sent, are portrayed as making sacrifices for their families.

Widespread protests by Filipino workers and supportive NGOs across the globe in the aftermath of the hanging reflected longer-term grievances at the way in which the state seemed to treat them as economic commodities rather than citizens and led to the immediate passage of the 'magna carta' of migrant worker rights. The Migrant Workers and Overseas Filipinos Act (Republic Act 8042) 1995 declared that the welfare and rights of its citizens was the primary concern of the state (not a means to support and revive the economy) (Article 27). It established new protections for migrant workers, including banning migration to 'unsafe' countries (section 4), stiff penalties for illegal recruiters and free legal advice to those affected, support for workers overseas, whether legal or in unauthorised positions, and the establishment of Migrant Workers Resources Centres in countries with large numbers of workers. The original 1974 institutional framework is thus substantially enhanced by the provision of protections for migrant workers. It covers all aspects of labour migration from advice on opportunities; matching with employers; mandatory pre-departure seminars on what to expect, how to adapt and workers' rights; advice and support while overseas; to return and reintegration advice and assistance. More recently, the state has extended rights to vote while overseas to its workers (Absentee Voting Act 2003 (Republic Act 9189) and also enabled citizens to hold dual citizenship (Dual Citizenship Act 2004 (Republic Act 9225)). The Philippines has also ratified the Palermo Anti-Trafficking Protocol and the UN International Convention on the Rights of All Migrant Workers and Members of Their Families. It ratified CEDAW in 1981.

This framework is seen as a model of managing migration positively although it is not seen in such an uncritical light by campaigners on behalf of OFWs (Philippines Migrants Rights Watch 2004). It attracts delegations from other countries supported by international agencies such as the ILO and IOM. The Philippines has sought to re-establish its position in the global market as an honest broker of protected but also regulated labour, leading some to suggest that the Philippines has become a 'deterritorialized' state with formal political activity extended outside state boundaries (Solomon 2005).

The assumption behind these measures is that the best protection for workers is the possession of skills. Women domestic workers are constructed within the Act as vulnerable workers in need of skills training before they travel abroad. They are now required to undertake a training and education programme and a certificate of attendance at an appropriate seminar, commissioned from NGOs, forms one of the mandatory pre-departure documents. At these seminars women are reminded of their responsibilities to act appropriately overseas by continuing to care for their families at home and to ensure the steady supply of remittances. State paternalism constructs women migrants as 'innocents abroad', an image that can be reproduced by some local and international women's organisations (Rodriguez 2005).

While women who work in private households are often particularly vulnerable to exploitation, including of a sexual nature (Parreñas 2001), Filipino women workers are noted for their ability to resist within households and to organise against their state's policies on issues relating to wages, conditions of employment and contracts (Solomon 2005). This is much easier when there are large numbers in one location. It is less easy in the isolated circumstance of migration to Europe, and particularly the UK, where their method of entry and conditions of employment on specific visas relating to foreign domestic workers enhance isolation and the potential for exploitation, discussed in the next chapter.

While international organisations such as the ADB argue that labour migration is a 'win win' situation for both exporting and importing Asian economies (ADB 2008a), others are more sceptical about the developmental benefits that have been gained from thirty years of overseas employment. Some workers' organisations argue for a radical change in priorities, which would put a stop to mass emigration and concentrate on policies that allow citizens to live and work in their own country. However, the depth of economic integration within the global migration market is probably such that it is now relatively self-sustaining. Migration has produced global social networks, social capital (language skills, abilities to adapt and work in different cultural contexts) and use of remittances.

'Filipino society has become migration-savvy' (Asis 2006: 8). So, for instance, entrepreneurs in the Philippines, having identified a potential international shortfall of nurses, have set up nursing schools to train specifically for the export market and in the process to 'upgrade' the value of export labour. Huge numbers have enrolled, not surprisingly when Filipino nurses earn US$3,000–4,000 a month in the US, compared with US$75–200 a month in the Philippines (ADB 2008a). However, markets are risky: they depend considerably on the economic and political contexts in other states. Filipino nurses in the UK now constitute the second largest group of overseas recruits (after India). (See Yeates 2009 chapter 4 for discussion of Asian nursing care chains and Buchan (2008) for discussion of the UK recruitment of Filipino nurses.)

Ghanaian nurses: market, state and family

Owing to the legacy of colonialism, some Africans have been constructed as commonwealth citizens, and as such, British subjects, with, in theory, claims to settlement, although in the immediate post-war era it was never expected that these claims would be exercised. Subsequently, notions of state loyalty to subjects have been overlaid by 'fear of admission of numbers of non-white people' (Clayton 2008: 12). Commonwealth citizens are now constructed as potential labour migrants who can fill shortages in particular sectors, one of which being skilled health care workers, including nurses. English-speaking Ghanaian nurses with recognisable professional and appropriate (Christian) values offer much.

Chapter 4 discussed gender relations and law in sub-Saharan Africa. This section is therefore restricted to a brief introduction to Ghana in West Africa to provide the context for the migrant body work chain. It focuses not on the majority of women who work in agriculture but on those who seek to access and work in the still very small formal sector of employment. Health care, along with education, is an important area of public provision in which, proportionately, many women are employed. We have seen how the public sectors of the state socialist societies have been restructured under liberalisation and that similar processes were implemented within Africa under SAPs in the 1980s and 1990s. Health sector reforms have had huge consequences for those working in the public sectors of African countries as well as for citizens in need of health care.

Ghana was the first country in Africa to gain independence from British colonial rule in 1957. It has a population of approximately 23 million. It is rich in mineral deposits (exporting gold, diamond, bauxite and manganese) and is the world's second largest producer of cocoa, the export of which is crucial to the economy. Like much of sub-Saharan Africa, it has faced huge economic and political difficulties in the period since independence and has been subject to the interventions of the IFIs as well as various forms of international development assistance. Stabilisation and SAPs were used to tackle hyper-inflation in the 1980s at the expense of incomes, wages and employment levels. When the harshness of this regime proved unacceptable, the policies were toned down by both IFIs and state governments. However, trade and financial liberalisation policies designed to open up developing countries to world markets remain the dominant ideological approach. Having experienced SAPs between 1987 and 1997, Ghana remained heavily dependent on the IFIs for assistance and opted for debt relief under the Heavily Indebted Poor Country programme in 2002, which it still receives (DFID 2008). The economy has improved since 2000 although it remains very vulnerable to fluctuations in primary commodity prices. The discovery of major offshore oil reserves in June 2007 is raising expectations of a brighter future. Although about a quarter of Ghanaians still live below the national poverty line, Ghana has one of the fastest rates of overall poverty reduction in Africa (Ghana Living Standards Survey 2005/6 quoted in DFID (2008); ODI 2010). Ghana is therefore relatively prosperous in the context of Africa with roughly twice the per capita output of the poorer countries in West Africa. It is nonetheless 135th on the UN Human Development Index (UNDP 2007–2008).

Women form almost half of the economically active population and are found in all sectors of the economy. Fewer than 10 per cent of economically active women work in professional and technical activities. As we have seen in sub-Saharan Africa, women work in subsistence-related agriculture and constitute the core of the temporary, seasonal and casual workforce, while men generally undertake the fewer permanent jobs. Women's work is associated with insecurity, risk and lack of employment or social protection. Women constitute many of the poorest sections of society who need access to health care, particularly but not exclusively, for care relating to their reproductive role (Grown et al. 2006).

Health sector reform in middle- and low-income countries has been a major focus for international policymakers (World Bank 1993). The preferred approach varied somewhat among countries but the influence of the World Bank in promoting its package of reforms was substantial, particularly in countries in need of international financial support. Mackintosh and Tibandebage (2004) summarise this package in Africa as involving the liberalisation of private clinical provision and pharmaceutical sales, and promotion of a 'mix' of public, private and voluntary providers; a reduction in the role of government to one of regulating and priority-setting and responsibility for direct provision of services in public health and for ensuring access to primary care for the poorest; an increased use of contracting-out of services funded by government to independent providers; decentralisation of health systems to local government control; increased autonomy of hospital management and finance; and some hospital privatisation. These reforms are accompanied by user charges for government health services, for government-provided drugs and supplies, and for community-based health services; and a shift towards insurance rather than tax-based financing mechanisms, including mutual insurance schemes.

The Ghanaian government, with assistance from the international policy community, has sought to implement reforms to its health sector. In 1996 the Ghana Health Service (GHS) was established as a Public Service body under Act 525. It is an autonomous Executive Agency responsible for implementation of national policies under the control of the Minister for Health through its governing Council – the Ghana Health Service Council. The GHS continues to receive public funds but its employees are no longer part of the civil service. This distancing of the GHS from direct government control aimed to provide staff with a greater degree of managerial flexibility. Teaching hospitals, private and mission hospitals are not part of the GHS.

The health sector reform model involves the greater commodification of health care through the provision of specific services for market payment or government purchase on behalf of citizens. These changes can have different impacts on women and men. The introduction of user fees for health services (and education) will affect those without access to cash hardest, whether they are men or women. However, women are clustered in poorer paying jobs in the informal and subsistence sector, so must rely on husbands to provide the cash. There may be schemes to exempt the poor from payment but these are often not well targeted or misused and unknown to those in need of them. Social insurance schemes are limited to those in formal employment. Mutual, community-based schemes, based upon voluntary prepayment arrangements, can be flexible and suited to those with fluctuating sources of income but they have had low participation rates (Ghana Health Service 2007: 65–67).

There are contradictions in these health service reforms. Fees and 'cash and carry' health schemes have a regressive impact on poor women. However, more targeted and increased spending on lower-level health care, because state responsibility is now focused on preventative services, has a progressive potential but user fees form a barrier to access to these public services for the poorest, including many women. These measures have been implemented in a time of economic crisis, which has generally involved cuts in government spending and the removal of subsidies from basic goods such as food products. Women, because of their social roles as carers and provisioners, have absorbed most of the cutbacks that have resulted from these policies (Molyneux and Razavi 2002: 3).

Basic statistics indicate some improvement in health provision in Ghana in recent years (Ghana Health Service 2007). In relation to women in particular, HIV infection rates are going down (the prevalence of HIV infection among pregnant women attending antenatal clinics declined to 2.6 per cent in 2007). Both fertility and maternal death rates have dropped since 1990 with the latter dropping to a 409 maternal mortality ratio (per 100,000 live births) in 2008 (ranked 145th in the world: the UK ratio is 8.2 and ranks 23rd). The mortality rate for children under five also dropped to 112 per 1,000 in 2000 but has not improved since (the equivalent figure for the UK is 7). 'Antenatal care coverage has been sustained at a high level of about 85% but deliveries by skilled personnel have declined from 44.5% in 2006 to 34.9% in 2007' (Ghana Health Service 2007: iv). The reason for this drop in skilled delivery is the cessation of a fee service at public health facilities. The service was to be replaced by Health Insurance but the GHS report that many pregnant women have not registered. Money to purchase essential consumables ran out. Other factors include the inadequate number of practising midwives and 'women in distressed labour face challenges getting to a health facility and even where they are able to reach a facility, they do so in a poor state' (Ghana Health Service 2007: iv). The World Health Organization (WHO) reported in 2006 a total spending on health in 2003 of US$ 16 per capita, of which US$ 5 was public spending (the UK equivalent was US$ 1,508). However, even in 2001, the WHO estimated that the 'cost of a set of "essential interventions" was US$ 34 per capita per year, much of which would need to be public spending, or $45 to include some additional hospital services' (Mackintosh and Tibandebage 2004: 9).

The provision of accessible levels and quality of health services therefore remains a major problem for countries in Africa. Although Ghana has received very substantial international support to assist with debt repayment, it must still service its debts, which are rising again. Trade liberalisation, which involves the increasingly free flow of goods and services in international markets, involves cutting trade tariffs (taxes levied on imports and exports from a country). These taxes constitute a significant source of revenue for developing countries and their reduction affects the funds available for public investment.

SAPs, health sector reforms and the liberalisation in the trade in services also have significant effects on the labour market. Generally the restructuring of the public sector in Ghana under the adjustment policies involved a huge reduction in public employment. Total formal sector employment fell from 464,000 in 1985 to 186,000 in 1991, a loss of 278,000 (The Statesman 2007). Many low-skilled women public-sector workers lost their jobs. According to the 2000 census data, only 4 per cent of Ghanaian women are found in public-sector employment while 6 per cent are in private formal employment. The Ghana Living Standards Survey in 2000 reported that 44 per cent of women as opposed to 21 per cent of men have no formal education. Formal-sector employment now requires secondary or higher levels of education making it available to fewer than 6 per cent of women (in comparison to 16 per cent of men).

More specifically, one of the major constraints on the ability of the health service to deliver even basic services is a chronic shortage of health professionals, with an estimated shortfall of 1,171 doctors (65 per cent) and 9,021 nurses (68 per cent) in 2002 (Buchan and Dovlo 2004). In 2007, there were sixty-nine nurses per 100,000 population in Ghana and about seven doctors. The doctor and nurse population ratios improved slightly between 2001 and 2007 but if they are compared with the equivalent figure in the UK of 166 for doctors and 497 for nurses, the scale of the problem emerges. One reason for the shortage of health professionals has been limited funds to train but a major problem is out migration. Liberalisation facilitated dual practice whereby doctors (and nurses) can work both in the state sector and in private practice. This can lead to a concentration on the latter, increasing the already severe shortage of staff and adding to the workload of those who remain. The problem is particularly severe in rural areas because staff move to take up better opportunities in urban areas. Generally, conditions for those working in this new world of public health provision have been very tough. Wages are low, working conditions and facilities are poor, and career prospects limited. The additional pressure of the HIV/AIDS pandemic in Africa contributes to the difficulties by reducing the available workforce, increasing demands on an already overstretched health system and its personnel and adding to the risks of health workers. Surveys of health professionals establish that over 60 per cent intend to migrate. They cite a range of reasons associated with the factors discussed: poor living conditions; the overall harsh economic context; poor salaries; lack of promotion; the desire to gain experience; and a general sense of despondency (Buchan and Dovlo 2004). The incentives, therefore for those with skills to migrate are substantial (Buchan and Dovlo 2004: section 5; Mensah et al. 2005: 20).

Liberalisation of the trade in services, which is explored in the next chapter, has contributed to the development of an international market, which enables health service workers to migrate with relative ease. There has been a history of large-scale migration of skilled personnel from Ghana. As economic and social conditions deteriorated in the 1960s, skilled workers started to migrate to the other countries in West Africa, particularly Nigeria. An estimated 2 million Ghanaians left between 1974 and 1981(Bump 2006). After the mass expulsions from Nigeria in the early 1980s, migrants turned to North America and Europe. By the mid 1990s it was estimated that between 10 and 20 per cent of Ghana's population was living abroad, many of whom were skilled. The UK has been a prime destination due to colonial history. The Ghanaian community, the longest-standing and largest African migrant community in the UK, has grown steadily over the last fifteen or so years (Bump 2006). One reason for the rise in these numbers was the employment opportunities offered to Ghanaian nurses by the NHS, which was seeking to expand in 1998 and was chronically short of trained personnel. Large numbers of nurses took up this opportunity: 2,468 had sought verification of their qualifications in order to migrate by 2003. Between 2003 and 2007, 1,097 Ghanaian nurses held initial registration with the Nursing and Midwifery Council. While the UK is a prime destination, it is not the only one. Over 3,000 nurses in total sought verification of their qualifications to migrate between 1998 and 2003. In 2000, more than 500 nurses left Ghana, representing more than double the number of graduates produced in Ghana that year (Gerein and Green 2006). The migration of doctors is equally large scale (Mensah et al. 2005; Buchan and Dovlo 2004).

The loss of this skilled labour has a substantial impact on the provision of health services to Ghanaian citizens in general but the loss of nurses and mid-wives can also have particular effects on women because of their reproductive health needs (Gerein and Green 2006). It is also a huge loss to the Ghanaian state: of the 702 general practitioners and medical officers trained in Ghana between 1995 and 2002, 487 emigrated, representing 69 per cent of the total. 20 per cent of trained nurses emigrated in the same period. The compensation comes in the form of remittances, which Ghanaians send over long periods of time (Bump 2006: 9). The official sum involved in 2004 was estimated at US$1.2 billion, which is thought to be about half the actual total. Remittances are the second most important source of foreign exchange. Ghana, like the Philippines, has recog-nised the importance of this diaspora and since 2002 has enabled Ghanaians to hold dual citizenship. In addition, some professionals return from overseas, bringing with them their enhanced social capital.

Ghanaian women seeking to migrate as nurses are in a relatively strong position although they join Filipina nurses in the competitive global market for health care service workers. They are equally vulnerable to changes in national policies and as the number of nurses from the Philippines has risen, the numbers of Ghanaian nurses registering with the Nursing and Midwifery Council (the official UK body) dropped from over 350 in 2003 and 2004 to 38 in 2008. The total number of overseas registrations (outside the European Union) fell from over 14,000 in 2004 to 2,300 in 2008. By 2008, Ghanaians had been replaced by nurses from the Philippines (249) and India (1020). Both countries have Bilateral Migration Agreements covering nurses. EU registrations increased from 1,033 to 1,872 in the same period, of which 456 were from Poland.

Conclusion

The location of a state within the global economic and political framework affects the way in which its citizens migrate while the state of gender relations within a particular society contributes to migration decisions and patterns. Many women, because of their local circumstances, migrate to provide body services as nurses, carers, domestic workers and as sex workers. Substantial numbers of women (although not all) migrate from all the countries under consideration as a survival strategy for themselves and their families. They do so within different forms of chain governance, which dictate the degree of legality involved.

Economies within the former Soviet Bloc were liberalised, privatised and opened up to those wishing to invest from outside and to trade. As a result about a third of all jobs in the region were lost. At the same time the state welfare systems were dismantled because of the financial crisis but also because of a changed ideological relationship between the state and its citizens in which the state's commitment reduced. The socialist emancipation project was based on investment in women's human capital to enable them to be productive workers although it did not change intra-household gender relationships significantly. The huge pressures on the economy and the reduction of state social rights to support women as working mothers encouraged an ideological reassessment of women's role, which sought to reposition unpaid family caretaking. Women's access to social entitlements from the state to support their roles as social reproducers is more closely associated with their position within the family, reinforcing social norms that support unequal gender relationships in the family and society. The formal rights associated with liberal democracy and rule of law ideology that now underpin the legal systems have varying degrees of legitimacy and efficacy. Restructuring has precipitated mobility, particularly among younger women who seek to improve their life chances.

Both Moldovan and Polish states relieve pressures on unemployment and reduce welfare costs through the migration and remittances of their citizens. Although they share this background, Moldovan and Polish women are integrated into different body work chains involving the UK. The interaction between issues of territoriality (the geographical spread of the networks of labour) and governance are of considerable importance here. Moldovan women want to migrate to 'Europe' but it is exceedingly difficult for them to do so 'legally' because Moldova is politically located on the edge of, not within, the EU. Many Polish women are also keen to migrate but because they are EU citizens they have a legal right to move within its boundaries. If we then add the input/output elements (education and training, recruitment, organisation of the body work system, travel to the site of service delivery and the service provision) we see that many Moldovan women are likely to be positioned within lower-valued body work chains than their Polish counterparts. They possess fewer educational and training 'inputs'. The Moldovan state is 'weak' while the Polish state is far more institutionally developed. The latter is able to provide its citizens with more inputs and more protection. The Moldovan state's inability to meet the needs of and protect its female citizens offers lucrative opportunities for the enterprising to exploit weaknesses in a very poor economy and is fertile ground for corruption. The UK market for social care workers sees Polish women as highly attractive workers who can add value to a poorly resourced sector without too much pressure on wage costs. Moldovan women are not in a position to offer these attractions. Domestic labour chains, which are often predicated on informal working arrangements in households, require differently constructed inputs, which Moldovan women may be more likely to meet. However, there is little effective demand for what would be construed as illegal and low-value input labour in the UK (but see for Italy Bodolica and Spraggon 2008).

The recruitment of body workers and travel to the site of service can therefore take very different forms for migrants from the two states. Local and international (criminal) networks of entrepreneurs can flourish in the Moldovan environment. Some women become caught up in highly dangerous, exploitative situations when they move or are moved across borders and find themselves forced to work in the illicit end of the sex industry in the UK and elsewhere in Europe. Moldova's unenviable reputation is defined by this process: it is seen as a source country for international criminal trafficking and therefore attracts a great deal of regional and international policy attention. Polish women are actively sought after by 'legitimate' UK recruitment agencies to work within the formal social care sector, which provides care both in public institutional and private domiciliary settings. Their movement is facilitated by a network of relatively low-cost flights, trains and coaches.

The Philippines is located within Asia with few historical connections with the UK. Unlike Moldova and Poland, it is an explicit 'service exporting' economy, which seeks to produce workers with appropriate inputs for export labour markets and to integrate them within body work chains through its governance strategies. Filipina women are therefore found across the world providing body work services but are particularly concentrated in certain countries such as Hong Kong (domestic workers), Japan (entertainers) and North America (domestic workers and nurses). While the UK government has been willing to facilitate nursing chains for skilled Filipina women to fill deficits in public provision, it severely restricts less-valued body work migration for non-European citizens, providing only limited opportunities for legal migration, predominantly into domestic work in private households. Nonetheless, Filipina women can use the extensive recruitment networks that exist in the Philippines and internationally and their social knowledge of migration processes to migrate outside the state governance structures.

Ghana is located in a poor region of the world with historical links with the UK created through colonialism. Such links include professional health care networks, which facilitate nursing chains. The Ghanaian state unlike the Philippines, is a more reluctant contributor to the global nursing care chain, which is experienced as a drain on its precarious local health provision. While remittances are a valuable source of revenue, they are not directly available to the state to support health services. On the other hand, the rapidly integrating global nursing chain provides considerable opportunities for Ghanaian women to improve their life chances. Nurses have high value from educational and training inputs but also due to their perceived social attributes. Ghanaian nursing chains have been attractive to the UK NHS and private nursing homes. As we shall see in more detail in the next chapter, governance of this particular body work chain has changed relative power relations and adversely affected Ghanaian nurses in comparison to their Filipina counterparts.

The 'vertical' relationships within each jurisdiction contribute to the construction of the particular migration identities described at the beginning of this chapter. The consequence is that, in relation to the UK, Moldovan women are involved in relationships associated with trafficking (trafficked victims); Polish women in those associated with social care (valuable flexible social carers); Filipina woman are involved in networks based around domestic labour (as vulnerable attractive domestics); while Ghanaian women access professional nursing networks, which are characterised as brain drains (skilled but expendable workers).

The next chapter moves on to consider in more detail the governance aspects of these body work chains; to assess who gains and who loses; and to consider the contribution of governance measures to strategies for fairer, more just distributions of benefits.

7

Global body work markets

Introduction

The global market in services is growing rapidly, constituting an increasing part of the global economy. Due to enduring gender assumptions, women form the majority of the service workers who provide body work. Women now migrate in substantial numbers from transitional and southern economies, not as 'dependent' family members but primarily to fill deficits in consumer economies. This chapter concentrates on elements in the governance of global body work chains: the 'external' macroeconomic and international institutional frameworks; state-based regulation of immigration and labour laws; the particular regulatory framework in which the body work is performed; and the 'internal' processes associated with the specific chains. These overlap and interact to create an often highly complex and plural framework of regulation that contributes to the distribution of the risks and benefits associated with body work chains. They may increase the vulnerability of women migrants to exploitation and ensure that most of the gains are reaped by Global North states, their citizens and a variety of entrepreneurs to the detriment of individual migrants, their home communities and states. Alternatively they may provide a degree of protection and support for migrant workers so that they benefit as individuals and also offset the depletion of social capital (the value of resources that arise from social relationships such as trust and reciprocity) which results when individuals leave their families and communities to work in another society. These 'horizontal' regulatory processes interact with the 'vertical' regulatory contexts in both the 'sending' jurisdictions (Chapter 6) and the 'receiving' one (Chapter 3). The domestic institutional context for the provision of the body work, whether supplied through a public body, such as a hospital or nursing home, or a private household, affects the forms of regulation associated with it and also the status of the suppliers of that care.

One outcome of this plurality of regulation is that one body worker may be a service supplier trading in a global service market; a migrant worker with human and labour rights; and kinswoman caring for transnational family members. Another body worker who supplies sexual services is unlikely to be recognised either as a (legal) migrant who works or as a member of a family. Instead she is seen as victim, denied her human rights. Governance of the global market in body

work, within trade, rights and care discourses, is contributing to the reconstruction of meaning of the activities involved. Services, particularly those associated
with body work, sustain life and enhance social and individual well-being. To be
traded on the global market, they must be commodified and economically valued,
and in the process the services are detached from their specific context and the
social relations in which they are embedded (Kelsey 2008: 13). New products and
relationships between the service giver and receiver are created. These regulatory
regimes mask wider injustices when they concentrate wholly on the perceived
harm or benefit to individuals as migrants supplying a service because the socio-
economic inequalities between citizens, including those who migrate, in the
supplying and receiving states are obscured.

   This chapter assesses the impact of these governance contexts on the social
relations involved in the specific body work networks associated with our archetypes: nurses, social care workers, domestic and sex workers. We will see the range
of ways in which these processes contribute not only to the injustices faced by
migrant women working in the UK body work sectors but also how the benefits
and risks within these networks are distributed. A relational approach to gender
justice, based on body-work-chain and feminist ethic-of-care analysis coupled
with a pluralist understanding of legal regulation, allows us to re-examine the
potential injustices involved in body work chains and move beyond a narrowly
construed understanding of exploitation that focuses on the individual rights
of the body worker. Such an approach allows us to raise questions such as: are
there ways of redistributing the benefits (value) within body work chains that
would recognise more fully the value of reproductive labour and why are women
obliged to migrate as a survival strategy in order to meet their own and their
family's needs?

Demand within a trade framework: migration as service supply

Services account for over 70 per cent of GDP in developed countries and on
average about 50 per cent within developing countries. Services play a key role
in the facilitation of trade. In northern consumer societies around 70 per cent of
workers are employed in service activities and the number is rising in developing countries (about 30 per cent in general), particularly in the new global
economies such as India. Informal service provision remains significant in the
developing world (UNCTAD 2005: 2). Changes in ways of providing services
also affect levels of poverty and gender equality, not least because service
providers, including governments, are traditional employers of women.

   Trade in services represents an increasing amount of the total trade of developing countries, estimated to be over US$ 1,700 billion in 2005 (Kelsey 2008: 10)
constituting more than 20 per cent of total cross-border trade. Least developed
countries have a tiny fraction of the world trade in services, mostly transport
and travel services, although they have a 'comparative advantage in exports of
labour-intensive services' (UNCTAD 2005: 3). Because the services provided by

developing countries are concentrated in a limited number of activities such as tourism and, in some cases, the provision of migrant service workers, these flows are particularly vulnerable to external shocks such as security measures due to threats of terrorism or natural disasters.

The services trade balances vary substantially: North America and Europe have large surpluses, while sub-Saharan Africa runs large deficits. Foreign direct investment by US and European transnational companies has played a very important role in the development of service trade. Developed countries remain the main source of outward foreign and direct investment (FDI), some of which flows into developing countries although 'FDI flows in services between developing countries are growing faster ... [More] than one third of the FDI in developing countries ... originate[s] in other developing countries, with India, China, Brazil and South Africa being among the main players' (UNCTAD 2005: 3).

The General Agreement on Trade in Services (GATS): disembodied service providers

The rapid growth in the market in services has stimulated, and been underpinned by, the development of a multilateral trade framework within the WTO. The GATS, the result of the Uruguay round of negotiations, aims progressively to liberalise all domestic service sectors (Article 1) although 'services supplied in the exercise of government authority' are excluded (Article 1.3(b)). The liberalisation of services raises different and potentially more problematic issues to those associated with the trade in goods (Chapter 5) because ' for a service to be liberalised it must first be privatised (Williams 2003: 75). The defamiliarisation and commodification of care (Chapter 3) is a prerequisite for the development of a global market in social care services. Equally, the SAP and fiscal measures promulgated by the IFIs over the last two decades have been geared towards the development of such markets within transitional and Global South countries (see Williams 2003: 85–87; Kelsey 2006; Razavi and Staab 2010).

Liberalisation of services highlights the relationship between the market and the state because the barriers to trade in services are regulatory and therefore often politically sensitive. Service regulations (including administrative, technical and licensing requirements) often protect very powerful and vocal vested interests such as professional associations. However, they also include those seeking to protect the hard-fought-for social and labour protections of workers. National legislation that requires equal treatment of all workers, including wage parity, causes concern for trade experts because of its cost equalisation effect, which undermines the comparative advantage of the foreign service provider. From this perspective it is economically rational for temporary service suppliers fulfilling a service contract (for example a migrant construction workforce provided by a foreign firm for a specific contract) to be governed by the terms and conditions, including wage levels, prevailing in their home, not host, country.

'The purpose of the GATS is to reduce and eventually eliminate domestic protectionism and, in the longer run, to rationalise distortions in the market (Matsushita et al. 2006: 604). GATS recognises the right of a country to regulate services for legitimate purposes, including the right to introduce new regulations in order to meet national policy objectives, as long as these do not constitute unnecessary barriers to trade (Article VI.4) and respect the spirit of Article VI.4 (Article VI.5(a)(ii)). These necessity and legitimacy tests are vague and the subject of much discussion.

GATS creates two categories of obligations: general obligations within the framework agreement, which contains general rules and disciplines, and specific commitments within the national 'schedules' 'under which individual countries list specific commitments on service sectors and on activities within those sectors' (Williams 2003: 79). General obligations bind WTO members even if they have undertaken no specific commitments. Thus, for instance, Article II, Most Favoured Nation (MFN), requires a WTO member to treat all nurses in the same manner even if it has made no specific commitment to open up its market to foreign nurses. In theory either a state has to admit all nurses under the same conditions or keep them all out. In their national schedules, WTO members can list whole service sectors for liberalisation or more specific elements within any sector. They can also specify the mode of supply through which this element will be liberalised. Article 1.2 GATS defines four modes of supply of services: Mode 1 cross-border supply when neither the service supplier nor the service consumer has to move; Mode 2 consumption abroad where the consumer moves to the country where the service is supplied; Mode 3 commercial presence when the service supplier establishes a *commercial* presence in the country where he/she supplies the service; Mode 4 presence of *natural person* (that is, not a legal entity) when the service supplier is established (temporarily) in a different country (Matsushita et al. 2006: 616). The complex and confusing architecture of GATS has not encouraged much activity. Some therefore argue that the best way to view GATS is 'as a vehicle for future liberalization, rather than as an instrument which failed to generate any liberalization' (Matsushita et al. 2006: 693).

The benefits of liberalisation of services and their trade are in any case heavily disputed. On the positive side, the processes can bring greater investment in ailing under-invested areas, increase access to new technical and professional expertise, increase employment and generally improve the efficiency and quality of service provision. The same policies give rise to much concern over poor people's, of which women form a majority, access to essential services such as water, education and health once they are privatised. Privatisation of services can undermine social solidarity because the shift from direct state provision of welfare services to more marketised forms of provision transfers care giving costs to household economies (and women in particular within these).

Our focus here is with women who migrate to provide a range of care services, which in trade discourse is classified as service supply via mode 4: the movement of natural persons. Mode 4 supply is a particularly contentious area within trade discussions. While Global North states focus on the liberalisation of capital flows, particularly within modes 1 and 3, which enables them to undertake cross-border transactions and to establish a commercial presence in other member countries, they resist such liberalisation when it comes to labour movement via mode 4 (Winters 2005). Most international and regional policy bodies along with some Global South countries argue that both factors of production, labour and capital should receive the same treatment and that GATS should tackle the wide range of obstacles imposed by countries on the former as well as the latter. They consider that migration within mode 4 is a 'win win' welfare situation for Global North and South countries (UNCTAD 2004b: 2). Some countries have labour shortages while others have a comparative advantage in abundant cheap labour, both skilled and unskilled, which cannot be absorbed within their very limited formal sectors. They claim that liberalisation of the movement of workers could produce substantial gains for developing countries (Winters et al. 2003; UNCTAD 2005: 5). They also recognise the significance for developing countries of remittances made by migrants amounting to US$ 167 billion in 2005. Unofficial remittances probably double or triple this figure (id21 Insights 2006: 2). Such remittances improve Least Developed Countries' ability to meet the MDGs and provide a more stable and direct method of investment (not reliant on trickle down effects) than FDI.

Mode 4 is viewed as having positive effects, specifically for women via the 'trickle-down multiplier effect' of migration care chains (Puri 2004: 226; Mahler 2006). Women do not require capital (although it can involve substantial costs in fees) and 'structural adjustment costs of economic reform and liberalization . . . are easier to bear because of the cushion' provided by women's income' (Puri 2004: 232). GATS mode 4 is therefore seen as a way of 'gender mainstreaming into service industries' (UNCTAD 2004a: 2). There is also some recognition of the potential disadvantages. UNCTAD, for instance, has called for the costs incurred by individual women when working abroad as independent service suppliers delivering services without a contract to be recognised. It has pressed for the standardisation of employment contracts and for both host and home governments to ensure that individual workers are provided with support facilities (Puri 2004: 234). However, such matters are not debated in terms of the overwhelming economic disparities, which motivate both skilled and unskilled women to migrate under often highly unequal and exploitative conditions (Williams 2003).

GATS negotiations over mode 4 operate within the domain of economic trade discourse, which sees labour as a commodity, as a factor of production. Within this framework national immigration controls act as trade barriers, undermining the principle of comparative advantage. There is a general assumption that mode 4 relates to *temporary* presence although, as Matsushita et al. point out, this is only an assumption given there is no reference to time frame in GATS Article 1.2 (Matsushita et al. 2006: 617). The aim, therefore, is to separate long-term migration, which involves settlement, from trade-related movements, which supply a specific service and entail no entry to the domestic labour market. A mode 4 visa would offer a streamlined national entry and work permit procedure to facilitate temporary cross-border movement covered by GATS commitments (UNCTAD 2003). Least Developed Countries argue that such a visa would support liberalisation on behalf of semi-skilled (rather than unskilled) workers (Kategekwa 2006: 1) and have the added advantage of managed movement within a trade framework (attenuating permanent or 'illegal' migration), given that there are an estimated 200 million migrant workers (both documented and undocumented) who are economically active in a country other than their own (Id21 Insights 2006: 1). A general 'GATS' visa is highly unlikely to emerge in the near future for political reasons. (It is estimated that GATS mode 4 only accounts for little over 1 per cent of the total world service trade (ILO 2004: 83).) Instead, states far prefer to enter into bilateral or regional agreements to meet specific skill shortages because multilateral trade discourse is far removed from the highly sensitive area of migration policies over which states are determined to retain national control (Nielson 2002; Wallach and Tucker 2006).

Regional liberalisation: the EU Services Directive

Within the EU, there is already a presumption of the free movement of workers, the majority of whom will be providing services if and when they cross national borders (Article 3(c) and Article 39(9) (ex 48) EC treaty) (Clayton 2008 chapter 6.) Recently the EU has sought to liberalise the trade in other aspects of service provision to strengthen the existing internal market in goods. The 2006 Directive on Services in the Internal Market (2006/123/EC) establishes a 'freedom to provide services' framework in which member states should not impose national requirements on incoming service providers that do not meet principles of non-discrimination on grounds of nationality or location; necessity (on grounds of public policy, security, public health, or environmental protection); and proportionality (Article 16). It therefore tackles the legal and administrative barriers that deter or prevent the provision of services in another member state country (European Commission 2009). When it was initially proposed, the draft Directive contained a 'country of origin principle' whereby a company or individual was entitled, for a limited period, to provide services in another member state on the basis of its home country laws. This principle was vigorously opposed by the trade unions, and some member states, because they feared it would lead to 'social dumping' whereby employers would bring in cheaper labour from another country to undercut wage levels (subject to minimum wage legislation) and social protections more generally, and increase profits. This principle was removed and the preamble now states that the Directive does not affect prevailing terms and conditions of employment, social security laws, or the fundamental rights within the EU Charter of Fundamental Rights. However, concerns remain that the implementation of the Charter will adversely affect countries with high standards of social protection.

UK GATS visa?

Despite the trade negotiators' desires to separate GATS temporary movement
from the state-level discussion relating to control of migration, the difficulties
of achieving this can be see in relation to the UK. The Department for Business,
Innovation and Skills (BIS) (formerly the Department for Trade and Industry)
is responsible for the GATS negotiations within Europe and is also keen to
ensure, along with the Treasury, that the labour supply matches the requirements of the economy. The BIS is interested in the development gains associated with migration and remittances and the Home Office is keen to protect
national security and also to forestall the political anxieties associated with
perceived uncontrolled or high levels of immigration. In its consultation on the
WTO GATS negotiations, the BIS acknowledges that liberalisation is extremely
sensitive politically for many countries, given the close link between work
permits and immigration policy and that policy and practice intertwine temporary entry with permanent settlement (2002).

New Labour was seen to be in the forefront of countries moving towards some
form of GATS visa system. The Home Office, through a series of White Papers
(Home Office 2002, 2005a) preceding legislation on immigration, started the
process of untwining temporary work-related and permanent migration and to
associate migration and citizenship with investment capacities and skills.
Migration associated with the GATS is now covered within Tier 5 of the points-
based immigration system under the general heading of 'temporary migration
under international agreements'. Employers who do not have a commercial
presence in the EU, but whose base is in a country that is a member of the
WTO and signed up to the GATS agreement, can sponsor a service worker.
This allows employees who meet the requirements to work in the UK on service
contracts awarded by British organisations. They can remain for up to twenty-
four months and apply for further extension. It is clear, however, that there is still a
lack of integration between trade, immigration and development discourse and
that (unskilled) female body workers, who command little economic value, do not
figure in the day-to-day reality of trade discussions, irrespective of the arguments
made on their behalf. Immigration controls presently try not only to prevent all
non-European unskilled workers from entering the labour market, but also to keep
temporary skilled service workers from outside Europe to an absolute minimum.

'Illegal' migrants who work in poorly or non-regulated sectors raise interesting tensions between the economics and politics of migration. On one level
their very invisibility and cheapness, due to lack of regulation, is an advantage
to the state, employers and consumers of services. On another level, the state
loses revenue through non-payment of taxes and experiences the social costs
that are reflected in the disquiet of citizens about the unfairness to themselves
but also, when high-profile accidents or cases of mistreatment surface, to the
migrants. Women working invisibly in domestic settings, in the sex industry or
in poorly regulated care sectors are particularly exposed to these tensions.

Migrant working as a human right? The contested rights discourses of migration

The market is far ahead of the trade governance framework with many more people migrating across the world than is recognised in trade statistics or through formal multilateral or bilateral agreements. Generally, it is estimated that there were 191 million migrants in 2005 of which most were workers and their families (ILO 2006a: 2).

There are a number of regulatory frameworks associated with such movements: international human and labour rights; trafficking; state immigration laws; and domestic labour laws. '[T]here is no human right to move to a particular country' rather '[s]tates have the right to a system of law which, within the constraints of international law, regulates who may enter' (Clayton 2008: 94, chapter 4). State-based immigration laws and policies create the degree of legality (documentation) with which migrants enter or remain in a particular country. The status of a migrant worker within immigration law deeply affects their position within domestic labour laws.

As discussed in previous chapters, labour laws are predicated on a male worker model whereby employment law protects those who are able to work full time in a formal economy with no care responsibilities. As a result of the activism by women in the trade union movement, the ILO has developed a greater understanding and recognition of women's rights as workers. The ILO recognises that workers migrate under conditions not of their own making and seeks to ensure that such migration is 'undertaken by choice and not by necessity'. Fully voluntary migration is achieved by 'generating full and productive employment and decent for all, especially in countries of origin' (2006a: 4). Its Decent Work campaign is based on the presumption that there are 'fundamental differences between trade in goods and the migration of labor, including service providers' (Martin 2006: 6). The ILO rights-based discourse clearly recognises the hardships and abuses faced by migrant workers, including 'low wages, poor working conditions, virtual absence of social protection, denial of freedom of association and workers' rights, discrimination and xenophobia, as well as social exclusion' (2006a: 4; see also ILO 2004) and identifies women migrant workers, especially domestic workers and trafficked persons, as the most vulnerable to abuse of human and labour rights.

Within this rights discourse, its 1998 Declaration on Fundamental Principles and Rights at Work has sought to elevate certain standards contained within core Conventions to fundamental principles that apply within member states, irrespective of ratification. These principles bind all members states. All ILO labour standards contained within ratified Conventions apply equally to migrant workers unless otherwise stated in the particular instruments. There are two ILO Conventions that apply specifically to migrants although they have attracted little international recognition: the Migration for Employment

Convention (no. 97) 1949 (forty-two ratifications, including the UK); and Migrant Workers (Supplementary Provisions) Convention (no. 143) 1975 (eighteen ratifications, not including the UK). However there seems to be considerable tension between the principle of state sovereignty and the protection of the human rights of all non-citizens (aliens) in another state.

There has been a division of labour at an international policy level between the UN, which has focused on the rights of aliens (which includes undocumented migrant workers), and the ILO, which has jurisdiction in relation to workers. The UN General Assembly, concerned with the vulnerabilities of all migrant workers, moved into the domain of the ILO with its 1990 International Convention on the Protection of the Rights of All Migrant Workers and Members of their Families, which provides 'a comprehensive legal framework for migration policy and practice' (ILO 2006a: 5). The ILO has subsequently drawn on its provisions to produce a non-binding Multilateral Framework on Labour Migration (ILO 2006b) to assist countries to improve migration policies. Article 2 of the 1990 Convention provides a relatively wide definition of migrant worker which extends to some forms of self-employment. It recognises the greater human hardships faced by undocumented migrants: Part III is concerned with the human rights of all migrant workers and their families, including undocumented workers, which include protections against violence, employment rights and access to emergency medical care. However, reflecting tensions relating to state sovereignty, Part IV grants additional rights to documented workers and their families. Article 44 requires States Parties to ensure the protection of family life and have regard to the need for the unity of migrant workers' families. This provision is very weak and provides no rights of entry to family members. Also, having regard to sovereignty there are no rights to remain or settle. A further tension exists between provisions that protect those who work in an undocumented way and provisions that place responsibilities on States Parties (in Part VI) to prevent clandestine movements and trafficking and to ensure that employers do not collude in such activities (Cholewinski 2003: chapter 4).

Women as migrant workers are not distinguished in either the ILO or the UN Conventions. Neither tackle the specific problems women face due to the international divisions of labour that result in women working in poorly regulated areas or as domestic or sex workers who fall outside international and national labour law (ILO 2004: 58–63, 86–91; ILO 2006b). Trafficking is recognized in the UN Convention as a problem but only in relation to state preventative obligations, not in relation to the position of the trafficked workers. The Convention has languished politically, lending support to Piper's argument that there is a lack of visibility on the position of migrants within general human rights discourse with a further invisibility of female migrants (Piper 2005).

Unlike these provisions the women's rights framework insists on the interrelationship between social, economic, cultural, civil and political issues. Article 11 of the CEDAW recognises the contexts in which women work and seeks to ensure that States facilitate women's access to employment. Some therefore argue that it is preferable to use the discourse of women's human rights to tackle the issues facing women migrant workers rather than the UN or ILO Conventions (Satterthwaite 2005; Piper 2005).

Trafficking and migration 'rights'

Migration is not a new global phenomenon and its most pernicious coerced form, slavery, provoked the first global social movement, the anti-slavery movement. Coerced labour continued in the form of colonial indentured (bonded) labour and persists in the twenty-first century as debt bondage and the activities that are recast as trafficking.

Trafficking is one aspect of migration, with strong gender associations, that has been singled out for intense international attention, including by human and women's rights activists. The discourse of trafficking constructs a particular migrant who is distinguished from other workers by the nature of the processes involved in his/her movement. Trafficked persons may be involved in bonded or forced labour but the processes associated with their movement are criminalised (as abuses of state immigration laws) and as such those involved are channelled through domestic criminal justice systems. The migrant becomes a victim of exploitative practices and is assumed to have exercised no agency. Trafficked migrants must seek protections, including human rights, as abused persons rather than as abused workers under the ILO Conventions and within domestic labour protections.

The concept of trafficking has emerged from an earlier discourse on the 'white slave trade', which has been distinguished in international law, some would argue inappropriately, from prohibitions on slavery (Reilly 2006). The international framework is now provided by the International Protocol to Prevent, Suppress and Punish Trafficking in Persons, especially Women and Children 2000 (the Palermo Anti-Trafficking Protocol), which supplements the UN Convention against Transnational Organized Crime. Trafficking in persons is defined as

> the recruitment, transportation, transfer, harbouring or receipt of persons, by means of the threat or use of force or other forms of coercion, or abduction, of fraud, of deception, of the abuse of power or of a position of vulnerability or of the giving or receiving of payments or benefits to achieve the consent of a person having control over another person, for the purposes of sexual exploitation. (Article 3 (a))

The definition incorporates two elements that distinguish it from other activities associated with the process of migration: consent is irrelevant and exploitation is recognised. Despite the explicit reference to other forms of exploitation (Article 3 (a)) such as forced labour and slavery, this Protocol is heavily associated, through the campaigns of women's organisations and in the media, with prostitution. 'Exploitation of the prostitution of others' and 'other forms of sexual exploitation' are not defined and are not terms recognised under existing international law. The vagueness was deliberate because there was no consensus among the states on the legitimacy of prostitution (Doezema 2005). The coercive elements (which override consent) distinguish trafficking from smuggling, the subject of another Protocol under the International Organised Crime Convention. 'Smuggling of migrants' involves 'the procurement, in order to obtain, directly or indirectly, a financial or other material benefit, of the illegal entry of a person into a State Party of which the person is not a national or a permanent resident' (Article 3 (a)).

The Trafficking Protocol does recognise the horrific abuse that women can experience. As a result the victim is not to be treated as an illegal migrant but as a victim of a human rights abuse. Kelly argues that the definition avoids an 'over inclusive definition which encompasses all foreign women involved in prostitution' which 'legitimates heavy handed law enforcement "clean up" campaigns that result in mass deportations, while ignoring the traffickers' but also avoids an under-inclusive one, which 'excludes anyone where there is no evidence of "force" at the initial recruitment stage' which 'results in women being denied access to redress and support' (2003: 14). However, many disagree. There has been much debate over the difficulties with the two definitions and the processes associated with their implementation (Anker and Doomernik 2006; Agustin 2007). Trafficking is associated with women who are constructed as victims of exploitation with no agency, duped by criminals. Smuggling is associated with the actions of male migrants, knowingly using illegal processes to cross borders. The two actions are sharply delineated whereas in practice the processes involved in assisted migration are fluid with no clear boundaries.

The International Crime Convention with its Protocol on Trafficking came into force in 2003 and has been ratified by 117 countries in stark contrast to the Migrant Workers Convention of 1990, which also came into force in 2003 and had thirty-six States Parties in 2007, all from 'exporting' nations (and therefore not the UK). At a European regional level, there is a Council of Europe Convention on Action against Trafficking in Human Beings 2005 (in force in 2008), which seeks to ensure a gender-sensitive human rights-based approach (Article 5). It also introduces an element of rights for the women involved, which temporarily constructs them as cooperative victims rather than illegal immigrants subject to deportation. It provides 'victims' with a degree of state-based social support while such victims decide whether they will give evidence against traffickers and more support for the period of the prosecution if they agree to do this. They will be granted up to six months' leave to remain. Thereafter they may be able to apply for refugee status, which, if successful, would result in permanent residence. These provisions (and their domestic-law equivalents within individual states) link the 'rights' of victims to their willingness to take part in prosecutions and clearly prioritise state security measures relating to organised criminality. As Adams argues '[i]f a woman's safety and welfare were really the priority why shouldn't a woman who has escaped from a situation where she faced threats, violence and/or rape and fears reprisals have the right to stay in the UK?' (2003:136).

The EU is itself a signatory to the International Crime Convention. There is a European Council Framework on Combating Trafficking in Human Beings (2002), which requires all EU states, including those who acceded in 2004 and 2007, to amend or introduce legislation incorporating trafficking measures (Council Framework Decision 2002/629/JHA). A 2004 Council Directive sets out the way in which member states are to treat trafficked persons. The UK is a party to both the International Protocol and the Council of Europe Convention and as a member of the EU complies with its directives. The UK is not a party to the Migrant Workers Convention.

The different approaches in the Migrant Workers Convention (based on pursuing human and labour rights) and Trafficking Protocol (structured around criminal investigations associated with irregular immigration or organised crime) construct a dichotomy between the oppressed forced labourer (epitomised as the prostituted woman) and the empowered free wage labourer (migrant female worker) (Anderson 2006: 25), which undermines a general analysis of the issues associated with female migrant labour, particularly unskilled body workers. In reality there is a 'continuum of experiences and exploitative relations' (Anderson 2006: 26). Trafficking enables the state to claim to be protecting the human rights of a particular group of victim migrants by prosecuting criminal gangs who exploit them while pursuing immigration policies in a world of huge economic inequalities, which produce both legal and undocumented (but not victimised) migrants.

Construction legality: channelling migrant workers in the UK

All aliens possess human rights. Because the UK is a State Party to the ECHR, which is now domesticated through the provisions of the Human Rights Act 1998, immigration decisions are subject to the rights contained therein and anyone present in the UK (irrespective of the lawfulness of their presence) can make a claim. Thus all migrants have a right to freedom from inhuman or degrading treatment (Article 3); freedom from slavery or forced labour (Article 4); and a (qualified) right to family life (Article 8). However, although a few individual immigrants have sought to exercise their rights, particularly in relation to the right to family life, there are huge obstacles to mounting a legal claim and as yet limited likelihood of much substantial gain (Clayton 2008: 122–135). For the overwhelming majority of women body workers, the UK human rights framework offers little or no protection.

To enter, remain and work legally in the UK, migrants must comply with state-based immigration laws. These laws are a product of a colonial history and the earlier use of Commonwealth migrant labour, the UK's membership of the European Community, and its position within the global economy. Those seeking to enter who are not British citizens, Commonwealth citizens with a right of abode or nationals from the European Economic Area require leave to enter. For those requiring such leave there are a range of entry routes which determine the conditions and length of stay (see Clayton 2008 for detailed discussion). Owing to the political prominence in recent years of issues that relate to immigration, there has been an outpouring of legislation, policy documents and initiatives. One aim has been to 'modernise' work- and business-related immigration control. This has been achieved through the move to a points-based system which provides the means to better manage work-related-migration. It can deny lawful entry to all economic migrants from outside the European Economic Area (EEA) or permit entry to whatever number of skilled workers is seen as necessary to meet acute shortages. It can block all unskilled workers (in any of the tiers described below), any shortages being met from within the EEA. Visitors, who are permitted to stay for a maximum of six months, are not allowed to work or provide a service, although a family visitor may be able to provide informal family care on a temporary basis (Clayton 2008: 349). Visitors must have no recourse to public funds and are not entitled to 'switch' (move to another immigration category).

Highly skilled individuals who 'contribute to growth and productivity' fall within Tier 1 and do not need a sponsor or a job offer to enter. Tier 2 covers sponsored skilled workers 'with a job offer to fill gaps in the UK labour force'. Because individuals in these categories 'contribute to the UK growth and output, developing the UK skilled workforce and filling shortages in the labour market', they will have a route to settlement (Home Office 2006a: 15). Tiers 3 to 5 are 'temporary categories where the expectation is that people will return home at the end of their stay'. In almost all cases they will not be able to apply for settlement, and apart from students in Tier 4, are not able to switch categories (Home Office 2006a: 15). All will require a sponsor and have no recourse to public funds. Tier 3 covers low-skilled workers and is 'quota based, operator led, time limited, subject to review and only from countries with which the UK has effective returns arrangements' (Home Office 2006a: 29). Tier 3 is unavailable and is likely to remain so. Tier 5 covers a range of situations, including entry under an international agreement (including under GATS discussed earlier); private servants in diplomatic households; and a youth mobility scheme, replacing a number of specific schemes such as au pairs and working holiday makers (Clayton 2008 363–367).

Two categories yet to be integrated into the points scheme involve those with UK ancestry and domestic workers in private households. About 17,000 visas are granted each year to the latter (from the non-EU countries) to accompany their employers to the UK (Wittenburg 2008: 4). A sustained campaign by women's organisations on behalf of domestic workers has resulted in the granting of more entitlements to this group than might have been expected. Currently a migrant domestic worker can leave her employer if she is abused or exploited and her visa as a worker can be renewed annually as long as she is employed as a domestic worker in a private household full time. She is entitled to apply for settlement after five years. The government has proposed to include such workers as 'domestic assistants' in Tier 5 of the new points-based system and to restrict them to a six-month business visa, tied to a particular employer, thereby removing their status as employees and denying a route to settlement. Vigorous campaigning by Kalayaan and other organisations has stalled these proposals, at least for the time being (Wittenburg 2008).

The other category, those with UK ancestry, is only explained by the UK's colonial history. A Commonwealth citizen who is over seventeen and who has a grandparent born in the UK can gain entry clearance with a visa, which enables them to work, although they must not have recourse to public funds. In 2008, 6,690 people fell into this category, a majority of whom will seek to become permanent settlers after five years (Home Office 2009b: 18). This category has been singled out in GATS negotiations as a problem, with calls for its abolition. This route has been seen as discriminating against (black) citizens from new Commonwealth countries in favour of (white) citizens from old Commonwealth countries whose ancestors originally emigrated from the UK during colonialism.

Once an individual reaches the status of being settled (with an indefinite right to remain), they presently start to enjoy similar rights to those of citizens, such as wider access to state resources, and can apply for citizenship, which now has higher hurdles under the Borders, Immigration and Citizenship Act 2009. Approximately 149,000 persons were granted settled status in 2008 of which 61,000 were employment-related grants. The bulk (69 per cent) relate to family settlement (Home Office 2009b: 33–36). There are likely to be further changes in the immigration system to impose greater restrictions on these forms of migration and to reduce entitlements to settlement and citizenship. Historical commitments to the Commonwealth will be reduced even further (Home Office 2005a; Home Office 2005b: Home Office 2006a) and low-skilled workers will be denied entry and settlement.

Body workers as migrants or embodied employees?

How do female body workers 'fit' into this range of categories? The points-based system of immigration seeks to delineate and value workers according to attributes associated with skill. Women who have these characteristics, such as nurses, may be able to enter through Tier 2 if sponsored by employers or Tier 5 if they enter under a bilateral agreement (discussed below). For those seeking to work as 'unskilled' carers from outside Europe there are limited possibilities. These include using the categories of ancestral rights; domestic worker in a private household; or youth mobility. Most categories have specific limits to the type of work undertaken, the hours involved and the initial length of stay.

Some women will have entered in a fully documented way but then undertake work in breach of their particular visa stipulations and therefore move into a twilight world of partial documentation; others will have overstayed or entered without the appropriate documents. Rules that prioritise skill inevitably create a continuum of legality and illegality with the unskilled care and domestic workers from outside Europe positioned at the latter end (Anderson 2006; Anderson et al. 2006; Datta et al. 2006). The interaction between employment and immigration rules can place women care and domestic workers in highly vulnerable positions (Anderson 2006). European women are able to move to the UK freely but are constructed as relatively low-value temporary workers. Workers from the A8 countries (central and eastern European countries that joined in 2004 and 2007) are required to register with the UK Border Agency if they wish to be employed for more than a month. The requirement to register ceases on completion of twelve months' continuous employment. It does not apply to those who are self-employed. Care employment agencies therefore are keen to promote the attractions of self-employment to European care workers.

The employment rights enjoyed by migrant women body workers depend, therefore, on both immigration and employment status. If they provide professional care in the formal sphere, as, for example, nurses working in the NHS, they will share similar employment rights to other workers including rights relating to equal pay and protection from sex and race discrimination. Equally, if a documented migrant woman works for a local authority or a private-sector employer who provides residential or domiciliary social care, she will enjoy the same rights as other workers even though working conditions and pay for all workers are poor in this sector. Employers face the prospect of a criminal conviction if they employ 'illegal' migrants, even if there are many incentives for both employer and worker to establish such a relationship, which nonetheless can place the worker in a vulnerable position.

As the campaigns relating to the status of domestic workers in private households show, immigration law has the potential to deny migrants the status of workers altogether even though 'local' domestic workers would be covered by labour laws. While the campaign has secured, for the time being, recognition of their status as employees who are entitled to receive basic employment law protection such as the National Minimum Wage, statutory holiday pay and a notice period, a woman's immigration status still makes her highly vulnerable in a private household. Any further irregularity in this status simply adds to her vulnerability despite potential labour protections (Wittenburg 2008). If a woman is 'trafficked' then she is a 'non-worker' victim rather than a bonded worker.

Because of the demand for care of the elderly and the transfer of responsibility to procure this to those who are in need of care, there is a growing demand for workers to undertake such work. Domestic and care work have both been defined by the ILO recently. A domestic worker is one who organises, carries out, and supervises housekeeping functions in private households, with or without the support of subordinate staff. The duties relate primarily to the day-to-day tasks that are necessary to manage a household but may include assisting in instances of minor illness or injury by taking temperature or applying a bandage (ILO 2008b). A care worker, on the other hand, 'provides routine personal care, such as bathing, dressing, or grooming, to the elderly, convalescent, or disabled persons in their own homes or in independent residential care facilities (ILO 2008b).

There is evidence, however, that social care work is increasingly being undertaken in private households by women workers who entered the UK on a domestic worker visa (Gordolan and Lalani 2009). Thus immigration laws that restrict the entry of non-European low-skilled social care workers may encourage the conflation of two different forms of body work when it is undertaken within the domain of the household and within the construction of domestic work (see Caruso 2002 for a discussion of the position in Italy). As care moves into the private sphere it becomes less valued, less 'work' and more 'help' within the domain of familial 'caring' and attracts less employment protection. A migrant woman worker faces problems in addition to those faced by white woman body workers, particularly in relation to racism. If she works within the home for a private employer, laws relating to racial discrimination are not available. This type of work may offer opportunities for those with irregular immigration status or formal restrictions on ability to work. However, these developments not only increase the potential to exploit vulnerable women migrant workers but also undermine attempts to improve the status of social care work through increased regulation and requirements for higher skill levels.

Care talk: working women as transnational family members

The 'home' contexts demonstrated the way in which gender relations contribute to the conditions under which women migrate. Women may migrate as an economic survival strategy for their family but also because they face discrimination in access to resources, violence or insecurity due to their status as single parents or being divorced or widowed or because they are deemed to have behaved inappropriately more generally.

Although the UK is not a State Party to the UN Migrant Workers Convention, which considers that family unity is a human right of migrant workers, the 1998 Human Rights Act provides a qualified right to family life. Nonetheless, the imperatives of state sovereignty ensure that in practice the UK state can be more concerned to prevent family unification than to promote it. Immigration status defines a migrant woman's ability to bring her family members with her. While skilled workers in the UK can usually, if they wish, bring family members who themselves have a recognised status, unskilled temporary workers cannot. However, if migrant women workers do have their families with them they can face further difficulties in meeting their caring needs. They may be care workers but they are not generally constructed by state social welfare or employment laws as workers who care. They have very limited access to public resources until they obtain indefinite leave to remain, a status which many will not be able to achieve. Caring for families is a particular problem for low-paid migrant women who must organise and finance their own care responsibilities. There can be very different levels of entitlements for different groups of migrant women in the welfare regimes of Europe (Kofman 2005). Many will be ineligible for, or have great difficulty accessing, the family-friendly, flexible employment rights and policies, discussed in Chapter 3, which go some way to support local female (and male) workers.

If their families are left at home out of choice or necessity then they face the problems associated with physical separation. Workers from outside Europe whose status is uncertain cannot risk leaving the country or will face further costs to secure (undocumented) re-entry. Equally, those who enter as temporary unskilled workers, who may have expended considerable sums to gain entry, may well be very reluctant to leave and jeopardise their chances of re-entry when they know that the state is imposing even tighter restrictions on this category. EU citizens, on the other hand, can travel back and forth with relative ease due to their more secure status and relative geographical proximity. 'Open channels' not only offer greater opportunity for family life but also are far more likely to encourage movement between the two states. Restrictions create permanence (and often increasingly undocumented and vulnerable workers).

Care is met primarily through remittances to families. Although there is evidence that remittances sustain and support the general well-being of families (NEF 2006: 8; Id21 Insights 2006), much less attention has been paid in mainstream debates to the cost of migration on social and gender relations, particularly within the families of migrant women (Piper 2005). While Hochschild (2000b) points to the expropriation of emotional labour by employers in care chains, subsequent studies of transnational families present a more complex picture of the effects of migration on family relationships (Bryceson and Vuorela 2002; Global Networks 2005; Pinnawala 2008). Women take on the breadwinning role through remittances (Parreñas 2005; Pinnawala 2008), which has a major impact on the 'gender contract' and family composition. In the Philippines, the families of male migrants are in general nuclear with female spouses continuing to take responsibility for care. In contrast, when women from both working-class and middle-class families migrate, there is a reconstitution of the division of labour through an extensive network of social relationships split solely among women. 'Fathers stay out of the picture, often avoiding any nurturing responsibilities by relocating to another island in the Philippines or, if around their family, by never asking about their children's emotional well-being' (Parreñas 2005: 332). Migrant women sustain their 'day-to-day' nurturing roles through the use of various channels of communication that are now available although their ability to maintain contact depends on availability within the home context and on the financial position of the migrant woman (Parreñas 2005). A woman in effect working as bonded labour in a brothel will have little opportunity to sustain her caring relationships. Despite the very substantial efforts made by migrant women to continue to nurture at a distance, their children still felt that it was not enough, reinforced by a continuing social norm that it is a women's job to provide proximate care in families. As Parreñas points out this is a 'no win situation' for women unless gender ideology within the Philippines changes (2005: 333).

A further argument that is made in favour of migration is that it increases the human resources to individuals and home countries through the skills and experiences gained during migration. In fact, women tend to find that their status as a migrant worker reduces the values of their skills and that they are obliged to work in less valued positions (Henry 2008). Thus skilled nurses may find themselves working as social care workers in private-sector nursing homes (Piper 2005). Many low-skilled social care and domestic workers have no access to skills development and so return home with few formally enhanced capacities. However, even if women face a reduction in their status in the host country, they may be empowered at home by their experiences of migration and their ability to contribute to household and community resources. This relative advantage may be retained on return although with no enhanced skills this will be difficult. They may also face real problems with reintegration and rebuilding broken family relationships.

The wider impact of the human and social capital costs of migration, which involve the depletion in socially reproductive resources in the home society, is often overlooked (Piper 2005). Within the UK, the various governance frameworks fail to recognise that migrant women are also family members who face more challenges than other working carers /parents in maintaining their caring relationships.

Fairer caring for body workers?

In trade discourse, migrants respond rationally to the market and move to enhance their comparative advantage: they are economic agents exercising choice. The subject is a highly autonomous agent, a disembodied factor of production, not a woman compelled by the vicissitudes associated with socio-economic survival to leave her home. She seems to be neither a 'human' nor a 'social' being. While being 'deterritorialised' through an ability to sell labour power anywhere, women gain minimal links with the state in which the service is provided. One type of worker, due to their political link with another territory, is separated out in a state in exchange for freer access to that state. Women's value here is associated with an ability to maximise comparative advantage as 'natural' service providers (mode 4) (see Rittich 2002). Contemporary forms of globalisation have challenged the wider regulatory framework of labour rights that have resulted from the efforts of the organised labour movement. State provision, including work-related and social benefits, is often viewed as an impediment to the operation of the free market, leading to pressures to liberalise labour contracts, including through the free market in services advocated by GATS, and thereby loosen the territorial base of labour laws. A universal GATS visa that was available to body work service providers could, it is argued on behalf of Global South women, greatly facilitate movement and in theory reduce the present costs associated with circumventing existing barriers. Such moves would remove, in the name of free trade, restrictive immigration rules and 'protectionism' (the inclusion of migrants in local social and labour law entitlements).

A universal rights discourse might seek to ensure that all workers are fully covered by human, social and labour law entitlements within a particular state. However the presence of increasing numbers of migrants clearly raises politically complex issues in relation to the territoriality of labour law (Mundlak 2009). Do workers bring their own labour laws with them or are they absorbed into the local framework? Can a home state 'interfere' to protect its citizens who are working under exploitative conditions in another jurisdiction? The discourse of state-based labour rights still relies on male models of work and does not fully recognise the interrelationship between work and care, between productive and reproductive roles, although there is growing recognition of shifting boundaries. The dominant international rights-based talk has not been about the protection of women as migrant workers, particularly those who are constructed by immigration controls as unskilled and unvalued for the economy. Their care labour is barely seen as work for the purposes of legal entry. Employment laws reproduce and reinforce their position as marginal workers with limited rights. They are migrants first and workers second.

The challenges to the discourses relating to trade and to rights are constructed around the benefits of migration for economic development and for the individual migrants and their families if migration is voluntary and provides decent and productive forms of employment. Little attention is paid to the social relationships and socially reproductive roles of female migrant workers who, because of societal norms, are not free of family responsibilities. They provide market-based care but they are not citizens who care and seemingly they and their families do not need to be cared about. Assessments of losses are restricted to the productive costs associated with skilled 'brain drains' rather than those associated with unvalued socially reproductive relations.

Chain analysis provides a way of determining the way in which the benefits and risks are distributed through the network of social relations with the aim of supporting positive redistribution. Within commodity chains (Chapter 5) these initiatives have focused upon aspects of corporate social responsibility such as ethical trading initiatives (voluntary codes of practice/private standards) and fair trading. The actions of networks of north and south civil society and women's groups have ensured that some of these initiatives have tackled the gender issues associated with women's involvement in production in the Global South. Are there similar initiatives when Global South women provide body work services in northern states? Is a discourse of 'corporate social responsibility', rooted in voluntary market-based (private) agreements and reliant upon consumer caring to stimulate change in the governance of chains, appropriate here?

Corporate social and ethical service provision?

Market-oriented voluntary initiatives seek to tackle some of the difficulties associated with the territoriality of labour law and accommodate state sovereignty over migrant working. However the self-regulatory approach of 'corporate' social responsibility in relation to migrant women providers of care services has focused on the actions of states as guardians of the national economy and as direct employers. In the UK, these involve two contrasting but interrelated initiatives: voluntary codes of practice on ethical recruitment and bilateral migration agreements. Ethical codes of international recruitment practice are a response to wider disquiet over the recruitment of skilled health professionals from countries with poorly resourced health services to meet the needs of individuals in generally well-resourced northern welfare states. They recognise that the home/exporting state loses skilled workers, who embody the capital invested in their education and training, contributing to severe skill shortages in some countries particularly in sub-Saharan Africa. At the same time, the receiving state gains the economic advantage of already trained labour.

Unlike the case with ethical concerns over global food policies, it was pressure primarily from professionals within the health sector and the wider development community that led to the NHS Code of Conduct on international ethical recruitment (NHS 2004), the first in the world although other health-related codes have followed (Mills et al. 2008: 687). The code prevents active recruitment by the health service employers (directly or through agencies) in specified countries unless there is an explicit agreement between states. Where permitted, no fees may be charged to professionals and all costs involved in their recruitment will be met by employers. Private-sector employers can have access to the NHS international recruitment programmes if they sign up to the code. The code covers 150 countries including a large number in Africa (including South Africa) as well as countries in Asia. There is now a similar Social Care Code of Practice for International Recruitment that has been developed for the recruitment of social workers and social care workers.

These codes do try to address to some extent the issues relating to the welfare of the individuals involved by seeking to ensure that migrant workers gain full access to training, to enhance skill levels, and to protection against discrimination, which could reduce existing skills or prevent the development of new. In so doing the host state invests in human capital, which will benefit not only the individuals and their families but also the home country on return (if they return). In exchange workers must meet a number of regulatory requirements, including language competency and supervised practice. They offer some formal protections to nurses, and possibly some social carers, who work in the formal sector but they provide nothing for most social care and domestic workers who do not have access to the underlying rights upon which these codes are based.

Mensah et al. (2005) argue in relation to the NHS code that while it is a welcome recognition of the impact of 'brain drains' on developing countries, it is generally ineffective and misdirected. In a robust international market it will not stop migration but simply add to its costs as migrants and intermediaries find ways of avoiding its effect (Mills et al. 2008: 685). It is also implicitly discriminatory. African nurses are denied access to well-paid labour markets while Australians are not. It is therefore not ethically satisfactory. Alternatives that would involve states seeking to block the emigration of its nationals are also highly problematic. The right to individual freedom of movement is pitted against another citizen's right to health although the former tends to 'trump' the latter (Mensah et al. 2005). Although the discourse of rights is increasingly being used in creative attempts to find ways of addressing the inequalities produced by this form of migration (Physicians for Human Rights 2004; Bueno de Mesquita and Gordon 2005), reducing the issue to a battle between one citizen's civil and political right to freedom of movement and another's economic and social right to health masks the far wider economic and social issues involved. It obscures the deep inequalities in service provision between states (Mills et al. 2008).

Are there ethical codes in sex chains? It seems an unlikely concept perhaps given the nature of many of the processes involved. However, the tourist industry, which has facilitated the expansion of international sex tourism, has developed in conjunction with ECPAT, a Code of Conduct for the Protection of Children from Sexual Exploitation in Travel and Tourism 1998 (www.the-code.org) and now operates through an independent steering committee of high-profile stakeholders from the tourism industry, UN agencies and NGOs. Signatories commit themselves to establish a corporate ethical policy against commercial sexual exploitation of children. A military presence is always associated with an increase in commercial sex markets (Truong 1990). The presence of international peacekeeping forces in South East Europe stimulated a thriving trade in women from regions across borders into Europe. With the arrival of troops in Kosovo in 1999 'a small scale local market for prostitution was transformed into a large scale industry based on trafficking run by organised criminal networks' (Amnesty International 2004: 7). Thus international peacekeepers, who were immune from local prosecution, were contributing to the problem, for which other elements within the same international community held individual states, such as Moldova, responsible. The response within the OSCE Mission to Bosnia and Herzegovina was to adopt Anti-Trafficking Guidelines and an expanded Code of Conduct for staff and secondees, which specifically required officials not to facilitate prostitution, traffic or have professional or personal relationships with any who were involved in such processes.

Bilateral migration agreements

Such codes are directed at voluntary compliance by service providers and commercial recruitment agents. In the UK the major health service provider is in fact the state while social care services are provided both in social and commercial sectors. The receiving state is involved as a direct employer. Bilateral migration agreements (BMAs), on the other hand, are products of arrangements between sending and receiving states that enable states to target and then manage the migration of particular groups of workers. They bypass the multilateral framework of GATS while providing a stronger institutional framework for migrants than that offered by voluntary codes. They are therefore viewed by some international policy and development bodies as positive developments (IOM/WorldBank/WTO 2004). By facilitating documented migration through state channels, they cut out commercial agents, thereby reducing costs and incentives for undocumented migration; relieve labour surpluses in supplying countries; offer some additional rights to overseas nationals, although they tend to focus on recruitment processes rather than subsequent employment relations; and arguably limit the effects of brain drains where the agreement is linked to the provision of development assistance. These agreements provide privileged access to those who meet identified labour market needs in receiving countries. Social security bilateral agreements can provide 'migration specific' arrangements relating to social security benefits for migrant workers, which provide similarity of treatment and portability, including the export of benefits, totalising (whereby contributions from working in each state are recognised) and cost-sharing between states. In general, existing BMAs lack a gender perspective and domestic workers are rarely included (Go 2007).

The Philippines has pursued a strategy of managed migration through such formal agreements and has successfully negotiated a social security agreement and also a recruitment-focused BMA to permit the NHS to recruit registered nurses (and other health care professionals) for the UK NHS (IOM 2008b). The UK has entered into a similar agreement with India. Generally, potential receiving states are either very reluctant, or refuse altogether, to enter into these binding agreements because of the potential breach of the principles of territoriality in labour laws. States argue that it is a private-sector responsibility to negotiate terms between workers and their employers. Furthermore, there is the fear of opening the floodgates to requests from other less 'desirable' state workers (Go 2007; Abashdze 2009).

Distributing value: multiple and overlapping governance discourses

What is the impact of these governance discourses on the distribution of value and power within body work chains?

Ghanaian nurses

Ghana has one of the stronger economies within sub-Saharan Africa, particularly in comparison to most of its West African neighbours. However, it is still economically vulnerable and heavily dependent on international financial assistance. Individual remittances of its citizens are major source of foreign exchange.

There are many incentives for those with the skills to seek employment in stronger economies. Women with nursing qualifications can join the international labour market in health/care services, which is integrating and commercialising rapidly (Grown et al. 2006; Kelsey 2006). Ghanaian women nurses are in a position to make informed choices in relation to migration. Governments contribute to the development of the market by standardising internationally recognised, but often privately provided, education and training requirements and ensuring that domestic professional regulations are kept to a minimum and standardised. A Ghanaian nurse's qualification is acceptable and she can register with the Nursing and Midwifery Council for a fee. Lowering the barriers to entry reduces both the costs and the risks involved in the chain, which thereby facilitates international movement.

The liberalisation of the service industries and the development of communication networks have enabled commercial recruitment agencies to establish themselves across the globe. These agencies manage the migration processes in exchange for fees and some offer loans to migrants to finance their move. Private recruitment agencies assist Ghanaian nurses to move to the UK for a substantial fee (roughly £3,000 in 2005 (Mensah et al. 2005: 13)). While commercial service-providers increase the cost of migration they make the process more manageable, with international job-seeking less dependent on informal contacts.

Due to wider socio-economic factors and government policies, the UK NHS has been short of nurses. It sought to meet this deficit through international recruitment. Due to Ghana's colonial history with the UK, replaced by association within the Commonwealth, there are strong health-related professional links between the two countries. A long history of Ghanaian migration to the UK contributes to their maintenance. Professional Ghanaian women have a range of social attributes, including language competence, which add to their formal skills. Ghanaian nurses therefore have been attractive to the NHS employers. There was a significant acceleration in the number of Ghanaian nurses joining the UK register until recently.

While the Commonwealth may contribute to the preservation of strong professional networks between Ghana and the UK, it is irrelevant to immigration policy. The value associated with being a Commonwealth 'citizen' is worth little. Loyalty to the Commonwealth has been submerged by wider political anxieties over uncontrolled numbers of non-European migrants. The points system for work-related migration for non-Europeans increases the value of skills but also provides stronger mechanisms to control their flow. With increased numbers of UK-trained nurses now available and a marked downturn in the economy, there is no longer an official shortage of nurses. Ghanaian nurses are not officially required and face far higher barriers (and costs) to documented entry. The potential for exploitation by intermediaries and agencies increases substantially.

Nonetheless, possession of professional skills remains an asset and has enabled nurses to migrate. Ghanaian nurses enter a formally regulated labour market and, as employees within the NHS or the private sector, they are covered through their contracts of employment by the UK labour laws and anti-discrimination laws. These formal rights offer them little substantive protection. Ethnic minority nurses generally experience significant levels of discrimination and also racial harassment (Henry 2008: 119; Yeates 2009: 117). One study found that Ghanaian nurses experienced substantial discrimination and consequent stagnation in their careers. They became 'alienated from their workplace and managers, and many became deeply demoralised'. They 'adopted what appears to be an increasingly instrumental attitude to their professional life by focusing on their job as a means to an end rather than gaining intrinsic satisfaction from it' (Henry 2008: 120), a process leading to a reduction in value for all involved.

Anxieties over the 'brain drain' from under-resourced health services in Africa contributed to the adoption of the NHS ethical code on international recruitment, which prevented active/direct recruitment by public employers of Ghanaian nurses, thereby increasing the barriers and costs of entry. The code exempted recruitment that results from specific agreements between states. The UK has bilateral agreements with the Philippines and India to provide nurses. Both the Philippines and India are in a stronger position to negotiate such agreements than Ghana: India has emerged as a major economic power and the Philippines is the world leader in state-backed provision of migrant labour. These agreements reduce the risks and costs for Indian and Filipina women migrants by removing immigration barriers, cutting out the need for intermediaries and providing some specific labour and social welfare entitlements that recognise the disadvantages of being a migrant worker. Their ability to remit funds home is increased. The combination of these two governance frameworks (the 'private' voluntary code and the public bilateral agreements) results in changed power relations within the social networks of the global nursing chain. Although most nurses continue to migrate outside either framework, recruited directly by employers and agencies, Ghanaian women lose out to Indian and Filipina women (Buchan 2008: 49).

The human rights discourse that underpins the private voluntary code seems to prioritise the socio-economic entitlements to the provision of health services due to Ghanaian nationals over the civil rights of Ghanaian citizens to free movement. However, it ends up justifying immigration controls and placing a moral responsibility on individuals rather than addressing structural injustices, as illustrated in such titles as 'Do visas kill?' (Clemens 2007) and 'Should active recruitment of health workers from sub-Saharan Africa be viewed as a crime?' (Mills et al. 2008). Rather than restricting immigration through these codes, the UK government (and therefore tax payers) could redistribute resources by paying compensation for the subsidies provided by Ghana (Mensah, Mackintosh and Henry 2005). It is estimated that Ghana lost around £35 million of its training investment in health professionals to the UK in 2004. The recruitment of Ghanaian doctors saved the UK roughly £65 million in training costs between 1998 and 2002. While family-based remittances benefit the Ghanaian economy substantially, they do not fund the health service and do not compensate for these losses. The net effect of this care-based migration is a perverse subsidy: a net flow of benefits from a poor country to a rich one.

Polish social care workers

Poland emerged from the collapse of the state socialist system with a relatively strong economy and secured entry to the EU. A corollary of liberalisation has been a large number of unemployed workers who relieve pressure on the economy if they migrate to work and also remit funds back home. Polish citizens face no immigration barriers to working in the UK apart from a registration requirement. The European Services Directive is further seeking to open up domestic provision of services to competitors within the EU through reducing national barriers to entry. Workers from the European Economic Area and A8 countries in particular provide an available source of labour for low-skilled jobs in the UK service sector, which are now almost completely denied by the points-based system to those outside this area.

Social workers (who do have recognised skills) and social care workers are recruited within Europe and internationally by both public- and independent-sector (commercial and social) providers of residential and domiciliary services, directly or through the use of commercial agencies (DH 2007b: 31; Welbourne et al. 2007). The Department of Health notes that the independent sector has become 'increasingly dependent on a migrant workforce, which does nothing to improve the stability of the sector' and expresses major concerns about 'hap-hazardly attracting would-be migrant workers desperate for employment even at low rates of pay' (2007b: 31).

The provision of social care has been very poorly regulated until relatively recently and its overwhelmingly female workforce is deemed to be low skilled. Local workers are not attracted to these tough and not well-respected jobs. The work is therefore more readily available to undocumented women workers from the periphery of Europe, who are obliged by their circumstances to accept adverse working conditions, although the services of intermediaries under these circum-stances can prove very costly. They can ensure the 'debt bondage' of migrant workers before they arrive in the UK (Anti-Slavery International 2008: 2). Both residential and domiciliary service provision and care workers are being increas-ingly subjected to regulation. This is a sector that could be seen as erecting more barriers to entry in an attempt to drive up the quality of provision although there are substantial constraints on funding the costs, such as better wages and working conditions, associated with such improvements. Pay rates in the social care sector are heavily influenced by what local councils are willing to pay because they make up 80 per cent of the purchasers of care services.

In this context, 'legal' Polish women with their range of educational and social assets, willingness to work full time and for low wages, are in great demand from service providers. Their status as European citizens and the relative ease and low cost of travel to Poland will ensure that most will not want to become permanent settlers, thereby increasing their value to the UK state. Recruitment agencies target young, single (that is, presumed not to have dependent children) women who may be willing to 'live in' on the site of their employment, undertaking body work that involves highly personalised relationships with supervisors and excessive hours. Young Polish women have been identified as a group of workers who are particularly vulnerable to not receiving the statutory minimum wage (Jayaweera and Anderson 2008).

Care 'assistants' are in any case one of the lowest-paid occupations in the UK. While those who are directly employed as care workers will be covered by labour laws and non-discrimination provisions, many are agency workers who have far more limited rights.

Social care is emerging as a specific body work activity within the international market. The increased public regulation of social care is constructing new forms of labour: paid and regulated care work and unpaid caring. However, much care work is still associated with informal provision within private households. As a consequence, care workers who migrate through the global social care chains to meet demand can find themselves in different institutional settings and very unclear regulatory contexts.

Filipina domestic (care?) workers

The Philippines is a labour-exporting state: trading in its people and the remittances they generate are a core business. The state facilitates this market by reducing the barriers to, and therefore costs of, migration through its governance framework. A flourishing commercial sector has developed to provide export-oriented education and training and other services that support the migration process, at a price to migrants. The attempts of the Philippine state to regulate this sector have met with limited success. Nonetheless, the governance of the social relations of body chains originating in the Philippines contributes to the reduction in risks involved, and potentially to the relative gains available, to migrants. The general 'social capital' of migration now available in the Philippines after a quarter of a century or more of experience adds value. Filipina women are marketed internationally as the 'world's favourite workers'. They are reliable, hardworking, caring and good value for money. Filipina women form a major part of the global domestic worker labour force but are also upgrading to undertake more formally skilled body work.

There are very limited opportunities for Filipina women to work in a fully documented way in the UK. The Philippines is a distant Asian state with no colonial ties with the UK. The governance of the network of social relations of migration involving the two states is more obviously associated with the development of a global services market. The UK is only interested in the Philippines' cheap skilled female body workers, a limited number of whom are enabled to enter and work on relatively favourable terms as a result of the bilateral agreement for health workers including nurses. The immigration barriers to documented entry for female domestic workers in private households, the most familiar construction of a Filipina woman in the UK, are high and, as we have seen, likely to become much higher in the future. At present, however, Filipina women can obtain a domestic worker visa if they accompany overseas employers to work in their households. While workers with such a visa are currently granted the status of employee and are therefore formally covered by local labour laws, their position within these private workplaces can be highly preca-rious. Migrant domestic workers 'frequently suffer from abuse (sexual, physical, and emotional), discrimination, low pay (or none), exceptionally long working hours, social isolation, and mental health problems arising from the extreme conditions of their employment ... such as having to sleep on floors and not being provided with bedrooms, and being given no time off, sick pay or access to healthcare' (Gordolan and Lalani 2009: 8). Anti-discrimination laws do not extend to those employed in private households but the obstacles to the enforce-ment of any rights that women may possess formally are very substantial (see Wittenburg 2008). Those with more ambiguous status and less access to work-ers' rights are even more vulnerable to potential exploitation (Gordolan and Lalani 2009: 24).

The social relations of body work are changing with a growing demand for paid care provided within homes, a process described as personalisation (Ungerson 2004). Although wage levels are very low, care is still costly to the individual, particularly if it is required throughout the day and night. 'Personalisation may foster the development of an informal market for care in which migrant workers, and particularly undocumented migrants, may become particularly desirable' (Ungerson quoted in Gordolan and Lalani 2009: 30). Because of the characteristics ascribed to them, Filipina domestic workers are becoming sought-after home-based carers. 'Many older people prefer the softer side of the Filipino. There is a big difference, you get a lot of lovely Indian women but they can be a bit harsh. Even Indians [employers] prefer Filipinos because they want someone more educated in their house, someone that has good English' (quote from an employment agency manager) (Gordolan and Lalani 2009: 32). Filipina women share employers' assessment of their attractions as clean and reliable, non-argumentative and affectionate workers. As a result, Filipinos 'tend to command the highest wages of all nationalities (Gordolan and Lalani 2009: 34). On the other hand, present domestic regulatory frame-works do not recognise them as care workers, thereby increasing their risks and reducing any benefits that may accrue from association with a potentially more skilled and regulated occupation. Unless a Filipina woman has settled status or has been in the country for more than three years, she is denied access to recognised training courses in care.

The social relations of body work involve intimate contact between service provider and recipient. It involves complex relations of power, exacerbated by personalised provision within the recipient's home. Establishing mutually agree-able content to the employment relationship may be very difficult, particularly if the worker lives in. Racism can be a major factor but anti-discrimination laws are unavailable. Although the 'Health and Safety Commission provides guide-lines for the safety of migrant workers, care workers in institutional settings, and health workers in general, it falls silent when it comes to specific provisions protecting paid care workers working in private households not hired by agen-cies' (Gordolan and Lalani 2009: 14).

Moldovan sex slaves

Moldova's post-state socialist eonomic position is very different from that of Poland. It is now located on the border of the EU but its citizens are shut out, particularly from the UK, which is not part of the Schengen agreement and maintains its own border controls. At the same time Moldova's economy relies on remittances from the export of its nationals. Its position in the global economy and weak governance structure mean that unlike the Philippines, it is unable to facilitate and support its nationals in the migratory process. There are few obvious 'legal' migration channels through which most Moldovan women could enter the UK to work, leading to a growing market for irregular migration services based on family networks or more commercial agencies. A Moldovan woman is therefore likely to need assistance from those who provide these services (Kelly 2002; Vulliamy 2004; Agustin 2007).

Intermediaries (traffickers) 'capitalize on permeable borders, political and military instability, economic dislocation, and rampant corruption to create efficient supply chains to satisfy the lucrative market for sex workers in Western Europe and the Balkans' (Lindstrom 2004: 46). Moldova's weak criminal justice system makes the risks involved in all forms of undocumented migration low. Expansion in the global market for commercial sex provision, associated with organised crime networks, has raised new grounds for concern rooted in the discourse of national security leading to international criminal measures aimed at curbing these activities. A Moldovan woman may therefore be smuggled and become an undocumented immigrant in the UK or she may be victim of trafficking. As a smuggled person she will need to seek employment in sectors that are informally organised and poorly regulated. Domestic or care work within the private sphere would be a possibility but there are strong cultural and social constructions of 'suitability' for this type of work: neither employers nor Moldovan women associate themselves with this work in the UK. The attractions of a 'Western' lifestyle make work in the hospitality industry more attractive to young women whose ascribed characteristics tend to revolve around their beauty and personal appearance. The sex industry offers possibilities: it is organised informally and, while it is subject to some criminal regulation, enforcement is weak and the actors within the sector have considerable expertise in operating within these conditions. A ready supply of migrant labour keeps costs down and profits up. Remuneration and risks may be considerably higher than other informal-sector jobs. She will have no employment protection, no access to welfare services and very limited access to the criminal justice system in the event of violence by purchasers or employers due to her undocumented status.

Can a Moldovan woman work legally as a prostitute? In theory, if she met the conditions for self-employment – not entering into an employment contract, having sufficient funds to maintain herself and having no recourse to public funds – she could obtain permission to enter as such a service provider. This is, of course, highly unlikely in the present context of the UK points-based system but the ECJ has ruled that prostitution is a provision of services for remuneration, that falls within the category of economic activities for self-employed persons.

Both the immigration and labour market controls generally deny Moldovan women the status of workers leading to the demands by women sex worker groups for legalisation of the industry to enable those working within it to protect themselves through access to employment rights and benefits including freedom of association and unionisation. It would also provide access to the police for protection. Would this regulation of the industry improve opportunities for Moldovan women? It could be seen in the discourse of service market liberalisation as an increase in protectionism and an attempt by a domestic service industry to protect itself against cheap migrant labour.

Some Moldovan women find themselves caught up in the highly exploitative and violent processes associated with trafficking. They fall within the regulatory framework established by the 2000 Trafficking Protocol as implemented by state parties. Within this framework they are trafficked persons within immigration controls, temporarily suspended from the status of undocumented/illegal migrants, not bonded labourers within international labour rights. They are entitled to stay within the country temporarily if they agree to cooperate with prosecutions. Many women do not do this and find themselves back in the category of undocumented migrant, rapidly repatriated with or without their consent. The public exposure involved in the trafficking process is in contrast to the twilight zones in which non-trafficked but undocumented workers exist.

The contest over the construction of trafficking continues. In whatever way the activity is seen, it represents a stark example of the wider costs of globalisation for Moldovan citizens. The exploitation associated with these forms of undocumented migration undermines individuals in a variety of ways. Their chances of gaining individually from the chain are minimal or indeed likely to lead to substantial economic social and emotional losses: their debts (including through bondage) prevents remittances to support families and they lose their potential to contribute social capital to their society though transferable skills acquisition. (The Criminal Injuries Compensation Authority has begun to recognise this loss in its guidelines, which provide compensation for 'a sustained period of sexual abuse'. Four trafficked women received awards in 2007 of between £6,200 and £16,500 and another 10,000 were estimated to be eligible (Townsend 2007).) In exchange, consumers purchase a cheap one-sided service, and intermediaries reap substantial rewards, both contributing nothing to the wider development of economic or social relations in Moldova.

Conclusion

The four examples demonstrate that the distribution of the benefits of body work chains depends on the particular power relations within the network of social relations. Ghanaian nurses are at one end of a spectrum and Moldovan (trafficked) women at the other. The first work in one of the more integrated global service markets, which is capital intensive, highly organised and has a strong institutional framework. Their labour is valued because it is skilled and they are well paid. The second work in a sector that is labour intensive, chaotically organised and unregulated. Their labour is denied value, considered unskilled and is poorly paid (if paid at all). Polish care and Filipina domestic/care workers are positioned between the two. Nurses face the least risk, the highest degree of agency and potentially the most gains from their involvement in the global body chains.

However, the examples also expose conflicting estimations of value based upon the demand for the services. There is a growing demand for (and therefore increased value to) care services, which, in economic theory, could be met effectively through a global free market in female migrant labour. UK employers could choose between Filipina and Polish workers for personalised care without consideration of migration status. Workers could compete on their (often ascribed) comparative advantages without the distortions of migration status that make their labour cheaper or more expensive. However the political threats posed to state sovereignty render such an approach inconceivable, even more so if the service provided is commercial sex. There are direct conflicts between the state and the market in the provision of such services. These variances are reflected in the governance of the particular chains, which deeply affect the power relations within. Intermediaries in sex chains can reap very substantial gains due to criminalisation, while the women involved can lose very substantially.

Generally the governance of particular body work chains contributes to the distribution of power within the social relations. The governance of sex chains is through the discourse of criminality. It is directed at the processes associated with the movement of bodies (by criminalised intermediaries) across borders and so is associated with state immigration controls. Both smuggling and trafficking are addressed through the criminal justice system. However, the rights discourse attached to trafficking provides a 'defence' by constructing the trafficked subject, a victim of rights violations lacking in any autonomy but also devoid of the status of worker. The active subject of migration is associated with the (male) smuggled person who breaches principles of state sovereignty and who is therefore denied a defence or rights. This gendered dichotomy obfuscates a continuum of exploitation that is associated with the network of social relations in body work chains but loses a sense of women as actors with varying degrees of agency who seek work to survive in a profoundly unequal world.

State immigration controls that restrict non-European labour for domestic/care work chains in a poorly regulated informal market contribute to the potential for women body workers to be 'illegal' migrants, and to work in a highly exploitative context. A merger between 'illegal immigration' and 'trafficking' results in migrants who are working in breach of immigration conditions being labelled as trafficked. Yet 'legal' migrants can be 'trafficked' in the sense that the context in which they work could lead them to be described as bonded or forced labourers.

Associating trafficking with immigration (the movement element) masks the way in which immigration status contributes to 'vulnerability and abusive employment relations. Perversely this means that immigration controls can be presented as a solution to human rights abuses' (Anderson and Rogaly 2005: 8–9). An alternative perspective would be to extend the 'rights' of trafficked persons to all those who are subject to forced or highly exploitative labour conditions.

UK immigration law mediates the relationship between a migrant worker and labour rights. The person is a particular type of worker. Human rights discourse has the potential to change this by ensuring that all migrants (as aliens) are fully covered by state-based labour laws. The UN Convention goes some way towards this position but still constructs a dichotomy based on immigration status. However, such a rights discourse could be developed further to encompass not just formal equality for all workers irrespective of migrant status (such as equal access to work-related social benefits), but substantial equality based upon the additional challenges faced by workers because they are migrants (such as the portability of such accrued benefits). However, the 'trumping' of the universalist principle of human rights over that of territoriality within labour law is contested.

One way around this impasse in the discourse of human and labour rights has been to shift to one of corporate social responsibility and to develop 'private' standards through international framework agreements or codes of practice. In this way MNCs agree to be tied into the wider institutional frameworks of rights throughout their global supply chain networks. However these developments are not so easy to replicate in the area of body work service chains, which involves the physical movement of workers into another jurisdiction. The provision of health/care services in the UK is very much bound up with the state as the principal provider or major funder (in the case of care services). Bilateral migration agreements offer the potential to provide migrant workers with substantial state-recognised and-facilitated rights and therefore to redistribute power relations. However women body workers are dependent not only upon their home state's economic and political clout in the global market place but also upon its commitment to negotiate with a gendered understanding.

Like the Ethical Trading Initiative in relation to the FFV chain, the NHS and Social Work/Care voluntary ethical codes are products of relationships between civil society actors. Trade justice initiatives are premised on the assumption that work relationships are a product of wider structural inequalities and that interventions in the governance of chains will improve the position of individual workers. However the health/care codes focus on the wider injustices to health/care in the home country by the recruitment of individual workers. As with the discourse of trafficking, the problem is associated with the movement of people, and is therefore controlled primarily via the voluntary adoption of immigration controls. The assumption seems to be that stemming recruitment through official channels will absolve UK society of responsibility for the accrued gains. A more just approach would involve the UK state employer compensating the Ghanaian people for these gains made at their expense while facilitating mutually beneficial working relationships between health workers in both countries.

One of the main reasons why workers who are migrants require 'additional' rights relates to the territorial division between productive and socially reproductive aspects of their lives. Given the prevailing gendered divisions of labour, women continue to take primary responsibility for socially reproductive activities. Many migrant worker families are transnational but women's migration in general does not lead to significant shifts in this division of labour; rather it reconstructs its form and incorporates a network of women into the chains. Both human rights provisions relating to migration and international labour rights have been built on the presumption that the worker is an unencumbered (male) subject who works in a formally regulated sector while state-based immigration laws tend to limit or deny access to the work-related social benefits that enable 'local' women workers to combine productive and socially reproductive roles. These rights discourses do not recognise the risks to, and potential losses of, caring relationships that migrant women workers face as transnational family members, nor the losses to wider communities, characterised as the 'social depletion' associated with women's migration. Economists can quantify the losses of skills to the health service in Ghana and estimate the levels of remittances to the Philippines and Moldova. They lack the conceptual framework to understand the losses to families and communities of women's unpaid socially reproductive labour (a care drain) when women's migration is not accompanied by a renegotiated gender contract, which would redistribute responsibility for nurture and care between women and men (and the state) in more just ways.

Is it possible to develop fair care or ethical trade (in body work services) initiatives that would start to tackle these losses to individuals and communities? While there is some activist discourse and networking in relation to migrant women workers, we do not see forms of wider consumer and civil society activism around the consumption of services that has developed for commodities such as the fair trade movement. Fair trade requires both producers and consumers to imagine and be attentive to lives lived on the other side of the world while fair care would involve imagining lives lived with us *and* on the other side of the world. The attentiveness required for an ethical caring approach to the provision of body work by migrant women might involve citizens ceasing to care so much about immigration controls, so that more women could come (and go) in a documented manner; ensuring that migrant status does not diminish access to labour protections; extending but also reconceptualising labour rights to cover body work relationships in personalised, family/household contexts; extending and reconceptualising social entitlements in ways that start to address the strains and losses to individuals and communities of caring at a distance. While these predominantly rights-based measures might start to address injustices associated with body work chains by redistributing some of the benefits and losses, a care approach requires us to consider the wider conceptual issues relating to the construction of the trade and rights discourses in the relocation of caring relations from the family/community to the market.

How would a care approach tackle the injustices associated with body work chains, which are frequently but not always based upon a survival strategy for women? At its most fundamental it poses the question: can caring that is provided through market-based body work services with the labour of migrant women workers ever be caring to all those involved? In the UK, expectations of caring are changing and increasing. Gaps emerge in direct relationships of care as women work more while men do not necessarily care more, which are filled predominantly by other women providing body work services. Once economically valued, it costs a great deal although women care workers are poorly paid because body work is not valued socially. Both the state, as a major funder of provision, and individuals, who need care themselves or for a family member, have incentives to reduce costs but want personalised services, provided in the home of the care recipient/customer, which encourages informal, unregulated provision.

The creation of a social market in care, with its rhetoric of independence for recipients of care, masks the interdependence involved. Can caring, which is based on trust, mutuality and reciprocity, be transformed into a discrete, costed service product and form the basis for a relationship of employment? The move from caring relationships to buying 'affects' (love/nurture) raises considerable challenges for many of the foundational assumptions of labour law. The 'normal' relationship between employer and employee does not pertain in the intimacy of body work relationships. How much of a care worker's identity or bodily integrity can be demanded in the provision of such services?

All benefit from expanding the body work services market with female migrant labour that has been 'produced' elsewhere and, due to state rules, has no recourse to public funds. Costs are kept down and workers bring acquired values and ascribed characteristics/identities, which may make them more willing to provide more of their being to their employers/care recipients. The interaction between restrictive immigration and labour laws can render such migrant women carers highly vulnerable to the complex power relationships involved in body work services (Datta et al. 2006). While these dilemmas are not restricted to migrant workers, their position is made more complicated by the racism they can experience from their care clients.

What are the true costs of the body work chains? These seem clear in relation to the provision of sexual services. The power relations underpinned by the governance structures ensure that too much of women's bodily integrity is extracted in meeting the desires of consumers. A woman's sense of self is undermined. Social/domestic care chains and even the professional nursing chains raise similar issues. Citizens in the UK are seeking to buy relationships (as affects/services) that will enable them to be nurtured and retain their sense of being. Without these, at worst they will die or at best experience a deeply impoverished existence. Women may want to migrate, and do so under conditions of their own choosing, but for most this is not the case. They migrate in order to care for their loved ones (or those for whom they have relations of obligation). In doing so, they face the attenuation of their sense of being and belonging. They may sustain these at distance, add to them or transform their sense of being and belonging through new enriching relationships, including with their employers. Local contexts often make this exceptionally difficult and more of their identity than they would wish may be absorbed in the service provision. So both they and their communities lose out.

Do those who receive the services gain? Possibly, but such a market in body work services does suggest that there is something amiss with the priorities in the UK consumer market, which has to rely on the extraction of the only asset available to many women, their embodied self, to provide care for the vulnerable. Although in the present global context, it would sound like protectionism, a utopian vision of redistributive justice would involve the ability of women and men to choose the communities in which they wish to live and work based on their sense of what relationships provide them with a sense of being and belonging. For most this will be within their families and communities. It would involve transformations in wider economic and gender relationships in both the Global North and Global South so that social reproductive activities are more evenly distributed between men and women and more valued within societies, which take more responsibility for caring relationships.

8

Constructing South Asian womanhood through law

Introduction

The next two chapters are concerned with transnational marriage chains. This chapter concentrates on the 'vertical' Global South jurisdictional pyramids in India, Pakistan and Bangladesh. The next shifts to the Global North to consider the UK, focusing firstly on the position of the communities that have origins in the countries discussed here; and secondly on the transnational social and economic relationships (the horizontal links between the two pyramids) involved when people move to meet the desire for particular marriage partners and the trading of contested norms, which contribute to the construction of the identities of spouses, that accompany them.

This chapter has two main objectives. The first is to introduce the South Asian jurisdictions which, in the language of chains, supply marriage partners. The three states share a history. Contemporary South Asian gendered legal identities, including those in the diaspora, result from the accretions of this history as well as present contexts. Colonialism redefined relationships between production and social reproduction in ways that confirmed women's position within a seemingly separate sphere of the family, not valued for their role as workers. Women gained recognition as equal citizens on independence in all three constitutions although nationalist discourses tended to construct women primarily as wives and mothers responsible for socially reproductive relationships, rather than as productive workers. The economies of India and (undivided) Pakistan on independence in any case presented few opportunities for women outside agriculture. Subsequently, the economic position of the different states has diverged significantly. India's recently emerged position within contemporary globalisation is creating a substantial consumer economy although, as we shall see, vast numbers of women are not integrated positively into 'Global India', a construct of the market, but live in 'Poor India', within the discourse of 'development' (DFID 2007). India's repositioning contributes to the reconstruction of gender identities, which is reflected in recent legal campaigns. The chapter explores the extent to which women are viewed as honourable (caring) kinswomen (within their particular community) or as valued consuming workers and autonomous (sexual) subjects supported by state rights.

Bangladesh offers few consumer-oriented opportunities although women work in significant numbers in the textile industry. Due to its highly vulnerable economic position since independence in the 1970s, Bangladesh has been the recipient of substantial intervention by the international development institutions. Gender relations in Bangladesh tend to be seen through the discourse of development not markets. However, as we shall see, these interventions have had an effect on legal strategies in relation to women. Women's involvement in any form of production is closely associated with community-based understandings of women's role within society. In Pakistan few women work in the small formal market or visibly within productive agriculture while international development discourse has increasingly been overtaken by that of 'security' and the politicisation of religion.

In many respects the discourses of law and development within the region have evolved separately. This is not to deny the wide-ranging actions associated with women's economic position in the rural and informal sectors, particularly in India and Bangladesh (Agnihotri and Mazumdar 2005: 67–73). As we shall see, much of the focus for the Indian independent women's movement has been on using state law to restructure power relationships between the state, communities and families in order to expand the 'civil space' available to women. However, any construction of a dichotomy between women as economic subjects who have not been the subject of specific legal campaigns and women facing violation of their civil rights who have, is misplaced because most women rely on the security gained through access to resources because of their socially reproductive relationships as daughters, wives, widows or community members. One of the economic and political legacies of colonialism is the absence of developed social welfare laws creating and then regulating 'public' aspects of family life. Across the jurisdictions, women find themselves using the criminal justice system to seek protection against exclusion from family resources or to contest unacceptable marriages without the option of 'exit' to live in a separate public sphere as citizens rather than as family members. There is, therefore, a direct and uneasy relationship between the authoritarian powers of the state and the family/community when women seek to secure their social and economic position within families through state-based law.

The limited civil, secular space of law has proven to be a challenge for feminist legal activists in South Asia, particularly in Pakistan. We see the extent to which women must be honourable or caring kinswomen in order to be citizens. Women's bodies matter because the social norms of being female in any society are inscribed on them. Women's sexuality is a source of power so their bodies are sites for contests over the exercise of this power, which takes place in and between relationships associated with the family, state and market. Within each of the South Asian 'vertical' contexts there is a fusion between polity and community (Baxi et al. 2006) which constructs a mediated, embodied citizenship for women, particularly when women attempt to exercise choice in matters of sexuality that are not community sanctioned.

This issue is explored initially through a discussion of 'honour' in the context of North India, (whence most BrAsian Indians originate). The chapter subsequently shows the ways in which women's sexuality is regulated within communities and in the legal systems of the subcontinent. Each country retains the colonial penal code, which criminalises many aspects of sexual activity, although we shall see that the different trajectories since independence, including the influence of Islamic law in Pakistan and Bangladesh, have made an impact on the plural regulatory regimes.

This discussion lays the foundation for the second more specific objective, which is to understand the way in which the norms and laws relating to the regulation of women's sexuality have been traded and contested in the marriage chains involving BrAsian communities with family links to often very localised areas of Pakistan, Bangladesh and India. The enduring importance of family networks is at the heart of the transnational marriage chain. The 'asset value' of potential spouses from South Asia is created by the previous migration of family and community members whose senses of well-being and belonging continue to be sustained through these networks. It is not only familiarity with a location that matters; it is the value of identities, moulded by the particular combinations of normative frameworks. Those who migrated, and in many cases two subsequent generations of family members, are established UK residents, positioned within a Global North post-colonial context that produces highly individualised gendered subjectivities as discussed in Chapter 3. Chapter 9 explores in more detail the effects of transnationalism on differently constructed subjectivities when South Asian women migrate to the UK as spouses and BrAsian women marry South Asian men.

Law's development in India

Domesticating women: constructing gendered laws in 'uncivil' colonial India

The development of economic relations under colonialism contributed much to the way in which women have become primarily positioned as non-productive or marginal contributors to the household and national economies. Here we consider briefly the impact of colonial economic interventions on agricultural and industrial production and on gender divisions of labour before moving on to consider more specifically the role played by law in constructing women primarily as family members rather than as workers and civil subjects.

The East India Company (EIC) 'ruled' India until 1858 when the British Crown took over. The pressure to produce specific raw materials led to the commercialisation of agriculture and an increase in the concentration of land in the hands of the few at the expense of the many (Nair 1996: 96). Agricultural production was organised in ways that resulted in 'corporate, kin related patterns of land settlement' (Washbrook 1981: 664). Anglo-Indian law imbricated itself within agrarian social relations: the 'public' relied on the 'personal'. The EIC administration found recognisable institutions and codes that were binding and had the force of law (Nair 1996: 19) including Hinduism, based on Hindu law, believed to be of divine origin; and Islam, another divinely inspired system with its shariat laws (Parashar 1992: 48–60 and generally) (see further Dhagamwar 1992; Agarwal 1994; Nair 1996). The colonial state distinguished between matters to be decided under its jurisdiction in each district and those that would be saved for application by Muslim and Hindu communities. The latter covered inheritance, marriage, caste and other religious matters, which have come to be described as 'personal laws'. For Hindus and Muslims, religious and 'personal laws' become synonymous.

After 1858 it became evident that 'the constraints on property relations imposed by the Hindu joint-family and corporate- and status-based forms of landholding stood in the way of Indian capital coming in to develop' a market based on 'freedom of the individual' not 'community trust and moral obliga- tion' (Washbrook 1981: 672). However, Hindu law was not dismantled in ways that would have facilitated freer markets. There were no root and branch legislative changes to the Hindu joint family system, which lay at the heart of agrarian property relations, because this normative system was defined as 'personal' law and untouchable. The colonial state did not invest in a modern administrative structure, which would have supported the courts in applying 'modern' law, nor did it develop an 'efficient and centrally-disciplined police force, to protect "legal" rights, safeguard the emancipation of the individual from community constraint and impose the rule of law' (Washbrook 1981: 677). Policing continued to be provided by locally dominant castes and the police acted as 'agents of local agrarian elites' (1981: 677).

While commentators offer different interpretations of these developments (see Nair 1996: 33–43; Spivak 1998), the implications for gender relations are clearer cut. Under Hindu textual rules women had very limited rights over property, and social practice based on customary norms offered little more (Agarwal 1994). Muslim women have significant scriptural rights to inherit although not equal to men's. However '[m]any Muslims appeared to have followed customary practi- ces of inheritance similar to those of the local patrilineal Hindu communities [for example in the Punjab] among whom women's rights were highly restricted' (Agarwal 1994: 98). A daughter, once married, must be located near to the natal home if she is to be granted a share in natal property (the route to property devolution) in order to maintain family control over it. Consequently, marriage customs and property rights evolved together customarily and were enforced by local community bodies (Agarwal 1994). Those with power within rural communities remoulded their position in the power struggles with the colonial state through these family property relations, leaving little space for women to manoeuvre between the state's involvement in the economic life of the com- munity and the family's assertion of control over the personal.

The exploitation of the unpaid labour of women and children in small peasant households facilitated the development of capitalist development of agriculture in rural India. From the 1860s onwards, as returns from agriculture dwindled, families were obliged to depend more heavily on household tasks geared to subsistence for survival. These tasks, undertaken mainly by women, received little recognition in the division of family resources. Holders of land and capital on the other hand were able to replace their family labour with hired labour. Women within more privileged sectors ceased to work in visibly productive activities; a move to seclusion and domesticity which signified higher status. Thus, despite differing economic positions, women's contributions became more invisible, less valued, while being associated with a desirable social outcome of withdrawal from the public domain. Women's value became more associated with the achievement of upper caste ideology of the sanctity of marriage, with chaste, modest and secluded demeanour, with enhanced social reproductive activities. Poor women who laboured publicly were associated with temporary marriages, frequent divorces and desertions. Domesticity, stripped of a labour element, was set against productive labour (Sen (S) 1999: 55). In these circumstances, the creation of a distinction between 'public' individual property rights enforceable in the domain of the state and 'private' marriage laws remaining under the purview of the community has the potential to cause conflict and to move the spotlight to the regulation of marriage practices and women's sexual behaviour.

By the beginning of the twentieth century, the colonial law 'project' became more embroiled in power struggles with landed interests. There was little appetite for improving the individual property rights of women in these contests between a male Victorian colonial state and rural Indian elites. Most aspects of laws governing inheritance and marriage among Hindus were not touched until after independence. However, the pressure mounted as the century moved on with the formation of several women's organisations and the election of a group of liberal lawyers to the government's Central Legislative Assembly in 1935. The Hindu Women's Right to Property Act 1937 granted more, although still limited, rights to Hindu widows but not daughters. Its provisions also explicitly excluded agricultural land, thereby protecting the key source of economic resources from any increase in entitlement for women.

Away from the economic sphere, there were some colonial legal interventions directed at 'uncivilised' customs, which seemed to expand the 'civil' space for some middle-class women within the sphere of the family (Nair 1996: chapter 3): the Abolition of Sati Act 1829, relating to the practice of widow immolation on a husband's funeral pyre; the Hindu Widows Remarriage Act 1856, improving the position of upper caste widows who were unable to remarry and consigned to a living death; the Age of Consent Act 1891, which raised the age of consent for intercourse for girls to twelve although it made no stipulation relating to the age of marriage; and the Child Marriage Restraint Act 1929, which fixed the age of marriage at fourteen (Sarkar 2000). The last high-profile measure relating to female infanticide was banned by a Special Act of 1870. These struggles within the context of colonial rule were constituted more by contests over who had the right to define women's position within

Indian society. As colonial interest in and power over social reform waned at the end of the nineteenth century, nationalists strengthened their discourse of the family as out of bounds for the colonial intervention and the family as a place of refuge from the state. The growing women's movement recognised the problems of petitioning a colonial state (Nair: 1996).

While the colonial state needed allies to force through changes in the agricultural sector, Indian industrialists sought out markets in competition with the metropolitan power and gave their support to nationalism. The number of women who worked in the industrial economy in the Bengal jute mills and Bombay textile mills declined rapidly as the industries grew more organised and lost markets (Nair 1996: 109–118). Women were not protected by upper-caste, male-led trade unions, and gender-specific protective or welfare-based legislation was perceived as expensive in the context of fierce global competition in the 1930s (Ramamurthy 2000: 562) (see further Washbrook 1994; Ramamurthy 2000; Mazumdar 2006).

Women's labour in both the agrarian and industrial sectors was repositioned at the margins, increasingly obliged to access resources through a 'family' wage or through family-based property entitlements. While Anglo-Hindu 'civil' law was an entanglement of statutory law, classical Hindu law and customary law interpreted through a body of case law developed in local colonial courts, the codification of the criminal law was a clear creation of the colonial state (see Dhagamwar 1992). The Indian Penal Code (IPC) and the Criminal Procedure Code (CrPC) were adopted in 1860 and 1861. The Laws of Evidence followed later. These Codes provided (and still provide with amendments) the criminal justice framework that applied to all individuals irrespective of community or religion, constructing women (and men) as individual colonial 'subjects'. They reflect Victorian British values and colonial anxieties through a range of finely drawn offences relating to property and the taking of life but broad-brush offences relating to the liberty of the individual (Dhagamwar 1992: 122–126).

Constituting 'civil' women: nation building 1947-1974

Economic women

India, after partition from Pakistan, achieved independence in 1947. The Congress party, in political control of the state, inherited a poor country shattered by physical and violent disruption involving the flight of up to 14 million refugees in both directions across borders, contributing hugely to economic difficulties. The entire manufacturing sector (mainly consisting of cotton and jute) accounted for just over 10 per cent of GDP. Congress adopted a socialist and modernist economic development approach with strong government involvement in the economy through five-year plans and state ownership of key industries. The public sector grew to be large and to influence most aspects of the economy. A modern industrial sector did not involve any measures to encourage the employment of women. While trade unions in the organised sector gained strength, their activities did not extend to support for women worker organisations. A nationalist ideology that valued women's 'work' contribution to the nation via the home and motherhood reinforced women's marginality in the public sphere of employment.

The nationalist state became heavily involved in support for the agricultural sector because of the need to provide greater food security for the population and to improve agricultural productivity. Development policies were not gender sensitive in this period so little, if any, attention was paid to the impact of these developments on women, who continued to be heavily involved in work as cultivators and labourers in the agricultural sector and the unorganised/informal economy more generally. The Green Revolution led to increased production of food crops overall but accentuated the gendered division of labour, with women being displaced as valued labour as technological development took place.

Constitutional women

The 1949 constitution establishes a secular state, with no official religion, in which everyone has the right to profess, practise and propagate their religion (Article 25) or none. It provides all persons with equality before the law (Article 14). Article 15(1) prohibits discrimination on grounds of religion, race, caste, sex or place of birth while subsection (3) retains the right of the state to make special provisions for women and children. Article 14 prohibits the state from denying any *person* equality before the law; Article 15 protects any *citizen* against the prescribed categories of discrimination. The constitution is divided into two parts: fundamental rights, which are justiciable, and directive principles of state policy, which are not. The former basically cover civil rights, including the rights to equality, while the latter provide the social and economic welfare aspirations of the nationalist government, such as the right to work, to education, to a living wage, the provision of free and compulsory education for children and so on. Article 44, located in the directive principles, states that the state will endeavour to secure the provision of a uniform civil code for all citizens.

The constitution also establishes the federal government structure. It constitutes the various states and Union Territories within the Union with their own executive, including a Governor, legislature and judiciary. Government within states at a local level is through the panchayat system in rural areas and municipalities in the urban areas. Legislative powers are divided between the Union and the states. Most taxes are collected through the statutory authority of Parliament. States have exclusive jurisdiction over some taxes but rely to a great extent on the distribution of central revenue funds and grants for specific programmes. Because states are responsible for the public control of land, including legislation, the Union government may issue directives relating to land to promote greater social and economic justice but cannot guarantee implementation.

Personal women

During the colonial era personal laws were largely unreformed. Those building the new India through an ideology of a strong state chose piecemeal reform of the existing pluralistic system primarily involving reforms involving the majority Hindu community. The state exercised its authority to enlarge the rights of Hindu women by using the concept of public equality, based upon the authority of the constitution, while maintaining the personal law construct (Parashar 1992). The comprehensive Hindu Code Bill was strongly supported by the emerging women's movement (Agarwal 1994: 205–210). The draft code, known as the Hindu personal law code, finally passed into law as a number of separate Acts (see Parashar 1992 Appendix for a succinct summary). These laws, with some significant modifications, are the current laws in force. The Hindu Succession Act 1956, which covers about 86 per cent of the Indian population, partly because 'Hindus' are defined to include Sikhs, Jains and Buddhists, significantly increased women's rights. It introduced equal inheritance rights within the law of succession for sons and daughters and brothers and sisters. All female heirs have absolute ownership and full testamentary rights over all property. In 2005 women's activists forced through amendments which give a daughter the same coparcenary rights to property (wherein a person has a right to the family property from birth) as a son.

Women's inheritance rights are governed by personal laws on all matters of property except where they relate to agricultural land when they depend on the specific laws prevailing in a state. The 1937 Hindu Women's Right to Property Act did not apply to agricultural land but the Hindu Succession Act 1956 does. State legislatures still have responsibility for other land laws, including those relating to tenancy. Tenancy rights are not covered by the Hindu Succession Act and can devolve differently, according to individual state laws and in ways that discriminate against women (Agarwal 1994: 216–218). Another area of discrimination (applying to all communities, not just Hindus) relates to the fixing of ceilings (the amount of land a family unit can hold) and the assessment of surplus land (to account for the needs of larger families).

Personal law and public land reforms, both pursued by state institutions, attribute different values to gender equality rights. The latter are clearly designed to promote redistributive justice, part of the directive principles of the constitution, but are not based on concepts of non-discrimination on grounds of sex, a fundamental right within the constitution. Gender equality rights are pitted against social reform measures, a dichotomy reinforced in the Supreme Court in 1980 when Justice Krishna Iyer argued that 'no submission to destroy this measure [the Uttar Pradesh Zamindari Abolition and Land Reforms Act 1950] can be permitted using sex discrimination as a means to sabotage what is socially desirable' (*Ambika Prasad Mishra* v. *The State of UP and Others* 1980 SCC 719 quoted in Agarwal 1994: 221).

The nationalist state was not willing to exert its authority to intervene in the religious laws of the minority communities. Reforms relating to the numerically small Christian and Parsee communities were only introduced recently (see Parashar 1992; Agnes 2000). Those relating to the Muslim community (accounting for about 12 per cent of the population) were politically problematic in the immediate aftermath of the trauma of partition. Muslims took advantage of the Government of India Act 1935 to secure the Muslim Personal Law (Shariat) Application Law 1937 which sought to impose shariat law on Muslims in those parts of the country that were following local (considered to be Hindu-influenced) customary laws. The 1937 Act enables individuals to opt to be governed by shariat or by customary law in regards to matters of adoption, wills and legacies, otherwise shariat law would apply. (Male) Muslim agriculturalists, particularly in the Punjab, were opposed to such measures. The Act explicitly excluded agricultural land, the devolution of which continued to be governed by local custom, and which constituted the bulk of the property.

In the aftermath of partition the government gave priority to the integration of this minority into the nation over the need to ensure legal equality for women. It accepted the claims of immutability of the shariat and declared itself incapable of making changes unless they were made by the community itself, thereby increasing the influence of religious law over the Muslim community (Parashar 1992: 150, chapter 4). No direct legislative reforms to personal laws have been forthcoming since. Hindu personal laws were reformed by the state to reflect the equality rights of women while those of other communities were placed beyond the powers of state legislators. There have been attempts to use the courts to infuse personal laws with the constitutional right to equality but these have not been successful (see Parashar 1992: 203–213).

Penalising community women

By the 1970s a belief that the state, in partnership with communities, would be able to deliver economic and social justice was draining away. The economy was stagnating; nearly half (300 million) of the population were poor. In 1975 Indira Gandhi's government declared a state of emergency, destroying a sense of the state as a benign and progressive force. The focus shifted, therefore, from a reliance on the state to deliver progress for all citizens to questioning why it had 'appropriated to itself the goodwill and struggle of an entire nation' (Chaudhuri 2005: viii). The position of women became very clear with the 1974 report (credited with creating the independent women's movement) of the Committee on the Status of Women in India (Guha 1974). The 'women's question' shifted from state paternalist attempts to improve women's position in the sphere of personal laws to the use of state power to support women as citizens who were vulnerable within the family.

At the same time the criminal justice system was exposed as a source of violence. The relationship between the state and communities had not developed in a way to provide women with 'civil' space to act as individuals. If women want to 'exit' the family and community they find themselves quickly within the domain of the criminal law and its institutions. Because women have such limited access to economic resources as citizens due to the lack of universal civil laws, they are obliged to rely on the criminal law for welfare when family laws, as interpreted by their communities, deny it to them (Basu 1999, 2008). The provision of maintenance to wives and divorced wives provides an example. Women can seek to enforce whatever right to maintenance they have through their particular personal law code. There are also provisions within the Criminal Procedure Code, designed to prevent destitution, to use summary proceedings to obtain maintenance from husbands, thereby ensuring that women were maintained within the family. These measures could offer the possibility of a speedier outcome. Muslim men have sought to avoid these provisions by arguing that they interfere with Muslim personal law. The issue exploded with spectacular effect in 1985 with the *Shah Bano* judgment (*Mohammad Ahmad Khan v. Shah Bano* AIR 1985 SC 945) which led to widespread public protest by Muslims and the Muslim Women's (Protection of Rights on Divorce) Act 1986 (Parashar 1992: 164–189; see Mullally 2004).

The urban women's movement subsequently identified another form of family economic violence: the torture, burning to death and suicide of women because their families had failed to meet demands in relation to dowry (gifts and valuables given by the bride's family to the groom at the time of or after marriage). Although the provision of dowry is illegal (Dowry Prohibition Act 1961), the practice is central to Hindu marriage processes. Campaigning led to changes to the IPC with the introduction of section 304B relating to dowry death and section 498A relating to cruelty. Both sections expose familial property relations to the criminal law (Gangoli 2007 chapter 4). Cruelty is defined as conduct that is likely either to drive a woman to suicide or to cause grave injury or danger to life, limb or liberty or harassment that is a result of coercion to meet unlawful demands for property or valuables. The second element is dowry related while the first is more widely drawn.

In India, the upper caste Hindu cultural construction of the chaste secluded woman, as reconstructed by nationalism, suggests that being a public woman involves derogation from prevalent values. Yet poor women are often, by necessity, in this space and far more vulnerable to violence. Lower-caste and tribal communities may not share these norms; women may marry informally and gain sexual experience at a young age. In these circumstances, the Penal Code provisions on rape and their interpretation within the courts were exposed as overwhelmingly hostile to women who were constructed as not complying with the normative framework of chastity and domesticity. Not only was the law unable to protect women, its institutions were a source of violence. Once in these public spaces and unprotected by communities, women were vulnerable to rape and violence perpetrated by state officials, including the police, as illustrated by the Mathura rape case (*Tukaram v. State of Maharashtra* AIR 1979 SC 185). The case hit a nerve in Indian society (see 'Open Letter' in Dhagamwar 1992: 328–333) and led to changes in the IPC relating to the offence of rape (although not to its definition) and in relation to procedural and evidential requirements (see

Dhagamwar 1992 chapter 8 for a detailed discussion). These include custodial rape: sexual intercourse with a woman while in the 'custody' of a public official (section 376 B, C and D). Women are given special protection because of their public vulnerability. A Sexual Offences Bill, which will thoroughly update these provisions, is under discussion. Measures relating to children are presently before Parliament (Protection of Children from Sexual Offences Bill 2011). An analysis of the 'violence of normal times' (Kannabiran 2005) has emerged more recently and shifted the focus to measures that can support women in their attempts to tackle violence in an expanded civil space.

Global India

Economic women or desiring subjects?

India is presently re-emerging as a 'major player' in the global market. Wide-ranging measures introduced since the mid 1980s reduced the dominant role that the state played in the economy and opened it up to the forces of global trade. Private-sector investment has flowed into the provision of utilities, transportation and telecommunications. Foreign investment is now encouraged. This has led to substantial year-on-year growth in some sectors of the economy but has created new insecurities, such as greater dependence on imports, fluctuations in balance of payments, reliance on debt and therefore vulnerability to externally determined economic policies.

India's service sector has expanded to become an important part of the economy, providing more work opportunities. While women only constitute 10 per cent of the formal labour market in India, they are gaining access to work within sectors integrated into the global market with its benefits. Women work in the special economic zones and in the outsourcing sector, which attracts young, predominantly unmarried, middle-class educated women. A consumerist culture is rapidly developing. In general, there has been a significant expansion in the economic well-being of the urban middle classes but the conspicuous consumption by the wealthy elite is a sign of emerging new divisions in society.

Despite recent economic developments, over 70 per cent of the population live and work in rural areas. Agriculture's importance to the economy has reduced somewhat but still accounts for about a third of GDP and employs two-thirds of the population. Although this figure is dropping, the proportion of women involved in the sector is increasing proportionately: in 2001 85 per cent of all rural female workers were in agriculture (Agarwal 2003: 192). Liberalisation within the WTO trade agreements is having a significant impact on the non-export agricultural sector, which no longer enjoys the same degree of state protection that it had under the earlier economic planning policies. Greater flexibilty has been achieved in India, as elsewhere, through casualisation and the intensification of labour adding to the already precarious position of the vast majority of workers. The overwhelming majority of women (and men) already work in the unorganised sector with informal arrangements of work and as 'micro entrepreneurs' (Jhabvala 2006: 37; Mazumdar 2006). The OECD in 2009 estimated that nine out of ten employees in India do not have a formal labour contract and social security benefits. 99 per cent of the workers in the agricultural sector are not members of a workers' organisation.

The Unorganised Workers' Social Security Act 2008 seeks to improve the position of informal workers through the provision of welfare measures, including health, life and disability insurance, old age pensions and group accident schemes. The aim is to reach 3.4 million workers over a five-year period although the design and implementation of the schemes are left to individual states. The Union government has also introduced an innovatory National Rural Employment Guarantee Scheme that gives a minimum of 100 days of employment to those in the unorganised sector.

Article 16(1) of the constitution states that all citizens shall have equality of opportunity in matters relating to employment or appointment to any office under the state and (2) no citizen shall on grounds only of . . . sex . . . be ineligible for or discriminated against in respect of any employment or office under the state. The provisions apply therefore to public offices not private institutions. A number of general and specific labour laws created after independence provide a patchwork of protection for formal employees although the Minimum Wages Act 1948 extends more broadly to workers in small and scattered industries and agriculture. In these labour laws women employees have tended to be constructed as in need of protection and in ways that restrict their access (see *Anuj Garg and others* v. *Hotel Association of India and others* 2007 INSC 1226).

When women move out of the 'private sphere' they face hostility. Only one in three women report that they can go to the market without family permission; likewise only one in four can visit friends (Gangoli 2007: 2). However, such community-based constructions of women, as wives, mothers or daughters, sit very uneasily with the construction of women as unencumbered, flexible workers in a global market economy. Equally, constructions of women within both family and criminal laws as chaste, sexually passive and in effect the sexual property of husbands offers little to a consumer market that is premised on the assumption that individuals construct their own identities and meet their desires through the goods and services they consume. In an era of globalisation, sections of the women's movement are increasingly challenging the prevailing constructions of sexuality within Indian society, offering alternative, active, understandings of passion and desire rather than victimhood (Kapur 2005). The wider context of the liberalisation of the market is therefore contributing to the restructuring of gender relations and the emergence of new contests in law over the construction of womanhood and over what constitutes the public and the private.

These can be seen in the social activism and prominent legal campaigning over the last ten years, which have contributed significantly to the expansion of the civil space in India. The international discourse on human rights, particularly relating to women, has played a central part in challenging community-based concepts of privacy, which seek to keep the state out of the personal laws but which have also allowed the state to enforce notions of community morality in the public arena. The recent campaigns require the state to take increased responsibility to protect the human rights of the individual.

Thus the campaign relating to sexual harassment in the workplace seeks to shift the discourse away from morality, where it would be seen as outraging the modesty of women (IPC section 354) or insulting the modesty of a woman (IPC section 509) to one that enforces women's human right to work in public without intimidation (*Vishaka* v. *State of Rajasthan* (1997) 6 SCC 241). Subsequent developments both in case law and the drafting of legislation have shown that the discourse of women's sexual rights can quickly slip back into the discourse of decency and morality and recast women as victims in need of protection and therefore a liability not an asset (*Apparel Export Promotions Council* v. *A.K. Chopra* AIR 1999 SC 625; see Kapur 1999: 353, 354–359).

The Protection of Women from Domestic Violence Act 2005 is a product of over ten years of struggle within the Indian women's movement to provide women with rights relating to violence in the home through a range of now 'orthodox' measures in the area (Jaising et al. 2009). The innovative section 17 grants the woman a right to reside in a shared household whether or not she has any property-based rights, and a right not to be evicted or excluded from the shared household. A residence order (section 19) can: restrain the respondent and his relatives from dispossessing the woman from the shared household; require him to leave and not to re-enter; prevent him from disposing of the property and direct him to secure (and pay for) alternative accommodation of a similar standard. Protection Officers (PO) (section 8), who are state employees, can draw up a Domestic Incident Report (DIR) or apply for protection order on behalf of a woman. A range of persons apart from the police can record a DIR.

While the Act draws its legitimacy from the international women's human rights framework, the legal response is clearly rooted in the analytical framework developed within the Indian women's movement (Kannabiran 2005). It contributes to the reconceptualisation of the family as a not wholly private space and the non-toleration of 'ordinary' violence. It seeks to ameliorate the lack of control over private and public space that women face – the 'civil death' that follows if a woman is ousted from, or seeks to leave, her marital family (Rajan 2004). The Act builds on the welfare role often ascribed to women's organisations in the absence of state welfare provision of housing or other benefits and to develop a state institutional framework for intervention in the family. POs provide a point of reference outside the family to assist the woman in her civil rights. Much depends on how the individual states respond to the mandatory requirements under the rules to establish POs and to provide them with resources (Lawyers Collective 2009). Overall the Act reduces the power of the family and increases that of state law. Such an Act cannot however redistribute property rights on a permanent basis.

Contesting sexual agency

The nationalist discourse on women constructed a new Indian 'woman'. She was not Western; she was neither an upper-caste conservative nor one of the masses of the poor. The more recent developments all point to further changes to the constructions of personhood. They suggest that globalisation is contributing to the integration of some women into forms of citizenship that entitle them to use public space as individuals and to exercise greater autonomy over their sexuality in a reconstructed private sphere. However, this conception of autonomy and individualism sits alongside Indian women's enduring status as kinswomen.

The 1860 IPC, still the basis for India's criminal law, reflects both the moral values of the Victorian drafters (modesty, virginity and chastity for women) and their understanding of the local norms (Kumari 1999).[1] It also reinforces the upper-caste discourse on the centrality of chastity, seclusion and domesticity for women and therefore the importance of regulating women's sexuality (Dhagamwar 1992: chapter 4). The concern is not with protecting vulnerable lower-caste propertyless women from 'public' violence or women seeking 'public' protection to enable them to exercise marital choices that are deemed to dishonour the 'private' family. The criminal justice system reinforces concepts of male control over women's sexuality.

This section considers the way in which these criminal justice provisions interact with local community and state governance contexts and changing constructions of personhood in North India. The discussion also provides the local context for the Indian element of the transnational chain.

Economies, polities and communities

The caste system, with its birth-based status hierarchy, forms the basis of social stratification in much of the Indian subcontinent. Caste historically has controlled group access to land and other productive resources. Marriages create family alliances and secure family positions within community hierarchies. Reproduction is a social act, inextricably linked to the political economy of communities and to the construction of community identity (Chakravarti 2005: 309). Any violation of the marriage codes is 'regarded as an attack upon *izzat* ('honour' or 'prestige'), a wide-ranging masculine concept underpinning patriarchal practices in India across all castes. Action to uphold *izzat* is always a male prerogative: women can only 'incite' action . . .' (Chakravarti 2005: 309). 'Dishonourable' conduct is seen as irreparably ruining a family. Those who transgress are punished to maintain the 'material structures of "social" power and social dominance' (Chakravarti 2005: 309). The goal of gaining and upholding 'honour' is shared by most communities in the subcontinent, and

---

[1] The provisions relating to rape and sexual assault are due to be replaced when the Sexual Assault Bill is enacted. These provisions will locate sexual assault firmly as a crime against the individual.

in the diaspora, whether Hindu, Sikh or Muslim, although here the focus is on Hindu communities in North India (Chakravarti 2005; Chowdhry 2004a, 2004b, 2007). The norms that establish acceptable marriages are highly complex and restrictive. Broadly speaking, women and men in the same village cannot marry each other (it would be incestuous) because they are deemed to be brothers and sisters by kinship rules, which create an idealised village and caste community (*biradari*). Marriages between men and women from different villages may well still break the rules. Both a self-arranged marriage and a marriage arranged inappropriately by the immediate family can reduce family honour. Although both the young woman and the young man are seen as at fault, the woman is the focus of attention. She is responsible for the dishonour because the 'idea of women as the sexual property of their communities is deeply internalised, mobilising not merely the family but also the community, frequently accompanied by violence' (Chakravarti 2005: 311).

None of these rules are recognised formally by the state. The constitution ensures universal adult suffrage and equality between men and women. Under the Hindu Marriage Act 1955 there are virtually no restrictions (apart from incest) on the marriage of two opposite-sex Hindu adults. Adults do not require any parental consent to marriage. Inter-faith or community marriages can be formalised via the secular Special Marriages Act of 1954. The legal age of majority and the minimum age for marriage for girls is eighteen. However, under section 375 of the IPC the age of consent for sexual intercourse is sixteen for unmarried and fifteen for married women. Sexual activity below these ages is illegal. An underage marriage arranged by a guardian will not trigger any action while an unsanctioned union will be challenged.

The plurality of normative frameworks (constitutional provisions, penal, 'state-sanctioned' personal and customary laws) is reflected in the diversity of contemporary governance structures in the villages. The *Biradari* turn to the traditional method of village governance, the panchayat, to settle disputes regarding caste and inter-caste matters, including transgressions relating to marriage and sexual liaisons (Chowdhry 2004a: 6). The traditional caste panchayat is constituted of men; women are not normally permitted to attend even though their activities are the focus of attention. Using its own normative framework it seeks to impose justice to restore honour. This will involve retrieval of the girl from her lover or husband and restoration to the guardianship of her father. Any marriage will be ignored. Once she is back within the family, she is at considerable risk of violence. At best she will be married to whomsoever will take her, given her dishonour; at worst she will be killed or persuaded into suicide. In any case her death will be described as suicide (Chakravarti 2005; Chowdhry 2004a, 2007). Her family and that of the young man may also face sanctions, such as fines or land dispositions or social boycott within the village, a very powerful collective punishment (Chowdhry 2004a).

This body is not recognised by the state and has no formal legal powers. It has been replaced by the statutory panchayat system, which provides for local governance in the villages, which encourages inclusive democratic processes through mandatory reservations for women and Dalits (Rai 2007). The official powers to deal with any crimes associated with these liaisons are held by the police and magistrates courts, which form the local state justice system. However, there is considerable hostility within village hierarchies to what is seen as interference by the state, granting young people, particularly women, individual agency in family and community affairs. Reduced profits from agriculture and increases in population have led to fragmentation of land owning, heightening fear of the impact of women's land rights. There are high levels of unemployment among men. Globalisation has brought consumerism to the villages, much of which is targeted on the young, including the exclusively male consumption of alcohol. Young men are seen as out of family control and there are anxieties about the potential increase in female independence as educated women find employment in service industries. Extremely unfavourable sex ratios result in a shortage of marriageable women at the lower end of the social scale and many young men who due to unemployment have difficulty obtaining brides in a dowry economy (Chowdhry 2004a: 36). In a culture that associates marriage and fatherhood with masculinity, a man with a reliable job, particularly outside agriculture, can command a high dowry which puts pressure on the bride's family funds.

The traditional power base operated by upper-caste senior males is vulnerable to these socio-economic changes (Chowdhry 2004a: 38). Villages have been politicised. The traditional patriarchs seek to maintain solidarity around caste-based social rules in circumstances where they have lost power. If they are unable to contain a particular marriage-related issue within their community domain, they move from private justice to public law to seek the support of the criminal justice system to protect male honour. This occurs particularly when a young couple elopes to pursue a 'love' marriage. As soon as it is clear the girl has 'run away' the woman's male guardian makes a complaint to the police who register a case of kidnapping (section 363: taking a minor out of the care of a guardian) or abduction (section 362: removal of a person from a place by means of force or by deceit) which applies to both minors and adult persons. The intent of the abductor has to be established: to murder under section 364; to secretly and wrongfully confine under section 365; to induce a woman into marriage in order that she may be forced or seduced to illicit intercourse under section 366; or to rape a woman under section 376. The age of the woman becomes a key fact but is not that easy to establish. Births are not necessarily registered; other records are patchy and not necessarily reliable. The judge, not the girl, decides on her age (Chowdhry 2004b).

The consensual and deliberate actions of the 'runaway couple', who will in many cases have married, are reconstructed within this legal framework. This is easier if the young woman is under age: the young man can be sought for kidnapping, if not for abduction and rape. Acting under these powers the police find the young couple, arrest the young man, who is not given bail, and return the young woman to her guardian. She is then persuaded to support the statements given by her guardian or others, which led to the arrest. The matter comes to court with all the parties – police, prosecutor, lawyers if present, and judge – knowing full well what the situation is but pursuing the matter as if it were as presented. The conviction of the young man (and any 'accomplices') for kidnapping/abduction, rape or other associated intent follows. On appeal the stories may not be accepted so readily. The women's statement is seen as false and the conviction may be overturned or the sentence reduced.

What are the implications of this use of state penal provisions for community-based norm enforcement? First, there is no use of the discourse of community honour. The issue is constructed as one involving a fundamental habeas corpus issue. Secondly, even if the magistrate or appellate court judge 'sees through' the story and does not convict the alleged perpetrators, the marriage is never recognised. Thus the woman's sexual behaviour is constructed still as 'illicit', that is outside marriage. Her 'promiscuity' has of course been established through the evidence that she is 'habituated' to sexual intercourse. Her position in law is close to that of a prostitute. If she has married a young man from within a forbidden *got* relationship she has the added stigma of an incestuous marriage. Thus, the pursuit of community honour and the protection of a system of alliance via the public state legal system construct the woman who has exercised agency as both morally and legally dishonourable. It denies her bodily integrity. Rather than protect her, the provisions make her acutely vulnerable to retribution from her family and the community, taking the 'honourable' way out of this situation. The young man is not similarly dishonoured although he may have spent considerable time in custody and experienced the rigours of the criminal justice process.

Thirdly, at the local institutional level, the state legal system is operating under the same norms as the community, with little separation between the laws of the community and the 'rule of law' by the polity (Baxi et al. 2006). In this context, the state-based penal provisions are fused with community values, allowing no space for the values associated with gender equality and constitutional rights to operate. The exercise of a sexual right, to have consensual sexual intercourse, either within marriage or without, is turned into an alleged 'sex crime'.

Feminists and activists in India have argued that these matters, like those associated with the debates more generally over domestic violence, are examples of custodial violence, bringing us back to an analysis of the power relations within families based upon a range of hierarchies, not only those associated with gender, but also with caste and class (Chakravarti 2005). Women's organisations support campaigns relating to women's right to choose if, when and whom to marry (Chakravarti 2005: 325). They highlight examples where judges throughout the court system have used values drawn from the discourse of rights and the rule of law to 'see through' the complaint and uphold women's autonomy (Chowdhry 2004b: 74, 2007: 203). In these circumstances, the rule of law ideology and constitutional morality of 'Global' India 'filters down' to reinforce local justice delivery.

Law's post-colonial development in Pakistan

Locating women's value

Pakistan had a population of approximately 170 million in 2009 (sixth largest in the world), 22 per cent of which live below the poverty line of one dollar a day. On independence, Pakistan was a very poor agriculture-based economy but has managed to develop what has been described by the World Bank (1997a) as a surprisingly resilient diverse economic base constituted by agriculture, manufacturing of textiles, chemicals and food processing, despite periods of mismanagement and a large range of internal and external shocks. Seven million Pakistanis live abroad, remitting US\$ 7 billion annually through formal channels, constituting the second largest source of foreign exchange after exports (Government of Pakistan 2010). Pakistan's strategic position in the 'war on terror' has ensured favourable international economic collaboration and its GDP grew between 6 and 8 per cent between 2004 and 2006. Poverty levels decreased, but growth has slowed subsequently. International political and military interventions have led to significant destabilisation and devastation, particularly within the regions abutting Afghanistan.

Agriculture still supports the majority of the population who live in rural areas directly or indirectly, employs 45 per cent of the labour force and accounted for 21 per cent of GDP in 2008–2009. Changes in agricultural production are leading to increased feminisation of the sector. Of those women who are defined as economically active, most work in agriculture, a third being family workers with little access to cash income and only 2 per cent owning land; under 20 per cent work in the service sector; and fewer than 10 per cent in industry (Shaheed 2009). Approximately 3 per cent of women of working age (aged ten or above) are paid employees (Government of Pakistan 2010; see further Shahid 2010). Women's work as family labour is, however, grossly under-reported, particularly in a society based on a strong ideology of purdah (see Mehdi 2001). The vast majority of women depend on familial distribution of assets although women are working harder in more informal labour contexts to fulfil family and farming responsibilities, which are made more time consuming by ecological degradation and conflict. The floods of 2010 have further undermined human security.

Pakistan ranks 141st of 182 countries on the human development index and 139th out of 157 on the gender-related development index. The positioning indicates substantial gender disparities, particularly in areas such as literacy (36 per cent compared to 63 per cent for men); access to education; lower life expectancy at birth; and low incomes (estimated to be one third of male earnings) (Shaheed 2009).

Constituting an Islamic identity

Pakistan achieved nation status in 1947 as a Muslim majority state. Originally it was constituted by two geographical areas, one to the east of India, which, after a civil war and the Indo-Pakistan war in 1971, seceded to become Bangladesh, and the other to the north-west. The partition of India involved massive death tolls and the mass migration of Hindus and Sikhs into India and Muslims into Pakistan. Disputes over the princely state of Kashmir and Jammu led to the first Kashmir War in 1948, after which India occupied approximately two-thirds of the state and Pakistan the remainder.

Pakistan was constituted as a secular democratic state but both these elements have struggled to take root. For much of its history Pakistan has been governed by military rulers installed after coup d'etats. (Pakistan inherited 30 per cent of the British Indian Army on partition, employing now half a million and constituting the sixth largest army in the world). After a period of civilian rule between 1972 and 1977 General Zia-ul-Haq became the third military president, introducing a policy of Islamification. In 1988 Benazir Bhutto was elected as prime minister on a secularist agenda and power alternated between her party and that of Nawaz Sharif's party, espousing Islamic politics, over the next decade. The country's economic position worsened and military tensions with India increased. A military coup in 1999 led to the installation of General Musharraf as leader and president in 2001. After parliamentary elections in 2002, executive powers were transferred to the prime minister. There has since been a gradual move towards democratic governance, which led, after the general election in 2008, to a civilian democratically elected government (see further Shaheed 2009).

The first prime minister, Jinnah, sought to establish a secular state where religious belief would not be part of political citizenship. Nonetheless, Islam had played a part in the nationalist ideology of Pakistani unity and was integral to the construction of Pakistani nationhood (Mullally 2007: 382). Women's conduct as Muslims was central to this fragile nation-building ideology, separating Pakistan from its Hindu neighbour but also seeking to unite the many linguistic and ethnic communities and socio-economic groupings within Pakistan. The fundamental rights provisions in the constitution provide for both freedom of religion (Article 20) and non-discrimination on the basis of sex (Article 25). There is no aspiration to a uniform civil code in the constitution. The Objective Resolution drawn up by the Constituent Assembly in 1949, which embodied the aims and objects of the constitution, became its Preamble providing that 'Muslims shall be enabled to order their lives in the individual and collective spheres in accordance with the teachings and requirements of Islam' (Mullally 2007: 381). This Preamble was not deemed to hold a supra-constitutional position thereby informing all aspects of the constitution, or to be justiciable. The 1956 constitution declared Pakistan to be an Islamic Republic and Article 198 required all laws to be brought into conformity with the injunctions of Islam. The National Assembly was to determine repugnance, instituting a political rather than judicial process. In 1973, Islam became the state religion.

Tensions in the relationship between the Shari'ah, the constitutional guarantee of equality and religion-based systems of personal law are evident generally in the legal system. Pakistan, like India, continued the plural legal system of colonial times on independence, with its separate personal law codes for different communities. We have seen the ways in which colonialism moulded these personal laws, fuelling a perception that the codes reflected customary practices more than the religious tenets upon which they were supposedly based. The demands of Muslim political leaders in the 1930s for codification to accord more with the Shari'ah led to the 1937 Muslim Personal Law (Shari'ah) Application Act, extending the application of Muslim Personal Law (MPL) to the whole of India, replacing customary understandings. This demand was continued after independence. In 1962 all Shari'ah Acts enacted by the various provincial legislatures in Pakistan were replaced by national legislation for West Pakistan although the Act was made subject to the provisions of enactments already in force, thereby protecting the position of the newly enacted 1961 Muslim Family Law Ordinance (MFLO). This Act sought to give women their proper place within society according to the fundamentals of Islam although this claim was hotly disputed by conservative elements because the Act restricted through procedural requirements, although did not prohibit, the practice of polygamy and the power of *talaq* (see Ali 2002, 2006). Challenges to the Act's constitutionality followed but were not supported. The vulnerability of the MFLO increased in the era of Islamisation, which underpinned a conservative nationalism after 1977, a process that focused on regulating women's sexuality far more tightly, shifting the emphasis to regulation through criminal provisions leading to the direct criminalisation of sexual relations outside marriage.

In 1977, Zia-ul-Haq suspended the fundamental rights chapter of the 1973 constitution. A Federal Shariat Court (FSC) was created under Article 203 C(1) with responsibility to examine laws for conformity with the injunctions of Islam. Initially the personal laws were shielded from the jurisdiction of the FSC. However in 1985 the Preamble to the constitution was incorporated as a substantive part of the 1973 constitution and therefore, conservatives argued, justiciable, enabling a review of MPL and the MFLO. Although the Supreme Court has resisted such an interpretation, and in so doing has preserved women's constitutional right to equality, the enduring legacy of this era lies in the reshaping of everyday norms to view not all citizens as equal (Mullally 2007; Shaheed 2009: 20).

Criminalising Pakistani women's sexuality

Pakistan retained the colonial criminal codes (Pakistan Penal Code (PPC) and Criminal Procedure Code (CrPC)) on independence. Zia set about 'Islamising' both codes. This process involves categorising the offences according to their punishments: hadd, qisas and tizar. 'Hadd (plural Hudood) offences are considered offences against God or against the interests of society as a whole.' Hadd punishments are mandatory (Ali 2007a: 376). The Hudood Ordinances 1979 established the offence of Zina which criminalises sexual relations outside marriage. It can be committed by both men and women and attracts a Hadd punishment (section 5, stoning to death in a public place) if proven. Section 6 covers Zina-bil-jabr, which can be committed by either a man or a woman (from the age of puberty) to whom he or she is not legally married. It involves sexual intercourse against the will or without the consent of the victim. If proven, it attracts a Hadd punishment. The level of proof for Hadd is exceptionally high, requiring at least four truthful and upstanding Muslim adult males to give eyewitness evidence. A raped woman therefore finds herself vulnerable to Zina if she cannot prove Zina-bil-jabr.

After the establishment of the FSC in 1980, parts of the Penal Code dealing with murder and bodily hurt were challenged. In the case of *Federation of Pakistan* v. *Gul Hussan* in 1989 the Supreme Court Shariat Appellate Bench found the sections of the PPC dealing with deliberate murder and deliberate hurt repugnant to Islam because there was no right of qisas (retaliation) or for provision for diyat (compensation). In contrast to the PPC and CrPC, the Koran and Sunna view murder and hurt 'first as a violation of the rights of an individual and his/her heirs and only then as a law and order issues and crime against the state' (Warraich 2005: 84). The Law of Qisas and Diyat were introduced in 1990.

Constructing and contesting honour

Reflecting the position in north India, the social and economic relations of power within family networks underpin the regulation of women's sexuality and lead to violence. Killings occur in all four provinces and the tribal areas adjoining Afghanistan. (4,101 were reported killed between 1998 and 2003 of which 2,774 were female; viewed as the tip of an iceberg by activists (Warraich 2005: 80)). The increasing politicisation of religion has added a further toxic dimension to family power relationships (Shaheed 2009). Although confined 'traditionally' to a response to the discovery of extra-marital sex by a woman family member, the ambit has extended to cover wider expressions of women's autonomy.

Honourable killing within the state criminal justice system

Under the pre-partition IPC, male relatives or husbands were able to make use of the exception contained within section 300 (on murder) relating to the deprivation of the power of self-control due to grave and sudden provocation. Such culpable homicide avoided the death penalty or life imprisonment under section 302. The PPC section 304(1) reproduced this exception. Inappropriate sexual behaviour by a wife or family member was regularly considered to amount to such provocation, 'granting male family members a virtual licence to kill their women on the pretext of "honour"' (Warraich 2005: 83). The provocation exception disappeared with the changed conceptual framework after 1990, which wove the Law of Qisas and Dayat into the PPC. Every unnatural death by another was now considered murder and four new categories of murder were introduced. Sentences now depended on the form of proof and the relationship of the offender to the deceased. A murderer is liable to qisas (the death sentence as retribution) if the accused confesses or there are sufficient credible eyewitnesses. If not, the murderer is liable to tazir, involving life imprisonment or death under section 302 (b) of the PPC. A spouse who murders the other spouse (where there is a surviving child of the marriage) is automatically exempted from qisas or tazir (Section 306 (c) PPC). In these cases a discretionary sentence under diyat is available. The new framework generally provides judges with possibilities for exercising broad discretion in sentencing where acts are seen as disrupting the social order or in circumstances where the facts and circumstances make the award of tazir appropriate (PPC section 311 and PPC section 338E) (Warraich 2005: 85).

Section 307 of the PPC states that qisas will not be enforced in circumstances where the Injunctions of Islam, which are not defined, make it inapplicable, providing further broad discretion to the judge. It is also possible for the heirs of a victim to forgive an accused or enter into a compromise in return for compensation (compounding). Compromise is likely where the killing is undertaken by close relatives and in communities in which marriages take place between relatives. These changes transformed the treatment of honour killings. The courts could now exercise their wide discretionary powers to demonstrate societal disapproval of such killings and some, within the Lahore High Court, have adopted a more progressive stance by utilising the human rights conceptual framework to prioritise women as citizens under the constitution rather than family members (Mullally 2007: 401–405; Ali 2007a). Many have failed to do so (Warraich 2005: 88–96). Judges, and therefore the state, validate the male family 'right' to police women's sexual conduct in the name of family 'honour'.

While guardians (father or husbands) are viewed as initiators of complaints, officers within the criminal justice system are responsible for pursuing them, either directly through cognisable offences or on a complaint by an aggrieved person in non-cognisable ones. Since 1990, the responsibility to initiate action has moved significantly from the state to the guardians/heirs of victims, although cognisable offences remain. Statistics show that a substantial proportion of honour killings are compromised before conviction. Of 'the 2253 "honour" killings in the Punjab since 1998, only 160 have resulted in trial court convictions'; many are overturned on appeal (Warraich 2005: 100).

The power of honour within communities

As in North India, regulation of sexuality takes place primarily within local communities, far away from the upper echelons of the judicial system. Both penal codes define sexual intercourse outside marriage as 'illicit' but stop short of criminalising such intercourse if heterosexual. The Zina Ordinance explicitly does so and passes on legally constructed responsibility to initiate the policing of social behaviour to families and communities. The law of Qisas and Diyat has enabled the merger between private tribal normative codes and state laws: '[i]n the tribal value system, retribution or punishment is codified in revenge, in the ideology of killing and dying for honour. . . . Retribution therefore, is private and this is often settled by a group of elders . . . through the imposition of fines' (Shah 2007: 148). The system hinges now on the Wali, the heir of the deceased or the victim (Shah 2007: 149). There is 'the deregulation of regulation, a transferring of legal resources to the private domain – of parent as Wali, of family as Wali and of tribe as Wali'. 'State law is penetrated by honour codes and tribalized' (Shah 2007: 149, 151).

The impact of these changes spreads far beyond killings. Women become 'criminals' caught up in the indiscriminate use of the Zina Ordinance. There is no 'civil' space for women in which to exercise their sexuality. The honour value system solidifies while the law fragments into subjective private concerns (Shah 2007: 151). Family control over the asset of women's appropriate behaviour is also used as a tool for extortion, to settle family feuds, or to exact revenge (Warraich 2005: 79). Families use the state penal code provisions relating to kidnapping and abduction and zina to implicate the local administration of justice system in the enforcement of local social values. 'The vast majority of cases registered under Hudood laws of zina and zina bil jabr are based on the personal and ulterior motives of near relatives . . . evidence is doctored and constructed, in collaboration with investigation agencies (in this case, invariably local police)' (Ali 2007a: 387). 'Honour accusations draw huge fines, and an exchange economy thrives within the politics of honour. People's pensions, house-building loans, advances on government salaries, traders' returns, fresh acquisitions of property, are all redistributed through honour accusations and the threats of violence' (Shah 2007: 139). A startlingly large number of women find themselves, as a consequence, convicted by the courts of first instance and imprisoned under the Zina Ordinance. Her 'male co-accused is acquitted for want of evidence while the woman is convicted for her pregnancy' (Ali 2007a: 390). Some cases make it into the spotlight of the superior courts where the judgments are almost invariably (although there are some notorious exceptions) overturned on appeal with admonishments, but with little effect on the subordinate courts. Huge damage is done to women in the process.

Much 'policing' takes place not within the polity of the local courts but within the sphere of community regulation in panchayats and jirgas. These bodies were provided with 'unchecked power' in the British period and still exercise much of it today within rural areas where the majority of the population lives. Judgments are based on customary practices and would be deemed illegal within common and shariat law. All participants are men. Women are not allowed to attend jirga meetings and may only be represented by male relatives so women hear of their adultery when they are summoned for punishment (Iqbal 2007). There are no appeals against verdicts. 'Shariat courts', established through the influence of religious right groups, operating outside the recognised state system and challenging community-based institutions, add to the complexities (Shaheed 2009: 27).

Dishonouring women, denying rights

Women's constitutional rights as citizens are precarious in the face of the determined efforts of conservative Islamist politicians and religious non-state actors. The control of family and community has expanded into a sphere previously occupied by post-colonial state law, which itself reflected family-based values but was secular in nature and based on a presumption of state protection for the individual. In these circumstances the struggle to expand civil space for women is hugely challenging.

A successful campaign led in 1996 to Pakistan ratifying CEDAW without reservations although making a general declaration invoking the Constitution of the Islamic Republic of Pakistan (Mullally 2007: 395–401). International human rights have been used in the courts to protect women's constitutional rights. Such rights, reinforced by constitutional provisions, have more resonance in the public sphere of employment as a means of tackling sex discrimination against the tiny minority of women who are able to access the formal sector than in relation to women as members of families. However the Commission of Inquiry for Women in 1997 supported CEDAW recommendations for a series of reforms to enhance women's rights within the family. In 2002, the National Commission on the Status of Women recommended the repeal of the Hudood laws using women's constitutional and human rights as justifications. Civil society organisations, both within and outside Pakistan, have used human rights discourse in attempts to combat the specific forms of violence enshrined in honour crimes and zina offences although they face challenges within 'civil' society from religious non-state actors.

These efforts have led to limited reforms. The Criminal Law (Amendment) Act 2004 amends the PPC and CrPC to provide more protection, including specific penalties, for crimes of honour. However, the crimes are still subject to the laws of Qisas and Dyat, thereby not tackling the basic problems identified above. Family members will still be able to avoid criminal sanctions by paying compensation or obtaining the forgiveness of the victim's family. The many years of struggle by activists within Pakistan and by international rights activists (see Amnesty International (USA) 1999) over the Hudood Ordinances led to the Protection of Women (Criminal Laws Amendment) Act 2006 which seeks to move zina-bil-jabr (the rape provisions) out of the Zina Ordinance and place it back within the secular PCC. Both measures, however, reflect the compromises necessary to stem opposition from the conservative Islamist parties who accused the government of carrying out a Western agenda to secularise Pakistan (Mullally 2007: 406).

Academic jurists, activists and some members of the judiciary, working with the tenets of Islam, tackle the conservative, and in their view incorrect, interpretations of Shari'ah that have been codifed into the state legal system (Ali 2007a). They argue that translation of scriptural text into law tends to reflect the prevailing objectives of those in power. They rely on an egalitarian rights-informed interpretation of Islam that can support a degree of increased space for women, an approach that has found favour in some instances in the courts.

Nonetheless, Pakistan's internationally strategic but highly vulnerable position in the 'war on terror', the legacy of Islamisation, the rise of politico-religious non-state actors, the poverty in which much of its population lives and the prevailing societal norms relating to gender equality in general, and violence in particular, make the struggle for the expansion of civil, or indeed religiously sanctioned, space a mountainous one for all women, irrespective of disparate forms of differences they face.

Law's post-colonial development in Bangladesh

We see a differently positioned struggle over women's embodied citizenship and the regulation of women's sexuality by state and community in Bangladesh, which reflects its position within the world market as a heavily donor-supported economy as well as its political history.

Constituting a Bangladeshi identity

Until partition in 1947, the area now forming the state of Bangladesh was part of the province of Bengal, located on the eastern periphery of India at the delta of two large rivers. The Bengalis maintained their own culture after the arrival of the Brahmin Hindus who located themselves in the western, more accessible, part of Bengal. The indigenous Bengalis were incorporated into the caste system at the lower end. The arrival of Islam in the thirteenth century provided a positive alternative although again the Bengalis found themselves perceived as lowly converts with poor understanding of Islam. Kabeer argues that in Bengal there were two forms of Islam: '[T]he Islam of the villages, a fusion of Hindu and Muslim traditions among cultivators and artisans' although it was difficult 'to disentangle the origins of various beliefs and customs ... which were shared by Muslim and Hindu peasant alike and were essentially Bengali beliefs' and 'the faith practised by the urban-based, foreign born Islamic elite who strongly resisted assimilation into indigenous Bengali culture' (Kabeer 1991: 118). The two belief systems coexisted uneasily. However, Bengali members of the Muslim League, who supported the demand for a separate Muslim homeland, espoused the latter.

Bengal was partitioned in 1947. West Bengal remained part of India with a Bengali Hindu majority while East Bengal, with its Bengali Muslim majority, became East Pakistan. Islam, as a fundamental element in the nation-building strategy of Pakistan, had its political centre in West Pakistan. 'State power ... was monopolised by a Punjabi-based, military-bureaucratic oligarchy whose policies towards the east wing reduced it to the status of a colony'(Kabeer 1991: 119). The tensions soon manifested themselves, particularly in struggles over cultural identity, resistance to which unified the population under a banner of Bengali nationalism. The cultural identity of Bengali women, as different from the Muslim women of West Pakistan, was an important element in this process and had tragic consequences in the war associated with the independence struggles. It is estimated that 30,000 Bengali women were raped by Pakistani soldiers in attempts to 'improve the genes' (Kabeer 1991: 122).

Bangladesh gained its independence from Pakistan in 1971 and was established under the Awami League as a secular, democratic, socialist state within the constitution of 1972. These values have changed in its subsequent turbulent politics. Bangladesh has been ruled 'by an unstable alliance between an under-developed national bourgeoisie and the military and civil bureaucracy', plagued by coups and counter-coups (Kabeer 1991: 122). In 1977, in a bid to distinguish his party from the Awami League and the nation from its West Bengal neighbour, General Rahman determined that citizens were Bangladeshis not Bengalis (Article 6 (2) of the constitution). Proclamation Order no. 1 inserted a declaration (Preamble) at the beginning of the constitution that it: was made in the name of Allah, the Beneficent, the Merciful; deleted the principle of secularism; and replaced it with trust and faith in the Almighty Allah; and inserted a clause that sought solidarity with other Muslim countries. In 1988 General Ershad declared Islam as the state religion although other religions 'may be practised in peace and harmony' (Article 2A).

In contrast to the process under General Zia in Pakistan, which introduced the Hudood Ordinances, this was not viewed as a very serious attempt at Islamisation of the state although it provoked opposition from many, including women's organisations. Nevertheless, there has been a significant growth in grassroots religious consciousness.

Valued women?

Bangladesh is one of the world's poorest and most densely populated countries. Partition in 1947 severely disrupted its position within the former colonial economic system as a producer of jute and rice for the urban industrial economy around Kolkota, now in India. On independence, Pakistan pursued a policy of development through industrialisation, which focused predominantly on West Pakistan, so while East Pakistan needed to replace its industrial base and modernise its agriculture, no policies materialised. The result was increased rural poverty. Bangladesh faced formidable problems on independence in 1971, which included the consequences of a violent conflict that had led to up to 10 million people fleeing to India and then returning; the highest rural population density in the entire world (159 million approximately in 2008) and a high population growth; the malnutrition of most citizens; a large illiterate and unskilled work force, resulting in mass underemployment; and a chronic shortage of experienced personnel to tackle these problems.

The socialist economic model which involved the nationalisation of much of what was left of the industrial sector was soon abandoned. From 1975 General Rahman pursued a more market-oriented, liberalising economic policy, while General Ershad, from 1982, set about implementing the IMF policy of structural adjustment, which formed international economic orthodoxy at the time and which sought to base economic liberalisation on export-led growth and the promotion of the private sector. The outcome was the development of the successful export-oriented garment industry, replacing jute production, which now provides 75 per cent of Bangladesh's total export earnings and a million formal-sector jobs for women (out of a total of about 2.2 million jobs). Bangladesh still turned to the IMF in 2003 for a three-year, US$ 490 million poverty reduction and economic reform programme and the World Bank approved US$ 536 million in interest-free loans. Prospects for growth are still not good.

The ready-made textile industry faces major competition and pressure to reduce costs. This sector is concentrated in export processing zones, which offer incentives to investors, including full repatriation of profits; all goods in the zone are exempted from export duties. Trade unions and strikes are prohibited. Textile workers are some of the worst paid workers in the world, often working in very poor conditions. Organised protests in recent years to increase the minimum wage finally led to a government Commission in 2006, which recommended a modest increase and urged employers to improve conditions.

Most Bangladeshis earn their living from agriculture. In comparison to countries with similar income levels, there are fewer women employed in agriculture due to the low demand for labour. Land holdings are small and productivity low (World Bank 2008: 57). Rural underemployment is a serious problem. Women work on farms owned by their husbands where they are providing increasing amounts of unpaid family help. Women are more involved in livestock rearing probably due to the success of micro credit schemes (World Bank 2008). The World Bank notes generally the very low level of participation of women in the labour market overall (26 per cent of women aged between fifteen and fifty-nine; second only to Pakistan in South Asia). However, it also highlights a recent significant increase in women's employment rates, particularly for young women, due to working in the garment industries but also in the community and social services sector. The latter employs almost one-fifth of all women workers. The employment of young men has decreased in the same period.

The formal sector of the economy overall is tiny and shrinking: only 10 per cent of women and 22 per cent of men aged between twenty and fifty-five receive cash wages (World Bank 2008: 62). For this work women are paid between 60 and 65 per cent of men's wages. At the same time only 4 per cent of women are reported as working as casual workers, of which about a quarter are housemaids. The attraction of the garment industries as a source of paid employment becomes obvious in this context.

Since independence in 1971, Bangladesh has received more than US$ 30 billion in grant aid and loans from foreign donors (about half of which has been provided) and donor aid constitutes more than half of its GDP. At national level, the IMF/World Bank conditionality, and at local level, multilateral and bilateral donor development programmes, have affected all aspects of people's lives. Once the commitment to Islam was established politically, aid from the Middle East, particularly from Saudi Arabia, began. These funds have disseminated values through 'Islamic non government organisations, the madrassa (religious education) system and the fundamentalist parties (Kabeer 1994: 134). Such NGOs are community oriented, working at the village level to provide basic health care, village administration and agricultural extension work. They affect the way in which women's sexuality is regulated collectively in rural areas.

Bangladesh depends on a range of external donors to support its highly vulnerable position within the world economy and they have brought with them their own gender agendas, which have contributed to alternative perspectives on rural development (see Kabeer 1994). Official government policies have clearly been influenced, as is evident from a recent World Bank report, which offers a very positive view of the way in which women's position has improved despite formidable odds (World Bank 2008). Fertility rates have dropped dramatically and education for girls increased significantly, both leading to the improvements in women's position within families and communities. Social attitudes, particularly among the younger generation, are changing, suggesting greater recognition of women's rights to participate in public and private affairs although the report cautions against over-optimism. Women still own virtually no property in their own right despite constitutional guarantees of equal rights to property. In 1996 under 4 per cent of the 17.8 million agricultural holdings were female owned. In 2006 fewer than 10 per cent of all women (under 3 per cent of younger women) had their names on marital property documents although young women were more likely to receive parental property, indicating perhaps that they are becoming less willing to give it up to brothers (World Bank 2008).

Donor support has opened up space for both the women's movement and Islamic NGOs. It has enabled a range of organisations to engage in development projects in rural areas that recognise the need to tackle hierarchies of power, including gender subordination. There has been significant external involvement in the governance of rural affairs supported by a state keen to extend its presence. Differing discourses relating to women's citizenship and sexuality are played out in these settings.

Legal constructions of women's bodies: criminalising sexual identities?

The tensions between public life, which follows norms of gender equality, and personal life, which follow religious norms not necessarily consistent with gender equality, are evident in the formal legal system. Bangladesh has ratified CEDAW with some reservations. The 1972 constitution (as subsequently amended) sets out the fundamental principles of state policy. Article 10 requires 'steps' to be 'taken to ensure participation of women in all spheres of national life' while Article 14 declares that it is the 'fundamental responsibility of the State to emancipate the toiling masses – the peasants and workers – and backward sections of the people from exploitation'. Under the justiciable fundamental rights provisions, all citizens are equal before the law (Article 27). Article 28(1) ensures that the state does not discriminate on grounds only of religion, race, caste, sex or place of birth while subsection (2) explicitly provides women with equal rights in all spheres of the state and of public life and (4) preserves the right of the state to make special provisions for the advancement of women. Freedom of religion is assured (Article 41). Laws inconsistent with the constitution are deemed void (Articles 7 and 26).

The private sphere is regulated through the personal laws of communities defined through religion. The 90 per cent of Bangladeshis who are Muslims are covered by the Muslim Personal Law; Hindus and Christians by personal laws inherited from the Indian colonial period; and tribal communities practise their own customary laws (Siddiqi 2005: 288–290). The state retained the 1961 Muslim Family Law Ordinance and the amended Dissolution of Muslim Marriages Act 1939. Under the Muslim Marriages and Divorces (Registration) Act 1974 the failure to register a marriage attracts criminal penalties. Adults do not require permission to marry. Guardians have the power to arrange the marriages and divorces of minors (twenty-one for men, eighteen for women), defined by the retained but amended Child Marriage Restraint Act 1929. While it is an offence to contract an underage marriage, the marriage is not invalidated. Early marriage at about sixteen to considerably older men is the norm although the rise in girls' education and the drop in fertility rates may be changing the gender relationships within marriage. More young women record that they have some say in a marriage partner (World Bank 2008: 13). Personal law is now administered in the state family courts under the Family Courts Act 1985.

The Penal Code is essentially the 1860 Indian Penal Code (Hossein 2001). We saw earlier the ways in which this Code constructs women's sexuality, including through the provisions relating to abduction and kidnapping (section 366). Despite the amendments to the constitution to ensure Islam as the state religion, no attempts have been made to introduce principles of Islamic criminal law. Instead there have been a number of specific criminal laws enacted to tackle issues relating to women. These laws result from the sustained focus on issues of violence by influential civil society organisations and the Bangladeshi women's movement, which have attracted wider public attention. Rape, which is seen by some groups as the most common form of violence against women, has been a major concern (Khan 2001). The original provisions within the Penal Code have been supplemented with a range of more comprehensive offences (the Repression Against Women and Children Prevention Act 2000 as amended in 2003) which reduced the draconian penalties attached to the crimes to encourage greater use of the law (Mansoor 2006).

A second area of concern is the rapid spread and spiralling amounts of dowry now being demanded and the violence associated with these demands even though the practice is contrary to Islamic law (World Bank 2008: 13). The reasons for its spread are attributed to the high unemployment rates of young men in rural areas seeking alternative sources of support (Khan 2001); the undervaluing of women's work on family farms; and fewer men in the marriageable market pool (World Bank 2008: 13). The giving or taking of dowry is officially prohibited (Dowry Prohibition Act 1980) and the more recent Repression Against Women and Children Prevention Act 2000 defines dowry in a way that tries to capture the processes involved; dowry-related violence attracts severe levels of punishment, including the death penalty for loss of life.

Acid attacks, predominantly on women, to disfigure and maim form the third high-profile issue (World Bank 2008; Khan 2001). This form of violence, which was virtually unheard of before independence, is associated with family or land disputes, vendettas and refusals to accept a man's marriage proposal or sexual relationship. The government response was the Acid Crime Act and the Acid Crime Prevention Act, both in 2002. The former provides the death penalty or life imprisonment for causing death by acid and long sentences for wounding. It also seeks to control the sale of the acids involved. The latter Act establishes procedures for dealing with such incidents and an Acid Crimes Prevention Tribunal to conduct the trials. Due to pressure from women's organisations, this legislation is beginning to be backed up by government initiatives to tackle violence, both in public and within the private sphere of the home (see World Bank 2008: 106–108; Mansoor 2006). However, a tiny fraction of women are willing or able to report violence publicly and when they do, they tend to approach the informal dispute settlement body, the shalish, and not the state institutions, such as the police or the courts, for very similar reasons to those we have seen in India and Pakistan.

Contesting community regulation

Despite some young women's entry into the public sphere as garment workers and providers of services, public space is perceived to be dangerous for women. It is the site for institutional violence, including rape by public officials as well as attacks (such as with acid) by individual men. A woman's reputation can be severely damaged by perceived inappropriate public association. Both women and men share this perception of public space, whether the setting is a village or a city (World Bank 2008: chapter 6 utilising research from Naripokkho and Bangladesh Mahila Parishad NGOs; Siddiqi 2006). More than 65 per cent of women believe that women and girls are harassed in the community. While a majority of women feel they cannot move alone in their village, they feel far more insecure in urban areas although wearing a borka may increase legitimacy (World Bank 2008: 102).

Codes of honour embedded within Pakistani and Indian systems of family alliances (*biradawi* or caste) do not prevail in Bangladesh. Nonetheless, the norms of modesty and the avoidance of shame are strongly held. Women who challenge conventional norms of appropriate behaviour feel more unsafe, both within the public realm but also within the sphere of the family, where they are indeed likely to experience more violence than women who accept the prevailing normative structure, which condones spousal violence. The majority of men and women consider that violence is justified for a 'major mistake' such as an unsanctioned sexual relationship or even too familiar behaviour. Challenges to acceptable behaviour are seen as challenges to wider social norms and punishable not only by a spouse but potentially by the community (World Bank 2008).

The formal state legal system is totally out of reach of the rural poor and has in any case very limited legitimacy (Alim 2006). The police and the magistracy are few in number and highly vulnerable to political pressures from rural elites or politicians. The state attempted to develop village-level justice through the establishment of statutory Village Courts in 1976. These bodies use local government representatives as adjudicators to resolve disputes informally. They have performed poorly, lack legitimacy and merge with the traditional body, the shalish (Biswas 2008). These bodies are of no fixed size or membership although they are dominated by the rural elite and local politicians who use them to resolve community disputes and to impose sanctions on community members. They consider a wide range of matters. Women attend, if at all, behind a curtain or are hidden in some other way (Golub 2003).

Shalish are not recognised by state law and their judgments or sanctions have no force of law although they may have community legitimacy. The powerful can impose their interests upon the less powerful, including women who are deemed to have transgressed the bounds of modesty and appropriate behaviour. They can use Islamic discourse to do this. Thus, women have been charged with zina (for sexual intercourse outside marriage), although it forms no part of Bangladeshi law, and issued with a fatwa as punishment (Shammy 2002; World Bank 2008 quoting Pereira and Nargis). Punishments range from social disgraces (such as shaving heads, parading around the village or ostracism) to physical mutilation (tied up in public, stoned or lashed) or even death. Such punishments, perpetrated by shalish members, are recognised neither within Islamic nor within Bangladeshi state law.

The emergence of this misinformed Islamic practice has been identified as part of a growing Islamic consciousness in the villages and has added to the concerns of women's organisations over the way in which women's sexuality is controlled in the shalish. The state in Bangladesh, and donors in alliance with the state or with NGOs, have sought to develop governance structures in the villages. These interventions utilise a range of normative frameworks but generally aim to bring village governance more in line with the state law and the principles of non-discrimination enshrined in the constitution. This has involved systematic attempts to strengthen the representation and voice of the weak and poor, including women. Since 1998, BRAC, a leading NGO, has been involved in initiatives with villagers to improve the quality of informal justice processes.

Other NGOs and external agencies are also involved in substantial intervention initiatives (Golub 2000; ADB 2008b).

What sets the women's movement's legal strategies apart from others in the region is that all these initiatives accept and work within the structure of the shalish rather than seeking to rely on state-based laws to expand civil space for women. There are two approaches: either 'to organise local/alternative *shalish* committees that are trained to carry out their own hearings within the framework of the law' or the more indirect methods adopted by Ain O Salish Kendra (ASK), whose staff observe, monitor and persuade. This organisation 'proceeds on the assumption that an equitable and representative *shalish* structure can be created and *sustained* only when there is an overall shift in community norms and practices of power' (Siddiqi 2006: 40). Strategies are limited to 'dispute resolution in matters that fall outside criminal jurisdiction' (Siddiqi 2006: 31). A challenge by the same NGOs to the use of extra-judicial punishment methods (beatings and lashings) in shalish resulted in a High Court ruling ordering the government to take effective preventative measures.

Conclusion

The economic and social processes associated with colonialism, nationalism and contemporary globalisation have interacted with relationships within family and community to produce complex constructions of difference in South Asia.

Nationalist projects, translated into constitutions, sought to create nations of equal citizens, irrespective of their affinities to religion, caste or class, while developing a sense of being and belonging to the new state through the construction of the family, which embodied the values of the nation. Women were ascribed a central role in this process of reproducing nationhood through their activities as social reproducers within the family. Thus women's bodies and behaviour have socially reproductive value to both family networks and wider society. While women, as holders of political citizenship, are autonomous individual subjects, they are also honourable and caring kinswomen, rooted within the connectedness associated with embodied familial and wider community relationships and access political rights as embodied citizens.

Struggles with the colonial state changed the relationship between production and social reproduction. As land moved more into the domain of the market, women's contribution to agricultural production became more associated with social reproduction and less valued as work. The nationalist ideological association of women with valued socially reproductive roles in the family reinforced this division. Even though across the subcontinent women worked on family-owned farms or as labourers for others and in other forms of informal production, there was limited policy recognition of women's contribution to the economy. Development programmes operate in the context of informal production and employment relations and through local community-based bodies. They are informed, to differing extents within the three states, by international macroeconomic and development policies. Constitutional jurisprudence and concepts of the rule of law (and now ideologies of 'good governance') have played a limited role in the governance of these programmes although this division has been addressed in recent times through a 'rights approach to development'.

Women access economic resources primarily through their social reproductive position within the family (Patel 2007). The status as a wife or mother is recognised as the basis for allocation of resources, including land, but the processes are contained within the personal law system rather than in 'public' processes of land law. Women's formal access to such resources has improved for the majority Hindu community in India through reforms of personal laws. However, attempts to improve women's access to resources more generally through the use of universal state laws have been met with resistance as interference with community (and family) matters. If women remain firmly within the accepted domain of their families and communities then as institutional members they are entitled to protection but if they move from being 'proper' family members, they face major difficulties. Across the subcontinent women, despite very different social and economic positions, have had very limited access to independent resources provided either through adequately remunerated and protected employment as workers or, as citizens, through state-based welfare provisions.

The contemporary context of globalisation is changing much. Some, particularly younger women, have been able to access formal employment in the expanding markets in services, particularly in India, and in the textile industry in Bangladesh. The interaction between women's identification with family-regulated behaviour and their role as employees is seen in the discourse over sexual harassment. Is women's sexuality to be 'policed' through a discourse of a sexually chaste family member or as an autonomous individualised worker or can she be an embodied and equal employee? The consumerist culture based upon the marketing of desires, including those based upon an active sexualised female identity, provides opportunities for new forms of identity-based politics, again particularly in India. It has increased the integration of the Indian women's movement into global discourses based upon rights. There is an expanded 'space' in which to argue for liberal notions of privacy, which provide freedom to individuals to conduct their lives as they choose. It is not clear that these constructions of identity in the market will provide a framework for tackling the diversity of economic and social injustices that women face as a result of globalisation. Market discourses offer little to the majority of women who are not formal employees and empowered consumers. They build upon gendered identities that are strongly moulded in the social relationships associated with family and community rather than that of individual political citizenship.

The differing effects on the governance of women's sexuality can be seen across the jurisdictions. The positive value of women's embodied citizenship, of being and belonging with nationalist discourse is transformed into the asset value of women's honourable bodies, legally constructed through combinations of community, religious and state normative frameworks, in wider family and community trading, which can be used to extort funds in Pakistan, excessive dowries in India and now also in Bangladesh. At the same time, power relationships within community networks and, particularly within Pakistan, with politico-religious groups, are challenged when women (and men) exercise sexual choice or behave badly, thereby damaging their value as social reproducers of perceived community and religious norms.

The power of kinship-based regulation derived from combinations of customary and religious norms is evident. The particular relationships between polity and community, which distribute power among actors, operate in different contexts: the village politics of North India, now suffused with market relationships; the Islamification of everyday norms in Pakistan; and contested development discourses in rural Bangladesh. The combination of colonial and post-colonial political economy has produced an uneasy relationship between constitutions based on a liberal modernist rule of law discourse; a criminal justice system retained from colonial times, reflecting its normative framework but amended in piecemeal ways to reflect often contested alternative values; and the various community-based 'personal' laws, themselves colonialist constructs, which regulate family relationships and religious norms.

The effects of the interaction between these discourses, with their differing normative underpinnings, vary according to location and context. The legitimacy of a particular discourse will depend on these factors. Higher courts on the whole maintain rule of law concepts, albeit constructed within particular contexts, and through their judgments seek to undermine the legitimacy of community governance by, for instance, asserting that caste panchayats do not exist or a shalish has no jurisdiction over criminal punishments. 'Judgments' promulgated by these latter bodies ignore state law provisions and use community-based norms even though their sanctions may be implemented (or not countered) by state officials. Criminal justice systems tend to reinforce subjectivities constructed within kinship-based relationships, which place high value on belonging in the community. The liberal 'rule of law' subjectivity, which values freedom to exercise individual choice, and therefore greater individual rather than familial agency in matters relating to caring relationships, is resisted.

In many South Asian contexts, there is little 'space' for women into which they can 'exit' from family regulation over their sexual identities. Women have limited access to 'citizen/political' resources if they are seen to transgress. States have not developed a large enough functional institutional space in which all women can act as citizens. Institutions can be captured by families, communities and other non-state actors. Women's movements have attempted to both critique and to use state law to open up such space for women by tackling violence both within private familial networks and the public institutions of the state such as the police and the workplace. They have also sought to counter social and economic relations of power within, not outside, family networks through the provision of greater rights for women. They are obliged to do this within legal frameworks, which predominantly place social issues within the domain of family 'personal' or religious laws and as such they meet with considerable resistance. They have also sought to use the discourse of human rights to improve women's position as embodied citizens of the state and insist that the legal system should operate within the normative values of the constitution, not those associated with abusive power relations within community governance institutions. This rights discourse is therefore developed creatively with regard to the enduring positive values associated with networks of familial and community relationships and the construction of a more relational subject than that normally associated with rights discourse (see Chapter 2).

The next chapter considers the implications of these developments within South Asian jurisdictions when BrAsian settled residents and citizens in the Global North are drawn into and draw on community, religious and state laws in the formation of transnational families.

Trading and contesting belonging in multicultural Britain

Introduction

Chapter 3 considered the impact of the UK's global economic positioning on changes in gender relations as more aspects of social reproduction are met through the market. It set the demand context for the food and body work chains in some detail and introduced the 'demand' involved in the transnational marriage (TNM) chain. In the language of chains, there is a demand in the UK for overseas spouses with the supply drawn from families and kin in South Asian homelands. Chapter 8 considered the broad jurisdictional contexts for the 'supply' of family members. This chapter brings us back to the UK to consider the contexts in which the TNM chains operate, although it might be more appropriate to describe the situation under consideration as a 'churn' rather than a 'chain' because we will consider the position of young BrAsian women who move to South Asia to marry as well as young South Asian women who move to the UK as spouses. However, the aim is not to reproduce the dominant discourse that views these movements through a dyad of culture and rights perspectives, narrowly focusing on abusive power relations.

As Phillips points out, the relationship between feminism and multiculturalism in contemporary Britain raises two contradictory political problems. The first is that 'anxieties about cultural imperialism [have] engender[ed] a kind of relativism that ma[kes] it difficult to represent *any* belief or practice as oppressive to women or at odds with gender equality' and leads to political paralysis. The second is that 'outside of feminist circles, principles of gender equality [are] being deployed as part of a demonisation of minority cultural groups. Overt expressions of racism [are] being transformed into a more socially acceptable criticism of minorities' (2007: 1, 2). This chapter seeks to find a way through this political conundrum by locating the chain within the political economy of UK multiculturalism. It takes seriously the agency used by communities with roots in the Global South as well as in the UK to secure economic and social reproductively-based well-being for their members. It locates TNMs within chain analysis to provide alternative perspectives on gender injustices without underestimating the abuses of power within family relationships, particularly in relation to the control of women's sexuality. It is important to stress clearly at the outset that there is no evidence to suggest that there is a greater prevalence of violence against women in UK minority communities than within those of the majority.

In orthodox economic terms it makes no sense to talk of commodities and value-creation here because this chain is organised primarily through the relationships of social reproduction, not the market. However, the framework and the concepts adopted in previous chains (inputs/outputs, territoriality and internal and external governance) remain valid. The supply of Kenyan products through a GVC illustrated the way in which TNCs operate territorially. In general, the GVC creates wealth for Europeans and access to waged but low-paid work for some women in source countries. The same process produces agricultural marginal areas on the periphery of these activities in which many of the families discussed here have their origins (Ballard 2003).

The global care chains showed the way in which women, affected adversely by these changes in global production processes, leave home to seek work as a family survival strategy while maintaining their social networks and family relationships. Here we are considering the position of those who migrate as family members, often as part of similar survival strategies. The focus is on the socially reproductive sphere of transnational practices associated with household formation rather than the 'production' focus of migrant workers, and encompasses the practices associated with long-established and settled communities (Yeoh et al. 2005; Charsley and Shaw 2006).

To avoid the political problems identified by Phillips and to understand the 'horizontal' trade, rights and care discourses associated with TNMs, it is very important to consider the governance of relationships within the 'vertical' pyramid in the UK from a BrAsian perspective. Rather than viewing communities through the lens of too much culture and finding patriarchal abuses of power, the chapter begins with a consideration of the relationship between BrAsian communities and the UK state and the impact on gender relations of varying degrees of recognition of group differences. The regulation of immigration, employment discrimination and family relations contributes to the construction of these relationships but takes place amidst wider contests over the merits of legal pluralism in a multicultural society. To focus solely on 'vertical' family issues reproduces the dominant construction of Asian women as 'trapped' within patriarchal family structures and denied access to labour markets because of family pressures rather than because they are excluded by market or state policies.

There are two closely linked, but for present purposes separable, aspects to the TNM churn/chain: the movement of people to meet the desire for particular marriage partners and the trading of the norms that construct the identity of the spouses. Family 'entrepreneurs in transnational space' (Ballard 1994) operate within a complex mix of the customary and religious codes, state legal systems of South Asia and the UK and international rights discourses, which are discussed in the second half of the chapter. In doing so, they circulate not only personnel and financial assets but also ideas and legal norms. The response of the state legal system to transnational family trading in belonging contributes significantly to the constructions of gender relations. The chapter concludes, therefore, with an assessment of the extent to which discourses of honour, constructed as a group identity, and women's rights, as associated with individuals, offer alternative, gender constructions of transnational belonging and demonstrates how they are traded transnationally in the marriage chain.

Repositioning family productivity and identity: from sojourners to transnational families

Introduction

This section considers the construction of one element of BrAsian identities through the 'vertical' impact of state immigration laws on labour market and family relations. Arguably, the state has contributed to the construction of a group identity though the negative use of state law: through the implementation of restrictive immigration law, which targeted specific groups, in particular Commonwealth Asian communities (Jones and Gnanapala 2000: chapter 1; Shah 2005: chapter 6).

There have been three phases in the establishment of the BrAsian communities in the UK, all of which have necessitated relationships with UK immigration law: the arrival of male workers (a state construction of migrant male productive (valued) worker); followed by women and children as family members for settlement (a female (unvalued) socially reproductive dependent); and, most recently, young women and men as spouses to further transnational family connection (gender-neutral equally unvalued male and female family members). The third phase forms the subject matter for the TNM chain discussed later.

Productive trading, male sojourners

There are a number of South Asian communities in the UK (see Ballard 1994; Gardner 2006; Shaw and Charsley 2006; McLoughlin 2009: the 'Writing British Asian Cities' project (www.leeds.ac.uk/writingbritishasiancities/); Change Institute 2009). The first, and numerically the largest, group, accounting for some two-thirds of all South Asians in Britain, originates from the Punjab. Fewer than half are drawn from the Indian side of the divide created by the partition of India in 1947. Most of the Indian Punjabis came originally from the Jullander Doab (Jalandhar district) and are Sikhs or Hindus. Most Pakistanis, about two-thirds, come from one distinct area in the Punjab, Mirpur in Azad Kashmir, and are Muslims. Well over half of the population of the villages in the Mirpur District and its immediate surrounding areas in Azad Kashmir live overseas; about a third of a million have settled in Britain (Ballard 2003). The second group has its origins in Gujarat in India, and consists of both Hindus and Muslims, some of whom have arrived in the UK via East Africa. They account for roughly a quarter of the BrAsian community. The third group are from Bangladesh, overwhelmingly from the Sylhet region and are Muslims (Gardner 1995).

Mostly the groups have their origins in rural areas. A number of single men who started to arrive in the UK during and at the end of World War 2 found employment in the munitions factories and then in the post-war booming industrial sector. There was considerable demand for unskilled labour to fill the jobs that the indigenous population increasingly did not want and until the 1960s there were no state-based immigration obstacles to this supply of labour. British governments actively encouraged migration from former colonies. However, early migrants were effectively excluded from jobs other than those at the bottom of the social order, irrespective of their own skills. The migrants, arriving from their local areas, lived and worked together near to the sources of employment, mainly in declining inner-city areas (see Samad and Eade 2002). Increasing numbers of kin arrived and together they started to build their own local communities based on their place of origin, producing 'ethnic colonies' of kinsmen and fellow villagers (Ballard 1994; Shaw 2001; Gardner 2006).

As the economic climate changed, migrants became threats to the indigenous labour markets (Brah, 1996: 74). The 1962 Commonwealth Immigrants Act brought regulation through immigration laws for the first time. From then on, a series of Immigration and Nationality Acts between 1968 and 1988 restricted access to labour markets so that migration for work became possible only with a work permit, which was limited in duration. These controls effectively obliged members of families who were in Britain to settle. While the state was increasingly intervening in families via immigration regulations, the communities were being deeply affected by recession and restructuring in the UK industrial sector, which, in the 1970s and 1980s, devastated heavy industries, creating mass unemployment in specific geographical areas. These events had an effect not only on the workers' financial ability to remit funds to families back home but also on their ability to bring their families to the UK.

Female settlers, limiting group social reproduction

By the 1970s these immigration laws had limited migration to 'dependents' of newly settled migrants and refugees. Men who sought to bring their wives and children faced increasing hurdles to achieve this reunion. There were differences in the speed with which this process was achieved with Indians first, followed by Pakistanis and lastly Bangladeshis who were most affected by the increasing restrictions (Shah 2002; Gardner 2006).

Men's relationship with the state was defined through their status as workers. Women's relationship with the state was through their status as family 'dependents'. However the South Asian women who eventually joined their spouses were not simply sitting waiting to be 'called for' by their husbands. As Gardner points out, Bangladeshi women's extensive socially reproductive activities are valued by their husband's family. They contributed actively to the process of transnational migration through 'wife work' within their father-in-law's household, work which they continued to carry out from a different location and in a different context when they migrated. '[I]t is not wives who are the dependants, but men, who rely on their wives for the work they have done in holding households and bodies together' (2006: 376).

As the processes of family reunion continued during a period of severe economic downturn and crises within welfare provision, the state became ever more suspicious of transnational family formation. The rules tightened and worked their ways into the interstices of family lives (Gill and Sharma 2007). They probed deeply into cultural and sexual arrangements, causing not only anxieties but also deep offence, given that a negative finding could brand a woman as adulterous, if her marriage was deemed invalid, or a child illegitimate, both of which outcomes would bring huge shame upon women and their families. 'The Immigration Rules governing the entry of foreign husbands and fiancés were changed five times between 1963 and 1983 with the primary aim of preventing black and migrant women from having their partners join them in Britain while allowing white women the right to do so' (Brah 1996; 75). As a result, men seeking to join wives or fiancées had to convince officials that their primary purpose was to marry; not to seek entry in order to obtain British residency (and therefore access to employment).

Each attempt to restrict family reunion via immigration procedures was modified or abolished due to the development of human rights laws (relating to the right to family life) in the UK (Jones and Gnanapala 2000: 15; Clayton 2008: 289–290). However, attempts by the Commission for Racial Equality (CRE), the body established to oversee the operation of the domestic race discrimination legislation, to apply this legislation to the implementation of the immigration laws failed.

Equally unvalued and dependent?

The primary purpose rule was abolished in 1997 by the incoming Labour government. However, the rules were in effect amended to give women equality on an equalling-down principle, making it equally difficult for a man to sponsor a wife or fiancée. The outcome is a gender-neutral construction of dependent family members. Because the sponsor of the person seeking entry clearance for marriage purposes must be able to demonstrate that they have sufficient resources to support their spouse and that they will not have recourse to public funds, young Asian women (and men) require evidence of paid employment. A desire for transnationalism ensures that families retain a close relationship with immigration control, an area of state regulation that is perceived to be draconian and partisan, operating to exclude members of these communities, in particular those who are unskilled which, given the original home areas, is the majority (Phillips and Dustin 2004; Wilson 2007).

Each community's ability to meet its aspirations on migration has been affected by racial exclusionism although some groups have fared better than others in overcoming the obstacles. Sikhs and Hindus have tended to fare well but, as Ballard (1994), Brah (1996), and Shaw (2001) caution, this has more to do with the accumulated resources that were available to these groups from their regions of origin than anything associated with faith. The Punjab is more prosperous than Mirpur and both are more prosperous than Sylhet. The 'twice migrant' (Bhachu 1985) East African Asians, who have origins in Gujarat but settled in East Africa before leaving or being expelled in the 1960s/1970s, have generally prospered. They arrived as complete family units and were settlers from the start unlike the other communities. They were generally better educated, spoke fluent English, with professional, technical or commercial experience.

Workers and family members in a multicultural state

Multicultural Britain: context

The 2001 British Census found 8 per cent of the UK's population (9 per cent of England's) belonged to an ethnic minority (ONS 2001). Minority ethnic groups tended to be concentrated in specific geographical areas with London having the highest proportion and diversity (Vertovec 2007). Those who identified themselves as of Pakistani origin (706,539 in England) lived in a limited number of areas (Yorkshire and the Humber (3 per cent of the population), Bradford (15 per cent), and the West Midlands (3 per cent)). About 2 per cent of the population of England and Wales were Indian, with Leicester having the highest proportion (26 per cent). Bangladeshis formed 0.5 per cent (283,000) of the population of England and Wales with 54 per cent living in London (nearly half within Tower Hamlets (Gardner 2006)). In England, 3 per cent of the population stated their religion as Muslim; 1 per cent Hindu; and 0.8 per cent Sikh.

Multicultural state

The UK is thus a multicultural society involving 'self conscious and more or less well organised communities entertaining and living by their own different systems of beliefs and practices' (Parekh 2000: 3). The ideological modern European state, however, accepts only one system of authority, sovereignty, 'the unitary, supreme and legally unlimited power from which all other powers are deemed to be derived' (Parekh 2000: 181–182). It offers individuals 'an unprecedented regime of personal liberties and rights. It is able to provide space for personal autonomy and cultural and religious freedom. . . and creates conditions for a relatively inviolate private realm, and autonomous civil society, and an autonomous public realm. . .' (Parekh 2000: 183–184). However '[a]ll its citizens are expected to privilege their territorial over their other identities; to consider what they share in common as citizens far more important than what they share with other members of their religious, cultural and other communities' (2000: 184).

This quest for homogeneity can transform the role of the modern state from a neutral arbiter to one of suppressor of diverse legal norms as far as minority communities are concerned. The British state does not recognise 'non-state' laws such as the customary practices of minority groups or religious codes, although there have been a number of specific 'concessions' granted through legislation (see Jones and Gnanapala 2000). Phillips argues that 'though not underpinned by any very conscious philosophy', the state 'stumbled onto a relatively robust version of multiculturalism' involving 'a series of smallish adjustments and accommodations that added up to a quite substantial practice' but that this limited form of multiculturalism is in 'sharp retreat' after the 2005 bombings in London. The 'language of multiculturalism' has been replaced by 'one of civic integration' (2007: 4–6).

The relationship between immigrant communities and the host society becomes more like a one-sided contract in which groups consent to the dominant way of life rather than a more balanced agreement with commitments on both sides (Kymlicka 1995). From this perspective, the British state is well aware of the communities it has chosen to admit. As a result, it has incurred the obligation to respect the fundamentals of their way of life. In return, the communities have an obligation to obey laws but they are entitled to be treated as equal citizens and the state is obliged to review its laws to accommodate community norms wherever possible (Parekh 2000).

As we have seen, the values and ideals underpinning Asian (and African) legal systems are different from those supporting the English state law – valuing 'the (trans-)local, kinship based, flexible, situation specific forms of justice, an area often inspired or supported by religious values and practices' (Shah 2005: 178). Diasporic communities bring with them a 'markedly sceptical attitude to the capacity and legitimacy of significant intervention by the state' (Shah 2005: 5). State intervention in the family is 'the sphere that most often comes into conflict with the official legal order which posits a rival form of social organisation premised on citizenship of the modern nation-state' (2005: 175). Arguably, within a multicultural society, these values should be accommodated (Shah 2005: 3–4). Those who chart the discrimination felt by specific BrAsian communities and the disillusion resulting from the perceived exclusion from the state system warn that the state is entrenching 'the very pluralism that it is seeking to avoid and precipitating the very instability and secession it seeks to prevent' (Parekh 2000: 185; Yilmaz 2000, 2001; Shah 2005).

There has been much debate about the relationship of multiculturalism to feminism (Phillips 2002a, 2007) reflected in the wider theoretical discussion in Chapter 2. The strand of feminism broadly associated with liberalism is wary of the political incorporation of the interests of women into discussions of multiculturalism that focus on the external relations between groups and the wider society, rather than the issues relating to gender relations within communities.

Such approaches pay insufficient attention to the role that the family plays in cultural reproduction and in the construction of gender relations (Okin 1998, 1999, 2002; Phillips 2002a). Minority women are obliged to choose between being insiders, defending beleaguered and misunderstood cultural practices, or being outsiders, identifying with the cultural practices of women within the majority cultures (Phillips 2007). However, despite evidence of deep-seated patterns of social exclusion of members of minority groups and limited understanding from the majority community of what constitutes a sense of belonging, the alternative assumption can be that 'exiting' the group altogether offers a positive strategy.

The political 'space' to debate these issues is profoundly affected by contemporary anxieties, which tend to drown out attempts to deconstruct this restrictive dichotomous approach (Phillips 2007). BrAsian women activists seek to avoid defining themselves through the discourse of a 'clash of cultures' and to find ways of supporting the interests of Asian women while making broader alliances with majority women's groups (Ali 2007b; Bano 2007, 2008; Ahmad 2008). In so doing, they challenge the wider community to listen carefully.

Productive employment, individual workers and group disadvantage

Although immigration rules initially constructed women as socially reproductive dependents, women entered paid employment (Bald 1995; Brah 1996; Kabeer 2000; EOC 2004; EOC 2006). A number of factors have had a significant effect on women's access to such work. These include the date of original migration, their particular kinship network, the local labour markets in which they found themselves, but also the way in which Asian women are perceived as constrained in their ability to work by family pressures.

Sikh brides quickly joined husbands and, not observing strict purdah rules, tended to find paid work. Compatible levels of educational achievement and professional status are seen as an important element in matching marital partners and a way in which to maximise position within family marital negotiations generally (Samad and Eade 2002). It is therefore not only in their own, but also in their family's, interests for daughters to gain qualifications. In contrast, the Mirpuri Muslim community took longer to reunite, partly because it was not as prosperous and remitted payments back home for longer but also because marriage is arranged between close family members. The incentive to join the UK spouse was reckoned to be less strong than for Sikhs or Hindus because the bride joined a close family household at home. Women observed purdah in Mirpur, adding a further disincentive for woman to work in public. Immigration laws were being tightened, slowing the whole process down. There may have been less incentive for women to seek paid work where close family ties of reciprocity are particularly valued and where women's education traditionally has not been expected to lead to employment outside the home. The Sylhetis faced the bleakest economic climate because they undertook family reunion much later than the other two groups in the 1980 and 1990s. Bangladeshi women who have been in the UK for a relatively short time have found it difficult to enter the public labour market, not only because of the requirements of purdah, but also because of the specific economic and spatial location of the community within declining areas of east London (Samad and Eade 2002).

Women who entered the labour market tended to work full time in low-paid semi-skilled and unskilled work in the manufacturing sector in the clothing and textiles industries. The decline in these industries led to a huge rise in unemployment among Asian women in the 1980s. The process of outsourcing a 'sweat shop economy' has occurred within the UK and has involved Asian women, particularly Bangladeshi women in east London, who work as home workers. This group of workers is seen as particularly subject to exploitation (Mitter 1985; Kabeer 2000).

Twenty-first century BrAsian women workers

BrAsian women join the consumer-based labour market described in Chapter 3. Although it is a complex picture, women from most minority ethnic communities fare worse than white women (EOC 2004, 2006, 2007; Botcherby 2006; Bradley et al. 2007). A person from an ethnic minority group is far more likely to be unemployed than a white person. Despite considerable regional variations, Pakistani women have an extremely high unemployment rate: five times the rate for white women (4 per cent) and more than double the rate for Pakistani men (10 per cent) (see Buckner et al. 2007b). Bangladeshi women, who live in one of the poorest of the UK's ethnic communities, are at least three times as likely to be unemployed as white women (Bradley et al. 2007: 12). Ethnic minority workers generally earn less per hour than workers from white backgrounds and this gap is increasing. Within the overall average for ethnic minorities, earnings are highest for Indian and lowest for Pakistani and Bangladeshi workers with Pakistani and Bangladeshi women being the lowest paid (Platt 2006). Over 50 per cent of Pakistani and Bangladeshi households with children live in poverty compared with 16 per cent of white households (Bradley et al. 2007: 12 quoting Platt 2006). There is, therefore, an 'ethnic penalty' (CRE 2006; Dex and Ward 2007).

The position of minority ethnic young women is changing (EOC 2006, 2007). They are increasingly well qualified, outperforming boys from the same ethnic origin and (in most cases) white boys. While the economic inactivity rate for younger women is still higher for Pakistani and Bangladeshi women than for white women, those in employment share the aspirations of their white contemporaries. Nonetheless sixteen-year-old Black Caribbean, Pakistani and Bangladeshi girls think it is harder for them to get a job than white girls and are more likely to exclude possible careers because of their sex, ethnicity or faith. Although young BrAsians have high aspirations, supported by their parents, of combining work and family life (Bhavnani 2006), there does not seem to be a significant shift away from the gender contract of the breadwinner and homemaker in Bangladeshi and Pakistani families, in contrast to the two-earner Indian and White households. Mothers from these communities are much less likely than white and Indian mothers to be working during pregnancy or to be in paid employment when their children are young (Dex and Ward 2007).

Group cultures: visible culture and invisible work cultures

The ethnic penalty means that BrAsian young women's investment in qual-ifications and educational success is squandered. There is a 'vicious circle of segregation' in that 'the lack of ethnic minority women in many workplaces and in many types of work means there are few positive role models' (EOC 2006: 8). Fear of discrimination may also restrict choice. A high proportion of under-thirty-five-year-old women in these groups say they experience sexism, racism and discrimination at work. One-third of BrAsian workers in a recent survey had experienced bullying compared to fewer than one in five white employees (CIPD 2006).

The requirement for minority ethnic women to 'fit into' particular work cultures is widespread (Kamenou and Fearfull 2006). Workplaces have a formal culture shaped by senior managers who increasingly recognise the 'business case' for promoting diversity (Bradley et al. 2007). They also have informal cultures, 'the way things are done around here' (Bradley et al. 2007 quoting Deal and Kennedy), which may not reflect the official management policy. Because 'fitting in' covers behaviour and personal appearance, Pakistani and Bangladeshi Muslim women experience problems with dominant work cul-tures. In the under-thirty-five age group, Bangladeshi and Pakistani women are three times as likely as their white counterparts to be asked about their plans for marriage and children at interviews. Faith issues have a strong effect on labour market chances (Bradley et al. 2007) with religious dress producing negative attitudes. Muslim women are 50 per cent more likely to have difficulty finding a job. (One in three have taken jobs at a lower level because no one would employ them at the level for which they were qualified, compared to one in twenty white women (EOC 2006: 5).) Pakistani women graduates are five times as likely to be unemployed as their white counterparts (Botcherby 2006; EOC 2006).

Given this bleak employment environment, considerable numbers of minor-ity ethnic women either work in ethnic-owned small businesses or have set up their own. Such businesses offer a more sheltered environment and the solidarity of family relationships, as well as freedom from external control and greater autonomy. However, small businesses are often financially risky, offer lower salaries and long working hours and 'in very small outfits there are no prospects of promotion and developing one's potential' (Bradley et al. 2007: 37).

Discrimination and intersectionality

Has the state recognised these penalties and exclusions experienced by BrAsian workers in general and by women in particular? There has been legislation prohibiting discrimination in the areas of employment and the provision of goods, facilities and services on grounds of race, nationality or ethnic or national origin since 1965 and on grounds of sex since 1975. Religion as a prohibited ground for discrimination in employment was added in 2003 and the provisions in the Racial and Religious Hatred Act 2006 may start to address the sense of injustice felt particularly by Muslims (Yilmaz 2001: 298), although the present context of heightened Islamophobia adds to the difficulties faced by these communities.

Discrimination law (now consolidated into the Equality Act 2010) is not discussed in detail here (see Fredman 2002; Collins et al. 2005: chapter 3; McColgan 2005). It is sufficient to point out that these provisions are firmly rooted in the liberal conceptual framework of individual direct or indirect discrimination, not group disadvantage or ethnic conflict (Shah 2005: 15). This framework has not been able to recognise the concept of 'intersectionality' (Crenshaw 1991; Grabham et al. 2009) which addresses the distinct and particular experience of one person or group when discrimination based on racism, racial discrimination, xenophobia and related intolerance intersects with gender, age, sexual orientation, disability, migrant, socio-economic or other status (UN 2001). 'The inability of anti-discrimination law to probe the structural disadvantages in society inevitably impacts more severely on those at the intersection of one or more disadvantaged social characteristics' (Hannett 2003: 83). Section 14 of the Equality Act 2010, which introduces the possibility of 'combined discrimination', goes some way towards addressing these limitations but is yet to be implemented.

Despite the establishment of a single body (the Equality and Human Rights Commission) in 2007 to oversee the various forms of legally recognised discrimination and the implementation of the Human Rights Act 1998 and the consolidated discrimination legislation, the objective is still to create a 'fair society with fair chances for everyone' through the protection of individual rights, not to tackle group disadvantage (Government Equalities Office 2009).

Reproducing connection, family members

Introduction

The pursuit of family well-being through community-based norms challenges liberal centralist state ideology. Families are of central social importance to South Asian communities. They are corporate entities that seek to ensure family social and economic well-being. Members owe reciprocal obligations to each other and the collective fortunes of the whole kinship network are closely bound up with family relationships. Marriages cement kinship networks and are therefore arranged between families rather than solely by the two potential spouses. For

Muslims, Islamic law provides the framework for family relations while Sikh and Hindu communities follow their religious laws. Religious codes tend, however, to be strongly interwoven with local community-based norms. This section concentrates on the 'vertical' relationship in a diasporic community between Muslim community/religious laws and UK state marriage law as an illustration.

Diverse families: pluralism in marriage

In the UK there are two forms of heterosexual marriage, romantic and arranged, and one form of civil partnership for single-sex couples. In romantic marriage and civil partnership, the individuals choose partners. In the latter, preferred by many within BrAsian communities, potential spouses are identified by parents or other third parties while the individuals involved make the final decision whether to marry or not. English law in principle only recognises marriages and divorces conducted in accordance with English state law. Arranged marriages and divorces, if they meet these requirements, will be valid but neither an Islamic marriage celebrated by British Muslim citizens in England nor an Islamic divorce has any legal status. While Islamic family law is not recognised in relation to matters conducted in the UK, it is fully recognised under private international law (Jones and Gnanapala 2000: chapter 4). Thus, overseas marriages and divorces conducted according to Islamic family law, as it operates within specific jurisdictions, such as Pakistan, India and Bangladesh, are the subject matter of UK legislation and court judgments. Because matrimonial matters continue to be conducted in both South Asia and the UK in many instances, the interactions between UK and the Muslim family law of these jurisdictions 'muddy the waters' of a purely centralist approach. For instance, an English Muslim citizen from a Pakistani family may marry in England a Muslim spouse who lives in Pakistan or they may marry in Pakistan. The legal consequences can be very different.

For the first generation of immigrants, the English matrimonial courts tended to be irrelevant because of the inevitable ignorance of its members to local legal norms. However, 'during the late 1960s and early 1970s English law moved further and further in the direction of recognising, through case law, that Muslims in Britain continued to act in accordance with what they took to be shari'a' (Menski and Pearl 1998: 58). This emerging recognition of legal pluralism was achieved through the courts' use of the distinction between residence and domicile. If the parties were domiciled in Pakistan then the court could address the issues via Pakistani Muslim family law. However, 'in line with increasing immigration restrictions ... English statute law began to demand, in effect, that the rules and procedures of the uniform domestic law were to be followed. 'English divorce law insisted on formal legal proceedings before an English court to bring about a legally valid divorce' (1998: 58). Thus Muslims to be married under English law were required to conduct the English civil marriage ceremony and, if necessary, divorce under English laws. Thereafter, in order to meet both sets of rules, Muslims generally marry and divorce twice. For English law, the civil law proceedings create and dissolve the marriage for state purposes while the religiously inspired procedures do this for the parties involved (see Carroll 1997).

The arrangements concerning marriages become very complex when the parties are operating within and between official and unofficial systems and across jurisdictions. There is concern that this plurality can be used by the more powerful, often husbands, to manoeuvre between jurisdictions and also between the formal and informal law systems (Carroll 1997). So, for instance, while polygamy is not recognised under English law, it is in Islamic law. Under Pakistani state law, a second marriage requires court permission, which takes account of the views of the existing wife. Nonetheless, the lack of registration does not invalidate the marriage. Only one wife can be resident in the UK. So the other wife has no chance of joining her husband unless and until he divorces his first wife. It is also possible that a man will marry a woman by nikah in the UK (the Islamic form unrecognised in English law) and another by a civil marriage or by nikah in Pakistan, which is subsequently recognised as a valid overseas marriage (Charsley 2006: 1173). While polygamous practices are not necessarily widespread they do involve a clear gender injustice not limited to the fact that this polyandry is only available to a man.

UK citizens and kinsfolk

Feminist legal critiques have shown how the construction of a private sphere outside of the regulation of the (state) law has contributed to the dangers all women can face within the family (O'Donovan 1985, 1993). Families can be very violent places and women's organisations have, with considerable success, forced the issue of domestic violence onto the public agenda over the last thirty years in an effort to obtain state intervention. Criminal and civil (family) laws relating to gender-based violence now reach deep into the family, and the police, as public law enforcers, as a matter of policy, if not always in practice, disregard the location of violence in their pursuit of perpetrators (Cowan and Hodgson 2007). As a result of women's activism, state intervention in the family is also increasingly legitimated through human rights discourse so that women's individual rights to life and liberty inform policy development.

The unjust treatment of women who kill violent men in attempts to defend themselves has been recognised by the judiciary through reinterpretations of the defence of provocation and within legislative provisions (Coroners and Justice Act 2009). Domestic violence, although not a specific criminal offence, is tackled in a range of civil law measures, which are backed by criminal sanctions (Cowan and Hodgson 2007). State agencies provide a range of services, including assistance from social services, access to public housing and welfare benefits. Civil society organisations run refuges and offer advice and assistance. Within the criminal justice system, there are specific procedures and guidelines for police and crown prosecutors and in parts of the country there are specialist Magistrates' courts. All these agencies are brought together through multi-agency committees at local level to assess risk and coordinate intervention (Home Office 2000; Cowan and Hodgson 2007). There are similar guidelines for dealing with sexual assault and rape and specialist institutional contexts for those who report rape under recently updated criminal provisions (see Wells and Quick 2010). The criminal law also provides offences of abduction and kidnapping (similar to those in South Asia). Parents who take a child abroad can be charged with child abduction under the Child Abduction Act 1984 or with the common law offence of kidnapping. There is an offence of false imprisonment. For a girl child (under eighteen) there are a range of child cruelty and education-related offences (such as absence from school) available.

Cultural violence or violence against women?

Does the violence experienced by BrAsian women in families 'fit' into this frame-work? Is it different? Manifestations of specific forms of violence include killings associated with 'honour', assault, confinement and imprisonment, and interfer-ence with choice in marriage (Welchman and Hossain 2005: 4). There is consid-erable contest over the definition of the problems facing BrAsian women, which are fought out among a range of sectional interests with different agendas (Siddiqui 2005; Reddy 2008). The language of honour crimes predominates in much public discourse. However, what do these terms honour and crime signify? For the media and in much public debate in a context of increased Islamophobia, honour crimes are perpetrated by families adopting foreign (and uncivilised) cultural practices. The association of such violence with 'other' cultures is resisted by minority women's organisations because of the familiar tendency to see violence against Muslim women by Muslim men as resulting from their culture while violence by British men against British women is devoid of culture and therefore different. Although government, community and religious spokespersons all make it clear that there is no justification within Islamic values for force, their voices are drowned out in the wider clamour to report lurid details of abuses. Women's human rights advocates recognise that the practices have roots within some communities but see them as forms of violence against women (Coomaraswamy 2005: xi). They point to the violence against young men who are caught up in honour-related crimes to highlight evidence of other hierarchies of power and that honour codes are concerned 'not only with the upholding of patriarchal hetero-sexual norms in relation to women, but also of broader norms of heteronorma-tivity which affect both men and women more generally' (Reddy 2008: 308).

From family to state crime

To what extent should cultural defences be recognised in criminal law if a young woman is killed by close family members because her behaviour is perceived to have brought dishonour to a family? A firm legal centralist or regulationist (Phillips 2007; Phillips and Dustin 2004) approach would argue one law for all: culture is no excuse. State law provides clear signals of the dominant cultural value of equality and encourages changes in behaviour (Carroll 1997). Muslim women (and men) are then able to seek redress outside (exit) their communities. Others argue that courts generally fail to do justice to minority citizens by not taking account of informal law systems, through in effect, not paying enough attention to 'cultural' issues and in particular not recognising the strength of, and therefore effect on, women's and men's behaviour, of the alternative normative systems (Shah 2005: chapter 7; Ballard 2006a, 2006b). These arguments can make feminists who have revealed the way in which 'cultural' defences have been used in criminal cases uneasy. They argue that gender and culture cannot be theorised as separate and distinct (Phillips 2003: 530–531). Prominent minority women's activist groups call for a 'mature multiculturalism', which recognises diverse cultural identities but also recognises that violence is an abuse of the fundamental rights of women, irrespective of cultural or religious contexts (Reddy 2008: 311). Within this approach, the rights of women in relation to violence are weighted more heavily than those related to group cultures. The criminal justice system has responded within a universal regulation framework by recognising and seeking to tackle honour killings, although not necessarily in ways that take full account of the discourse of women's rights (Reddy 2008: 313–317).

Exiting family codes, entering civil society: adapting state law?

There is, however, considerable resistance to replacing a family discourse of honour with a state criminal one which led to strong opposition to the creation of a specific offence of forcible marriage (Wilson 2007). A clear distinction between culturally acceptable arranged marriages and culturally abhorrent forced marriages is insisted upon by all policymakers, judges and Islamic scholars (Ahsan 1995: 23). In practice, there is a continuum of attitudes, with consent and coercion standing at two opposing ends, which operates in the wider context of gendered inequalities (Anitha and Gill 2009: 180) and intergenerational perspectives:

> [T]he elderly [in the Pakistani community in Bradford and Bangladeshi community in Tower Hamlets] appear exasperated by their inability to enforce or impose their decisions of marriage on young men and women. . . . Middle aged participants argue that forced marriage is a problem which will eventually die out. . .they distinguish between culture and Islam . . . forced marriage is unIslamic [and] accept that they have to accommodate the wishes of their children . . . There is a degree of ambiguity over the understanding of coercion . . . Force is unacceptable but emotional and psychological pressure appears to be condoned. Young people consider any form of coercion to be completely unacceptable. (Samad and Eade 2002: 110)

A forced marriage is constructed within two legal contexts: in English marriage law, in which duress renders a marriage voidable, and in the Forced Marriage Act 2007 (Phillips and Dustin 2004; Anitha and Gill 2009; Enright 2009). Most recent cases on the content of duress suggest that very little pressure may be required for evidence when parental arguments stress personal affection, duty, religious beliefs and powerful cultural norms and familial obligations (Enright 2009: 343). This judicially constructed definition is now based on a concept of consent with a high individual will content, which would probably invalidate many arranged marriages if they were to come before a court although courts still recognise consent that is reluctant or resentful as valid (Anitha and Gill 2009: 172). The Forced Marriages (Civil Protection) Act 2007 defines such a marriage as one without free and full consent. Force includes to 'coerce by threats or other psychological means' (Family Law Act 1996 section 63A(6)). Powers to prevent the removal of young girls from the jurisdiction have been greatly strengthened by the introduction of a specific protection order (Part 4A within the Family Law Act 1996). Actions can be instigated by relevant third parties (see Enright 2009: 344). Orders can be made ex parte and generally can be enforced against secondary as well as primary perpetrators (Enright 2009: 344–345). These features, and the civil nature of the provisions, make it clear that 'the current law around forced marriages is designed to take some account of those cultural factors which contribute to the problem' (Enright 2009: 345) and are examples of 'mature multiculturalism' (Reddy 2008: 318).

These measures presume very high levels of agency and, if utilised, are likely to result in the young women's exclusion from family and community. There are potentially two policy frameworks through which to provide support: those relating to domestic violence and the other relating to child protection for those under the age of eighteen. Neither offers at present an adequately resourced, culturally sensitive response to the growing number of such marriages. One report estimates between 5,000 and 8,000 reported incidences, of which 62 per cent were threats of forced marriages and the remainder were marriages that have taken place (Kazimirski et al. 2009: 2). Indeed, as minority women's groups point out, their ability to provide such support has been adversely affected by recent government policies (Phillips and Dustin 2004; Anitha and Gill 2009; Enright 2009). Exit comes at great personal cost to women's sense of belonging and is not a course of action that many are able or willing to undertake (Enright 2009).

Keeping it in the family or tackling through dialogue?

While the aim may have been to 'assimilate' BrAsian family laws within the state system, communities have moulded their religious and community laws to fit around the dominant legal system. This process is described as angrezi (English) Hinduism, angrezi Shariat (Menski and Pearl 1998) and ingreji Shoriyot for the Bangladeshi community (Shah 2005).

Muslim communities, in particular, have been developing their own responses, which are designed to accord with the 'traditional Muslim way of dealing with family matters outside the state interference' (Yilmaz 2001: 303). One such response has been the establishment of Shari'a councils in England devoted to the informal settlement of disputes between Muslims according to Muslim law (Shah-Kazemi 2001). These bodies can now be recognised as providing binding arbitration under the Arbitration Act 1996 and voluntary agreements concerning matters that do not conflict with state law can be enforced through a consent order in county courts and the High Court. Decisions are subject to national law and can be enforced only when the body acts as an arbitrator under the Arbitration Act 1996. Councils therefore operate as 'alternative dispute resolution' bodies on family and financial affairs, although there are suggestions that, in practice, many informal unrecognised bodies are making decisions beyond their remit (MacEoin 2009).

Councils are products of the diaspora, not totally separated from state law or from local community norms and values (Bano 2007). They have focused specifically on problems created by the plurality of normative systems within which Muslim communities live (Shah-Kazemi 2001; Bano 2004, 2007). The Muslim Arbitration Tribunal (established in 2007 and comprising 'courts' in five cities) has warned on the basis of its own experience that forced marriages constitute a crisis for young Muslims and that more than 70 per cent of marriages involving a foreign spouse have some element of coercion or force (2008). It argues for both community action to deal with the problem and dialogue with the government.

Women who initiate the majority of referrals use the councils to pursue justice for themselves. They seek a fair hearing and rely upon the positive values of Islam. For some women, these bodies provide a way of dealing with their family problems that does not require them to reject their identity as BrAsian Muslim women (Bano 2004). They are, in effect, seeking to combine the discourse of Islam with that of human rights. Others suggest ways of combining the recognition of informal family law systems with additional supportive provisions to prevent injustices to women (Carroll 1997; Shachar 2001). These provisions would involve the injection of women's human rights into the informal institutional setting, thus seeking to expand 'civil' space within community or religious normative contexts. However, some women's organisations are not confident that, as presently constituted, these bodies provide an effective response to the difficulties women face because they give too much recognition to existing communal cultural or religious identities at the expense of rights (Patel 2008).

There are some within the UK minority communities who seek recognition for a separate 'Muslim personal code'. Politically, there is no likelihood that the UK state will cede authority in the present climate of suspicion over 'separatist' activities. The existing arrangements have already generated considerable hostility and alarmist discussion in the media (Bano 2008). The present context of heightened mistrust, racism and Islamophobia is contributing to the solidification of group identities around religion. It is argued that government policy is shifting from multiculturalism to 'multi faithism' (Patel 2008). Such developments are leading to a contraction of secular/civil space within many communities. Undermining the social capital of a community by devaluing its normative structures reduces trust, and the potential for dialogue between the state and a range of constituencies, including minority women, is made all the more difficult (Phillips and Dustin 2004; Phillips 2007).

Transnational marriage chains

Introduction

The socially reproductive activities of families form the core of this chain involving the movement of people and the flow of norms between the Global North and South. They are not directly market driven, although communities have used 'private enterprise' in the form of family-based emigration as their local industry: kinship as capital (Ballard 2003) in contrast to state-organised export of citizens to manage a national economy (as in the Philippines). Family networks, built on concepts of reciprocity, enable communities to gain access to labour markets in the North for family members but also to transfer resources, generated in the North, to families located in the Global South. Southern states gain through family remittances and a reduction in the number of potentially unemployed young persons. However the transnational family (TNF) not only 'derives its lived reality' from 'the material bonds of collective welfare among physically dispersed members' but also from a 'shared imaginary of "belonging", which transcends particular periods and places to encompass past trajectories and future continuities' (Yeoh et al. 2005: 308; Vertovec 2007). Globalisation is producing 'normative transnationalism': 'in many parts of the world it has become the norm for family members to travel abroad and maintain numerous forms of contact with kin and communities of origin' (Vertovec 2007: 20).

Transnational marriages remain very popular within some BrAsian communities. In 2006 of the 47,000 overseas spouses, 17,000 came from Pakistan, Bangladesh and India and accounted for 13,265 of the 42,110 grants of settlement to spouses (Enright 2009: 353). They constituted the majority of marriages in a study of Pakistani Punjabi families in Bristol (Charsley 2006), '50% of marriages [in the predominantly Mirpuri community] in Bradford while in Oxford the proportion of these alliances is estimated to be as high as 71%' (Samad and Eade 2002: 48–49, references omitted). There is no research evidence in relation to Bangladeshis in Tower Hamlets but the patterns are thought to be similar (Samad and Eade 2002).

This discussion adopts the chain concepts of input/outputs, territoriality and governance to identify the gender issues involved. TNF-based networks, in contrast to the activities of TNCs, can be seen as 'bottom up' rather than 'top down'. By valuing and prioritising activities associated with the socially reproductive domain of care they can present a challenge to Global North consumer market economies and modern, albeit multicultural, European states. The 'demand' at the heart of this chain to choose spouses/partners from specific locations in the Global South can be seen as a normatively transgressive act. The discourses (trade, rights and care) associated with the governance contribute to the distribution of the benefits and risks associated with the chain in complex ways and reflect contests over the construction of the values involved.

Territorially, the chains channel benefits to families and support a wider set of commercial services to peripheral areas in the Global South although the relationship between these and wider social and economic development depends on local contexts. Because of the migration history discussed above, spouses tend to come from highly localised areas. For the Pakistani Muslim population, marriages to consanguineous family members, (first or second cousins) living in Pakistan have always been significant (Samad and Eade 2002). While the British Pakistani population is heterogeneous in socio-economic status in Britain and origins in Pakistan, the Mirpur district, which is situated in Azad Kashmir in the foothills of the Himalayas, accounts for the overwhelming majority of UK Pakistani emigrants, most of whom come from two small towns. In total, 50 per cent of the region's population emigrates. Despite appearances in Mirpur city, it is a rural agricultural and impoverished area which, in contrast to the neighbouring Jalandhar region in the Punjab, has not had a green revolution. Over the years families have remitted payments back, which have resulted in wealth for individual families and a boom in construction as money has been used to build luxurious dwellings. A service industry has developed to cater for the needs of emigrants and their families but despite the availability of capital from remittances, no industrial or agricultural development has taken place. The Pakistani state has not invested in the necessary infrastructure, such as education, bridges and roads, to trigger such developments. As a result land prices have boomed, fuelled by speculation and prestige building projects, but have also suffered downturns with changes in the economic circumstances of migrants. Because the area is locked into transnational family-based enterprises and has not developed much local capacity for economic development, migration remains a necessity for the region. It is socially conservative with a strong Barelwi Islamic tradition, despite the outward manifestations of wealth produced by the investments of transnational families, and is in many respects marginalised within Pakistan due to its geographical and political positioning in Azad Kashmir, a region that seeks independent recognition (Ballard 2003, 2005).

For the Bangladeshi community, there is a finite number in a small population in the UK of suitable brides or grooms within appropriate kinship networks. Cousin marriages, not traditionally associated with this community, seem to be increasing (Gardner 2006). Sylhet is the source of most of the Bangladeshi overseas migrants, including to the UK. This region in the north-east is often portrayed as different from the rest of Bangladesh with an economy based on tea cultivation on plantations. The flow of remittances by non-resident Bangladeshis to relatives in Sylhet is a major source of foreign currency and the only source of income for some families. This flow of money has again stimulated a building boom in luxury homes:

> Today it is common in 'Talukpur' to find homesteads or *bari* (a collection of separate households on one site, usually with a common patrilineal ancestor going back two or three generations) that have experienced vastly different economic fortunes – a reflection of whether or not the heads of the households migrated. (Gardner 2006: 377)

This differential access to wealth has created local tensions over land ownership and further enhances the desirability of alliances with a diasporic family. The region is considered to be a socially and religiously conservative area in which women's behaviour is closely regulated. There is very limited acceptability of seeing women in public (World Bank 2008: 103–104).

There is anecdotal evidence that the Sikh and Hindu communities, who do not favour close family marriages, now search within their diasporic community as a whole. They go 'off shore' as families seek to trade up to find spouses in the USA although increasing prosperity in India may be changing perceptions again. However, the Punjab remains a key source. This part of India is the homeland of the Sikhs who comprise about 60 per cent of its population, with Hindus constituting the vast majority of the rest. The Jalandhar district, where most family networks are based, does not rely on remittances for its main source of income although these have undoubtedly enriched individual families. The Punjab is a relatively more prosperous state providing much of the wheat and rice for India as a whole. However, 66 per cent of the Punjabi population live in rural areas where there are very high levels of unemployment, particularly among the young, including those with educational attainments. The Punjab is socially conservative. Women's literacy is significantly lower than men's (64 per cent compared to 76 per cent). The drop-out rate of girls from school is very high. There are only 876 females per 1,000 males compared to 933 for India as a whole, indicating gender-differentiated foeticide and infanticide.

Capital from remittances has been used to increase investment in agricultural development but in contrast to Pakistan, the Indian state has contributed to infrastructural developments in this economically and politically important state. Some remittances are used to fund charitable projects, including religious buildings but also schools and hospitals, which supplement state services, thus providing more enduring and positive flows of income than the land-based investments in Mirpur and Sylhet (Ballard 2005).

The dominant marital ideology in the UK of companionate partnerships has not displaced the value of the family-arranged marriage system for young adults brought up in the UK, although the practices in crafting a 'home from home'

model are clearly evolving (Ballard 1994; Shah 2002). Shaw and Charsley
caution against a 'dominant image of ... unsuitable matches ... "forced"
upon unwilling young people in response to socio-economic, cultural and
psychological pressure by parents from working-class uneducated rural backgrounds' in Mirpur (2006: 406). It is no longer the norm that the bride is located
in South Asia and the groom in the UK: sex ratios have roughly evened up,
including recently within the Bangladeshi community (Samad and Eade 2002;
Gardner 2006).

Transnational connections are not hangovers from the past but a product of
the contemporary UK context. In their present form such marriages enable
families within the various communities to secure 'material and social advantage' (Shaw and Charsley 2006: 419). Connections are reinforced: the British
household maintain links with its homeland while creating direct links with
Britain for the South Asia household (Gardner 2006: 385). Although serving
these wider strategic advantages, they also create 'emotional connections between
people divided by geographical distance' (Shaw and Charsley 2006: 419). They
can renew a sense of belonging that may have been attenuated among family
members who have been physically separated by earlier migration (Gardner
2006). 'Marriage to close and trusted kin is seen as a way of reducing the social
and emotional risks of making a transnational marriage' (Gardner 2006: 385).
Cousin marriages involve 'the children of loved and trusted siblings' and
'strengthen consanguinity with affinity ... and, at least from the perspective of
parents, thus offer multiple routes to trust, security and support' (Shaw and
Charsley 2006: 411).

Do these motives coincide with the aspirations of the potential spouses?
Generalisations are risky but while young BrAsians are clearly seeking to develop
their own identities, it is also argued that they are not rejecting the values that
underpin these connections (Samad and Eade 2002). Shaw and Charsley's
research with young British Pakistanis found that both sexes saw positive
advantages in transnational marriages involving close kin who are known to
them and whom they may have met, facilitating a discourse of romance leading
to arranged love marriages. They considered that partners from Pakistan were
likely to be better life companions and committed to the marriage because of
the values they were seen to embody: more rooted in religious values and less
identified with UK consumer market motivations.

Young women wanted their future partners to be respectful to them and their
elders and not obsessed by money. They thought their Pakistani kin would be
less likely to be unfaithful. The young men wanted wives who were not too
assertive and pushy and who would reinforce religious and cultural values in
their children. Both sexes were wary of matches with British Pakistanis, including their UK cousins, whom they considered, reflecting the dominant discourse
of disapproval, to be too familiar or close to them. Transnational spouses are
genealogically close but distant enough (Shaw and Charsley 2006: 413–415).
From this perspective, differing inter-generational motives and gendered

constructions can be contained within the same process (Shaw and Charsley 2006: 419). While the older (first) generation prioritise an amalgam of values involving customs and traditions associated with their place of origin in South Asia, such as, for instance, identity as a Punjabi, the younger second and third generations are remixing the elements to increase the significance of an Islamic identity.

There is therefore a complex relationship between 'value addition', territoriality and identity construction. Rootedness in a locality, both in South Asia and the UK, adds values associated with transnational economic and ontological security for families, particularly among older generations. However, the same rootedness is seen as decreasing the value of the spouse as a potential consuming worker/citizen in the UK. This form of transnational trading is not seen as valuable to the state because it seemingly supplies persons based upon their self-defined socially reproductive contribution. Further, because state controls explicitly prevent a productive focus (this is family not economic migration) to the immediate process, the potential for these new family members to contribute to production is also seen as limited.

As in the care chain, the inputs are associated with the persons involved, in particular their ascribed characteristics or identities as suitable potential spouses. They are seen as embodying values that will strengthen family relationships and senses of belonging. These identities have been constructed through family and community relationships in the home state, whether this is the UK or within South Asia. Women's behaviour, particularly relating to their sexuality, is a crucial marker or symbol of community identity (Anthias and Yuval-Davies 1992). Even though transactions now involve the movement of both men and women, the inscribed value of women's sexual bodies remains central. Parental desires may not coincide with those of children who may wish to embrace dominant discourses of sexual freedom and individual expressions of sexual identities.

Marriage breakdown, which seems to be increasing, causes wider community concern and intervention (Badawi 1995; Shah-Kazemi 2001; Samad and Eade 2002: chapter 4). The consequences can be particularly severe because conflict between the parties involves conflict within a close family network with a lot at stake (Shaw and Charsley 2006: 419). Allegiances are broken, which can have disastrous effects on the spouses involved (and their families (see Hussain and Jenkins 2010)) particularly because these events take place within the context of immigration controls. The disintegration of a marriage can lead to deportation, a powerful weapon in the hands of disgruntled spouses and family members (see Siddiqui et al. 2008).

Governance discourses of care, rights and trade

State immigration controls contribute to the creation of value and the risks in the chains by denying or permitting entry, and thereafter access to permanent settlement. This external institutional framework seeks to suppress or at least disrupt demand, raising interesting comparisons with the governance of trafficking chains. It does not take place within a market-related trade discourse, rather it involves the regulation of the socially reproductive arrangements of a community, superseding earlier controls relating to the group as migrant workers. In a context where rights to family formation take second place to migration control, the state is able to intrude very substantially into the 'private' area of family life of citizens based upon their group identities.

Since the 1970s, the pattern of migration to the UK has changed substantially with a marked reduction of migrants from the old and new Commonwealth. They have been replaced by migrants from the EU and also by newcomers with origins in countries and communities across the world. The consequential 'superdiversity' presents new worries for policymakers over issues of social cohesion and competition over access to resources (Vertovec 2007: 9). These anxieties are reflected in a plethora of legislative intervention: there have been eight separate Acts since 1990 dedicated to immigration and nationality matters.

This external governance context suggests that the UK does not value transnationally constructed identities, particularly, although not exclusively, within the BrAsian Muslim communities because they seem now to represent resistance to an acceptable construction of belonging to the British state. There is a suspicion over the motives of families because the majority community finds it hard to accept that young British citizens brought up in a Global North consumer culture would choose (and therefore value) an arranged marriage to a 'foreigner' from what could be a 'backward' part of Pakistan or Bangladesh, particularly if s/he is a close relative. This continued engagement of BrAsian settled communities with immigration laws take place in a context of heightened political tension relating to global insecurity and an increased focus on 'securing borders'. A wider discourse of suspicion and protection of national security, not only increases barriers and therefore costs but also contributes to the risks for the individuals involved.

The state immigration rules are increasingly narrowing the target for interventions to focus on South Asian Muslim transnational family arrangements. Earlier perceived risks were curbed through bans on male primary migration followed by restrictions on (female) family unification. The discriminatory primary purpose rule, which led to most marriage migrants being female, was replaced in 1997 with similar requirements for women and men wishing to enter on a spousal settlement visa. The suspicion remains that marriages of South Asian-based men to UK women could be 'bogus'. In recent years, a new construction has been added to this state suspicion of transnational marriage: that the marriage has been forced upon one of the parties by the families. The concern, and the primary focus for intervention, relates to the potential abuse of BrAsian young women whose marriages involve South Asian-based men and which tend to take place within the man's home country (Enright 2009: 332). These young women are then coerced into sponsoring spousal visas.

There is little consensus on the relationship between immigration and forced marriages and disputed statistics on the scale of the problem (see Phillips and Dunstan 2004; Khanum 2008). Enright (2009) reports that the Foreign and Commonwealth Office Forced Marriage Unit deals with approximately 400 cases a year. Although some argue very strongly that there is no evidence that families are pressurising their children to marry to enable a family member to obtain access to the UK (Samad and Eade 2002; Ballard 2006b), the connection is made consistently by policymakers and in the media. Headlines reporting a 2009 baseline survey on the issue of forced marriages undertaken by SACH (a Pakistan-based NGO) in collaboration with the British High Commission in Pakistan read '96.6% marriages take place to attain foreign nationality' although there is no substance at all in the body of the reports to substantiate this claim (Imran 2009). It has, however, been quoted extensively, including on the website of the British National Party. Within some quarters there is a further elision with other forms of extremist behaviour that threaten border security such as 'terrorism' (Wilson 2007) but also with trafficking (involving underage 'child' marriages) (Bokhari 2009).

The concern more generally over 'suspicious' marriages involving foreign nationals has led to further regulation via immigration laws. Such marriages require notification and, once accepted, they must take place at a designated registry office to allow for efficient monitoring of the individual subject to immigration control (see Toner 2007). Denmark, in particular, has led the way by amending its immigration rules to try to stop perceived forced marriages, which, although race neutral, clearly target the Pakistani community (Aliens (Consolidation) Act 2002; Bredal 2005: 343). While many see the motivation for these rules as limiting Asian immigration generally, the Danish state justifies them on gender equality grounds as protecting young women by removing the immigration incentive for marriage (Bredel 2005). The British government measures are somewhat less draconian although many of the Danish requirements are already incorporated into Immigration Rules. Since December 2008, the minimum age to sponsor a spouse's visa if they are from outside the EU is twenty-one. (UK citizens can still marry at sixteen with parental consent.) Since March 2009 the Home Office has issued a Code of Practice to enable officials to spot individuals who may be vulnerable to a forced marriage and to encourage them to refuse a visa on this ground or review permission to stay in the UK (Home Office 2009a). They will therefore be looking for the potential for vulnerability and exploitation (not the genuineness of the marriage). The overall aim of this new policy is clear from the Home Office consultation policy that preceded these changes: to encourage young people to think long and hard about transnational marriages (2006b: 6). Many, particularly in the BrAsian communities, see these measures as an excuse for ever tighter immigration controls and ineffectual (Samad and Eade 2002; Siddiqui 2005; Ballard 2006b). There is no reason to suggest that tackling the issue through state immigration rules will do anything more than antagonise communities that feel under attack from the state and inadequately protected against racism (Phillips and Dunstin 2004; Wilson 2007; Enright 2009). The procedures may add considerably to the difficulties faced by the majority who continue to want to marry transnationally. Young people generally will be obliged to wait longer if they wish to marry abroad, putting more pressure on their behaviour prior to this event occurring.

In this governance context, transnational arrangements are risky for families and for the individual spouses, particularly for the young women who are separated from their natal families. Satisfying entry clearance requirements based on marriage is becoming increasingly difficult and has its consequences. First, women whose marriages are arranged with Pakistani nationals may find themselves 'immigration widows' if the men are refused entry clearance (Charsley 2006: 1169). Even if the visa is finally granted this may occur many months later, creating a very substantial hiatus in the development of relationships. Secondly, the restrictions on primary migration may add pressures to the negotiations with families in Pakistan to enable another member to migrate and can lead to husbands absconding, bringing shame on the family. Thirdly, for a young man to be sponsored by his wife and to be in effect dependent on her and her family for a significant period of time can be challenging to masculine identities and adversely affect gender relationships within the household (Charsley 2005). Fourthly, the whole process takes place under a shadow of suspicion and increasingly intrusive surveillance.

Socially reproductive care

Entrepreneurial family agency involves activities that maintain connection and solidarity. Internal governance is organised as a 'bottom up', socially reproductive activity through the discourse of care unlike the bureaucratic governance within TNCs and GVCs. Families adapt marriage rituals and ceremonies more generally to 'fit' around English and Islamic marriage law requirements to minimise their effects (Charsley 2006: 1171). Such adaptations are aimed at minimising risks to daughters in particular (Charsley 2006). Families divide up the stages of the wedding to try to ensure that the formalities are undertaken to satisfy immigration requirements and to signal a firm commitment but also to avoid the unwelcome consequences of the marriage not working out. Consummation will only occur when the spouse arrives in the UK on a spousal visa. Even then the rituals may be delayed if there are doubts about suitability. A permanent right to remain only occurs after two years while the acquisition of citizenship takes a further three years. If there are doubts a (male) spouse may return to Pakistan speedily and the woman, although requiring a divorce under either English law and/or Islamic law, is in fact still a virgin. A woman thus can avoid unwanted sexual intimacy and she is in a better position in relation to any future marriage.

These arrangements avoid the far less welcome possibilities such as the formal marriage arrangements being completed overseas and the wife returning home pregnant. Thereafter, if entry clearance is not granted, she becomes a single parent in the UK. Alternatively, the husband joins her and the marriage subsists until citizenship has been obtained, then she is divorced by him. Or, he may refuse to divorce her under religious law. He is able to stay in the UK and marry again causing considerable loss of family honour.

Differential human rights and individual agency

There is an alternative, but not altogether separate, governance perspective that focuses less on the 'trading' for family-based social and material advantage and more on issues of individual identity and constructions of belonging. Here marriages are seen more as sites of intergenerational and gendered conflict over constructions of sexuality. A forced marriage prevents young women and men exercising choice over sexual partners or, more generally, demonstrating independent (understood often as replicating the mores of the majority community) behaviour. They involve a differently constructed violation of (human) rights: forced marriages are primarily abusive exercises in family power and perpetrations of violence against women.

Differential human rights

Incomers

The focus on forced marriages obscures wider forms of abuse that take place in the context of migration to the UK, such as those involving 'non-resident Indian (NRI) marriages' between Indian men with rights of residence or citizenship in Britain (and elsewhere) and Indian (often Punjabi) women. These include abandonment in India shortly after the marriage, after receipt of the dowry; abandonment on arrival in the UK, again after the receipt of the dowry; discovery of another wife and that the husband has been forced or obliged by his family to undertake this arranged marriage; discovery of deceit relating to financial or other circumstances; and threats of violence to produce more dowry (NCW 2006).

South Asian women who migrate to join their husbands are in a particularly vulnerable position as new arrivals who can be deported at the end of the two-year probationary period imposed by immigration controls if they are separated from their husbands. A spouse must also support their immigrant spouse's application to remain indefinitely; if not the person commits a criminal offence as an overstayer once the spousal visa has expired. In these circumstances, due to their isolation within the home with their abusive spouse, young women are unlikely to make applications to the Home Office, which would lead to the regularisation of their residency. Until she obtains a permanent right to remain a woman is covered by the 'no recourse to public funds' rule, which denies her access to welfare benefits, social housing, public funds or facilities funded by public funds. The vulnerability created by her immigration status thus reinforces power relations within the family and limits the potential for 'exit'. As a result of campaigns by women's organisations, concessions were introduced in 1999 for women who can claim a right to stay for an indefinite period provided they are able to prove that the marriage has broken down due to domestic violence. (Between 500 and 600 immigrant women generally experience domestic violence each year (Gill and Sharma 2007: 184)). The evidential burden, although lowered in 2003, is still high. Women must have acquired a caution, court order or conviction against the spouse or more than one piece of publicly attested evidence of violence.

The practical difficulties involved in seeking help from the state faced by a woman who is unfamiliar with the country, its language and the dominant culture are enormous, further complicated by her inability to access public resources. She must exit her family networks, thus being seen as bringing shame on herself and her family, which may also have close links with her spouse's family, back home. Domestic violence is defined as an act perpetrated by intimate partners or 'associated persons' who 'have or have had an intimate personal relationship' of 'significant duration' (Domestic Violence Crime and Victims Act 2004, section 4) (Siddiqui 2005) although the courts have used the 1997 Protection from Harassment Act to tackle violence by a mother-in-law. In *Singh* v. *Bhakar* [2007] 1 FLR 880, violence covered 'a campaign of bullying and humiliation' and led to a £35,000 award of compensation (Jones 2006).

While the Home Office has issued guidelines to policymakers on tackling domestic violence within Black and minority communities, which shows awareness of specific cultural contexts (Parmar and Sampson 2005), it is not clear that immigrant women are supported to 'enter' the dominant society (Shah-Kazemi 2001; Wilson 2007; Kazimirski et al. 2009). There is a shortage of specialist services for minority women and reluctance within government policies prioritising the creation of social cohesion to support projects that focus on single communities (Wilson 2007; Enright 2009). Under present public funding regimes, refuges for women who face violence are not able to recoup their costs for women subject to the 'no recourse to public funds' rule and therefore are unable to assist.

Finally, the consequences of being deported can be dire for women. They may be returned to overwhelmingly hostile circumstances, which include honour killings and the offence of zina in Pakistan (see previous chapter). The families involved may be prominent members of the community who have a great deal to lose (Wilson 2007). However, appeals against deportation on grounds of violation of human rights or claims for asylum are increasingly being turned down (Gill and Sharma 2007; Wilson 2007; Siddiqui et al. 2008 although see *SN (Pakistan)* v. *Secretary of State for the Home Department* [2009] EWCA Civ 181). Thus as non-citizen transnationals, South Asian women are not protected from violence and abuse within the UK. They remain firmly trapped within the power relations of the family without effective access to civil protections. Their human rights are 'trumped' by the imperatives of immigration control. They 'fall victim to the quadruple whammy of marginalisation resulting from their immigration status, gender, ethnicity and abuse' (Gill and Sharma 2007: 189).

Outgoers

UK public policy on forced marriages is primarily driven by the Foreign and Commonwealth Office, which has focused concern on the plight of female UK citizens taken overseas to marry. The Forced Marriage Unit (FMU) assists those who are at risk of, or have been forced into, such marriages and the issue has gained a high profile as a consequence. Abroad, the FMU works with embassy staff to rescue victims who may have been held captive, raped or forced into having an abortion. In the UK it assists professionals working in the social, educational and health sectors and has developed a relatively comprehensive policy framework for tackling the issue (Phillips and Dustin 2004; Enright 2009). The FMU works very solidly within a human rights framework, stressing that the actions associated with forced marriages are violations of the women's rights and constitute violence against women (Home Office/FCO 2006).

Families may assume that Mirpur, Sylhet or the Punjab will offer safe havens for their actions, away from UK state laws and within the legal contexts described in the previous chapter. The discourse of 'forced' marriages is exemplified by a young UK woman of Sylheti origin who is persuaded by her family to visit for a family event and finds herself about to be married to a local man against her will, possibly because she has an 'unsuitable' boyfriend in the UK or is behaving in ways that are considered likely to jeopardise her marriage chances (Siddiqi 2005). The young woman may seek to access the state penal provisions relating to abduction and kidnapping to regain her liberty from her family. However, unless she can access external assistance from friends, family or a civil society organisation she is very unlikely to be able to use the Bangladeshi legal machinery to gain her liberty. There are major practical obstacles to obtaining justice, including limited professional legal skills locally and gender bias in the police, who consider these personal not public matters leading to inadequate investigations (Hossein 2001).[1] If the young woman is a dual citizen, she may be in a better position if she can access the consular protection offered through the FMU. The outcome in these circumstances is usually that the police retrieve the girl and hand her over to the British High Commission (Siddiqi 2005: 296). If they come to know of the situation, the High Commission may mount with local police a 'rescue operation'. 'Such events initiate considerable social discussion and gossip. In contrast, local women/girls being forced into marriage with local men tends to be seen as a "normal" or everyday event, not newsworthy' (Siddiqi 2005: 295).

However, the plight of BrAsian women forcibly taken to Mirpur has become the focus for UK state policy relating to transnational forced marriages. The FMU estimate that 70 per cent of their cases originate there. The state legal framework for dealing with the activities associated with forced marriages, in particular abduction involving writs of habeas corpus, is very similar to that of

[1] In 2008, lawyers in the UK and Bangladesh took action in the High Court in Dhaka to obtain the release of a Bangladeshi woman doctor living in London. Action was also taken in the UK under the new forced marriage provisions to restrain her parents from further actions.

Bangladesh. Judges have on occasion expressed their condemnation of the practices, which they see as rooted in (backward) traditions and contravening Islamic values (Hossein 2001). They will issue orders requiring that the family produce the missing person in order to establish whether she is being held against her will. The same practical difficulties pertain but are more formidable given the state endorsement of Islamic precepts of zina. Considerable efforts are made by the special unit specifically established within the British Consulate in Islamabad to support young BrAsian women caught up in these processes but the political conditions in Azad Kashmir often make it too dangerous to conduct many 'rescue missions', although they are undertaken, leading to the repatriation of hundreds of young people. The consulate works with local NGOs to support a refuge for 'rescued girls' and to undertake educational programmes relating to forced marriages, which stress the violation of rights involved.

Much less appears in the UK popular media about the problems BrAsian women from the Jalandhar district of the Punjab face although the same consular rescue services are provided within India. The issue has a high profile in the Indian press. Thus, while the British government seeks to support its nationals in India, it is noticeable that the Indian state is far more proactive than its neighbours in its response to the abuses of power experienced by Indian women in transnational marriages, particularly abandonment and divorce overseas. The National Commission for Women (NCW), the co-ordinating-agency dealing with these issues, commissioned a report on the problems and held high-profile meetings in conjunction with the Ministry of Overseas Indian Affairs in the Punjab and Kerala in 2006 (NCW 2006). It has published advice leaflets for NRIs and potential spouses and in August 2009 established an NRI cell to deal with complaints, make recommendations to government such as for the compulsory registration of marriages, and to carry out awareness campaigns. It has established an overseas office in the Indian embassy in London. The welfare of its nationals is obviously the focus for this intervention but there is no doubt that the greater degree of civil space available to women in India has its impact on the development of these initiatives.

Conclusion

This chapter has considered the interrelated themes of trading and belonging through a discussion (using the vertical pyramid concept) of the often uneasy relationships between the state and BrAsian families, which have a significant gender dimension. The communities are not homogeneous. Some have fared better economically than others; the marriage norms and aspirations of some are more affected by immigration controls than others; and the importance of religious norms within family and community regulation are stronger for some communities than others. However, state interventions have contributed both to the relationships of production and social reproduction and to the construction of gendered identities.

BrAsian communities have adapted and consolidated their transnational identities built around networks of social relationships, which produce alliances and create social solidarities. We have seen the interaction between and contests over the constructions of trade, rights and care discourse in the transnational family chains and how the benefits and risks associated with transnational families are distributed. The inputs are associated with the persons involved in the chain and in particular their acquired characteristics and ascribed identities as suitable potential spouses. They are seen as embodying values that will strengthen family transnational relationships and senses of belonging. These identities have been constructed through their family and community relationships in their particular home state. Territorially, their move to a household located in a more prosperous state adds value to them as far as their home family is concerned, providing a network of social relationships that tie the two families together socially and economically.

The internal governance of this chain is organised as a 'bottom up', socially reproductive activity, rather than as a productive one, primarily through networks of social relations within transnational families and their communities. It is conducted through the community and religious normative frameworks associated with marriage, through the discourse of care. As we saw in relation to the body work chains, while trade discourse may champion free movement of labour to meet demand, states use immigration controls in an attempt to limit access to their labour markets to those whom they view as priority workers. The external governance here does not take place directly within this trade discourse even though the activity involves the movement of persons. It is regulated through state controls over immigration rather than rights to family formation. The UK state contributes to the creation of value and the risks in the chain by permitting or denying entry and thereafter access to permanent settlement. The increasing entry requirements, framed through the discourse of suspicion and the protection of national security, not only increase barriers and therefore costs but also contribute to the risks for the individuals involved.

State family laws, including protective measures against abuse, provide at a formal level the domestic regulatory framework in which subsequent relationships are conducted. However, migrant status affects access to family and wider welfare provision, limiting the protections available to recently arrived family members. The interaction between immigration controls and family law can increase risks to individual migrants, particularly young women, and to wider family relations. Families seek to minimise these through adaptation in religious and community norms.

The state is able through its immigration laws to intrude very substantially into the 'private' area of family life of citizens based upon their group identities. However, the regulatory discourses are complex, reflecting potentially conflicting normative assumptions. Communities with histories of involvement with state immigration controls tend to see the present context as a continuation of narrow productive-focused restrictions, while their objective is to preserve and, where possible enhance, a sense of transnational identity and belonging, which encompasses economic well-being but extends much wider.

Partly in response, a state-based discourse of suspicion is extending beyond concerns relating to production into those at the heart of the socially reproductive sphere. The state is also concerned not only with work but also care. In relation to production, transnational family trading can be seen as not contributing to productive enterprise because it can involve a supply of inappropriate persons who are not recruited through their productive skills, which the state is not able to prevent. Restricting migration based upon family formation or reunion, which involves its own nationals who choose to form a union with an overseas spouse, is far more difficult to accomplish because such restrictions raise issues of human rights, which protect against the intrusion of the state into private life. Because of the overall socio-economic positioning of many BrAsian families, partners are often joining households with less consumer capacity, which are seen as potentially more demanding of state resources. While young men might be offering unwanted labour, women are seen as less willing or able to adopt the consuming worker model, now underpinning the consumer economy, by not joining the paid labour force in sufficient numbers.

The state does not recognise the evident entrepreneurial skills shown by all the communities in their different ways in migrating to the UK and prospering in relative terms. The first generations within the communities 'traded' without an expectation of state assistance (from the home or the receiving state) but are now formally required to show, at least for a significant period of time, that they will take financial responsibility for the incoming transnational members of their families. In the UK's modern multicultural state with its liberal values and support for freedom and choice, they could reasonably have expected that their children would fare better through access to UK education and employment opportunities. This expectation has not been fully realised.

The interventions of the UK's modern multicultural state have affected minority women's identities and position within the labour market. Chapter 3 explored the impact of wider socially reproductive norms (segment C in the pyramid) on women's position within production and the relationship between the labour and gender contracts in a northern consumer economy. The normative move from the gender-specific breadwinner/homemaker model to the universal (possibly caring) worker/consumer model can create specific intersectional effects for BrAsian women whose relationship with the labour market is constructed through a culturalist understanding that assumes that they are kinswomen deterred by community values or unable to 'fit' because they embody such values rather than workers facing discriminatory or hostile work environments. BrAsian young women exercising agency meet with resistance. As a result, employment discrimination shapes BrAsian identities, adding new layers to an earlier perception, moulded by the state through immigration policies, that women were dependent carers.

The legal response to group-based penalties and specific gender injustices has been through provisions that construct the problem as discrimination against an individual: as difference rather than disadvantage. Intersectional injustice based on complex identities has not been tackled. At the same time an attempt to challenge the dominant assumption that prioritising caring over labouring is not contributing appropriately to society is made politically more complex by the dominant perceptions of contemporary BrAsian families. There is little recognition in practice of socio-economic rights, making agency within the social reproductive sphere all the more difficult to exercise.

'Trading' in desires for family solidarity is viewed as securing the well-being-of the transnational family as a whole, through not only material, but also non-market affective ties. It seems to prioritise social reproductive values, produced in the family, based upon the 'traditional' gender contract. This form of trading is not only not valued but is looked upon with suspicion because it is seen as not reproducing dominant consumer cultural values, although it usually involves a range of 'modern' market processes such as transnational communications technology. Because the activities are seen as reproducing values relating to family solidarity rather than civic solidarity and cohesion, immigration laws aim at disputing demand. It could be argued, therefore, that the communities are being singled out for not being modern enough, for prioritising relationships based upon kin and religion (particularly Islam) over loyalty through individual consumer/worker identity to the state.

Communities have not 'fitted in' in this sense leading to a particularly tense relationship between the multicultural state and family regulation. BrAsian family networks tend to minimise involvement with state-based institutions in this area and regulate their affairs through frameworks that provide more community-based power. Increasingly those communities that follow the Islamic faith, and their younger members in particular, are defining themselves as Muslims and not as South Asians, which can raise tensions between customary and religious sources of normative regulation as well as with the state-based legal system. Muslim BrAsian communities now experience considerable Islamophobia, which permeates and obfuscates their relationships with the state in a variety of contexts but in particular in relation to plural practices of law.

The presumption that young BrAsian women, in particular, are not marrying close family or kin out of choice but to meet trading priorities of families becomes reconstructed as a challenge to liberal values. They are encouraged to support the liberal values of free choice in marriage partners, to shift from group solidarity to individual desire. The state immigration code of practice and other documentary requirements associated with transnational marriage formation are designed to produce 'ethical marriage' that is compliant with liberal standards and individual human rights values. However, such state actions seem to provoke change through paternalism, replacing a family-based form transacted through community/religious laws with another through the exercise of state laws and policies. Young women are constructed as social reproducers (marriage partners) who are not trusted to exercise sufficient agency to be involved in marriage arrangements until twenty-one rather than as individuals exercising their human right to family formation. They are denied agency in order to encourage an alternative exercise of agency.

However, a care approach requires us to be attentive to the full range of power relationships involved here. Transnational family trading constructs identities and senses of being and belonging that continue to place particular family- and community-constructed values on women's sexual bodies. Women's 'inappropriate' agency can lead to loss of value (honour) to an extended network of social relationships. Family-based honour codes are shaped not only 'vertically' as we saw in both this and the last chapter but also through trading across jurisdictional boundaries (horizontally). While the discourse of honour is associated with the socially reproductive sphere of care, feminist care discourse requires relationships to be reciprocal, voluntarily entered into and attentive to abuses of power. However, the challenge to honour has been through the use of the women's human rights discourse on violence against women, which values women's autonomy and seeks to provide protection against risks of abuse. Governance of this chain involves these two competing discourses, which construct women's agency and subjectivity differently.

We have seen the state and community responses to the violence that ensues when young women (and men) transgress community social norms in the exercise of their sexuality around marriage in the 'supply' contexts in South Asia and also in the 'demand' context of the UK. Because of transnationalism, some family members will have had their sexual identities and senses of belonging formed and regulated within the normative frameworks of South Asia until they migrate as young adults, while BrAsian citizens' sense of self will be constructed through discourse of individualism and autonomy, reflected in state regulatory frameworks, as well as family connection. Young adults with sexual identities formed within post-colonial contexts find themselves within settings that do not necessarily value their subjectivity in similar ways and will experience engagements with the respective regulatory institutions differently.

The law and policy on forced marriages operates in two distinct but interrelated contexts for the communities under consideration: the first takes place in the UK and usually involves the forced union of two British nationals living locally; the second involves a transnational arrangement. There are two constructions of young women. The first, popular with the mass media, is explicitly associated with exiting: here the young BrAsian woman defies (outmoded) family values in her desire to live a richer life as a worker and consumer in the UK market society (Seal and Wiseman 2009). Although these stories detail the painful processes and losses of relationship involved, the values of citizenship do triumph. The second does not focus on the exit element but constructs the young BrAsian woman as a passive and helpless victim who is rescued by the British state, pursuing its responsibilities as guardian of liberal values, from the abusive behaviour of family members overseas (Anitha and Gill 2009:

178–179). The first involves considerable agency and autonomy, the second very little.

When a young BrAsian woman finds herself in Mirpur or Jalunder, being held against her will or being forced to marry, her position is deeply affected by the prevailing local values and their translation into the legal processes. The same can be said for the young Sylheti woman who is subjected to violence by her spouse on arrival in the UK. Both will carry with them not only their understandings of family relationships but also their expectations of the state. For those arriving in the UK, their experience of the British state will be from the perspective of immigration control; for those finding themselves in South Asia they might expect assistance as rights-holding British citizens. The construction of the valued identity in young women is constructed through the interaction between the 'vertical' (within the jurisdiction) and 'horizontal' (across jurisdictions) discourses that govern women's sexual bodies.

While much state and civil society concern is directed at protecting the human rights of BrAsian women citizens when they find themselves unwillingly located in South Asia, the objective of restricting immigration seems to take priority over the protection of the human rights of South Asian migrant women caught up in forcible and violent relationships in the UK. Their immigration status as non-British citizens firmly roots them in the power relations of the family, although in a legal centralist state they are presumed to have access to criminal and family laws. Although the discourse of human rights is being used to 'trump' community regulation of marriage practices, it is not being used to protect all women against violence in the face of other state priorities. It is being used in ways that once again accentuate a dichotomy between Women and Culture.

The impact of traded (and transformed) family 'legal codes' constructed within a global discourse of 'honour' presents challenges to the women's movement and to policymakers in the UK. The construction of honour and women's perceived subordinate position is closely tied to a growing Islamophobia, which sees certain South Asian Muslim communities as dysfunctional and not producing appropriate citizens, and public constructions of terror. Traded and transformed family legal codes are challenged generally through the universalist discourse of human rights with its autonomous subject. The question remains whether women's human rights provide a caring conceptual framework through which to tackle the abuses of power that are associated with such trading of belonging without destroying the very basis of solidarity upon which the relationships are built.

Conclusion

Introduction

Who do we care about and how? My aim has been to provoke new ways of thinking about the nature of gender inequalities in the context of contemporary globalisation and to enrich feminist legal scholarship so that it can better tackle global inequalities.

The book has deployed a framework that investigates the social and economic processes that link jurisdictions. These chains are governed by a range of discourses, which operate 'horizontally' in the terminology adopted by this book. Forms of governance, however, interact with the 'vertical' contexts within the particular jurisdictions. The domestic contexts construct gender relationships that both affect, and are affected by, the transnational governance discourses. This conclusion provides a summary of the way in which this plurality of discourses impacts both on understandings of gender relations and on the distribution of power. It then reviews the core conceptual framework adopted in this book through a consideration of three interrelated ways in which the concept of care has been used; as an activity; as a value; and as a method. I finish with some pointers on how to answer the question posed at the outset: who do we care about and how?

Discourses of care

Trade, rights and care have been used throughout this book to structure ways of thinking about regulation in relation to gender relations, both 'vertically' within jurisdictions and also 'horizontally' through the governance of the chains. Each has been associated with an institutional context and an identity: trade with market and consumer; state with rights and citizen; care with family/ community and carer. I have associated each with a particular form of analytical approach: trade with neoliberal forms of economic analysis and practice; rights with liberal Enlightenment thought; and care with ethics of care analysis. Each has been interrogated from a feminist perspective.

I have explored many instances of pluralism in action within jurisdictions: from multicultural UK with its largely unrecognised customary and religious laws; through constitutions, customary and state laws in post-colonial Africa;

to the personal laws, penal codes and constitutions in South Asian jurisdictions. I have generally associated customary and religious laws with the conceptual framework of care because these systems tend to be based on status in family and community settings and embody values of connectedness. I have considered the concepts as transnational discourses through discussion of the WTO trade framework, international human rights and labour laws, and non-state 'soft laws' associated with corporate social responsibility but also within specific community and personal laws. I have considered the effects of these plural discourses on the distribution of power within social relations particularly focusing on their effects on gender.

Certain trends have emerged. The discourses associated with care are being incorporated into the market as more aspects of social reproduction are marketised. We have seen this in the ethical codes and personal standards initiatives. We also saw how those who support the development of land markets in Africa are now considering alliances with communities based upon customary systems of landholding. This represents one example of a wider trend towards 'non-state' law processes supported by international policymakers. Such initiatives are often seen as offering 'spaces' for women's voices to be heard and their interests to be recognised. Women's customary usage of land can be valued, thereby avoiding the devaluation associated with formal land titling through the state. Therefore it could be argued that these alliances between community and market, which combine care and trade discourses, offer potential for some restructuring of gender relationships. Some post-colonial feminists have also seen the positive potential in moves to marketise aspects of culturally constructed sexuality (Tamale 2006, 2008). These alliances offer opportunities for women to avoid the reconstruction of their subjectivity as autonomous unembodied subjects, the foundation of state-based rights discourses, and thereby provide opportunities for more positive constructions of community cultural identities. Rights based upon abstract identities have often failed to deliver justice to women, whether this is in state, land, employment or family laws. We could interpret the desire for arranged BrAsian transnational marriages in this context.

These coalitions between market and community do not seek to reinforce existing gender hierarchies within communities but to use the opportunities offered by the 'neutral' market to produce more freedom and redistribute power within community social relations. In many respects, therefore, they conceptually 'leapfrog' an economically inspired, ideological developmental process which involves moving from kin-based 'pre-modern' forms of organisation to liberal democracy and unfettered markets in which identities become ever more abstracted, the subject of Carol Gilligan's original critique and the foundational building block for ethics of care analysis. Economic development and the empowerment of women through community-based cultural identities become linked in positive ways. It is argued that marketisation can be a force for good and therefore the objective is to ensure that women have sufficient control within its forms.

Much of the substantive discussion in this book suggests that though power is determined within specific contexts, women are seldom in a position to mould markets to their advantage. An alternative view is that markets build new desires on existing gender hierarchies within communities rather than promoting new positive subjectivities. While markets allow for more freedom to express diverse sexual identities, specific forms of these sexualised desires, which cater for predominately male consumers, seem to gain power rapidly. Without a relatively well-developed rights-based discourse, which recognises women's right to express a positive sexual identity and to be treated with equal dignity, the challenge to such market developments can take the form of a reassertion of morality based upon women's roles within family and community relations. Again we could interpret the development of 'honour' crimes in global markets in this way.

We have seen that women's movements in South Asia have focused on expanding the civil 'space' available for women by using state-based legal strategies to counter the gender hierarchies entrenched in family and community structures while recognising all the problems with seeking to use state power in post-colonial states. There are real problems for women when polity and community relations coalesce (Baxi et al. 2006). Women need state entitlements to challenge both community and market-based gender hierarchies, although the existing conceptual basis for many of these rights has often proved inadequate for the task.

The growth in the global market has reconstructed the role of states and reduced sovereignty significantly in many areas, particularly those relating to economic regulation. We have seen the way in which states have been restructured in the transition from state socialism to market liberalism and the impact on women's position. We have also seen the effects of SAP on women's position in sub-Saharan Africa. Some women have been in a position to benefit from these developments but many have not. Ethical codes of practice may offer some women in the formal agribusiness sector in Kenya greater enforcement of state labour rights and additional entitlements that may add up to decent work, to use the ILO's terminology. However, these soft laws by definition do not extend beyond the particular supply chain unless voluntarily adopted by others. They lack the universality of state laws. They offer little or nothing to those not directly linked to global processes. The reconstituted role of states as facilitators of markets within a trade discourse that can construct policies in relation to labour standards or the regulation of service sectors as barriers to trade makes the development of state-based gender policies far more difficult to achieve and to implement. The international women's human rights discourse, which requires states to take responsibility for ensuring women's equality in productive and socially reproductive spheres and which recognises the links between the two, has an important role to play in valuing the contribution of state actions to the development of women's capabilities.

A corollary of state sovereignty is that non-state forms of regulation 'travel' better. So we have seen that the personal and community laws that originated in South Asia provide the normative framework for BrAsian communities in the UK. Soft laws based upon corporate social responsibility travel well because they emerge from organisations that have in many respects broken free of states. The discourse of women's human rights, although more anchored to state sovereignty for implementation, has also moved across the world to provide women with ways of challenging gender hierarchies within personal and community laws, though it has proven less robust in challenging the gender inequalities generated in markets.

Care as a gendered relation or commodity

Identifying the activity of care might seem straightforward but as this book has shown, this is not necessarily the case. As a species, we must biologically repro- duce ourselves to survive but we need much more to make us into social beings and productive workers. We need food, love and affection including physical and sexual nurture and a sense of being and belonging to flourish. These activities form the basis for our global chains. They have been discussed within the wider analytical relationship between production and social reproduction because although many aspects of caring are undertaken outside the market within the socially reproductive sphere of the family and community, more are being provided through the market, in commodified forms as a result of worldwide economic and social developments. The changing relationship between social reproduction and production has marked effects on gender relationships because, however social reproduction is organised in any local context, it is generally assumed to be the primary responsibility of women. These assumptions prevail even when caring becomes the subject of commodification or marketisation (see Ertman and Williams 2005), ensuring that women maintain their responsibilities within the family and community while undertaking much of the work associated with the provision of care services. As a result, the ideological construction of these gender contracts, through which the division of labour is organised, is under pressure.

The dominant European model of the male paid breadwinning/female unpaid homemaking household is being replaced by newer forms more akin to a two- (or one-and-a-half) worker model with an unresolved reconstruction of the 'home- making' responsibility. We see the ways in which welfare and labour laws in the UK contribute to this reconstruction through support for workers as parents and carers, encouraging women to join and remain in the labour market while suggesting a changed division of labour within the family through the use of the gender-neutral terminology of parenting and caring. These assumptions, or perhaps more likely encouragements, in relation to changed roles are not borne out in practice, with women still undertaking substantially more responsibility than men for these activities.

In some communities, the model based upon clearer divisions of labour, and their location, is more firmly entrenched. In some of the BrAsian families considered in this book fewer women work outside the home. The reasons are complex, a mixture of preferences structured within family/community norms and the presence of high entry barriers to formal employment and substantial disincentives to remain when BrAsian female identities are constructed as not 'fitting' dominant work cultures. Many workplaces and measures such as anti-discrimination laws fail to protect due to weaknesses in their concept framework. However, the seeming resistance to moving towards an adult working consumer household is transposed within policy circles and in dominant cultural contexts from not 'fitting in' to work to not belonging sufficiently in society more generally. Thus the socially reproductive duty of women to embody and transfer this aspect of the dominant cultural norms is questioned and reconstructed as the dominance of too much community-based culture.

In the UK, households on the whole depend on an income from waged work undertaken in formal, regulated contexts although as we have seen there is still a considerable amount of informal working. Households therefore sustain themselves through this income with additional social benefits provided through the state. For most of the households in the other jurisdictions considered in this book, survival depends on gaining income from a far wider range of activities because their economies are heavily dependent on agricultural production, have small formal industrial and service sectors and few public sector jobs. The nature and size of the formal economies differ in the countries we have considered. They have been affected by neoliberal policies in different ways. Poland and Moldova have moved from a state socialist economy to liberal markets, leading to major restructuring of more widely available state-based employment into more scarce private employment. In sub-Saharan Africa macroeconomic policies have sought to marketise land and commercial agricultural production but with limited success and formal waged employment remains very scarce. Agriculture is very important in South Asia as well, although the economies differ, with India increasingly able to offer more of its population more access to paid work, particularly in the service sector, albeit huge numbers of the population have no access to these jobs. Households, depending on their geographical and economic positioning, must survive on a range of activities involving subsistence farming, informal casual and seasonal labour and petty trading. Many more activities are undertaken in the socially reproductive sector, including general household provisioning through unpaid labour, much of which is provided by women. The divisions of labour in the gender contract vary but generally men seek productive employment and production-focused farming while women take responsibility for family provisioning (growing the bulk of household food in sub-Saharan Africa) and wider caring, while seeking any opportunity that may be available for paid work.

For some, international migration offers a way of gaining access to more formal markets although women can find themselves once again in informal contexts in Global North economies. Changes in global production processes have led to the development of formal employment opportunities in the Global South as mass production and contracted-out services have been relocated from the Global North and have provided women with access to formal labour markets. In the Global North the same changes have led to women joining the labour market because a breadwinner wage can no longer sustain the lifestyles desired by the majority of the population and required to fuel the consumer economy. These developments have been underpinned by changes in the way in which work is organised with increased use of 'flexible' work so that formal production encompasses relationships once more associated with informal working, which do not attract the labour law protections available to those holding the status of employee. Such work is therefore flexible but also precarious. While flexible work offers women in the Global North ways of combining work and care when backed by wider social welfare provisions relating to child and increasingly elder care, it provides women who work and care in the Global South with limited employment law protection in contexts where labour law is not combined with many work-related, more socially oriented rights and where broader socially reproductive-focused measures are not available. Equally, migration does not guarantee access to the wider benefits that underpin the relationship between production and social reproduction in the Global North.

We have seen the rapid expansion of service economies in Europe, and also increasingly elsewhere in the world, as more aspects of social reproduction are commodified and the development of multilateral and regional governance frameworks to facilitate further integration of markets. With the development of these markets, the social relationships through which the caring activity takes place become 'things'. Caring needs become consuming desires. In the Global North food can be bought as a 'meal in' in packets from a supermarket for home consumption or a 'meal out' in a restaurant. It is not grown, harvested, prepared and cooked by the women (and men) who will eat it. Relationships of care involving bodily needs, whether these relate to sexual satisfaction or a clean body, become services to be bought. Relationships of care in the socially reproductive sphere become affective labour and body work in the productive sphere. Once care becomes affect, no longer anchored in the 'local' social relationships of the family, it can be provided by a far wider range of people, including women, who, through migration, are able to turn their 'local' social relationships of care into valued labour, provided through market relationships far from home. So once care becomes a 'thing' new concepts of distance and proximity are constructed. Food can be produced and prepared thousands of miles away from where it is consumed. While bodily care still requires intimacy, it can involve market relationships between the carer and the cared for, which draw together people whose socially reproductive relationships have been formed thousands of miles apart and oblige the migrant worker to find ways of sustaining her socially reproductive relationships at long distance.

A plurality of values: meeting needs, ensuring entitlements, buying desires

The second way in which care has appeared in this book is as a value. Generally care has been posed in opposition to the market. Within neo-classical economics, the market is liberating. It sweeps away 'pre-modern' forms of relationships dependent on kin and family and the discretionary and paternalistic forms of allocation associated with (welfare) state provision. The market in this way of thinking provides everyone with the freedom to satisfy their desires. If there is a willing buyer and a willing seller, anything and everything can be bought and sold (Ertman and Williams 2005: 2). This form of analysis is grounded in a 'defense of private culture' (Radin and Sunder 2005: 10). The market has no moral values, individual preferences are formed somewhere else. It simply acts as a neutral tool, as a rational way of meeting desires (Radin and Sunder 2005: 10). The market liberates and what everyone needs, therefore, is an ability to commodify. Law's role here is to facilitate trades in everything for everyone including women and the poor.

Post-modernist schools of thought have muddied the waters by suggesting that cultures and commodities are not in opposition, rather meanings are marketised. 'The cultural study of "commodities in motion" focuses on the changing meanings of the commodity as it passes through various local and global circuits, including markets' (Radin and Sunder 2005: 13, references omitted). So because commodities do not have fixed meanings, commodification can be liberating, a path to freedom not to subjugation. Rather than dwelling on the way markets may objectify women and subordinate them in the process, the object of commodification can be liberty and equality. 'More commodification can mean more *equality* not inequality' (Radin and Sunder 2005: 15, original emphasis). Although they seem to occupy different political positions, there is a close affinity here between laissez-faire economics, which has informed the development policies discussed above, and post-modern cultural studies (Radin and Sunder 2005: 15; Fraser 2009).

Many do not see the same benefits. The counter view, therefore, is that by encroaching on the territory associated with social reproduction, the market destroys the world if all that we value can only be conceived as a gain from trade (Radin and Sunder 2005: 11). It has malign effects on cultures, leading to resistance and the reassertion of the values of particular constituencies (such as the cultural value for conservative Christians of monogamous heterosexual marriage in developed sexualised markets). Feminists who adopt a universalist rights-based approach recognise that the market is not a neutral and unmitigated force for good. However, human flourishing is more often associated with ensuring access to political as well as economic entitlements (Nussbaum 1999a, 1999b). Women need substantial and reconstituted rights to enable them to exercise freedom of choice, to gain equality (Mullally 2006).

Such feminists would not deny the value of the market or necessarily oppose its expansion into areas of social reproduction if it were regulated in ways that ensured substantive equality to women (through the deconstruction of the boundaries between the public and the private sphere). The overall role of law, therefore, is to regulate those trades in commodities that restrict freedoms for individual subjects. Although rights are put to different uses, reflecting the differing evaluations of the capacity of the market to deliver freedom, within neoliberalism and more enlightened justice, both approaches rest on the same construction of subjectivity.

The feminist analysis of care, built not only on the importance of relationships to the construction of individual identity but also on the centrality of their associated values of attentiveness, responsibility, competence and responsiveness to the organisation of decent societies more generally (Tronto 1994), is less likely to view commodification as a positive moral development. Here law can be deployed to protect against the encroachment of the market. 'Commodification of some important things of value could have a "domino effect" on others, and overrun nonmarket cultures in which some parts of life – including love, babies, sex, and freedom – are not for sale' (Radin and Sunder 2005: 11).

Ethics of care feminism insists that individual subjectivity is not legislated into existence through the application of abstract reasoning as liberal thought would have us believe. While liberalism acknowledges that relationships based upon emotional concepts of love, trust and mutuality may exist in the private sphere, it requires public life to be conducted by abstract autonomous individual subjects, unimpeded by particular identities as women or men. Although care analysis has focused on the proximate and intimate relationships associated with family and community life, it has extended its reach to public, and more tentatively, market relationships (Tronto 1994; Robinson 1999; Held 2006), the underlying assumption being that care thinking, which is associated with women's way of being and doing, is undervalued in the public world of rights thinking, which is associated with that of men. Happily, engagements between universalist and difference feminist analysis are producing creative new ways of addressing these differences over the construction of subjectivity: such as valuing the deliberations of 'real' people in the determination of guiding abstract principles (Benhabib 1994, 2002b; Mullally 2006) and recognising the value of justice principles to caring relationships (Held 2006).

While feminism addresses these conceptual differences, the wider battle lines within both the theoretical and policy domains have tended to be drawn up along the divide between 'an economic arena dominated by rational self-interest and self-interest alone ("the market"), and a sharply different arena of intimacy and altruism that must be protected from the kind of instrumental behaviour that is appropriate in market contexts', with both camps viewing any overlap as corruption (Ertman and Williams 2005: 4). We have charted these battles between macroeconomic development policies that champion the unbridled market and those that would value human freedom as the goal of development (Sen (A) 1999) and through the struggles to increase the value of human rights and the role of the state in their enforcement.

Despite the use of the conceptual dichotomy of production and social reproduction and an organising theme that poses a question couched in terms of care
(who do we care about?) rather than rights, the aim of this book has been to
avoid dichotomous and evaluative constructions such as: is the commodification
of care a good or a bad thing; are rights better for women than care; and is
multiculturalism bad for women? While I argue that care matters and that care
values provide the criteria for an assessment of the impact of global developments
on gender relations, I concentrate on the processes involved in various forms of
marketisation of care in contemporary forms of globalisation. My argument is
that while it is important to assess the extent to which these processes can provide
the type of caring relations needed to make a decent and fair society for all, the
best way of addressing this issue is through a consideration of the way in which
power is distributed within social relationships when they take place in the
market. The aim, therefore, is not to lose sight of relationships in an ideological
world of things and neutral tools.

As a result we see that markets are not neutral. They affect men and women,
rich and poor differently. Because of the unequal distribution of wealth in the
world, the poor are more likely to find themselves the objects of commodification rather than its subjects, obliged through lack of power to offer too much of
their identity or bodily integrity in the transaction. Thus poor women are far
more likely to be sellers and richer men buyers of questionable commodities
such as sex. Viewing commodification as a process involving the distribution
of power in relationships enables us to see that while commodification under
these conditions is unacceptable, interventions that control individuals who
create and enter such markets in order to survive, and thereby potentially
reduce their power, are equally inappropriate (Radin and Sunder 2005: 12).

This book demonstrates in a number of ways that constructed dichotomies of
social/ community life and market as separate spheres are conceptually flawed.
Markets are increasingly structured on the relationships and the values associated with care. Affective labour is at the heart of consumer capitalism (Hardt
1999; Hardt and Negri 2000). Consumers demand care services. Businesses are
managed as caring organisations. Manifestations of caring, through fair trade
concepts, sell products. Body work, which is inextricably tied up with relationships of intimacy, trust and mutuality, is performed in myriad forms in the
market. Equally we have seen that intimate transactions such as marriages
have economic dimensions and that identities are manifested through abilities
to trade norms. 'Objects' such as land rights have multiple meanings: as security
for the creation of land markets; as a means of providing sustenance for a
household; as a means through which women can improve their social position.
All meanings are contained in the same object at the same time but embody
different distributions of power, including through constructed gender identities within relationships. Given that any object may have many meanings, what
is of interest to issues of gender justice is the question: who has control over the
creation of meaning (Radin and Sundari 2005: 16–17)? To what extent do

material and social inequalities reinforce dominant meanings over more redistributive ones? Do markets entrench prevailing relations of inequality?

Regulation through legal discourses contributes to the construction of meaning and degrees of commodification. Power is distributed through the governance of networks of relationships. I have contended that the overlapping and
unstable governance discourses of trade, rights and care all contribute to the
construction of gendered meanings and identities and affect the distribution of
power. By exploring the way in which these discourse are deployed, by whom
and in which arena provides a way of thinking more creatively about feminist
interventions to tackle global injustices. We can ask to what extent care values
are valued in the market and whether they are reconstituted when they shift
from social reproduction to production. By whom are they valued?

Thus we are able to see three paradigmatic constructions of women's sexuality
that have featured in this book. They interact in particularly complex ways in the
discussion of the transnational marriage chain. The first associates identity with
'belonging to the family/community'. Here, dominant social values assume
that women's behaviour, in particular the exercise of their sexuality, is a matter
primarily for family regulation supported by community structures. The family
fortunes, and those of the kinship group, are very much tied up in appropriate
marriages because physical and social reproductive functions take place within
heterosexual marriages. Discourses of social reproduction focus on kinship and
status-based values. A woman is seen as embodying the honour and purity of the
family so justifying the monitoring of her behaviour to avoid bringing shame
to everybody. Because virginity is important, early marriages will probably be
encouraged. These values will be reflected in interpretations of customary and
religious laws that regulate family relationships. In societies that are organised
around such values of family solidarity, the state may police morality through the
penal system, reinforcing community control over women's sexuality. While the
state may formally embody liberal rule-of-law concepts, it may possess little
legitimacy within the community, which can in any case be sanctioned through a
plural legal system to enforce its own rules. Alternatively the community may
bypass state laws or 'capture' them with the result that the practice of local state
officials reflects community rather than state values.

Family relationships nurture and provide a solid sense of identity but may
not tolerate behaviour that is seen as transgressive and there may be very little
'civil space' for women outside of family structures: no state-provided financial
support or accommodation; few legal protections against the violence that may
result; no safe havens such as women's refuges; and, more generally, little public
support for the autonomy of women to make individual choices. Women's
organisations have struggled long and hard in these contexts to create civil
space for women to exercise greater autonomy over their sexuality.

In the second paradigm the boundaries are redefined between family and
state. Women's identity is reconstructed as embodying the values of the state –
it therefore belongs to the state rather than the family. In nationalist contexts,

women become responsible for 'reproducing the nation and for mothering patriots' (Anthias and Yuval-Davis 1992: 113–114). In European liberal states, women's bodies are not relevant to their relationship with the state within liberalism wherein individual abstract subjects enjoy equality through law in their public dealings. Family norms are relegated to the private sphere, and are not the concern of the state unless they conflict with state values. Subjects demonstrate their loyalty to the state through their espousal of liberal values, even in their family relationships, in exchange for the recognition of entitlements or rights. Socially reproductive norms are expected to reflect state priorities. Citizenship constructs a civil space for freedom of expression, including of sexuality, by individuals. Liberalism provides individuals with rights to family life, including free choice of marriage partner, but the family is protected from the state by non-intervention in this private sphere. The state no longer polices 'personal' morality. Liberalism also assumes that state law reigns supreme and is applicable to all. Alternative normative systems, such as customary or religious laws, that hold sway over family relationships become often troubling social (cultural) practices if they do not function as guardians of state values. The aim is to support or even encourage women to exit these social practices into what is presumed to be the protective environment provided by majority civil society.

The feminist critiques that demonstrate the limitations of liberalism for women are by this point familiar. The Enlightenment narrative is deeply flawed. Activists have demanded the extension of rights to protect against family-based abuse and violence. Women's organisations internationally have developed the international human rights framework so that it is starting to recognise sexual as well as reproductive rights. States have been challenged to deliver freedom of expression and to protect the rights of gay, lesbian, bisexual and transgendered individuals to form partnerships and family units of choice. The liberal construction of the unencumbered body upon which these claims have been based has also been the subject of a range of feminist critiques, including from those in the Global South.

We have also seen that post-colonialist feminists have been particularly wary of extending state power into family relationships in contexts that bear too much similarity to the one described in the first paradigm and which take little or no account of the adverse effects on gendered power relationships within the community when pluralism is ignored. State paternalism, or worse state violence, can replace that of the family. Campaigns to tackle sexual violence have increasingly been overlaid, therefore, with a demand for sexual rights and for an *erotic justice*, which seeks to tackle the injustices associated with social, legal and economic systems that constrain expressions of sexuality (Kapur 2005).

The third paradigm is firmly rooted in contemporary globalisation, reflecting the triumph of market-driven desire. Women's bodies are centre stage again as the site for the consumption of desires. Here women's sexual identity is constructed through the market as individuals express their sexuality and satisfy their desires freely as consumers, not as family members or citizens. The market recognises no limits other than those associated with a willing buyer and seller. In practice, it ignores discourses of family values, 'morality' or 'public interest', but would also seek to remove, or at least minimise, regulatory frameworks that incorporate such values. In this discourse, women have the right to buy their way out of (exit) oppressive family relationships to exercise freedom and equality in the market. The state, however, seeks to ensure that social solidarity, usually based upon conceptions of liberal family values in the Global North, is not undermined by the abuses of power created by market relationships.

Radical feminist discourse in particular has critiqued the sexualisation and exploitation of women's bodies in these processes and has been used by states to seek to disrupt some forms of market provision. Women's movements more generally have attempted to find a way of expressing a sense of women's belonging that recognises the importance of caring relationships, which are neither exploited within the family nor in the market and which are supported by responsive state policies. For many, this has involved the use of the discourse of human rights and a focus on state action. A sense of belonging through state rights is traded against a sense of belonging to family. In this battle between states and communities, the voices of women, particularly those from, or with family roots in, the Global South who seek to develop and express their own constructions of sexual identities based on more culturally embodied subjectivities are drowned out, whether it is in the transnational family context of abusive family relationships (described as crimes of honour and forced marriages) or in relation to commercial transactions involving trafficking and sex working.

The women's movement internationally has focused on law-related and rights-based strategies to tackle violence against women. In post-colonial societies this involves finding ways through the complexities of law and its relationship to community norms. The international rights movement, with its universalist stance and focus on violence against women, has been critiqued by Global South feminists wearied of their totemic association with 'exotic' forms of such violence, such as female circumcision and 'bride burning/dowry related' deaths. One contemporary focus for this exoticism is 'honour' crimes. The analysis and campaigns of Global South feminists to challenge this 'othering' have made a significant impact on the sophistication of jurisprudence and policy development associated with the implementation of women's human rights in the area of VAW (Merry 2006). However, it is essential that the voices that raise questions about the construction of identity, which underpins rights relating to the exercise of sexuality, are listened to with care. Must such rights be culturally unmarked and exercised within a framework of absolute autonomy or can there be a more embedded concept of rights that recognises the values of care?

Women are: female kin often with honour to protect but also persons whose sense of identity and belonging is constructed in relation to others within family and community; citizens with entitlements to bodily integrity and rights to exercise choice over the expression of their sexuality; and consumers free to meet their desires. They can be all these at the same time but possibly in different domains. Wider social and economic processes will contribute significantly to the way in which these discourses interact and determine who has the power to deploy which to whose relative advantage. Poor women in Moldova find themselves objects in the market because their lack of power in the network of relationships associated with sex chains ensures that in many instances they are unable to exercise sufficient control over the transaction and are obliged to sell too much of their bodily integrity. States-based regulatory discourse in relation to immigration control further constructs them as without agency in order to locate them outside the framework governing commodified work relationships (forced labour) but within a rather strange agency-less human rights discourse.

The debates over the nature and value of culture, which have engaged a huge amount of feminist energy, are reflected in the discussions throughout this book. The main fault line for these debates over culture is usually between law and culture or rights and care. We have seen the various constructions of 'culture' and the way in which women's human rights discourse has attempted to recast itself in a framework of culturally sensitive universalism. However, too much energy has been devoted to the politics of culture, and not enough to its economics. This book considers the culture of the global market and assesses the extent to which and the ways in which cultural identities are marketised within it. Therefore the governance discourses of rights, care and trade all contribute to the construction of the meaning of 'cultures'. Dominant trade discourse seeks to portray the market as strictly neutral – without a culture. In this view markets offer the mechanism through which exogenous and private culture (understood as tastes and distastes) is realised. This view is challenged by feminists (and others) through the discourses of rights and care. At the same time markets make culture the subject of commodification (Radin and Sunder 2005: 10). In some contexts '[m]arkets are a primary means of distributing and debating cultural representations' (Radin and Sunder 2005: 19). Those in positions of power within the market can therefore mould the meaning of culture and in the process construct cultural identities. The Philippines state gains market position for Filipina female workers on the basis of their gendered cultural attributes. As a result, individual women command higher wages than other less-valued identities and market themselves on the basis of their cultural identities. Women within transnational BrAsian families tend to lack the power to construct a positive account of their 'cultural' desires to marry overseas kin while women's organisations are reconstituting, in a somewhat unstable alliance with the UK state, the culture of 'honour' crimes as a culture of violence against women by using the relatively powerful human rights discourse.

The book has therefore been based upon the presumption that it is preferable to assess the impact on the distribution of benefits and losses involved when the culture of socially reproductive care moves to the commodified culture of the market before considering whether that process should be resisted. The framework adopted nevertheless is predicated upon the value of relational methods, drawn from ethics of care and commodity supply chains analysis.

Relations of care: the chain method

The third way in which care has been used in this book has been as a method to show the way in which relationships change within the global market place and the effect that these changes have on gender relations. There are a number of obvious relationships created when I go to my local supermarket to buy a pack of pre-prepared mangetout, not least of which is the temporary social one with my neighbour on the checkout till. However, does the 'thing', the commodity, create one between the woman who prepared it and myself? She knows that I live in the UK and shop at a particular chain of supermarkets and that I will only buy this product if it meets particular standards relating to quality of presentation and freshness. There is no legal relationship between us. I am not liable if the woman develops an allergic rash on her body or if she is not paid the Kenyan statutory minimum wage. Yet I have checked the packet to see where it has come from. I chose it because it was labelled organic and therefore not sprayed with chemicals that could affect the sprayer's health. I speculate that at least part of the 'value added' price for being organic might be captured by the producer and might possibly be reflected in wage levels. I spend some time pondering on whether to buy a 'local grown' regionally produced cabbage instead. Why have I identified myself to the retailer's market intelligence team (via the bar code swiped by my neighbour) as in the category of consumer who receives promotional literature on the retailer's foundation, which works 'in partnership with farmers in Africa to produce development' and a set of vouchers worth £2 each for any organic product purchased over the next month? I am a consumer who, through the exercise of choice, constructs my own sense of identity as well as another, deduced by my behaviour. I am part of the network of social relations created by the first of the chains considered in this book and incorporated into its governance. The development of agribusiness through commodity chains has created new relations of production, which encompass the consumer. Although production takes place at distance, the processes create proximity through the governance of the chains. The values that would once have been associated with provisioning of food within the socially reproductive sector are transposed into the desires of 'concerned' consumers. The discourse of care incorporated into consumer choices and care (for the safety of the product, the conditions under which it is produced) is marketised in Ethical Trading Initiatives and Fair Trade products.

The chains facilitate a discourse of responsibility, the dominant form of which is corporate social responsibility, not worker solidarity based around campaigns for improved global labour rights. They shift the discourse from caring through working to caring through buying. The governance of the chains produces new wider alliances between activists, including consumer and worker organisations, development policymakers and private enterprises, which have resulted in the development of private 'soft law' standards (such as ETI codes of conduct). These developments have enabled the discourse of gender justice to gain some recognition. They have been used to tackle the disadvantages that women face when they become southern global production workers as we have seen through the discussion of our gender pyramid.

Through wider activism, supported by more attentiveness from consumers to the distribution of benefits within the network of relationships, the discourse of responsibility has the potential to be recast and expanded in ways that improve women's position as caring workers within agribusiness. It can extend to a requirement not to use informal forms of work, which enables women to become formal employees with greater access to state-sanctioned labour protections and benefits. It can recognise the particular vulnerabilities of women who combine paid work and the extensive care responsibilities that wider social norms place upon them in contexts where there is little social welfare support from the state. Such initiatives can recognise also the impact of wider social norms, such as gendered assumptions relating to skills and abilities and tolerance of sexual harassment, on women's position at work. In these ways it may be possible to reshape the discourse of corporate social responsibility to a wider concept of political responsibility on the basis of new coalitions of actors brought together through the social and economic processes associated with global supply chains (Young 2004).

Do I think about the migrant women from sub-Saharan Africa whom I see going to and fro along my street at the end of their shifts in the local care homes in the same way as I think about the purchase of vegetables? How did I think about the Malawian woman whom my mother and I employed to care for her in her last two years of life in my home (Stewart 2005)? Was it as a purchaser of services; as an employer requiring an employee to carry out duties specified in her employer's care plan; as a daughter, seeking to replace love and demanding physical labour while I prepared earlier drafts of this book? Did I think of her as a mother and grandmother? Although I am not a consumer of commercial sexual services, I am very familiar with one neighbour who used to provide on-street services and another who works in a 'sauna'. Do I feel responsible for their work conditions or indeed for the invisible women who feature in 'raids' by local police?

We have seen that the body work chains that involve the movement of people not products have not produced the same level or form of interventions based on coalitions of market actors despite existence of the soft-law ethical recruitment codes for health professionals and some social care workers. Yet some of the social relationships involved are far more transparent because they involve the intimate proximity of the workers to the purchasers of their services. Thus the marketisation of care into care services provided through affective labour generally, and body work specifically, has not generated marketised care discourses in relation to the workers. This may not be surprising because the immediate, visible relationship is in theory protected by well-developed Global North, hard, that is, state, labour laws. In addition, caring for bodies, labour associated with women's invisible social reproductive activities in the private sphere of the family, attracts very little value in the market place. It is considered demeaning and often unpleasant work. Thus the care value content of this form of affective labour is low. Proximity in the market place produces a new form of distance.

There seems, therefore, no need to care differently (or much) about a worker who is a migrant body worker. However, as our discussion of the chain has shown, they, like many women workers in Kenya, tend to work in informally organised markets, either because their immigration status denies them access to the formal work or because the work is organised in this way or both. Thus they are particularly vulnerable because they are not able to access the regulatory protection offered under employment law nor the wide social benefits that the status of employee tends to attract. State immigration restrictions on access to the public funds add to these differences. In addition, their productive activities and socially reproductive role, which, due to wider social norms, generally remain relatively unchanged by migration, are separated spatially.

Care migration produces new sets of social relationships in relation to what Tronto (1994) describes as the care giving and care receiving elements of care but not those aspects associated with caring about, that is taking responsibility for, care. Part of this is marketised through remittances but much is not. We have seen that the corporate social responsibility-inspired soft codes can, if they are backed by sufficiently vigorous gender activism, offer ways of recognising some of the more direct deleterious effects of ignoring social reproduction on women's access to and involvement in labour markets. These effects are differently constructed for women migrants and require creative ways of enabling women to sustain, but also reconstruct in more positive ways, their identities as transnational family members. The focus for the existing ethical codes is on recruitment activities and the effect of migration on health and care service provision. They are less well developed as a means of caring for the migrant workers. As we have seen, bilateral migration agreements between specific states can offer more potential for positive measures to support migrants but they lack gender perspectives. Their location within inter-state trade negotiations limits the potential for the sort of wider alliances of civil society actors, including women's activists, seen in the first chain.

In the body work chain associated with sex the development of a global market has provoked an explicit state-backed discourse of criminal responsibility, which does not emanate from the direct governance structure of the chain. While it is a result of marketisation, the response is not therefore organised around market-reconstructed caring interventions. The sense of connectedness here is imposed through the criminal law on the consumers of commercialised sex services provided through trafficking chains although the measure is a result of coalitions of activists and state policymakers acting on a feminist-inspired agenda.

Those who purchase sex from persons whom they are expected to know are providing this through coercion will be guilty of a criminal offence. Why is this particular consumer singled out to take more responsibility and face state sanctions if he acts irresponsibly? Because in this area the trade discourse which views the market as a neutral tool through which private preferences are exercised, is directly challenged by the state discourse of suppression of the market in the wider interests of society.

In my neighbourhood customers purchasing such services may face criminal sanctions. It is very unlikely that the arrival of a new member of a neighbour's family will be noticed by many outside the specific community concerned unless their arrival involves new registration at the doctor's surgery. There will be few shared social opportunities to exchange neighbourly 'gossip' between communities about such an arrival and in any case not many would be interested in finding out more. Our third chain involving transnational marriages and diasporic belonging is predicated on strengthening existing relationships within families and communities. The transactions involved have been described in this book through the discourse of trading but they do not involve the marketisation of a social relationship into a commodity or a service. However, families do make use of the market to facilitate these transnational transactions and as we have seen in the earlier section there are strong elements of marketised forms within these socially reproductive activities.

The connectedness created by the internal governance discourse of this chain through community and religious norms creates strong senses of responsibility through the network of social relationships. Again we see a divergence between internal and wider governance discourses. Here the external governance discourse of immigration controls seeks to loosen or possibly disrupt the transnational network of social relations. Unlike in the other market-based chains, the governance discourse encourages localism, as individuals (and families) are encouraged to choose spouses from the pool of national residents and in so doing reconstruct a sense of responsibility to the state rather than the family, to reconstruct identity as a citizen rather than as a family member.

The development of private 'soft law' exposes the conceptual limitations of labour law within the present context of globalisation (Mundlak 2009). This takes two forms, relating to its reach, which are of particular interest to the discussion in this book: the territorial scope and the nature of the labour relation covered. While both affect all workers, they can have a differential effect on women. The first relates to matters horizontal in this book. Labour law does not 'travel': it is based on the principle that it is determined and applied universally within the jurisdiction of a particular state. In our first chain, large northern retailers require all actors in their chains to meet detailed specifications. The response, as we have seen, has been for local actors to add to their value by taking over responsibility for compliance with these requirements. These private standards incorporate core labour standards and local state employment laws. They can, by voluntary agreement, add additional employment-related rights and benefits. In this way it is possible to avoid the general conditionality of adding labour standards determined by standards in the North into the WTO trade framework and a challenge to the territorial principle. The argument, therefore, is that private standards offer a vehicle through which women tied into global chains can benefit from better labour conditions and claim a little more of the value created.

The same principle of territoriality applies to women migrants who work in the Global North. However, here we see that it is 'trumped' by the exercise of another form of state sovereignty through immigration laws. While the trade discourse is based on the 'win win' of the demand and supply of labour as a factor of production, state immigration controls seek to regulate the market, ensuring that those who enter without the correct documentation or who subsequently cease to have it, are denied protection from many formal employment law protections and benefits. In addition, home states are unable to 'interfere' in the work relations of their citizens in another state. This state is unable to compensate, therefore, for any disadvantages its citizens face due to the determination of their migrant status by the receiving state unless there is a formal agreement between the two states to do so on such matters, for instance, as the portability of social security benefits.

In the first chain, private standards are proffered as a way forward. Here one response has been to use the discourse of human rights to 'elevate' some core elements of labour law into universal rights and in this way dilute the concept of sovereignty somewhat. Human rights could also be used to compensate for the disadvantages experienced by the worker due to the movement/distance element by prioritising alien status, with entitlement to an increased range of rights, or worker status, with entitlement to full employment protection, over that of migrant. In the latter context, the worker becomes entitled to protection on the basis of their labour relation alone not on the basis of hybrid identity as a migrant worker, thus reducing the vulnerability of undocumented workers obliged to work in informal settings.

However, these measures do not tackle the second conceptual limitation of labour law, which is highlighted by the increased marketisation of caring relationships into services and the use of female migrant labour. As we have seen, the labour rights approach has not catered well for women because it is based upon male models of work and does not recognise the interrelationship between work and care generally. It has not yet managed to recognise fully the changed nature of the labour relation that occurs when caring is performed in the market through relationships that are personalised, less time bound and conducted in 'private' workspaces. As a result, the conditions in which the content – 'affect' – is performed can result in more extraction of the worker's labour than is acceptable. Workers have difficulty, in these contexts, exercising control over the boundaries of their bodily integrity. This inability to control the boundaries to the work relation has been transposed for one group of migrant women into the discourse of trafficking but in the process denies them both agency and the status of forced worker, which in itself requires to be rethought. It is necessary in an era of globalisation, with its dramatic increase in labour mobility and new forms of working, to move beyond the present construction of the 'universal worker' towards one that recognises the whole identity of a person who is engaged in new forms of social relationships (Ontiveros, 2002).

We have seen a second example of the way in which the sovereignty of immigration controls has interacted with domestic laws in the UK to reduce the protection of migrants and to increase the vulnerability of women to abuse, this time in the family rather than the workplace, in the transnational marriage chain. The discourse of suspicion that is attached to transnational marriage migration is policed through immigration controls, which reduce migrant women's effective access to protection against domestic violence. Until women have moved out of their status as migrant spouses, whose right to remain depends on evidence of a continuing marital relationship, and into the status of settled resident, they have very limited access to public funds and are very vulnerable to the relations of power that prevail within the family network of social relations. The discourse of human rights has been used here to some effect to gain greater access to domestic-law protections against violence and to neutralise the effects of immigration law. However, the regulatory discourse of suspicious immigrants trumps the protective discourse in relation to dangerous families and leaves those who migrate into the UK exposed to violence from their kinsfolk without effective access to protections available to citizens.

In this area, we also have a specifically gendered discourse, in relation to forced marriages, which constructs women as victims. However, unlike trafficking, which is directly located within the domain of immigration law and incorporated into the state criminal processes, not abusive and exploitative labour processes, forced marriage is tackled through civil processes and offers potentially more agency to the women involved. At present, however, it is heavily associated with transnational forms of marriage and immigration controls.

Can immigration status be separated from that of work or care, which would enable precarious migrant workers and precarious migrant kinsfolk to be protected as citizens with human rights rather than denied the status of employee because they have been 'trafficked' into sex work or denied the status of potential citizen (and protection from violence) because they have been coerced into marriage?

Utopian care?

The introduction to this book ended with reflections on the relationship between feminism and contemporary capitalism. Fraser (2009) suggests that the feminist critiques developed in and for an era of state-organised capitalism have been 'resignified' in the era of neoliberal economics that has followed. Second wave feminism was based upon a combination of economic, cultural and political analysis of gender injustice. In post-war welfare states and third world development states, in what I have described in this book as the nationalist phases in discussions of sub-Saharan Africa and South Asia, the state sought to take political control of the economy to produce forms of redistribution in the name of solidarity. The state socialist system took a different path but was based on an ideology of redistribution and solidarity. It also ensured that feminism as a political project did not emerge.

Feminist critiques in the Global North exposed a far wider range of injustices. They exposed the limitations to economic solidarity, based on a breadwinning and family man, earning a family wage and unvalued and invisible female contributions within the family dependent on private distribution of resources. The demand for redistribution of economic resources between women and men was accompanied by a demand for recognition of differences and identities between and among women and for representation for women within all institutional contexts. The feminist project, however, did not give up on the state, rather its aim was to reconstitute its institutions to achieve greater redistribution, recognition and representation. Post-colonial feminism was less enthusiastic about separatist politics of recognition and, after periods of nationalism, more wary of the role of post-colonial states, but still sought ways of using the state. The main focus for struggles on all fronts was therefore state based, with limited internationalism.

In the subsequent neoliberal era, the market tames politics and states. Collective responsibility for forms of redistribution is replaced by the personal responsibilities of private actors. During this era feminism has flourished, leading to a far wider recognition of differences and identities. However, issues of redistribution became increasingly separated from cultural politics. Markets, as we have seen, have taken over feminist concepts such as care and have in effect destroyed the family wage. So men and women exercise their freedoms through working and consuming with the benefit of 'customer care'. Undoubtedly women have gained access to the market as workers but the feminist objective of redistribution and increasing the value of women's caring labour has not occurred. Women grind away at jobs in the market out of necessity not as an expression of liberation. Men take little more responsibility for unvalued socially reproductive caring.

The feminist critiques of state welfarist provision, which sought to transform discretionary allocation of state defined needs into entitlements based on an understanding of caring needs as universal, has found echoes in the recasting of needs as a specific neediness in those who fail in the market place. Feminism has, like capitalism, globalised, making innovative connections across the world and developing an influential discourse on women's human rights. However, as we have seen, the focus has been on violence and reproductive issues and not on the processes of impoverishment.

So, as Fraser suggests, feminism has spread as a discourse but in the process some of its values have been absorbed into more powerful discourses and consequently have been changed. I would argue, on the basis of the work presented in this book, not completely. We do need to recapture the relationship between economic, political and cultural injustices in a global market: to reconnect the struggles against traditional forms of authority with those created and built upon in this market. I would argue that there are forms of political responsibility that can be 'recaptured', which moves us closer to solidarity and away from personal responsibility, and that are less rooted in a conceptual framework of state sovereignty, while recognising that state power is essential to tame the market and to create the civil space for vast numbers of women across the world. If we place care at the centre of this project we can start to reverse the priority between production and social reproduction, between activities that are valued and those that are not. We could start to see relationships built on values of attentiveness, responsibility and responsiveness and based on mutuality, reciprocity and equality as the core project for social, economic and cultural solidarity.

In terms of this book it can be summed up in Figure 5, which takes us back to the original framework. There is a need to wrest the discourse of care back from the domain of the market, not for the purpose of retreating into the traditional spheres of authority such as the family, but to harness some of the power it has achieved outside feminism to move forward. So the utopian feminist project is to care more about care. We need to care less about immigration and more about social solidarity with those who seek to work or live in culturally diverse ways. We need to care more about food, care and sex so that the relationships upon which they are based are conducted with dignity and equality, with all those involved maintaining the maximum control over their bodily integrity in the process. Utopian care thinking would lead us to care more by putting the value of social reproduction not production at the centre of policy objectives. It is essential that this thinking moves beyond state boundaries.

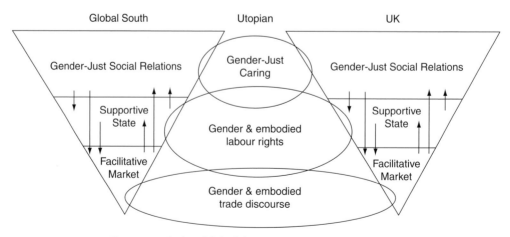

Figure 5: Gender-just global relations.

This book has used care method and care values to argue that feminism needs to be attentive to the way in which the benefits of global social and economic processes are distributed. We have seen the profound gender-based inequalities that exist. We need to encourage the development of care values within market discourses that are rooted in the concept of responsibility. We need to continue to develop concepts of fair or caring trading to displace the construction of the market as a neutral culture-free arena and to tackle the conceptual limitations within rights discourse in ways which encourage the development of a more relational construction of the subject and to develop further the concepts associated with care so that it provides a solid foundation for analysing not only intimate relationships but also the full range of social and economic relationships that exist.

References

ABA/CEELI 2006. *CEDAW Assessment Tool Report for Moldova*. Washington DC: American Bar Association.

Abashdze, Archil 2009. 'Labour Migration from Georgia and Bilateral Migration Agreements: Needs and Prospects', *CIPDD Policy Review*. Available at: www.isn.ethz.ch/isn/Digital-Library/Publications/Detail/?ots591=0C54E3B3–1E9C-BE1E-2C24-A6A8C7060233&lng=en&id=105090

Abiala, Kristina 2006. 'The Republic of Moldova: Prostitution and Trafficking in Women', in Geetanjali Gangoli and Nicole Westmarland (eds.), *International Approaches to Prostitution: Law and Policy in Europe and Asia*. Bristol: The Policy Press, pp. 91–111

ADB 2008a. *Asian Development Outlook 2008*. Manila: ADB

ADB 2008b. Gender and Social Justice, Ain O Salish Kendra – ASK Background of the project. Available at: www.adb.org/gender/working/ban001.asp accessed on 10/08/08, last accessed 10 August 2008

Adams, N. 2003. 'Anti-trafficking Legislation: Protection or Deportation?', *Feminist Review* 73 (1): 135–139

Agarwal, Bina 1994. *A Field of One's Own: Gender and Land Rights in South Asia*. Cambridge University Press

Agarwal, Bina 2003. 'Gender and Land Rights Revisited: Exploring New Prospects via the State, Family and Market', *Journal of Agrarian Change* 3 (1&2): 184–224

Agnes, Flavia 2000. *Law and Gender Equality*. Oxford University Press

Agnihotri, Indu and Mazumdar, Vina 2005. 'Changing Terms of Political Discourse: Women's Movement in India, 1970s–1990s', in Mala Khullar (ed.), *Writing the Women's Movement: A Reader*. New Delhi: Zuban (in collaboration with EWHA Women's University Seoul), pp. 48–79

Agustin, Laura 2007. *Sex at the Margins: Migration, Labour Markets and the Rescue Industry*. London: Zed Books

Ahmad, Fauzia 2008. 'From Another Shore – The Calumniator Credited: "Honour" and Spin in Islamophobia times', *The Muslim News*, 28 March 2008, Issue 227

Ahsan, Manazir 1995. 'The Muslim Family in Britain', in King, Michael (ed.), *God's Law versus State Law: The Construction of an Islamic Identity in Western Europe*. London: Grey Seal, pp. 21–30

Alexander, M. Jacqui and Mohanty, Chandra T. 1997. 'Introduction: Genealogies, Legacies, Movements', in M. Jacqui Alexander and Chandra T. Mohanty (eds.), *Feminist Geneaologies, Colonial Legacies, Democratic Futures*. New York: Routledge. pp. xiii–xlii

Ali, Shaheen Sardar 2002. 'Testing the Limits of Family Law Reform in Pakistan: A Critical Analysis of the Muslim Family Law Ordinance 1961', *International Survey of Family Law*. Cambridge University Press, pp. 317–335

Ali, Shaheen Sardar 2007a. 'Interpretative Strategies for Women's Human Rights in a Plural Legal Framework: Exploring Judicial and State Responses to Hudood Law in Pakistan', in Anne Hellum, Shaheen Sardar Ali, J. Stewart, and A. Tsanga (eds.), pp. 377–398.

Ali, Shaheen Sardar 2007b. 'Religious Pluralism, Human Rights and Citizenship in Europe: Some Preliminary Reflections on an Evolving Methodology for Consensus', in T. Leonon and J. Goldschmidt (eds.), *Religious Pluralism and Human Rights in Europe*. Utrecht: Insertentia, pp. 55–79

Alim, Abdul Mohd 2006. *Shalish and the Role of BRAC's Federation: Improving the Poor's Access to Justice*. Working Paper Series. http://ssrn.com/abstract=905745

Amnesty International 2004. 'Kosovo (Serbia and Montenegro): "So Does That Mean I Have Rights?" Protecting the Human Rights of Women and Girls Trafficked for Forced Prostitution in Kosovo.' www.amnesty.org/en/library/info/EUR70/010/2004

Amnesty International (USA) 1999. *Pakistan: Violence Against Women in the Name of Honor*. New York: Amnesty International

Anderson, Benedick 1991. *Imagined Communities*. London: Verso

Anderson, Bridget 2001. *Reproductive Labour and Migration*. Rotterdam: Sixth Metropolis Conference, 26–30 November 2001

Anderson, Bridget 2006. *A Very Private Business: Migration and Domestic Work*. University of Oxford: Centre on Migration, Policy and Society, Working Paper 28

Anderson, Bridget and O'Connell Davidson, Julia 2003. 'Is Trafficking in Human Beings Demand Driven: A Multi Country Pilot Study.' Geneva: IOM Migration Research Series No. 15. www.compas.ox.ac.uk/fileadmin/files/pdfs/Bridget_Anderson/BA1_Anderson %20IOM%20report.pdf

Anderson, Bridget and Rogaly, Ben 2005. *Forced Labour and Migration to the UK*. COMPAS and TUC. www.tuc.org.uk/international/tuc-9317-f0.pdf

Anderson, Bridget, Ruhs, Martin, Rogaly, Ben and Spencer, Sarah 2006. *Fair Enough: Central and East European Migrants in Low-Wage Employment in the UK*. University of Oxford: Centre on Migration Policy and Society Research Report

Anitha, Sundari and Gill, Aisha 2009. 'Coercion, Consent and the Forced Marriage Debate in the UK', *Feminist Legal Studies* 17 (1): 165–184

Anker, Christien L. van den and Doomernik, Jeroen (eds.) 2006. *Trafficking and Women's Rights*. Basingstoke: Palgrave Macmillan

An Na'im, Abdullahi 1990. 'Islam, Islamic Law and the Dilemma of Cultural Legitimacy for Universal Human Rights', in C. Welch, and V. Leary (eds.), *Asian Perspectives on Human Rights*. Boulder: Westview, pp. 31–54

An Na'im, Abdullahi 1999. 'Protecting Human Rights in Plural Legal Systems of Africa: A Comparative Overview', in An Na'im (ed.), *Universal Rights, Local Remedies: Implementing Human Rights in the Legal Systems of Africa*. London: Interights, pp. 39–64

An Na'im, Abdullahi and Hammond J. (eds.) 2002. *Cultural Transformation and Human Rights in Africa*. London: Zed Books

Anthias, Flora and Yuval-Davis, Niral 1992. *Racialized Boundaries: Race, Nation, Gender, Colour and Class and the Anti-racist Struggle*. London: Routledge

Anti-Slavery International 2008. *Opportunities and Obstacles: Ensuring Access to Compensation for Trafficked Persons in the UK*. Prepared by Janice Lam and Klára Skrivánková. London: Anti-Slavery International

Aphane, Doo, Manzini, Nomcebo, Mthembu, Lenca, Vilakazi, Philisiwe, Dlam-ini, Thenbayena, Magwaza, Maureen and Mkhonta, Faith 1995. 'Widow: Status or Description?' in Welshman Ncube, and Julie Stewart, (eds.), *Widowhood, Inheritance Laws, Customs and Practices in Southern Africa*. Harare: Women and Law in Southern Africa Research Project, pp. 39–40

APJRF 2009. *Searching for Success in Judicial Reform*. Asia Pacific Judicial Reform Forum. New Delhi: Oxford University Press

(APWLD) Asia Pacific Forum on Women Law and Development 2008. *Fundamentalisms in Asia-Pacific: Trends, Impact, Challenges and Strategies Asserting Women's Rights*. Chiang Mia, Thailand: APWLD

Armstrong, Alice 1992. *Struggling over Scarce Resources: Women and Maintenance in Southern Africa*. Harare: University of Zimbabwe Publications

Armstrong, Alice 2000. 'Rethinking Culture and Tradition in Southern Africa: Research from WLSA' in Stewart, Ann (ed.), pp. 87–100

Arthurs, Harry 2002. 'Private Ordering and Workers' Rights in the Global Economy: Corporate Codes of Conduct as a Regime of Labour Market Regulation', in Conaghan, J., Fischl, R. M. and Klare, K. (eds.), pp. 472–489

Ashiagbor, Diamond 2006. 'Promoting Precariousness? The Response of EU Employment Policies to Precarious Work', in Fudge Judy and Owens Rosemary (eds.), pp. 77–79

Asis, Maruja M. B. 2006. 'The Philippines' Culture of Migration.' www.migrationinformation.org/profiles/print.cfm?ID=364

Badawi, Zaki 1995. 'Muslim Justice in a Secular State', in Michael King (ed.), *God's Law versus State Law: The Construction of an Islamic Identity in Western Europe*. London: Grey Seal, pp. 77–79

Badgett, M. V. Lee and Folbre, Nancy 1999. 'Assigning Care: Gender Norms and Economic Outcomes', *International Labour Review* 138 (3): 311–326

Bair, Jennifer 2005. 'Global Capitalism and Commodity Chains: Looking Back, Going Forward', *Competition and Change* 9 (2): 153–180

Bald, Suresh R. 1995. 'Coping with Marginality: South Asian Women Migrants in Britain', in Marianne Marchand and Jane Parpart (eds.), *Feminism/Post-Modernism/Development*. London: Routledge, pp. 110–126

Ballard, Roger (ed.) 1994. *Desh Pradesh: The South Asian Presence in Britain*. London: Hurst and Co.

Ballard, Roger 2003. 'A Case of Capital-rich Under-development: The Paradoxical Consequences of Successful Transnational Entrepreneurship From Mirpur', *Contribution to Indian Sociology* 37 (1 and 2): 49–81

Ballard, Roger 2005. 'Migration, Remittances, Economic Growth and Poverty Reduction: Reflections on Some South Asian Developments', in Tasneem Siddiqui (ed.), *Migration and Development: Pro-Poor Policy Choices*. Dhaka: University Press Limited, pp. 333–358

Ballard, Roger 2006a. 'Ethnic Diversity and the Delivery of Justice: The Challenge of Plurality', in Prakash Shah and Werner F. Menski (eds.), *Migration Diasporas and Legal Systems in Europe*. London: Routledge and Cavendish, pp. 29–56

Ballard, Roger 2006b. 'Forced Marriages: Just Who is Conspiring Against Whom?', University of Roehampton. www.casas.org.uk/papers/networks.html

Banda, Fareda 2003. 'Global Standards: Local Values', *International Journal of Law, Policy and the Family* 17: 1–27

Banda, Fareda 2005. *Women, Law and Human Rights: An African Perspective*. Oxford and Portland: Hart Publishing

Bano, Samia 2004. *Complexity, Difference and 'Muslim Personal law': Rethinking the Relationship Between Shariah Councils and South Asian Muslim Women in Britain.* UK: University of Warwick Ph.D thesis

Bano, Samia 2007. 'Muslim Family Justice and Human Rights: The Experience of British Muslim Women', *Journal of Comparative Law* 1 (4): 1–29

Bano, Samia 2008. 'In pursuit of Religious and Legal Diversity: A Response to the Archbishop of Canterbury and the Sharia Debate in Britain', *Ecclesiastical Law Journal* 10: 283–309

Barker, Gary 2009. *Engaging Men and Boys in Caregiving: Reflections from Research, Practice and Policy Advocacy*. New York: UN Commission on the Status of Women Fifty-Third Session 2–13 March

Barnett, Hilaire 1998. *Introduction to Feminist Jurisprudence*. London: Cavendish

Barrientos, S., Dolan, C. and Tallontire, A. 2001. 'Gender and Ethical Trade – A Mapping of the Issues in African Horticulture.' www.nri.org/NRET/genderet.pdf

Barrientos, Stephanie, Dolan, Catherine and Tallontire, Anne 2003. 'A Gendered Value Chain Approach to Codes of Conduct in African Horticulture', *World Development* 31 (9): 1511–1526

Barrientos, S. and Dolan, Catherine (eds.) 2006. *Ethical Sourcing in the Global Food System*. London: Earthscan

Barrientos, S. and Smith, Sally 2007. 'Do Workers Benefit from Ethical Trade? Assessing Codes of Labour Practices in Global Production Systems', *Third World Quarterly* 28 (4): 713–729

Bassett, Ellen M. 2007. 'The Persistence of the Commons: Economic Theory and Community Decision Making on Land Tenure in Voi, Kenya', *African Studies Quarterly* 9 (3): 1–29

Basu, Srimati 1999. 'Cutting to Size: Property and Gendered Identity in the Indian Higher Courts', in Rajeswari Sunder Rajan (ed.), *Signposts: Gender Issues in Post-Independence India*. New Delhi: Kali, pp. 248–291

Basu, Srimati 2008. 'Separate and Unequal; Muslim Women and Un-Uniform Family Law in India', *International Feminist Journal of Politics* 10 (4): 495–517

Baxi, Pratiksha, Rai, Shirin M. and Ali, Shaheen Sardar 2006. 'Legacies of Common Law: "Crimes of Honour" in India and Pakistan', *Third World Quarterly* 27 (7): 1239–1253

Belsar, Patrick 2005. *Human Trafficking: Estimating the Profits*. Geneva: ILO Working Paper 42

Beneria, Lourdes, Floro, M., Grown, C. and MacDonald, M. 2000. 'Introduction: Globalization and Gender', *Feminist Economics* 6 (3): vii–xviii

Benhabib, Seyla 1992. *Situating the Self: Gender, Community and Postmodernism in Contemporary Ethics*. Cambridge: Polity Press

Benhabib, Seyla 1994. 'Deliberative Rationality and Models of Democratic Legitimacy', *Constellations* 1 (1): 25–53

Benhabib, Seyla 1996. *Democracy and Difference: Contesting the Boundaries of the Political.* Princeton University Press

Benhabib, Seyla 2002a. *The Claims of Culture: Equality and Diversity in the Global Era.* Princeton University Press

Benhabib, Seyla 2002b. 'Sexual Difference and Collective Identities: The New Global Constellation', in Susan James and Stephanie Palmer (eds.), *Visible Women.* Oxford and Portland: Hart Publishing, pp. 137–158

Bentzon, Agnete Weis, Hellum, Anne, Stewart, Julie and Ncube, Welshman 1998. *Pursuing Grounded Theory in Law: South–North Experiences in Developing Women's Law.* Oslo: Tano-Aschehoug

Berman, Paul Schiff 2007. 'Global Legal Pluralism', *Southern California Law Review.* http://ssrn.com/abstract=985340

Beveridge, Fiona 2005. 'Feminist Perspectives in International Economic Law', in Doris Buss and Ambreena Manji (eds.), *International Law: Modern Feminist Approaches.* Oxford and Portland: Hart Publishing, pp. 173–201

Bhachu, Parminder 1985. *Twice Migrants: East African Sikh Settlers in Britain.* London: Tavistock Publications

Bhavnani, R. 2006. *Ahead of the Game: The Changing Aspirations of Young Ethnic Minority Women.* Manchester: EOC

Biswas, Zahidul Islam 2008. 'A neglected but potential rural justice forum', *The Daily Star* www.thedailystar.net/law/2008/08/01/index.htm

Bodolica, Virgina and Spraggon, Martin 2008. 'Work Experiences of Moldovan Women in Italy: Bearing the Double Identity Strangeness', *Equal Opportunities International* 27 (6): 537–558

Bokhari, Farhat 2009. *Stolen Futures: Trafficking for Forced Child Marriage in the UK.* London: ECPAT

Botcherby, S. 2006. *Pakistani, Bangladeshi and Black Caribbean Women and Employment Survey: Aspirations, Experiences and Choices.* Manchester: EOC.

Bradley, Harriet, Healy, Geraldine, Forson, Cynthia and Kaul, Priyasha 2007. *Workplace Cultures: What Does and Does Not Work.* Manchester: EOC

Brah, Avtar 1996. *Cartographies of Diaspora: Contesting Identities.* London and New York: Routledge

Braithwaite, John and Drahos, Peter 2000. *Global Business Regulation.* Cambridge University Press

Bredel, Anja 2005. 'Tackling Forced Marriages in the Nordic Countries: Between Women's Rights and Immigration Control', in Lynn Welchman and Sara Hossain (eds.), pp. 332–353

Brooks-Gordon, Belinda 2006. *The Price of Sex: Prostitution, Policy and Society.* Cullompton: Willan Publishing

Bryceson, Deborah and Vuorela, Ulla (eds.) 2002. *The Transnational Family: New European Frontiers and Global Networks.* Oxford: Berg

Buchan, James 2008. 'New Opportunities: UK Recruitment of Filipino Nurses', in John Connell (ed.), *International Migration of Health Workers.* Abingdon: Routledge (Taylor and Francis), pp. 47–61

Buchan, James and Dovlo, Delanyo 2004. *International Recruitment of Health Workers to the UK: A Report for DFID.* London: DFID Health Systems Resources Centre

Buckner, Lisa and Yeandle, Sue 2005. *We Care: Do You?* Sheffield Hallam University

Buckner, Lisa and Yeandle, Sue 2007. *Valuing Carers – Calculating the Value of Unpaid Care*. London: Carers UK. Available at www.carersuk.org

Buckner, Lisa; Yeandle Sue; and Botcherby Sue 2007. *Ethnic Minority Women and Local Labour Markets*. Manchester: EOC

Budlender, Debbie 2008. *The Statistical Evidence on Care and Non-Care Work across Six Countries*. Geneva: UNRISD Gender and Development Programme Paper no. 4

Bueno de Mesquita, J. and Gordon, M. 2005. *The International Migration of Health Workers: A Human Rights Analysis*. London: Medact

Bugaric, Bojan 2008. 'Populism, Liberal Democracy, and the Rule of Law in Central and Eastern Europe', *Communist and Post-Communist Studies* 41 (2): 191–203

Bujra, Janet 1982. 'Women "Entrepreneurs" of Early Nairobi', in Colin Sumner (ed.), *Crime, Justice and Underdevelopment*. London: Heinemann, pp. 122–161

Bump, Micah 2006. 'Ghana: Searching for Opportunities at Home and Abroad.' www.migrationinformation.org/profiles/print.cfm?IS=381

Burca, Elena 2006. *The Alternative Report of Evaluation Regarding the Implementation of Convention on the Elimination of All Forms of Discrimination Against Women*. Chisinau. www.iwraw-ap.org/resources/pdf/Moldova_SR.pdf

Buss, Doris and Manji, Ambreena (eds.) 2005. *International Law: Modern Feminist Approaches*. Oxford and Portland: Hart Publishing

Byrnes, Andrew and Connors, Jane 2010. *The International Bill of Rights for Women: The Impact of the CEDAW Convention*. Oxford University Press

CAFOD 2003a. *Rough Guide to Globalisation*. London: CAFOD.

CAFOD 2003b. *Rough Guide to Economic Partnership Agreements*. London: CAFOD.

Carasciuc, Lilia 2007. *Measuring Corruption: From Survey to Survey*. Chisinau: Transparency International Moldova

Care Council 2007. 'Skills for Care.' www.skillsforcare.org.uk/research/research_reports/research_reports_introduction.aspx

Carothers, Thomas 1998. 'The Rule of Law Revival', *Foreign Affairs* 77 (2): 95–106

Carothers, Thomas 2006. *Promoting the Rule of Law Abroad: In Search of Knowledge*. Washington: Carnegie

Carroll, Lucy 1997. 'Muslim Women and "Islamic Divorce" in England', *Journal of Muslim Minority Affairs* 17 (1): 97–115

Caruso, B. 2002. 'Immigration Policies in Southern Europe: More State, Less Market?', in Conaghan, J., Fischl, R. M. and Klare, K. (eds.), pp. 299–319

CEDAW Committee 2006. 'Consideration of Combined 5th and 6th Reports of States Parties for Kenya.' www.un.org/womenwatch/daw/cedaw/reports.htm

CEDAW Committee 2007. *Concluding Remarks on (Poland) 37th Session, 15th January–2nd February*. CEDAW/POL/CO/6

Chakravarti, Uma 2005. 'From Fathers to Husbands: Of Love, Death and Marriage in North India', in Welchman, Lynn and Hossain, Sara (eds.), pp. 308–331

(The) Change Institute 2009. *Understanding Muslim Ethnic Communities: Summary Report*. London: Department for Communities and Local Government

Chanock, Martin 1982. 'Making Customary Law: Men, Women and Courts in Colonial Northern Rhodesia', in M. J. Hay and M. Wright (eds.), *African Women and the Law: Historical Perspectives*. Boston University, African Studies Center, pp. 53–67

Chanock, Martin 1985. *Law, Custom and Social Order: The Colonial Experience in Malawi and Zambia*. Cambridge University Press

Chanock, Martin 1991. 'Paradigms, Policies and Property: A Review of Customary Law of Land Tenure', in K. Mann and R. Roberts(eds.), *Law in Colonial Africa*. London: Heinemann, pp 61–84

Charlesworth, Hilary and Chinkin, Christine 2000. *The Boundaries of International Law: A Feminist Analysis*. Manchester University Press

Charsley, Katherine 2005. 'Unhappy Husbands: Masculinity and Migration in Transnational Pakistani Marriages', *Journal of the Royal Anthropological Institute* 11: 85–105

Charsley, Katherine 2006. 'Risk and Ritual: The Protection of British Pakistani Women in Transnational Marriage', *Journal of Ethnic and Migration Studies* 32 (7): 1169–1187

Charsley, Katherine and Shaw, Alison 2006. 'South Asian Transnational Marriages in Comparative Perspective', *Global Networks* 6 (4): 331–344

Chaudhuri, Maitrayee 2005. 'Introduction', in Maitrayee Chaudhuri (ed.), *Feminism in India*. London and New York: Zed Books

Chodorow, Nancy 1978. *The Reproduction of Mothering: Psychoanalysis and the Sociology of Gender*. Berkeley: University of California Press

Cholewinski, Ryszard 2003. *Migrant Workers in International Human Rights Law*. Oxford: Clarendon Press

Chowdhry, Prem 2004a. 'Caste Panchayats and the Policing of Marriage in Haryana: Enforcing Kinship and Territorial Exogamy', *Contributions to Indian Sociology* 38 (1): 1–42

Chowdhry, Prem 2004b. 'Private Lives, State Intervention: Cases of Runaway Marriage in Rural North India', *Modern Asian Studies* 38 (1): 55–84

Chowdhry, Prem 2007. *Contentious Marriages, Eloping Couples: Gender, Caste, and Patriarchy in Northern India*. New Delhi: Oxford University Press

Christian Aid undated. *Trade Justice: Turning Words into Action*. London: Christian Aid

Chua, Amy 2003. *World on Fire: How Exporting Free Market Democracy Breeds Ethnic Hatred and Global Instability*. London: Heinemann

CIPD 2006. *How Engaged are British Employees?* London: CIPD

Clayton, Gina 2008. *Textbook on Immigration and Asylum Law*. Oxford University Press

Clemens, Michael A. 2007. *Do Visas Kill? Health Effects of African Health Professional Emigration*. Center for Global Development Working Paper No. 114.' http://ssrn.com/abstract=980332

Clements, Luke and Thompson, Pauline 2007. *Community Care and the Law*. London: Legal Action Group

Collins, H. 2002. 'Is There a Third Way in Labour Law?', in Conaghan, J., Fischl, R. M. and Klare, K. (eds.), pp. 449–469

Collins, Hugh, Ewing, Keith D. and McColgan, Aileen 2005. *Labour Law: Text and Materials*. Oxford and Portland: Hart Publishing

Community Care 2009. 'Vacancy Rates: the Rates in Full.' www.communitycare.co.uk/Articles/2009/04/15/111285/vacancy-rates-the-figures-in-full.html

Conaghan, Joanne 2002. 'Women, Work, and Family: A British Revolution?' in Conaghan, J., Fischl, R. M. and Klare, K. (eds.), pp 53–74

Conaghan, Joanne 2006. 'Time to Dream? Flexibility, Families and the Regulation of Working Time' in Fudge, Judy and Owens, Rosemary (eds.), pp. 101–129

Conaghan, Joanne, Fischl, R. M. and Klare, K. (eds.) 2002. *Labour Law in an Era of Globalisation*. Oxford University Press

Conaghan, Joanne and Rittich, Kerry (eds.) 2005. *Labour Law, Work and Family*. Oxford University Press

Conn, David 2007. 'Supermarket sweep-up', *The Guardian*, 25 July

Connell, John (ed.) 2008. *International Migration of Health Workers*. Abingdon: Routledge (Taylor and Francis)

Coomaraswamy, Radhika 2005. 'Violence against women and "crimes of honour"' Preface in Welchman, Lynn and Hossain, Sara (eds.), pp. xi–xiv

Cornwall, Andrea, Jolly, Susie, Correêa, Sonia (eds.) 2008. *Development with a Body: Sexualities, Human Rights and Development*. London: Zed Press

Cornwall, Andrea and Molyneux, Maxine 2006. 'The Politics of Rights-Dilemmas for Feminist Praxis: An Introduction', *Third World Quarterly* 27 (7): 1175–1191

Cornwall, Andrea and Nyamu, Celestine 2005. *What is the 'Rights-based Approach' All About? Perspectives from International Development Agencies*. Sussex University: Institute of Development Studies Working paper no. 234

Cowan, Sharon and Hodgson, Jacqueline 2007. 'Violence in a Family Context: The Criminal Law's Response to Domestic Violence', in Rebecca Probert (ed.), *Family Law and Life: Under One Roof*. Ashgate: Aldershot, pp. 43–60

Coy, Maddy, Horvath, Miranda and Kelly, Liz 2007. *'It's Just Like Going to the Supermarket': Men Buying Sex in East London*. London Metropolitan University: Child and Woman Abuse Studies Unit (CWASU) Report for Safe Exit Tower Hamlets

Coyle, Angela 2003 'Fragmented Feminisms: Women's Organisations and Citizenship in "Transition" in Poland' *Gender and Development* 11 (3) 57–65

Coyle, Angela 2007. 'Has Transition Left Women Behind? Polish Women's Labour Markets at "Home" and "Abroad"', *Development and Transition* 08. www.developmentandtransition.net/index.cfm?module=ActiveWeb&page=WebPage&DocumentID=660

CRE (Commission for Racial Equality) 2006. *Employment and Ethnicity*. London: Commission for Racial Equality.

Crenshaw, Kimberley 1991. 'Mapping the Margins: Intersectionality, Identity Politics and Violence against Women of Color', *Stanford Law Review* 43 (6): 1241–1299

Datta, Kavita, McIlwainy, Cathy, Evans, Yara, Herbert, Joanna, May, Jon and Wills, Jane 2006. *Work, Care and Life Among Low-Paid Migrant Workers in London: Towards a Migrant Ethic of Care*. Department of Geography, Queen Mary, University of London

De Soto, Hernando 2000. *The Mystery of Capital: Why Capitalism Triumphs in the West and Fails Elsewhere*. New York: Basic Books

Department for Work and Pensions 2010. 'Households Below Average Income (HBAI).' http://statistics.dwp.gov.uk/asd/index.php?page=hbai

DFID 2002. *Safety, Security and Accessible Justice: Putting Policy into Practice*. UK Department for International Development, July

DFID 2007. *Ending Poverty in India*. New Delhi: DFID India

DFID 2008. *Ghana Factsheet*. London: DFID. www.dfid.gov.uk

DH 2005. *Independence, Well Being and Choice: Our Vision for the Future of Social Care for Adults in England.* London: Department of Health

DH 2007a. *Annual Report.* London: Department of Health

DH 2007b. *Collaborative Recruitment Solutions in Social Care – Getting and Keeping Your Workforce.* London: Department of Health

DH 2008. *Carers at the Heart of 21st Century Families and Communities.* London: Department of Health. www.dh.gov.uk/en/publicationsandstatistics/publications/publicationspolicyandguidance/DH_085345

DH 2009a. *Working to Put People First: The Strategy for the Adult Social Care Workforce in England.* www.dh.gov.uk/publications

DH 2009b. 'Shaping the Future of Care Together.' Green Paper. www.dh.gov.uk/en/Publicationsandstatistics/Publications/PublicationsPolicyAndGuidance/DH_102338

Dhagamwar, V. 1992. *Law, Power and Justice: The Protection of Personal Rights in the Indian Penal Code.* New Delhi: Sage

Dex, Shirley and Ward, Kelly 2007. *Parental Care and Employment in Early Childhood: Analysis of the Millennium Cohort Study (MCS) Sweeps 1 and 2.* Manchester: EOC

Djordjevic, Jelena 2008. 'Social and Political Inclusion of Sex Workers as a Preventive Measure Against Trafficking: Serbian Experiences', in Andrea Cornwall, Susie Jolly, and Sonia Correêa (eds.), *Development with a Body: Sexuality, Human Rights and Development.* London: Zed Books, pp. 161–177

Doezema, Jo 2005. 'Now You See Her, Now You Don't: Sex Workers at the UN Trafficking Protocol Negotiations', *Social and Legal Studies* 14 (1): 61–89

Dolan, Catherine, Humphrey, John, and Harris-Pascal, Carla 1999. *Horticulture Commodity Chains: The Impact on the UK Market of the African Fresh Vegetable Industry.* University of Sussex: IDS Working Papers 96

Drakapoulou, Maria 2000. 'The Ethic of Care, Female Subjectivity and Feminist Legal Scholarship', *Feminist Legal Studies* 8: 199–226

DTI (Department for Trade and Industry) 2002. *Liberalising Trade in Services – A New Consultation on the World Trade Organization GATS Negotiation.* London: DTI

Dwasi, Jane 1999. 'A Study in International Labor Standards and their Effect on Working Women in Developing Countries: The Case for Integration of Enforcement Issues in the World Bank's Policies', *Wisconsin International Law Journal* 17: 347–462

Ehrenreich, Barbara and Hochschild, Arlie R. (eds.) 2003. *Global Women: Nannies, Maids and Sex Workers in the New Economy.* London: Granta Books

Elson, Diane 1999. *Gender-neutral, Gender-blind, or Gender-sensitive Budgets? Changing the Conceptual Framework to Include Women's Empowerment and the Economy of Care.* London: Commonwealth Secretariat Gender Budget Initiative – Background Papers

Elson, Diane 2000. *Progress of the World's Women.* New York: UNDP-UNIFEM Biennial Report

Elson, Diane 2002. 'Gender Justice, Human Rights and Neo-Liberal Economic Policies' in M. Molyneux and S. Razavi (eds.), *Gender Justice, Development and Rights.* Oxford University Press pp. 78–114

Elson, Diane 2004. 'Feminist Economics Challenges Mainstream Economics', *Newsletter of the International Association for Feminist Economics* 14 (3): 6–9

Elson, Diane and Cagatay, Nulifer 2000. 'The Social Content of Macroeconomic Policies', *World Development* 28 (7): 1347–1364

Engle, Karen 2005. 'International Human Rights and Feminisms: When Discourses Keep Meeting', in Buss, Doris and Manji, Ambreena (eds.), pp. 47–66.

Engster, Daniel 2004. 'Care Ethics and Natural Law Theory: Toward an Institutional Political Theory of Caring', *Journal of Politics* 66 (1): 113–135

Enloe, Cynthia 1989. *Bananas, Beaches and Bases: Making Feminist Sense of International Politics*. London: Pandora

Enright, Mairead 2009. 'Choice, Culture and the Politics of Belonging: The Emerging Law of Forced and Arranged Marriage', *Modern Law Review* 72 (3): 331–359

EOC 2004. *Ethnic Minority Women and Men*. Manchester: EOC

EOC 2006. *Moving on up? Bangladeshi, Pakistani and Black Caribbean Women and Work*. Manchester: EOC

EOC 2007. *Moving On Up? Key Statistics*. Manchester: EOC

EPZA (Exporting Processing Zone Authority) 2005. *Horticultural Industry in Kenya 2005*. Nairobi: EPZA. http://www.epzakenya.com/UserFiles/File/Horticulture.pdf

Ertman, Martha M. and Williams, Joan C. 2005. 'Preface: Freedom, Equality and the Many Futures of Commodification', in Martha M. Ertman and Joan C. Williams (eds.), *Rethinking Commodification: Cases and Readings in Law and Culture*. New York University Press, pp. 1–7

European Commission 2009. 'Quick Guide: Services Directive.' http://ec.europa.eu/internal_market/services/services-dir/guides_en.htm

Falk Moore, S. 1978. *Law as Process: An Anthropological Approach*. London: Routledge and Kegan Paul

Faundez, Julio 1997. 'Introduction' in Julio Faundez (ed.), *Legal Technical Assistance in Good Government and Law: Legal and Institutional Reform in Developing Countries*. London: Macmillan, pp. 1–24

Faundez, Julio, Footer, Mary E. and Norton, Joseph (eds.) 2000. *Governance, Development and Globalization*. London: Blackstone

Ferguson, Ann and Folbre, Nancy 1981. 'The Unhappy Marriage of Patriarchy and Capitalism', in Lydia Sargent (ed.), *Women and Revolution*. Boston: South End Press, pp. 313–338

Fodor, Eva 2002. 'Gender and the Experience of Poverty in Eastern Europe and Russia After 1989', *Communist and Post-Communist Studies* 35 (4): 369–382

Fodor, Eva 2005. *Women at Work: The Status of Women in the Labour Markets of the Czech Republic, Hungary and Poland*. New York: UNRISD Occasional Paper 3 February

Folbre, Nancy 2009. 'Varieties of Patriarchal Capitalism', *Social Politics* 16 (2): 204–209

Fox, Tom and Vorley, Bill 2006 'Small Producers: Constraints and Challenges in the Global Food System', in Barrientos, Stephanie and Dolan, Catherine (eds.), pp. 163–177

Fraser, Nancy 1989. *Unruly Practices: Power, Discourse and Gender in Contemporary Social Theory*. Cambridge: Polity Press

Fraser, Nancy 1995. 'From Redistribution to Recognition? Dilemmas of Justice in a "Post-Socialist" Age', *New Left Review* 1 (212): 68–93

Fraser, Nancy 1997. *Justice Interruptus: Critical Reflections on the 'Postsocialist' Condition*. London: Routledge

Fraser, Nancy 2000. 'Rethinking Recognition', *New Left Review* 3: 107–120

Fraser, Nancy 2001. 'Recognition without Ethics', *Theory, Culture and Society* 18 (2–3): 21–42

Fraser, Nancy 2009. 'Feminism, Capitalism and the Cunning of History', *New Left Review* 56: 97–117

Fredman, Sandra 2002. *The Future of Equality in Britain*. Manchester: EOC Working Paper Series no. 5

Fredman, Sandra 2006. 'Precarious Norms for Precarious Workers', in Fudge, Judy and Owens, Rosemary (eds.), pp. 177–200

Fudge, Judy and Owens, Rosemary (eds.) 2006. *Precarious Work, Women and the New Economy: The Challenge to Legal Norms*. Oxford and Portland: Hart Publishing

Fudge, Judy and Owens, Rosemary 2006. 'Precarious Work, Women, and the New Economy: The Challenge to Legal Norms' in Fudge, Judy and Owens, Rosemary (eds.), pp. 3–27

Fuszara, Malgorzata 2005. 'Between Feminism and the Catholic Church: The Women's Movement in Poland' *Czech Sociological Review* 41 (6) 1057–1075

Gabriel, Yiannis and Lang, Tim 2006. *The Unmanageable Consumer*. London: Sage

Gaidzanwa, R. 1992. 'Bourgeois Theories of Gender and Feminism and their Shortcomings with reference to Southern African Countries', in R. Meena (ed.), *Gender in Southern Africa: Conceptual and Theoretical Issues*. Harare: SAPES Books, pp. 92–125

Gangoli, Geetanjali 2007. *Indian Feminisms: Law, Patriarchies, and Violence in India*. Aldershot: Ashgate

Garcia, Zoraida 2005. *Impact of Agricultural Trade on Gender Equity and the Position of Rural Women in Developing Countries*. Roskilde University Denmark: Department of Social Sciences, Federico Caffè Centre Research Reports n. 9/2005.

Gardner, Katy 1995. *Global Migrants: Local Lives*. Oxford: Clarendon

Gardner, Katy 2006. 'The Transnational Work of Kinship and Caring: Bengali–British Marriages in Historical Perspective', *Global Networks* 6 (4): 373–387

Gereffi, Gary 1994. 'The Organisation of Buyer-driven Global Commodity Chains: How US Retailers Shape Overseas Production Networks' in Gereffi, Gary and Korzeniewicz, M. (eds.), pp. 95–122

Gereffi, Gary, Humphrey, John and Sturgeon, Timothy 2005. 'The Governance of Global Value Chains', *Review of International Political Economy* 12 (1): 78–104

Gereffi, Gary and Korzeniewicz, M. (eds.) 1994. *Commodity Chains and Global Capitalism*. Westport, CT: Praeger

Gerein, N. and Green, A. 2006. 'Midwifery and Nursing Migration: Implications for Maternal Health in Low-income Countries', in Grown, Caren, Braunstein, Elissa and Malhotra, Anju (eds.), pp 235–260

Ghai, Y. 1993. 'Constitutions and Governance: A Prolegomenon', in S. Adelman and A. Paliwala (eds.), *Crisis in Law and Development*. Oxford: Hans Zell, pp. 51–74

Ghana Health Service 2007. 'Annual Report 2007.' www.ghanahealthservice.org/

Ghencea, Boris and Gudumac, Igor 2004. *Labour Migration and Remittances in the Republic of Moldova*. Chisinau: Moldova Microfinance Alliance and Soros Foundation

Gill, Aisha and Sharma, Kaveri 2007. 'Response and Responsibility: Domestic Violence and Marriage Migration in the UK' in Thomas Spijkerboer and Sarah Van Walsum (eds.), *Women and Immigration Law: New Variations on Classical Feminist Themes*. Abingdon: Routledge Cavendish, pp. 183–221

Gilligan, Carol 1982. *In a Different Voice*. Cambridge, MA: Harvard University Press

Global Networks 2005. Special Edition 5 (4)

Go, Stella P. 2007. *Asian Labor Migration: The Role of Bilateral Labor and Similar Agreements*. Manila, Philippines: Regional Informal Workshop on Labor Migration in Southeast Asia

Goetz, Anne Marie and Hassim, Shireen 2002. 'In and Against the Party: Women's Representation and Constituency-Building in Uganda and South Africa' in Molyneux, M. and Razavi, S. (eds.), pp. 306–343

Golub, Stephen 2000. 'From the Village to the University: Legal Activism in Bangladesh', in Mary McClymont and Stephen Golub (eds.), *Many Roads to Justice: The Law-related Work of Ford Foundation Grantees around the World*. New York: Ford Foundation, pp. 127–158

Golub, Stephen 2003. *Non-state Justice Systems in Bangladesh and the Philippines*. UK: DFID Paper

Gordolan, Lourdes and Lalani, Imtaz 2009. *Care and Immigration: Migrant Care Workers in Private Households*. London: Kalayaan

Gould, Carol 2004. *Globalising Democracy and Human Rights*. Cambridge University Press

Gould, Carol 2007. 'Transitional Solidarities', *Journal of Social Philosophy* 38 (1): 148–164

Government Equalities Office 2009. *A Fairer Future: The Equality Bill and Other Action to Make Equality a Reality*. London: Government Equalities Office. www.equalities.gov.uk

Government of Pakistan 2010. *Pakistan Economic Survey 2009–2010*. Ministry of Finance. www.finance.gov.pk/survey_0910.html

Government of Philippines 2008. *Labour Force Survey*. Manila: National Statistics Office

Grabham, Emily, Cooper, Davina, Krishnadas, Jane and Herman, Didi (eds.) 2009. *Intersectionality and Beyond: Law, Power and the Politics of Location*. London: Routledge Cavendish

Griffiths, Anne 1997. *In the Shadow of Marriage: Gender and Justice in an African Community*. Chicago and London: University of Chicago Press

Griffiths, Anne 2002. 'Legal Pluralism', in R. Banakar and M. Travers (eds.), *An Introduction to Law and Social Theory*. Oxford: Hart Publishing, pp. 289–310

Griffiths, John 1986. 'What is Legal Pluralism?', *Journal of Legal Pluralism* 24: 1–55

Grown, Caren, Braunstein, Elissa and Malhotra, Anju (eds.) 2006. *Trading Women's Health and Rights? Trade Liberalisation and Reproductive Health in Developing Countries*. London: Zed Press

Guha, Phulrenu 1974. *Towards Equality: Report of the Committee on the Status of Women in India*. India: GOI, Dept. of Social Welfare. www.cscsarchive.org:8081/MediaArchive/Library.nsf/(docid)/8D5818C7A2C38D7965257132002AFB95?OpenDocument&StartKey=Towards&count=50

Hammer, Nicolaus 2005. 'International Framework Agreements: Global Industrial Relations Between Rights and Bargaining', *Transfer* 11 (4): 511–530

Hannett, Sarah 2003. 'Equality at the Intersections: The Legislative and Judicial Failure to Tackle Multiple Discrimination', *Oxford Journal of Legal Studies* 23 (1): 65–86

Harcourt, Wendy 2009. *Body Politics in Development*. London: Zed Press

Harding, Sandra. G. 2008. *Sciences from Below: Feminisms, Postcolonialities and Modernities*. Durham: Duke University Press

Hardt, Michael 1999. 'Affective Labour', *Boundary* 2 26 (2): 89–100

Hardt, Michael and Negri, Antonio 2000. *Empire*. Cambridge MA: Harvard University Press

Harrison, James 2007. *The Human Rights Impact of the World Trade Organisation*. Oxford: Hart Publishing

Hartstock, Nancy C. M. 1997. 'The Feminist Standpoint', in Linda Nicholson (ed.), *The Second Wave*. New York: Routledge, pp 216–235

Hartstock, Nancy C. M. 2006. 'Experience, Embodiment, and Epistemologies', *Hypatia* 21 (2): 178–183

Harvey, David 2005. *A Brief History of Neoliberalism*. Oxford University Press

Hassim, S. 1993. 'Family, Motherhood and Zulu Nationalism: The Politics of the Inkatha Women's Brigade', *Feminist Review* 43: 1–25

Hassim, Shireen and Razavi, Shahra 2006. 'Gender and Social Policy in a Global Context: Uncovering the Gendered Structure of "the social"', in Shahra Razavi and Shireen Hassim (eds.), *Gender and Social Policy in a Global Context: Uncovering the Gendered Structure of' the Social*. Basingstoke: Palgrave Macmillan

Held, David and McGrew, Anthony 1999. *Governing Globalization: Power, Authority and Global Governance*. Cambridge: Polity

Held, David, McGrew, Anthony, Goldblatt, David and Perraton, Jonathan, 1999. *Global Transformations: Politics, Economics and Culture*. Cambridge: Polity

Held, Virginia 2004. 'Care and Justice in the Global Context', *Ratio Juris* 17 (2): 141–155

Held, Virginia 2006. *The Ethics of Care: Personal, Political and Global*. Oxford University Press

Hellum, Anne 1999a. 'Women's Human Rights and African Customary Laws: Between Universalism and Relativism – Individualism and Communitarianism', *European Journal of Development Research* 10 (2): 88–104

Hellum, Anne 1999b. *Women's Human Rights and Legal Pluralism in Africa: Mixed Norms and Identities in Infertility Management in Zimbabwe*. Oslo: Mond Books

Hellum, Anne, Ali, S. S., Stewart, J. and Tsanga, A. (eds.) 2007. *Human Rights, Plural Legalities and Gendered Realities: Paths are Made for Walking*. Harare: Weaver Books

Henry, Leroi 2008. 'Disengagement and Demoralisation: The Roots of Ghanaian Nurses' Responses to Discrimination in the NHS', in V. Tschudin (ed.), *The Globalisation of Nursing: Ethical, Legal and Political issues*. Oxford: Radcliffe Medical, pp 116–125

Herring, Jonathan 2009. *Older People and the Law*. Oxford University Press

Himmelweit, Sue and Land, Hilary 2007. *Supporting Parent and Carers*. Manchester: EOC

Hochschild, Arlie Russell 2000a. 'Global Care Chains and Emotional Surplus Values', in N. Hutton and A. Giddens (eds.), *On the Edge: Living with Global Capitalism*. London: Jonathan Cape, pp 130–146

Hochschild, Arlie Russell 2000b. 'The Nanny Chain', *The American Prospect*, January 3

Hochschild, Arlie Russell 2003. 'Love and Gold', in Barbara Ehrenreich and Arlie Russell Hochschild (eds.), *Global Woman: Nannies, Maids, and Sex Workers in the New Economy*. London: Granta Books, pp 15–30

Home Office 2000. 'Domestic Violence: Break the Chain. Multi Agency Guidance for Addressing Domestic Violence.' London: Home Office. www.nationalarchives.gov. uk/ERORecords/HO/421/2/domesticviolence/mag.pdf

Home Office 2002. *Secure Borders, Safe Haven: Integration with Diversity in Modern Britain.* London: HMSO Cm 5387

Home Office 2004. *Paying the Price: A Consultation Paper on Prostitution.* http://news.bbc.co.uk/nol/shared/bsp/hi/pdfs/16_07_04_paying.pdf

Home Office 2005a. *Controlling Our Borders: Making Migration Work for Britain.* London: HMSO Cm 6472

Home Office 2005b. *Selective Admission: Making Migration Work for Britain.* London: Home Office Consultation Document

Home Office 2006a. *A Points-Based System: Making Migration Work for Britain.* London: HMSO Cm 6741

Home Office 2006b. *Marriage to Partners from Overseas.* London: Home Office Borders and Immigration Agency consultation paper, December

Home Office 2007. 'UK Action Plan on Tackling Human Trafficking' www.ungift.org/doc/knowledgehub/resource-centre/Governments/UK_Action_Plan_to_Combat_Human_Trafficking_en.pdf

Home Office 2008. 'Tackling the Demand for Prostitution: A Review.' www.homeoffice.gov.uk/documents/tackling-demand?view=Binary

Home Office 2009a. 'A Code of Practice on forced marriage.' www.ukba.homeoffice.gov.uk/sitecontent/documents/policyandlaw/IDIs/idischapter8/section1/annexa2.pdf

Home Office 2009b. 'Control of Immigration Statistics: United Kingdom 2008.' Home Office Statistical Bulletin. www.homeoffice.gov.uk/rds/pdfs09/hosb1409.pdf

Home Office and FCO 2006. *A Wrong not a Right: Summary of Responses to the Consultation on the Criminalisation of Forced Marriages.* Forced Marriage Unit, London: HO/FCO

Hoskyns, Catherine 2006. *Gender in Global and Regional Trade Policy: Contrasting Views and New Research.* UK: Workshop Report 5–7 April 2006. Centre for the Study of Globalisation and Regionalisation, Warwick University

Hoskyns, Catherine and Rai, Shirin M. 2007. 'Recasting the Global Political Economy: Counting Women's Unpaid Work', *New Political Economy* 12 (3): 297–317

Hossein, Sara 2001. 'Abduction for Forced Marriage: Rights and Remedies in Bangladesh and Pakistan', *International Family Law*, April, 15–24

Howard-Hassmann, Rhoda, E. 2005. 'The Second Great Transformation: Human Rights Leapfrogging in the Era of Globalization', *Human Rights Quarterly* 27: 1–40

Hughes, Donna M. 2002. 'The Use of New Communications and Information Technologies for Sexual Exploitation of Women and Children', *Hastings Women's Law Journal* 13 (1): 129–148

Hunt, Diana 2005. 'Some Outstanding Issues in the Debate on External Promotion of Land Privatisation', *Development Policy Review* 23 (2): 199–231

Hussain, Zahid and Jenkins, Russell 2010. 'Pakistani Family is Buried Amid Tight Security after Honour Killings', *The Times* 22 May

Id21 Insights 2006. 'Sending Money Home: Can Remittances Reduce Poverty?' *Id21 Insights* 60 (January) Institute of Development Studies Sussex. www.id21.org/insights

Ikdahl, Ingunn, Hellum, Anne, Benjaminsen, Tor A., Kaarhus, Randi and Kameri-Mbote, Patricia 2005. *Human Rights, Formalisation and Women's Land Rights in Southern and Eastern Africa.* Studies in Women's Law, number 57, Institute of Women's Law, University of Oslo

Ilumoka, Adetoun O. 1994. 'African Women's Economic, Social and Cultural Rights – Toward a Relevant Theory and Practice', in Rebecca F. Cook (ed.), *Human Rights of Women*. Philadelphia: Pennsylvania University Press, pp. 307–325

ILO 2004. *Towards a Fair Deal for Migrant Workers in the Global Economy*. Geneva: ILO

ILO 2006a. *International Labour Migration and Development: The ILO Perspective*. Geneva: Report to 61st Session of the General Assembly High Level Dialogue on International Migration and Development, New York 14–15 September

ILO 2006b. *Multilateral Framework on Labour Migration: Non-Binding Principles and Guidelines for a Rights-based Approach to Labour Migration*. Geneva: ILO

ILO 2007. *Global Employment Trends for Women*. Geneva: ILO

ILO 2008a. *Draft ISCO-08 Group Definitions: Occupations in Cleaning and Housekeeping. Updating the International Standard Definition of Occupations* (ISCO). Geneva: ILO

ILO 2008b. *Global Employment Trends for Women*. Geneva: ILO

Imran, Myra 2009. '96.6 per cent marriages take place to attain foreign nationality', *The International News*, Saturday, 22 August.

IOM 2007a. *Remittances in the Republic of Moldova: Patterns, Trends and Effects*. Chisinau: IOM Mission to Moldova

IOM 2007b. Background Paper for Trade and Migration Seminar. Geneva 4–5 October www.wto.int/english/tratop_e/serv_e/sem_oct04_e/background_paper_e.pdf

IOM 2008a. 'In Moldova, Women Receiving Remittances Save More than Men', *Gender and Migration News*, 31 July

IOM 2008b. 'Compendium of Good Practice Policy Elements in Bilateral Temporary Labour Arrangements.' www.iom.ch/jahia/webdav/shared/shared/mainsite/published_docs/studies_and_reports/compendium_version_2.pdf

IOM/World Bank/WTO 2004. Background paper; Trade and migration seminar. Geneva 4–5 October. www.wto.org/english/tratop_e/serv_e/sem_oct04_e/background_paper_e.pdf

Iqbal, Nasira 2007. 'Legal Pluralism in Pakistan and its Implications on Women's Rights', in Jennifer Bennett (ed.), *Scratching the Surface: Democracy, Traditions, Gender*, Pakistan/Afghanistan (Lahore): Heinrich Böll Foundation pp 101–118

Jackson, Melissa 2006. 'Polish workers plug health care gap', BBC News Online. http://news.bbc.co.uk/go/pr/fr/-/2/hi/health/3819231.stm

Jaising Indira, Basu, Asmita and Dutta, Brototi (eds.) 2009. *Lawyers Collective Handbook on Law of Domestic Violence*. Nagpur: LexisNexisButterworths Wadhwa

Jayawardena, K. 1986. *Feminism and Nationalism in the Third World*. London: Zed Books

Jayaweera, Hiranthi and Anderson, Bridget 2008. 'Migrant Workers and Vulnerable Employment: A Review of Existing Data', TUC Commission on Vulnerable Employment. www.vulnerableworkers.org.uk/wp-content/uploads/2008/08/analysis-of-migrant-worker-data-final.pdf

Jeffries, Stuart 2004. 'I'm Rich and I'm Living Well. Shopping Here is Part of That', *The Guardian*, 12 March, G2 Comments and Features p. 2

Jhabvala, Renana 2006. 'Globalization, Liberalization and Women in the Informal Economy', in Veena Jha (ed.), *Trade, Globalisation and Gender – Evidence from South Asia*. Geneva: UNIFEM-UNCTAD, pp. 35–88

Jones, Richard and Gnanapala, Welhengama 2000. *Ethnic Minorities in English Law*. London: Trentham Books and School of Oriental and African Studies

Jones, Sam, 2006. 'Bullying Mother-in-law Must Pay £35,000', *The Guardian*, 25 July

Kabeer, Naila 1991. 'The Quest for National Identity: Women, Islam and the State in Bangladesh', *Feminist Review* 37: 38–58

Kabeer, Naila 1994. *Reversed Realities: Gender Hierarchies in Development Thought.* London and New York: Verso

Kabeer, Naila 2000. *The Power to Choose: Bangladeshi Women and Labour Market Decisions in London and Dhaka.* London and New York: Verso

Kabeer, Naila 2004. 'Globalisation, Labor Standards, and Women's Rights: Dilemma of Collective (In)Action in an Interdependent World', *Feminist Economics* 10 (1): 3–35

Kamenou, N. and Fearfull, N. 2006. 'Ethnic Minority Women: A Lost Voice in Human Resources Management', *Human Resources Management Journal* 16 (2): 154–172

Kannabiran, Kalpana (ed.) 2005. *The Violence of Normal Times: Essays on Women's Lived Realities.* New Delhi: Women Unlimited in association with Kali for Women

Kaplinsky, Raphael 2000. *Spreading the Gains from Globalisation: What Can Be Learned From Value Chain Analysis.* Sussex: Institute of Development Studies Working Paper 110

Kapur, Ratna 1999. '"A Love Song To Our Mongrel Selves": Hybridity, Sexuality and the Law', *Social and Legal Studies* 8 (3): 353–368

Kapur, Ratna 2005. *Erotic Justice: Law and the New Politics of Postcolonialism.* London: Glasshouse Press

Kategekwa, Joy 2006. *Extension of Mode 4 Commitments to Include Unskilled Workers in the WTO. A Win Win Situation, Especially For LDCs.* Geneva: South Centre for the OECD Development Centre Panel on Migration and Development

Kaur, Amarjit 2006. 'Order (and Disorder) at the Border: Mobility, International Labour Migration and Border Controls in Southeast Asia', in Amarjit Kaur and Ian Metcalfe (eds.), *Mobility, Labour Migration and Border Controls in Asia.* London: Palgrave Macmillan, pp. 23–51

Kazimirski, Anne, Keogh, Peter, Kumari, Vijay, Smith, Ruth, Gowland, Sally, Purdon, Susan and Khanum, Nazia 2009. *Forced Marriage: Prevalence and Service Response.* UK: National Centre for Social Research Report No DCSF-RR128 on behalf of Department for Children, Schools and Families

Kelly, Liz 2002. 'Journeys of Jeopardy: A Review of Research on Trafficking in Women and Children in Europe.' Geneva: IOM

Kelly, Liz 2003. 'The Wrong Debate: Reflections on Why Force is Not the Key Issue With Respect to Trafficking in Women for Sexual Exploitation', *Feminist Review* 72: 139–144

Kelsey, Jane 2006. 'Taking Nurses and Soldiers to Market: Trade Liberalisation and Gendered Neo-colonialism in the Pacific'. Sidney: Opening Plenary Paper to the 15th annual conference on feminist economics

Kelsey, Jane 2008. *Serving Whose Interests? The Political Economy of Trade in Service Agreements.* London: Routledge-Cavendish, Glasshouse

Kenya Land Alliance 2004. *Women, Land and Property Rights and the Land Reforms in Kenya.* Nairobi: Kenya Land Alliance/Fidakenya

Khan, Saira Rahman 2001. 'Reflections on Women and Violence in Bangladesh', Asia Pacific News, 24 June. www.hurights.or.jp/asia-pacific/no_24/05Saira.htm

Khanum, Nazir 2008. *Forced Marriage, Family Cohesion and Community Engagement: National Learning Through a Case Study of Luton.* Luton: Equality in Diversity.

Kittay, Eva Feder 1999. *Love's Labor: Essays in Women, Equality and Dependency.* New York: Routledge

Klein, Naomi 2000. *No Logo.* London: Harper Collins

Kofman, Eleonore 2005. *Gendered Migrations, Livelihoods and Entitlement in European Welfare States.* Geneva: UNRISD paper on Gender Equality: Striving for Justice in an Unequal World

Kouvo, Sari 2005. 'The United Nations and Gender Mainstreaming: Limits and Possibilities' in Buss, Doris and Manji, Ambreena (eds.), pp 237–252

Kraamwinkel, M. 2002. 'The Imagined European Community: Are Housewives European Citizens?', in Conaghan, J., Fischl, R. M. and Klare, K. (eds.), pp. 321–338

Kritzinger, Andrienetta, Barrientos, Stephanie and Rossouw, Hester 2004. 'Global Production and Flexible Employment in South African Horticulture: Experiences of Contract Workers in Fruit Exports', *Sociologia Ruralis* 44 (1): 17–39

Kuenyehia, Akua 1994. 'The Impact of Structural Adjustment Programs on Women's International Human Rights: The Example of Ghana', in Rebecca J. Cook (ed.), *Human Rights of Women.* Philadelphia: Pennsylvania University Press, pp. 442–436

Kumari, Ved 1999. 'Gender Analysis of the Indian Penal Code', in Amita Dhanda and Archana Parashar (eds.), *Engendering Law: Essays in Honor of Lotika Sarkar.* Lucknow: Eastern Book Company, pp. 139–160

Kymlicka, William 1995. *Multicultural Citizenship: A Liberal Theory of Minority Rights.* Oxford University Press

La Strada 2008a. 'Executive Summary: Research on Public Opinion in Regards to Domestic Violence.' www.lastrada.md/actiuni_currente/en.html, last accessed 31 August 2008

La Strada 2008b. 'Moldova Fell to One Tier Down in the US Department of State Trafficking in Persons Report.' http://www.lastrada.md/agenda/en.html% 20 last accessed 31 August 2008

Lacey, N. 2004. 'Feminist Legal Theory and the Rights of Women', in K. Knopp (ed.), *Gender and Human Rights.* Oxford University Press, pp 13–55

Lair, Craig 2006. 'Toward an Application of Global Commodity Chain Analysis to the "Production" of Service Work Providers: The Case of Domestic Workers and Flight Attendants', The American Sociological Association, Montreal Convention Center, Montreal, Quebec, Canada (Paper presented at the annual meeting 10 August www. allacademic.com/meta/p105178_index.html

Law Commission, The 2011. *Adult Social Care.* Report 326 HC941 London: Stationery Office

Lawrence, Felicity 2003. 'Growers' market', *The Guardian*, 17 May

Lawrence, Felicity 2004. 'Force Fed: How Our Newly Industrialised Food System Leads to Environmental and Human Degradation', The Rachel Carson memorial lecture, 3 December

Lawyers Collective 2009. *Staying Alive.* Delhi: Lawyers Collective, Women's Rights Initiative, Third Monitoring and Evaluation Report 2009 on the Protection of Women from Domestic Violence Act, 2005

Lewis, Jane and Giullari, Susanna 2005. 'The Adult Worker Model Family, Gender Equality and Care: The Search for New Policy Principles and the Possibilities and Problems of a Capabilities Approach', *Economy and Society* 34 (1): 76–104

Lewis, Jane and Campbell, Mary 2008. 'What's in a Name? "Work and Family" or "Work and Life" Balance Policies in the UK since 1997 and the Implications for the Pursuit of Gender Equality', *Social Policy and Administration* 42 (5): 524–541

Limanowska, Barbara 2005. *Trafficking in Human Beings in South Eastern Europe*. New York: UNDP on behalf of UNICEF, UNOHCHR and OSCE/ODIHR

Lindstrom, Nicole 2004. 'Regional Sex Trafficking in the Balkans: Transnational Networks in an Enlarged Europe', *Problems of Post-Communism* 51 (3): 45–52

Luce, Stephanie 2005. *The Case for International Labour Standards: A 'Northern' Perspective*. Sussex: IDS Working Paper 20

Maboreke, Mary 2000. 'Understanding Law in Zimbabwe' in Stewart, Ann (ed.), pp. 101–116

MacEoin, Denis 2009. *Sharia Law or One Law for All*. London: Civitas, www.civitas. org.uk

Mackintosh, Maureen and Tibandebage, Paula 2004. *Gender and Health Sector Reform: Analytical Perspectives on African Experience*. Geneva: UNRISD Report on Gender Equality: Striving for Justice in an Unequal World Report

Mahler, Sarah J. 2006. *Gender Matters*. Sussex: *Id21 Insights*, January Institute of Development Studies. www.id21.org/insights

Mama, Amina 1997. 'Sheroes and Villians: Conceptualizing Colonial and Contemporary Violence Against Women in Africa', in M. Jacqui Alexander and Chandra T. Mohanty (eds.), *Feminist Genealogies, Colonial Legacies, Democratic Futures*. New York: Routledge, pp. 46–62

Mandelstam, Michael 2001. *Community Care Practice and the Law*. London: Jessica Kingsley Publishers

Manji, Ambreena 2006. *The Politics of Land Reform in Africa: From Communal Tenure to Free Markets*. London: Zed Books.

Mansoor, Taslima 2006. 'Justice Delayed is Justice Denied: Women and Violence in Bangladesh', *The Daily Star* http://www.thedailystar.net/law/2006/03/02/index.htm

Martin, Philip L. 2006. *GATS, Migration, and Labor Standards*. Geneva: International Institute for Labour Studies, Discussion paper on Decent Work Research Programme, DP/165/2006

Massey, Doreen 1994. *Space, Place and Gender*. Cambridge: Polity Press

Matembe, Miria 2002. *Gender, Politics and Constitution Making in Uganda*. Kampala: Fountain Publishers

Matsushita, Mitsuo, Schoenbaum, Thomas J. and Mavroidis, Petros 2006. *The World Trade Organization: Law, Practice and Policy*. Oxford University Press

Matthews, Roger 2005. 'Policing Prostitution: Ten Years On', *British Journal of Criminology* 45 (6): 877–895

Mazumdar, Indrani 2006. 'Impact of Globalisation on Women Workers in Garment Exports – The Indian Experience', in Veena Jha (ed.), *Trade, Globalisation and Gender– Evidence from South Asia*. UNIFEM-UNCTAD, pp. 91–152

Mbilinyi, Majorie 1988. 'Runaway Wives in Colonial Tanganyika', *International Journal of Sociology of Law* 16: 1–29

McAuslan, Patrick 1998. 'Making Law Work: Restructuring Law Relations in Africa', *Development and Change* 29 (3): 525–552

McAuslan, Patrick 2003. *Bringing the Law Back In: Essays in Land, Law and Development*. Basingstoke: Ashgate

McClintock, Annie 1992. 'Screwing the System: Sexwork, Race, and the Law', *Boundary* 2 19(2): 70–95

McClintock, Annie 1993. 'Family Feuds: Gender, Nationalism and the Family', *Feminist Review* 44: 61–80

McColgan, Aileen 2005. *Discrimination Law: Text, Cases and Materials*. Oxford: Hart Publishing

McDonald, Ann 2001. 'Care in the Community' in Lesley-Anne Cull and Jeremy Roche (eds.), *The Law and Social Work: Contemporary Issues of Practice*. Buckingham: Palgrave and Open University, pp. 146–154

McLoughlin, S. 2009 'Writing British Asian Cities', *Contemporary South Asia* 17 (4): 437–447

McNeill, Desmond and St Clair, Asuncion Lera 2009. *Global Poverty, Ethics and Human Rights: The Role of the Multilateral Organsations*. London: Routledge

Mehdi, Rubya 2001. *Gender and Property Law in Pakistan: Resources and Discourses*. Copenhagen: DJØF Publishing

Mehra, Madhu 2007. 'Women's Equality and Culture in the Context of Identity Politics', in *Journal of Comparative Law* 2 (2): 1–32

Melissaris, E. 2004. 'The More the Merrier: A New Take on Legal Pluralism', *Social and Legal Studies* 13 (1): 57–79

Mensah, K., Mackintosh, M. and Henry, L. 2005. *The 'Skills Drain' of Health Professionals from the Developing World: A Framework for Policy Formulation*. London: Medact

Menski, Werner 1993. 'Asians in Britain and the Question of Adaptation to a New Legal Order: Asian Laws in Britain?', in M. Israel and N. K. Wagle (eds.), *Ethnicity, Identity, and Migration: The South Asian Context*. University of Toronto, pp. 238–268

Menski, Werner and Pearl, David 1998. *Muslim Family Law*. London: Sweet & Maxwell

Menski, Werner and Shah, Prakash (eds.) 2006. *Migration, Diasporas and Legal Systems in Europe*. London: Routledge Cavendish

Merry, Sally Engle 1988. 'Legal Pluralism', *Law and Society Review* 22 (5): 869–896

Merry, Sally Engle 1991. 'Law and Colonialism', *Law and Society Review* 25 (4): 889–992

Merry, Sally Engle 2001. 'Rights, Religion, and Community: Approaches to Violence Against Women in the Context of Globalization', *Law and Society Review* 35 (1): 39–88

Merry, Sally Engle 2006. *Human Rights and Gender Violence: Translating International Law into Local Justice*. The University of Chicago Press

Mills, E. J., Schabas, W. A., Volmink, J., Walker, R., Ford, N., Katabira, E., Aranka, A., Joffres, M., Cahn, P. and Montaner, J. 2008. 'Should Active Recruitment of Health Workers from Sub-Saharan Africa Be Viewed as a Crime?', *The Lancet* 371 (23): 685–688

Ministry of Lands and Housing (Kenya) 2005a. *Draft National Land Policy*. Nairobi: MLH

Ministry of Lands and Housing (Kenya) 2005b. *Issues and Recommendations Report*. Nairobi: MLH

Ministry of Lands (Kenya) 2007. *National Land Policy (May)*. Nairobi: National Land Policy Secretariat Ministry of Lands. www.ardhi.go.ke/

Minnesota Advocates for Human Rights 2000. *Domestic Violence in Moldova*. www.mnadvocates.org

Mitter, Swasi 1985. 'Industrial Restructuring and Manufacturing Homework: Immigrant Women in the UK Clothing Industry', *Capital and Class* 9 (3): 37–80

Moffat, Graham 2007. 'Work-Life Balance and Employment Law', in Rebecca Probert (ed.), *Family Law and Life: Under One Roof*. Ashgate: Aldershot, pp. 135–158

Mohanty, Chandra. T., Russo, A. and Torres, Lourdes (eds.) 1991. *Third World Women and the Politics of Feminism.* Bloomington: Indiana University Press

Molyneux, Maxine 1985. 'Mobilization Without Emancipation? Women's Interests, the State and Revolution in Nicaragua', *Feminist Studies* 11 (2): 227–254

Molyneux, Maxine and Razavi, Shahira 2002. 'Introduction' in Maxine Molyneux and Shahira Razavi (eds.), *Gender Justice, Development and Rights.* Oxford University Press, pp. 1–42

Muchlinski, Peter 2007. *Multinational Enterprises and the Law.* Oxford: The Oxford International Law Library

Mullally, Siobhan 2004. 'Feminism and Multicultural Dilemmas in India: Revisiting the Shah Bano Case', *Oxford Journal of Legal Studies* 24 (4): 671–692

Mullally, Siobhan 2006. *Gender, Culture and Human Rights.* Oxford: Hart Publishing

Mullally, Siobhan 2007. 'Women, Islamisation and Human Rights in Pakistan', in Javaid Rehman and Susan C. Breau (eds.), *Religion, Human Rights and International Law: A Critical Examination of Islamic State Practices.* The Hague: Martinus Nijhoff, pp. 379–408

Mundlak, Guy 2009. 'Deterritorialising Labor Law', *Law and Ethics of Human Rights* 3 (2): Article 4

Muslim Arbitration Tribunal 2008. 'Liberation from Forced Marriages.' www.matribunal.com/

Naffine, Ngaire 2002. 'In Praise of Legal Feminism', *Legal Studies* 22 (1): 71–101

Nair, J. 1996. *Women and the Law in Colonial India: A Social History.* New Delhi: Kali for Women

NCW (National Commission for Women), India 2006. *Report on Problems Relating to NRI Marriages: Legal and Other Interventions on NRI Marriages.* Delhi: National Commission for Women

Nedelsky, Jennifer 1993. 'Reconceiving Rights as Relationship', *Review of Constitutional Studies* 1: 1–26

Nedelsky, Jennifer 1997. 'Embodied Diversity and the Challenges of law', *McGill Law Journal* 42: 91–117

Nedelsky, Jennifer 2000. 'Communities of Judgment and Human Rights', *Theoretical Inquiries in Law* 1 (2): 245–282

NEF (New Economics Foundation) 2006. *Migration and the Remittances Euphoria: Development or Dependency?* London: NEF. www.neweconomics.org

NHS 2004. 'Code of Practice for the International Recruitment of Health Care Professionals.' www.dh.gov.uk/prod_consum_dh/groups/dh_digitalassets/@dh/@en/documents/digitalasset/dh_4097734.pdf

Nielson, Julia 2002. *Current Regimes for Temporary Movement of Service Providers: Labour Mobility in Regional Trade Agreements.* Paris: OECD hosting joint WTO-World Bank Symposium on Movement of Natural Persons (mode 4) Under the GATS on 11–12 April. Reported at www.wto.org/english/tratop_e/serv_e/symp_apr_02_nielson1_e.doc

Nnaemeka, Obioma 2003. 'Nego-feminism: Theorizing, Practicing, and Pruning Africa's Way' *Signs: Journal of Women in Culture and Society* 29 (2): 357–385

Noddings, Nel 1984. *Caring: A Feminine Approach to Ethics and Moral Education.* Berkeley: University of California Press

Nussbaum, Martha 1999a. 'Women and Equality: The Capabilities Approach', *International Labour Review* 138 (3) 227–245

Nussbaum, Martha 1999b. *Sex and Social Justice*. Oxford University Press.

Nussbaum, Martha 2002. 'Women's Capabilities and Social Justice', in Maxine Molyneuz and Shahira Razavi, (eds.), *Gender Justice Development and Rights*. Oxford University Press, pp. 45–77

Nussbaum, Martha and Glover, J. 1995. *Women, Culture and Development: A Study of Human Capabilities*. Oxford: Clarendon Press

Nyamu, Celestine 2000. 'How Should Human Rights and Development Respond to Cultural Legitimization of Gender Hierarchy in Developing Countries?', *Harvard International Law Journal* 41: 381–408

Nyamu-Musembi, Celestine 2002. 'Are Local Norms and Practices Fences or Pathways? The Example of Women' Property Rights' in An Na'im and Hammond (ed.), pp. 126–150

Nyamu-Musembi, Celestine 2006. *Breathing Life into Dead Theories about Property Rights: De Soto and Land Relations in Rural Africa*. Brighton: Institute of Development Studies Working Paper 272

Obbo, Christine 1989. 'Sexuality and Economic Domination in Uganda', in Nira Yuval Davis and Flora Anthias (eds.), *Women, Nation, State*. London: Macmillan Press, pp 71–91

O'Connell Davidson, Julia 1998. *Prostitution, Power and Freedom*. Cambridge: Polity Press

O'Connell Davidson, Julia 2002. 'The Rights and Wrongs of Prostitution', *Hypatia* 17 (2): 84–98

O'Connell Davidson, Julia and Anderson, Bridget (eds.) 2006. 'The Trouble with "Trafficking"' in Christien L. van den Anker and Jeroen Doomernik (eds.), *Trafficking and Women's Rights Series – Women's Rights In Europe*. London: Palgrave Macmillan, pp. 11–26

ODI (Overseas Development Agency) 2010. *Millenium Development Goals Report Card: Measuring Progress Across Countries*. London: ODI

Odgaard, Rie and Bentzon, Agnete Weis 2007. 'Rural Women's Access to Landed Property: Unearthing the Realities within an Eastern African Setting', in Hellum, Anne, Ali, Shaheen Sardar, Stewart, J and Tsanga, A (eds.), pp. 202–235

Odonga Mwaka, Beatrice 1998. *Widowhood and Property Among the Baganda of Uganda: Uncovering the Passive Victim*. UK: Warwick University thesis

O'Donovan, Katherine 1985. *Sexual Divisions in Law*. London: Weidenfeld & Nicolson

O'Donovan, Katherine 1993. *Family Law Matters*. London: Pluto Press

OECD 2000. *Employment Outlook*. Paris: OECD

OECD 2009. *Is Informal Normal? Towards More and Better Jobs in Developing Countries*. Paris: OECD

Okin, Susan Moller 1982. 'Women and the Making of the Sentimental Family', *Philosophy and Public Affairs* 11 (1): 65–88

Okin, Susan Moller 1998. 'Feminism and Multiculturalism: Some Tensions', *Ethics* 108 (4) 661–684

Okin Susan Moller 1999. 'Is Multiculturalism Bad for Women?' in Joshua Cohen, Mathew Howard and Martha Nussbaum (eds.), *Is Multiculturalism Bad for Women?* Princeton University Press, pp. 7–24

Okin, Susan Moller 2002. '"Mistresses of Their Own Destiny": Group Rights, Gender and Realistic Rights of Exit', *Ethics* 112: 205–230

Oloka-Onyango, Joseph and Tamale, Sylvia 1995. '"The Personal is Political," or Why Women's Rights are Indeed Human Rights: An African Perspective on International Feminism', *Human Rights Quarterly* 17: 691–731

Ong'wen, O. 2008. 'Understanding Kenya: Post-election Crisis, Land and the Interim EPA', International Centre for Trade and Sustainable Development, *Trade Negotiations Insights* 7 (5) 9–10. http://ictsd.net/programmes/epas/

Onoria, Henry 2002 'Introduction to the African System of Protection of Human Rights and the Draft Protocol', in W. Benedick, E. Kisaakye and G. Oberleitner (eds) *The Human Rights of Women: International Instruments and African Experiences* London: Zed Books, pp. 231–242

ONS 2001. *Living in Britain: General Household Survey 2001*. London: HMSO

ONS 2002. *Carers 2000*. London: HMSO

ONS 2008. *Labour Force Survey*. London: HMSO

Ontiveros, M. L. 2002. 'A New Course for Labour Unions: Identity-Based Organizing as a Response to Globalization', in Conaghan, J. Fischl, R. M. and Klare, K. (eds.), pp. 417–428

Orford, Anne 2002. 'Feminism, Imperialism and the Mission of International Law', *Nordic Journal of International Law* 71: 275–296

Otto, Dianne 1999. 'A Post-Beijing Reflection on the Limitations and Potential of Human Rights Discourse for Women', in Kelly D. Aksin and Dorean M. Koenig (eds.), *Women and Human Rights*. Ardsley, NY: Transnational Publishers, pp. 115–135

Oxfam 2004. *Trading Away Our Rights: Women Working in Global Supply Chains*. Oxford: Oxfam. www.maketradefair.com

Pantiru, Maria Christina, Black, Richard and Sabates-Wheeler, Rachel 2007. *Migration and Poverty Reduction in Moldova*. Sussex: Development Research Centre on Migration, Globalisation and Poverty: Working Paper C10

Parashar, Archana 1992. *Women and Family Law Reform in India*. New Delhi: Sage

Parekh, Bhikhu 2000. *Rethinking Multiculturalism: Cultural Diversity and Political Theory*. Basingstoke and New York: Palgrave

Parmar, Alpa and Sampson, Alice 2005. *Tackling Domestic Violence: Providing Advocacy and Support to Survivors from Black and Other Minority Ethnic Communities*. London: Home Office Development and Practice Report

Parpart, Jane 1988. 'Sexuality and Power in the Zambian Copperbelt 1926–1964', in S. Stichter and Jane, L. Parpart (eds), *Patriarchy and Class: African Women in the Home and Workforce*. Boulder, Colorado: Westview Press, pp 141–160

Parpart, Jane 2000. 'The Widow Refuses: Embodied Practices and Negotiations over Inheritance', in Gillian Youngs (ed.), *Political Economy, Power and the Body: Global Perspectives*. London: Macmillan, pp. 159–179

Parreñas, Rhacel 2001. *Servants of Globalisation: Women, Migration and Domestic Work*. Stanford University Press

Parreñas, Rhacel 2005. 'Long Distance Intimacy: Class, Gender and Intergenerational Relations between Mothers and Children in Filipino Transnational Families', *Global Networks* 5 (4): 317–336

Patel, Pragna 2008. 'Faith In The State? Asian Women's Struggles for Human Rights in the U.K.', *Feminist Legal Studies* 16 (1): 9–36

Patel, Reena 2007. *Hindu Women's Property Rights in Rural India: Law Labour and Culture in Action*. Aldershot: Ashgate

Pearson, Ruth 2003. 'Feminist Responses to Economic Globalisation: Some Examples of Past and Future Practice', *Gender and Development* 11 (1): 25–34

Pearson, Ruth 2007. 'Beyond Women Workers: Gendering CSR', *Third World Quarterly* 28 (4): 731–749

Philippines Government 2008. 'Labour Force Survey 2008.' www.census.gov.ph/data/pressrelease/2008/lf0801tx.html

Philippines Migrants Rights Watch 2004. *Philippine Migration: Challenges to Hurdle. An Alternative Report.* New Manila: Philippine Migrants Rights Watch. www.pmrw.org

Phillips, Anne 2002a. 'Feminism and the Politics of Difference. Or Where Have All the Women Gone?', in Susan James and Stephanie Palmer (eds.), *Visible Women: Essays on Feminist Legal Theory and Political Philosophy.* Oxford: Hart Publishing, pp. 11–28

Phillips, Anne 2002b. 'Multiculturalism, Universalism and the Claims of Democracy' in Molyneux, M. and Razavi, S. (eds.), pp. 115–138

Phillips, Anne 2003. 'When Culture Means Gender: Issues of Cultural Defence in the English Courts', *Modern Law Review* 66 (4): 510–531

Phillips, Anne 2007. *Multiculturalism without Culture.* Princeton and Oxford: Princeton University Press

Phillips, Anne and Dustin, Moira 2004. 'UK Initiatives on Forced Marriage: Regulation, Dialogue and Exit', *Political Studies* 52 (3): 531–551

Physicians for Human Rights 2004. *An Action Plan to Prevent Brain Drain: Building Equitable Health Systems in Africa.* Boston, MA: Physicians for Human Rights

Pinnawala, Mallika 2008. 'Engaging in the Trans-local Management of Households', *Gender, Technology and Development* 12 (3): 439–459

Piper, Nicola 2005. *Gender and Migration.* Geneva: Global Commission on International Migration.' www.gcim.org

Platt, L. 2006. *Pay Gaps: The Position of Ethnic Minority Women and Men.* Manchester: EOC.

Pogge, Thomas (ed.) 2001. *Global Justice.* Oxford: Blackwell

Pogge, Thomas 2002. *World Poverty and Human Rights.* Cambridge: Polity Press

Prada, Juan Martin 2006. *Economies of Affectivity.* www.vinculo-a.net/english_site/text_prada.html

Puri Lakshmi 2004. 'Trade in Services, Gender and Development: A Tale of Two Models', in Anh-Nga Tran-Nguyen and Americo Beviglia Zampetti (eds.), *Trade and Gender: Opportunities and Challenges for Developing Countries.* UN Inter-Agency Network on Women and Gender Equality Task Force on Gender and Trade. New York and Geneva: UNCTAD, pp. 223–250

Purvanneckiene, Giedre 2009. *Equal Sharing of Responsibilities Between Women and Men: Reflection on European Policies.* New York: Interactive Expert Panel on Capacity-building for mainstreaming a gender perspective into national policies and programmes to support the equal sharing of responsibilities between women and men, including care-giving in the context of HIV/AIDS, at the UN Commission on the Status of Women, 53rd Session

Radin, Margaret Jane and Sunder, Madhavi 2005. 'Introduction: the Subject and Object of Commodification', in Martha M. Ertman and Joan C. Williams (eds.), *Rethinking Commodification: Cases and Readings in Law and Culture.* New York University Press, pp. 8–29

Rai, Shirin M. 2002. *Gender and the Political Economy of Development.* Cambridge: Polity Press

Rai, Shirin M. 2007. 'Deliberative Democracy and the Politics of Redistribution: The Case of the Indian Panchayats', *Hypatia* 22 (4): 64–80

Rajan, Rajeswari Sunder 2004. 'Rethinking Law and Violence: The Domestic Violence (Prevention) Bill in India 2002', *Gender and History* 16 (3): 769–793

Ramamurthy, Priti 2000. 'The Cotton Commodity Chain: Women, Work and Agency in India and Japan: The Case for Feminist Agro-Food Systems Research', *World Development* 28 (3): 551–578

Ramesh, Randeep 2010. 'Food Standards Agency to be abolished by Health Secretary', *The Guardian*, 12 July. www.guardian.co.uk/politics/2010/jul/11/food-standards-agency-abolished-health-secretary

Ranger, Terence 1983. 'The Invention of Tradition', in T. Ranger and E. Hobsbawm (eds.), *The Invention of Tradition*. Cambridge University Press, pp. 1–14

Rawls, John 1971. *A Theory of Justice*. Cambridge MA: Harvard University Press

Rawls, John 1999. *The Law of Peoples*. Cambridge MA: Harvard University Press

Razavi, Shahra 2003. 'Introduction: Agrarian Change, Gender and Land Rights', *Journal of Agrarian Change* 3 (1–2): 2–32

Razavi, Shahra 2007. *The Political and Social Economy of Care in a Development Context: Conceptual Issues, Research Questions and Policy Options*. Geneva: UNRISD Gender and Development Programme Paper no. 3

Razavi, Shahra 2009. *Sharing Care More Equally in an Unequal World*. New York: Interactive Expert Panel on Capacity-building for mainstreaming a gender perspective into national policies and programmes to support the equal sharing of responsibilities between women and men, including care-giving in the context of HIV/AIDS, at the UN Commission on the Status of Women, 53rd Session

Razavi, Shahra and Staab, Silke 2010 'Underpaid and Overworked – A Cross-National Perspective on Care Workers', *Special Edition of International Labor Review* 149 (4): 000

RCP (Regional Clearing Point) 2003. *First Annual Report on Victims of Trafficking in South Eastern Europe*. IOM/Stability Pact for South Eastern Europe/ICMC. www.iom.hu/PDFs/First%20Annual%20Report%20on%20VoT%20in%20SEE.pdf

Reddy, Rupa 2008. 'Gender, Culture and the Law: Approaches to "Honour Crimes" in the UK', *Feminist Legal Studies* 16 (3): 305–321

Reilly, Adrienne A. 2006. 'Slavery Legislation vs Trafficking Legislation in Prosecuting the Crime of Female Sexual Slavery: An International Law Perspective', in Anker, Christien L. van den and Doomernik, Jeroen (eds.), pp. 89–137

Rittich, Kerry 2002. *Recharacterizing Restructuring: Law, Distribution and Gender in Market Reform*. The Hague: Kluwer Law International

Robinson, Fiona 1999. *Globalizing Care: Ethics, Feminist Theory and International Relations*. Oxford: Westview Press

Rodriguez, Robyn 2003. 'Globalization and State "Experimentalism": International Migration and the "Labor Brokering" Philippine State', Paper presented at the American Sociological Association, Atlanta, annual meeting. www.allacademic.com/meta/p107193_index.html

Rodriguez, Robyn 2005. *Domestic Insecurities: Female Migration from the Philippines, Development and Subject-Status*. California: Centre for Comparative Immigration Studies, University of California, San Diego, Working Paper 114

Rwezaura, Bart 1989. 'The Changing Role of the Extended Family in Providing Economic Support for an Individual in Africa', *Bayreuth African Studies Series* (BASS): 57–89

Samad, Yunas and Eade, John 2002. *Community Perceptions of Forced Marriage*. London: FCO.

Sanchez-Taylor, Jacqueline 2001. 'Dollars Are a Girl's Best Friend? Female Tourists' Sexual Behaviour in the Caribbean', *Sociology* 35 (3): 749–64

Sandbu, Martin 2009. 'The Tobin Tax Explained', *Financial Times*, 27 August. www.ft.com/cms/s/0/6210e49c-9307–11de-b146–00144feabdc0.html

Santos, Boaventura, De Sousa 2002. *Toward a New Legal Common Sense: Law, Globalization, and Emancipation*. London: Butterworths

Santos, Boaventura, De Sousa and Rodriguez-Garavito, Cesar (eds.) 2005. *Law and Globalization from Below: Towards a Cosmopolitan Legality*. Cambridge University Press

Sarfaty, Galit A. 2007. 'Doing Good Business or Just Doing Good: Competing Human Rights Frameworks at the World Bank', in Bronwen Morgan (ed.), *The Intersection of Rights and Regulation: New Directions in Sociolegal Scholarship*. Aldershot: Ashgate Press, pp. 93–106

Sarkar, Tanikar 2000. 'A Prehistory Of Rights: The Age Of Consent Debate In Colonial Bengal', *Feminist Studies* 26 (3) 601–622

Sassen, Saskia 2002. 'Women's Burden: Counter Geographies of Globalization and the Feminization of Survival', *Nordic Journal of International Law* 71: 255–274

Satterthwaite M. 2005. 'Crossing Borders, Claiming Rights: Using Human Rights Law to Empower Women Migrant Workers', *Yale Human Rights and Development Law Journal* 8: 1–66

Schech, Susanne and Dev, Sanjugta Vas 2007. 'Gender Justice: The World Bank's New Approach to the Poor?', *Development in Practice* 17 (1): 14–26

Seal, Rebecca and Wiseman, Eva 2009. 'Abducted Abused Raped Survived'. *The Guardian* 11 January. available at www.guardian.co.uk/world/2009/jan/11/british-asian-forced-marriages

Sen, Amartya 1999. *Development as Freedom*. Oxford University Press

Sen, Amartya 2009. *The Idea of Justice*. London: Allen Lane

Sen, Samita 1999. *Women and Labour in Late Colonial India: The Bengal Jute Industry*. Cambridge University Press

Sevenhuijsen, Selma 1998. *Citizenship and the Ethics of Care: Feminist Considerations on Justice, Morality and Politics*. London: Routledge

Sevenhuijsen, Selma 2003. 'In Place of Care: The Relevance of the Feminist Ethic of Care for Social Policy', *Feminist Theory* 4 (2): 179–197

Shachar, Ayelet 2001. *Multicultural Jurisdictions: Cultural Differences and Women's Rights*. Cambridge University Press

Shaffer, G. 2003. *Defending Interests. Public Private Partners in WTO*. Washington DC: Brookings Institution Press

Shah-Kazami, Sonia Nurin 2001. *Untying the Knot: Muslim Women, Divorce and the Shariah*. London: Nuffield Foundation

Shah, Nafisa 2007. 'Making of Crime, Custom and Culture: The Case of Karo Kari Killings in Upper Sindh', in Jennifer Bennett (ed.), *Scratching the Surface: Democracy, Traditions, Gender*. Pakistan/Afghanistan (Lahore): Heinrich Böll Foundation pp. 135–156

Shah, Prakash 2002. *Bangladeshis in English Law*. London: Guildhall University Conference 'Bangladeshis in Britain: Changes and Choices, Configurations and Perspectives'

Shah, Prakash 2005. *Legal Pluralism in Conflict: Coping with Cultural Diversity in Law*. London: Glass House

Shaheed, Fareda 2009. *Gender, Religion and the Quest for Justice in Pakistan. Final Research Report for Religion Politics and Gender Equality*. Geneva: UNRISD

Shahid, Ayesha 2010. *Silent Voices, Untold Stories: Women Domestic Workers in Pakistan and their Struggle for Empowerment*. Oxford University Press

Shammy, Farah Jabin 2002. 'Fatwa and the Helpless Women in Bangladesh', *New Nation*, 18 December

Shaw, Alison 2001. 'Kinship, Cultural Preference and Immigration: Consanguineous Marriage among British Pakistanis', *Journal of the Royal Anthropological Institute* 7: 315–35

Shaw, Alison and Charsley, Katherine 2006. 'Rishtas: Adding Emotion to Strategy in Understanding British Pakistani Transnational Marriages', *Global Networks* 6 (4): 405–421

Shivji, Issa 1993. *The Concept of Human Rights in Africa*. London and Dhaka: CODESRIA

Siddiqi, Dina M. 2005. 'Of Consent and Contradiction: Forced Marriages in Bangladesh', in Welchman, L. and Hossain, S. (eds.), pp. 282–307

Siddiqi, Dina M. 2006. *Ain o Salish Kendra: Twenty years on the Frontline*. Dhaka: Ain o Salish Kendra (ASK) www.askbd.org/

Siddiqui, Hannana 2005. 'There Is No "Honour" in Domestic Violence, Only Shame! Women's Struggles Against "Honour" Crimes in the UK', in Welchman, L. and Hossain, S. (eds.), pp. 263–281

Siddiqui, Nadia, Ismail, Sajida and Allen, Meg 2008. *Safe to Return? Pakistani Women, Domestic Violence and Access to Refugee Protection*. South Manchester Law Centre in conjunction with Manchester Metropolitan University

Silbey Susan, S. 1997. '"Let Them Eat Cake": Globalization, Postmodern Colonialism, and the Possibilities of Justice', *Law and Society Review* 31 (2): 207–235

Skills for Care 2007. *National Survey of Care Workers. Final Report* JN 142079 November TNS UK

Sklar, Judith 1990. *The Faces of Injustice*. New Haven, CT: Yale University Press

Smith, Sally, Auret, Diana, Barrientos, Stephanie, Dolar, Catherine, Kleinbooi, Karin, Njobvu, Chosani, Opondo, Maggie and Tallontire, Anne 2004. *Ethical Trade in African Horticulture: Gender, Rights and Participation*. Institute of Development Studies, University of Sussex

Snyder, Francis 1999. 'Governing Economic Globalisation: Global Legal Pluralism and European Law', *European Law Journal* 5 (4): 334–374

Solomon, Scott 2005. 'Migration, the State and Democracy: The Case of the Philippines', Paper to the Annual meeting of the International Studies Association. www.allaca demic.com/one/prol/prol01/index.php?cmd=prol01_search&offset=0&limit=5&multi_ search_search_mode=publication&multi_search_publication_fulltext_mod=full text&textfield_submit=true&search_module=multi_search&search=Search&sea rch_field=title_idx&fulltext_search=Migration%2C+the+State%2C+and+Democracy %3A+The+Case+of+the+Philippines

Spivak, Gayatri Chatrovorty 1998. 'Can the Subaltern Speak', in Cary Nelson and Lawrence Grossberg (eds.), *Marxism and the Interpretation of Culture.* Abana and Chicago: University of Illinois Press, pp. 271–315

(The) Statesman 2007. 'The Informal Sector in Ghana' 30 April 2007.

Steiner, Henry J., Alston, Philip and Goodman, Ryan 2008. *International Human Rights in Context: Law, Politics, Morals.* Oxford University Press

Stevens, Christopher 2005a. *Impacts and Challenges of Multilateral and Bilateral Trade Agreements on Africa.* Tunis: African Development Bank Economic Research Working Paper 79

Stevens, Christopher 2005b. *Creating a Development Friendly EU Trade Policy.* Sussex: IDS Briefing Paper

Stevens, Christopher and Keenan, Jane 2000. *Will Africans' Participation in Horticulture Chains Survive Liberalisation?* Sussex: IDS Working Paper 106

Stevens, Christopher and Keenan, Jane 2004. *Making Trade Preferences More Effective.* Sussex: IDS Briefing Paper

Stewart, Ann 1993. 'The Dilemmas of Women's Legal Development', in Abdul Paliwala and Sam Adelman (eds.), *Law, Crisis and Underdevelopment.* London: Heinemann, pp. 219–242

Stewart, Ann 1996 'Should Women Give Up On The State?', in S. Rai and G. Lievesley (eds.), *Women and the International State.* London: Taylor & Francis, pp. 23–44

Stewart, Ann (ed.) 2000. *Gender, Law and Social Justice.* Oxford: Blackstone

Stewart, Ann 2004. *Aspirations to Actions: 25 years of CEDAW.* London: British Council

Stewart, Ann 2005. 'Choosing Care: Dilemmas of a Social Market', *Journal of Social Welfare and Family Law* 27 (3–4): 299–324

Stewart, Ann 2007. 'Home or Home: Caring About and For Elderly Family Members in a Welfare State', in Rebecca Probert (ed.), *Family Law and Life: Under One Roof.* Aldershot: Ashgate, pp. 159–177

Stewart, Julie 1998. 'Why I Can't Teach Customary Law', in J. Eekelaar and T. Nhlapo (eds.), *The Changing Family: Family Forms and Family Law.* Oxford: Hart Publishing, pp. 217–229

Stewart, Julie and Tsanga, Amy 2007. 'The Widows' and Female Child's Portion: The Twisted Path to Partial Equality for Widows and Daughters under Customary Law in Zimbabwe', in Hellum, A., Ali, S., Stewart, J. and Tsanga, A. (eds.), pp. 407–436

Stiglitz, Joseph 2002. *Globalization and Its Discontents.* London: Allen Lane

(The) Strategy Unit 2008. *Food Matters: Towards a Strategy for the Twenty First Century.* London: Cabinet Office. www.foodsecurity.ac.uk/assets/pdf/cabinet-office-food-matters.pdf

Sutherland, Stewart 1999. *With Respect to Old Age: Long Term Care – Rights and Responsibilities.* London: HMSO Royal Commission on Long Term Care

Tallontire, Anne 2007. 'CSR and Regulation: Towards a Framework for Understanding Private Standards Initiatives in the Agri-food Chain', *Third World Quarterly* 28 (4): 775–791

Tamale, Sylvia 1999. *When Hens Begin to Crow: Gender and Parliamentary Politics in Uganda.* Kampala: Fountain Publishers

Tamale, Sylvia 2006. 'Eroticism, Sensuality and Women's Secrets Among the Baganda', *IDS Bulletin* (Sexuality Matters) 37 (5): 89–97

Tamale, Sylvia 2008. 'The Right to Culture and the Culture of Rights: A Critical Perspective on Women's Sexual Rights in Africa', *Feminist Legal Studies* 16: 47–69

Tamanaha Brian Z. 2000. 'A Non-Essentialist Version of Legal Pluralism', *Journal of Law and Society* 27: 296–321

Tamanaha Brian Z. 2008. 'Understanding Legal Pluralism: Past to Present, Local to Global', *Sidney Law Review* 30: 375–411

Tarkowska, Elzbieta 2002. 'Intra-household Gender Inequality: Hidden Dimensions of Poverty Among Polish Women', *Communist and Post-Communist Studies* 35 (4): 411–432

Taylor, Mathew 2007. 'Family Tributes to Polish Care Worker Gunned Down in London', *Guardian* 5 October. www.guardian.co.uk/uk/2007/oct/05/ukguns.world

Taylor, Rebecca 2007. 'London's Twenty First Century Slave Trade.' *Time Out*, March www.timeout.com/london/big-smoke/blog/2729/London-s_twenty-first-century_slave_trade.html

Tett, Gillian 2009, 'Could "Tobin tax" reshape financial sector DNA?' *Financial Times*, 27 August www.ft.com/cms/s/0/980e9ec8-92f2-11de-b146-00144feabdc0.html

Teubner, Gunter 1992. 'The Two Faces of Janus: Rethinking Legal Pluralism', *Cardozo Law Review* 13: 1443–1462

Third World Quarterly 2006. Vol 27 (7) (special edition)

Tiraspol Times 2008. 'Moldovan Sex Slaves Released in UK Human Trafficking Raids' 22 April

Toner, Helen 2007. 'Immigration Law and Family Life – a Happy Marriage', in Rebecca Probert (ed.), *Family Law and Life: Under One Roof*. Aldershot: Ashgate, pp. 197–221

Townsend, Mark 2007. '"Sex Slaves" Win Cash in Landmark Legal Deal', *The Observer*, 16 December

Tripp, Aili Mari 2002. 'The Politics of Women's Rights and Cultural Diversity in Uganda', in Maxine Molyneux and Shahira Razavi (eds.), *Gender Justice, Development and Rights*. Oxford University Press, pp. 413–440

Tronto, Joan 1994. *Moral Boundaries: A Political Argument for an Ethic of Care*. London: Routledge

Trubek, David 2006. 'The Rule of Law in Development Assistance' in David Trubek and Alvaro Santos (eds.), *The New Law and Economic Development: A Critical Appraisal*. New York: Cambridge University Press, pp. 74–94

Trubek, David 2009. 'The Political Economy of the Rule of Law: The Challenge of the New Developmental State', *Hague Journal on the Rule of Law* 1: 28–32

Trubek, David and Galanter, Marc 1974. 'Scholars in Self-Estrangement: Some Reflections on the Crisis in Law and Development Studies in the United States', *Wisconsin Law Review* 4: 1062–1101

Truong, T. 1990. *Sex, Money and Morality: Prostitution and Tourism in Southeast Asia*. London: Zed Books

Tsuma, Lawrence 2000. 'Political Economy of the World Bank's Legal Framework', in Faundez, Julio, Footer, Mary E. and Norton, Joseph (eds.), pp 7–27

Turner, Bryan S. 2001. 'Risks, Rights and Regulation: An Overview', *Health, Risk and Society* 3 (1): 9–18

Twining, William 2000. *Globalisation and Legal Theory*. London: Butterworths

Ungerson, Clare 2004. 'Whose Empowerment and Independence? A Cross-national Perspective on "Cash for Care" Schemes', *Ageing and Society*, 24: 189–212

Ungerson, Clare and Yeandle, Sue (eds.) 2007. *Cash for Care in Developed Welfare States*. Basingstoke: Palgrave Macmillan

Ungureanu, Larisa 2006. 'Gender Barometer in the Republic of Moldova: An unprecedented project'. www.azi.md/news?id=42243

UN 2001. 'Background Briefing on Intersectionality'. Working Group on Women and Human Rights, 45th session of the UN CSW

UNCTAD 2003. *Increasing the Participation of Developing Countries through Liberalization of Market Access in GATS Mode 4 for Movement of Natural Persons Supplying Services*. Geneva: UNCTAD Secretariat to the Trade and Development Board Note

UNCTAD 2004a. *Trade and Gender: Opportunities and Challenges for Developing Countries*. New York and Geneva: UN

UNCTAD 2004b. *Report of the Expert Meeting on Market Access Issues in Mode 4 (Movement of Natural Persons to Supply Services) and Effective Implementation of Article IV on Increasing the Participation of Developing Countries*. New York and Geneva: UNCTAD Note, Ninth Session 71: TD/B/Com.1/

UNCTAD 2005. *Trade in Services and Development Implications*: Note by UNCTAD Secretariat for the Trade and Development Board; 9th Session, Geneva, 14–18 March. TD/B/COM.1/71, 20 January 2005

UNDP 2007–2008. *Human Development Report 2007–8: Fighting Climate Change: Human Solidarity in a Divided World*. New York: UNDP

UNICEF (Somalia) 2004. *Eradication of female genital mutilation – An advocacy paper*. www.unicef.org/somalia/SOM_FGM_Advocacy_Paper.pdf

UNIFEM 2006. *The Story behind the Numbers: Women and Employment in Central and Eastern Europe and the Western Commonwealth of Independent States*. UNIFEM Central and Eastern European regional office

UNRISD 2005. *Gender Equality: Striving for Justice in an Unequal World*. www.unrisd. org/unrisd/website/document.nsf/0/1FF4AC64C1894EAAC1256FA3005E7201? OpenDocument

Vachudova, Milada Anna 2000. 'Eastern Europe as Gatekeeper: The Immigration and Asylum Policies of an Enlarging European Union', in Peter Andreas and Timothy Snyder (eds.), *The Wall Around the West: State Borders and Immigration Controls in North America and Europe*. Lanham, MD: Rowman and Littlefield, pp 153–166

Vertovec, Stephen 2007. *New Complexities of Cohesion in Britain: Super-Diversity, Transnationalism and Civil-Integration*. Wetherby: Commission on Integration and Cohesion

Villarreal, Marcela 2006. *Changing Customary Land Rights and Gender Relations in the Context of HIV/AIDS in Africa*. Montpelier: International Colloquium paper. www. mpl.ird.fr/colloque_foncier/Communications/PDF/Villarreal.pdf

Vosko, Leah F. 2006. 'Gender, Precarious Work, and the International Labour Code: The Ghost in the ILO Closet' in Fudge, Judy and Owens, Rosemary (eds.), pp. 53–75

Vulliamy, Ed 2004. 'Majlinda was just 13 when she was snatched from her Albanian village and sold into the sex industry', *The Observer*, 3 October

Walkowitz, Judith 1980. *Prostitution in Victorian Society*. Cambridge University Press

Wallach, Lori and Tucker, Todd 2006. *Debunking the Myth of Mode 4 and the US H-1B Visa Program*. Public Citizen's Global Trade Watch. www.citizen.org/trade/wto/gats/

Wallerstein, I. and Smith J. 1992. 'Households as an Institution of the World Economy' in J. Smith and I. Wallerstein (eds.), *Creating and Transforming Households*. New York: Cambridge University Press, pp. 3–26

Warraich, Sohail Akbar 2005. '"Honour killings" and the Law in Pakistan' in Welchman, L. and Hossain, S., (eds.), pp. 78–110

Washbrook, David A. 1981. 'Law, State and Agrarian Society in Colonial India', *Modern Asian Studies* 15 (3): 649–721

Washbrook, David A. 1994. 'The Commercialisation of Agriculture in Colonial India: Production, Subsistence and Reproduction in the "Dry South", c.1870–1930', *Modern Asian Studies* 28 (1): 129–164

Welbourne, Penelope, Harrison, Gai and Ford, Deirdre 2007. 'Social Work in the UK and the Global Labour Market: Recruitment, Practice and Ethical Considerations', *International Social Work* 50 (1): 27–40

Welchman, Lynn and Hossain, Sara (eds.) 2005. *'Honour': Crimes, Paradigms, and Violence Against Women*. London: Zed Press

Welchman, Lynn and Hossain, Sara 2005. 'Introduction: Honour Rights and Wrongs' in Welchman, L. and Hossain, S. (eds.), pp. 1–21

Wells, Celia and Quick, Oliver 2010. *Reconstructing Criminal Law*. Cambridge University Press

Wengi, Jennifer Okumu 1997. *Casting a Stone into the Bush: Structural Adjustment Programmes and the Family in Uganda: Weeding the Millet Field: Women's Law and Grassroots Justice in Uganda*. Kampala: Uganda Law Watch Centre

West, Robin 1997. *Caring for Justice*. New York University Press

Westmarland, Nicole 2006, 'Shifting Perspectives on Street Prostitution in England and Wales', in Geetanjali Gangoli and Nicole Westmarland (eds.) *International Approaches to Prostitution: Law and Policy in Europe and Asia*. Bristol: Policy Press, pp. 21–43

White, Julie A. and Tronto Joan, C. 2004. 'Political Practices of Care: Needs and Rights', *Ratio Juris* 17 (4): 425–453

White, Luise 1987. 'Vice, and Vagrants: Prostitution, Housing and Casual Labour in Nairobi in the mid 1930s', in Snyder, Francis and Hay, Doug (eds.), *Labour, Law, and Crime*. London: Tavistock, pp. 202–227

White, Luise 1990. *The Comforts of Home: Prostitution in Colonial Nigeria*. University of Chicago Press

Whitehead, Ann and Tsikata, Dzodzi 2003. 'Policy Discourses on Women's Land Rights in Sub-Saharan Africa: The Implications of the Re-turn to the Customary', *Journal of Agrarian Change* 3 (1–2): 67–112

Williams, Fiona 2001. 'In and Beyond New Labour: Towards a New Political Ethics of Care', *Critical Social Policy* 21 (4): 467–493

Williams, Mariama 2003. *Gender Mainstreaming in the Multilateral Trading System*. London: Commonwealth Secretariat

Williams, Patricia 1991. *The Alchemy of Race and Rights*. Cambridge MA: Harvard University Press

Wilson, Amrit 2007. 'The Forced Marriage Debate and the British State', *Race and Class* 49 (1): 25–38

Winrock International 2005. *Women at Risk in the Republic of Moldova*. Arkansas: Winrock International

Winters, L. Alan 2005. *Developing Country Proposals for the Liberalization of Movements in Natural Service Suppliers*. London: University of Sussex, Development Research Centre on Migration, Globalisation and Policy, Working Paper T8

Winters, L. Alan, Walmsley Terrie, L., Wang, Zhen Cun, Grynberg, Roman 2003. *Liberalizing Labour Mobility under the GATS, Economic Paper No 53*. London: Commonwealth Secretariat

Wittenburg, Vanina 2008. *The New Bonded Labour?* Oxford: Oxfam and Kalayaan

Wolfenshohn, James 1999. *A Proposal for a Comprehensive Development Framework*. New York: World Bank

Wolkowitz, Carol 2006. *Bodies at Work*. London: Sage Publications

Women Working World Wide 2007. *Promoting Women Workers' Rights in African Horticulture*. Manchester: Women Working Worldwide. Available at www.women-ww.org/index.php/programmes/past-projects

Woodman, Gordon 1998. 'Ideological Combat and Social Observation: Recent Debates About Legal Pluralism', 43 *Journal of Legal Pluralism*, pp. 21–59

World Bank 1993. *World Development Report: Investing in Health*. New York: World Bank

World Bank 1997a. *World Development Indicators*. Washington, DC: World Bank

World Bank 1997b. *World Development Report 1997: The State in a Changing World*. Oxford University Press

World Bank 2003. *Land Policies for Growth and Poverty Reduction*. Washington DC: World Bank

World Bank 2008. *Whispers to Voices: Gender and Social Transformation in Bangladesh*. Washington DC and Dhaka: The World Bank Bangladesh Development Series Paper no. 22

Wylie, G. 2006. 'Doing the Impossible? Collecting Data on the Extent of Trafficking', in C. Van den Auker and J. Doomernik (eds.), *Trafficking and Women's Rights*. Basingstoke: Palgrave Macmillan, pp. 70–88

Yeates, N. 2004. 'Global Care Chains: Critical Reflections and Lines of Enquiry', *International Feminist Journal of Politics* 6 (3): 369–391

Yeates, Nicola 2009. *Globalising Care Economies and Migrant Workers*. Basingstoke: Palgrave Macmillan

Yeoh, Brenda S. A., Huang, Shirlena and Lam, Theodora 2005. 'Transnationalising the "Asian" Family: Imaginaries, Intimacies and Strategic Intents', *Global Networks* 5 (4): 307–315

Yilmaz, Ihsan 2000. 'Muslim Law in Britain: Reflections in the Socio-legal Sphere and Differential Legal Treatment', *Journal of Ethnic and Migration Studies* 20 (2): 353–360

Yilmaz, Ihsan 2001. 'Law as Chameleon: The Question of Incorporation of Muslim Personal Law into the English Law', *Journal of Ethnic and Migration Studies* 21 (2): 297–308

Yilmaz, Ihsan 2002. 'The Challenge of Post-modern Legality and Muslim Legal Pluralism in England', *Journal of Ethnic and Migration Studies* 28 (2): 343–354

Young, Iris Marion 2004. 'Responsibility and Global Labour Justice', *Journal of Political Philosophy* 12 (4) 365–388

Zuckerman, Elaine and Qing, Wu 2005. *Reforming the World Bank: Will the Gender Strategy Make a Difference? A Study with China Case Examples*. Washington: Heinrich Böll Foundation

Index